WHAT SHOULD I DO WITH MY LIFE?

Po Bronson is a feature writer for *Wired* and has written about high-tech culture for *The New York Times Magazine*, *The Wall Street Journal* and *Forbes ASAP*. His first novel, *Bombardiers* was translated into ten languages and became an international bestseller. His second novel, *The First $20 Million is Always the Hardest*, was a *New York Times* bestseller. Bronson grew up in Seattle, graduated from Stanford in 1986, and lives in San Francisco.

I'm writing from Shreveport, Louisiana, five hours north of New Orleans. I had such a strong internal reaction while reading your book this morning, the only thing I can think of to compare it to is a tornado touching down in my . . . soul? . . . self? . . . core? I don't know what I want to do with these feelings yet, but thank you for being the catalyst for this activity.

ANN PAYNE

Something from Mexico: It is hard for me to say this, but until not so long ago I thought my reality was very much different than what it is now. I am struggling with not only my inside demons (as I call them), but I feel as if [I] have some- how lived in someone else's shoes and know I am trying to recuperate myself and my dreams and my peace. Sometimes I feel like the oldest twenty-eight- year-old in Mexico and sometimes I feel like a ten-year-old boy. Best Regards and thank you for the Soul Searching.

SERGIO MONTIEL
Ixtapa

Our local library has fourteen copies with seventeen on the waiting list. I had to go to a distant suburb to get a reserved copy. Our local library in Centerville, Ohio, has never had a bestseller with this type of response. Your book is helping everyone take a good look at themselves. Your book does a profound job of lead- ing the reader to answer this question to themselves and No one Else. You chose everyday people not "textbook or Hollywood Types." You will be blessed by this book now and in the years to come. Hope you had a good Father's Day.

A fan and friend,
JOHN D.S.

I am an Indian working at India's largest passenger car manufacturer in New Delhi, since last six years. It was all vacuum and purposelessness around me. Then, someone referred me your book, which indeed has brought a gust of fresh air in my life. Thank you for writing such a book which I call is a "cerebral panacea."

SHANTANU CHATTERJEE
New Delhi

You don't know me, although it seems like you interviewed my subconscious for your book. Thank you for writing a book which has caused my soul to resonate, ache, laugh, and cry all at the same time. I can only take so many chapters at one sitting, which is strange for a guy who typically reads fifty books a month. Reading *What Should I Do with My Life?* has become a nightly session with my dreams seated comfortably nearby, smiling back at me to bring them to life.

JEFF GREGORY
Washington, D.C.

Po, reading the stories in the book made me feel part of a community, however distant and disparate. There's a part of me in many of those stories and there's a part of them and you in me too. There's a wonderful analogy to this in Buddhism, where they liken people to brilliant jewels that reflect light and color to one another in a vast network of shining jewels. I know this sounds a bit "New Age" coming from a guy who grew up in the 'hood, but it makes me feel human.

Pura vida,
JOHN-PAUL RIVERA
Costa Rica

Quite honestly, at the end of most of the chapters, I cried. Primarily because I could identify with the people you chose to write about, but also because their stories didn't provide me with answers to my own questions about what I should do with my life. Each chapter forced me to acknowledge that I am going to have to find the answers to my own questions. You warned us readers that your book was not a self-help nor a how-to book—and you were right. It was a wake-up call to start relying on myself, rather than others, to answer the question of what I should do with my life.

Sincerely,
HEIDI
Kansas City

Instead of wasting my time watching the Stanley Cup Playoffs or MLB Saturday, I caught the C-Span Los Angeles Times Book Fair. A few hours later, I bought your book at Books-A-Million, where I never buy anything. Now I know what to do with my life, and I'm sixty-three! I can't put the book down.

RUSS WHITE
Lake Mary, Florida

Dear Po,
My name is Curline. I live in Madrid, Spain. I'll tell you this and I know you'll understand what I mean: I felt we were face to face, you speaking to me. I miss that freshness, openheartedness in writers and journalists today, so many seem

to be hiding behind metaphors and the latest jargon instead of writing what they truly feel or live. Know you've got a friend here. Count on it.

I don't own a computer. I'm writing you from one at the local library. I've spent the past fifteen years raising my four children, mostly by myself, and going from one shit job to another at barely more than minimum wage. I read your book as a starving person would devour a meal. I've enrolled in college thanks to Pell Grants and student loans. I refuse to give up.

PAM
Ironton, Missouri

You were able to take the question and provide a response that I have never seen before. Instead of simply forcing things into fake categories you illuminated what is behind the decision. I think your work will stand the test of time.

Take care,
JOHN LESALLE
Connecticut, USA

Ya'ateeh Waashindoondee! Greetings from the Navajo Nation. I bought your book after reading a review of it in a newspaper while on the road from D.C. to Window Rock, Arizona. I finished it last night and what food for thought! Your book, I hope, will allow me to find out that I am not my work. I can have something different. And that's OK. Your book has given me places where I never thought of searching before. *Ahe'hee!*

Best wishes,
CHRISTOPHER J. PAISANO

I hate to be cliché, but I have never felt the urge to write an author and thank him for his story. I also very much enjoy that not all of your stories have happy endings. I think that reality, in which someone can venture down a new path and either not achieve any more happiness or any more success, is what really makes the book so provoking. You show the yin and the yang—which is refreshing in a society of microwave books that all have been reduced to some form of "chicken soup" for the soul/career/relationship.

JOE BRUNETTI
Chicago

My name is Ann Wilson and I'm reading your book here in Atlanta. It is truly a buoy in a very turbulent sea for me (it's intimidating to write a writer but I plunge ahead—pedestrian metaphors everywhere, watch out). Your book is so amazingly right-this-minute in my life. The questions, the observations, my gosh, they take my breath away. You dove into the confusion, fear and joy of what it is to be a free person with choices and honored the condition, not with platitudes and slogans, but with courage and bone-honest truth about life searches. I am deeply moved by your integrity and your wisdom and the stories, the stories.

Hey: I got a copy of your book on my way back to the Philippines from a family reunion. I had given up on the capital letter questions (i.e., "What Is the Meaning and Purpose of Life") a long time ago, but a curiosity on how you were going to approach it or, to be more exact, on what level you (or to be less personal—"the Author") would fail and validate my belief that this is a stupid question. I was gearing up for a long flight and was looking for any kind of amusement.

In any case—the book has turned out to be satisfying. I like it that you had a diverse range of stories. Your book got me revisiting the capital letter questions all over again. I don't know if it's the sandwich I had for lunch but that thought is also oddly comforting. Good work, chap! Chop-chop!! Carry on!!

FERMIN TARUC
Manila, Philippines

Dear Po,
I have lived my life in reverse. At age twenty-four, I was diagnosed with a life-threatening illness. Doctors gave me between two and ten years to live. At a time when most young people are laying the foundation for their careers, I was focused on improving my health and increasing my chances of staying alive. Next year I will be fifty!

Your book is feeding my soul. And while I am only halfway through, it made me feel what I believe people who are adopted feel when they finally meet their birth parents.

KYM KING
Houston

Hi Po,
Is Australia too far away to be interesting? I used to lie in bed at night knowing I was meant to be doing something, but not quite remembering what it was. Like on the transit to this life I fell asleep at the vital moment when the man driving my bus was giving out the final instructions. Po, it's a bit akin to being gay and coming out when I talk about this stuff. No bull! Good on you for being authentic and following your inner voice! Doing so gives so many other people permission to do the same.

Cheers, and all the best,
NICOLE

my name's trina and my aunt gave me your book. i put it on the shelf with her other self-helpers. on sunday, i picked your book up again because (seriously) i wanted something to put me to sleep. i haven't put it down since (which gets complicated in the shower) and will probably finish the damn thing tonight (the hardcover is heavy on the train). the thing is, you didn't write a book of winners. you wrote about people doing dumb things, thinking crazy ways, and going to extremes trying to figure it out. you wrote about people like me. Through your book, I have rediscovered new ways to view the question and not more ways to answer it. but this is good.

Next to the sea, sitting with my colleagues, I saw my dreams flowing away with the waves. I'm a wiser man now. I believe that your book would be a spiritual experience for the reader because your thoughts are (coincidentally) very similar to what the great Indian spiritual masters—Swami Vivekananda and Jiddu Krishnamurti have propagated all their lives.

NINAD VENGURLEKAR, a like-minded soul in India

I was brought up in the wake of people who knew what they wanted in life, got it and explained their actions by "it needed to be done." I, on the other hand, focused on the eggs and could not enjoy the taste of the omelette. My failure has been not having the courage of my emotions. I am working on a way to make my anger have a positive outcome and my lost years count for something. Your book was quite helpful.

Best wishes,
DOMINIQUE LASALLE
London

Hello from Brazil. How are you? I had a quite hard time in getting your book in the States last month—it was sold out many places. I must tell you I was very touched by it. Thank you so much for the energy you put in looking for new answers for these new times. The book makes so much sense—and it seems to make sense independently of the geography.

Sincerely,
LUCIANA STEIN

I am a U.S. Marine major recently returned from combat in Iraq. I have sent you a photo from the second day of the war. I just finished your book yesterday on a plane flight from Oklahoma City to San Diego. Actually, I *almost* finished it on the plane . . . I was so hooked that I walked off the plane at my destination, and instead of going to get my car I sat in the airport and finished it right there. I would love to buy you a beer.

S.C.

Po Bronson

WHAT SHOULD I DO WITH MY LIFE?

The True Story of People Who
Answered the Ultimate Question

VINTAGE

Published by Vintage 2004

2 4 6 8 10 9 7 5 3 1

Copyright © Po Bronson 2003

The picture of Noah Goldfader on p. 40 was taken
by Kym Hoblitzell

First published in the United States in 2003 by
Random House Inc.

First published in Great Britain in 2003 by
Secker & Warburg

Vintage
Random House, 20 Vauxhall Bridge Road,
London SW1V 2SA

Random House Australia (Pty) Limited
20 Alfred Street, Milsons Point, Sydney
New South Wales 2061, Australia

Random House New Zealand Limited
18 Poland Road, Glenfield,
Auckland 10, New Zealand

Random House (Pty) Limited
Endulini, 5A Jubilee Road, Parktown 2193,
South Africa

The Random House Group Limited Reg. No. 954009
www.randomhouse.co.uk

A CIP catalogue record for this book
is available from the British Library

ISBN 0 09 943799 6

Papers used by Random House are natural, recyclable
products made from wood grown in sustainable forests.
The manufacturing processes conform to the environmental regulations of the country of origin

Printed and bound in Great Britain by
Bookmarque Ltd, Croydon, Surrey

For Michele and Luke

||| Contents

xiv | Contents

Introduction:
Obvious Questions Don't
Have Obvious Answers

FROM YOUR FEARS COME MISCONCEPTIONS

We are all writing the story of our life. We want to know what it's "about," what are its themes and which theme is on the rise. We demand of it something deeper, or richer, or more substantive. We want to know where we're headed—not to spoil our own ending by ruining the surprise, but we want to ensure that when the ending comes, it won't be shallow. We will have done something. We will not have squandered our time here.

This book is about that urge, that need.

I began this project because I hit that point in my life. The television show I'd been writing for was canceled. The magazines I wrote for had thinned their pages. My longtime book editor had quit to pursue theater and film. I was out of work, I had a baby on the way (my first) and I was worried: how to be a good father, how to make money to support my family, and how to keep growing as a writer. I probably could have hustled up an assignment (the freelance writer's equivalent of following the advice "just go get a job") but I wasn't sure I should. I felt like the kinds of stories I'd been telling no longer worked. They no longer mapped the depth and drama of human life as I experienced it.

Looking for guidance and courage at this crossroads, I became intrigued by people who had unearthed their true calling, or at least those who were willing to try. Those who fought with the seduction of money, intensity, and novelty, but overcame their allure. Those who broke away from the chorus to learn the sound of their own voice. Nothing seemed more brave to me than facing up to one's own identity, and filtering out the chatter that tells us to be someone we're not.

What might I learn from those who had confronted this question?

I decided on the simplest approach possible: I would express my curiosity to whoever would listen, trust this would provoke some leads, and travel the country tracking down the people whose stories spoke to me. I had no idea that sticking to this simple method would soon take me to so many places I'd never been, and far deeper into people's lives than I'd ever gone as a writer.

I hit on an incredible wellspring of honest sentiment. Complete strangers opened their lives and their homes to me, confessing feelings and events they hadn't revealed to their closest friends. This was at a time when we were losing our respect for corporate leaders, we no longer believed new technology would make our lives better, and the attack on our freedom made life precious and weighty. People were reassessing what mattered to them and what they believed in.

I heard some nine hundred stories, spent countless hours corresponding and on the phone, and came to know about seventy people closely. I spent time with them all in person, which was absolutely necessary. (About fifty are included in the book.) The word "interview" doesn't describe the emotional exchange that usually occurred. None were friends when I started, but most were by the time I was done. These were microwave friendships, forged with fast blasts of revelation and bonding, like those formed quickly in a freshman dorm, remembered for years. I let them cry in my arms. I slept on their couches. I sat in their musty attics, looking through old photo albums. We went running together. We traded secrets. I met their parents and held their children. I went to one's wedding. I became symbolically associated with their turning points. Many people described how much it helped them to have me listen; they talked their way into a greater understanding of what had transpired and why.

The people in this book are ordinary people. By that I mean they did not have available to them resources or character traits that gave them an uncommon advantage in pursuing a better life. Some have succeeded, many have not. They're not famous. Over half are parents. Over half participate actively in their church. They're a diverse assortment of ages and professions. Most (but not all) are educated, but a fair number earned that education later in life, as one step upward in their chosen transformation. A handful had spent years earning a high salary before they woke up to what their life was all about, but only a couple of them saved any of that money—most spent what they earned, just like anyone else, and as a result didn't have a safety net when they changed their life. Only two asked me not to use their real names. I've chosen stories that I hoped would encourage reflection and offer solace, not ones that merely entertained.

Most important, when I say that these are ordinary people, I mean they're real. They're messy and complicated. You hold in your hands the *antithesis* to all those books which pretend their one-size-fits-all formula will result in rosy, happily-ever-after Hollywood endings. I'm a chronicler; this is (foremost) a social documentary of people's lives; it just so happened that I learned a ton in the observation. The result might lack the comforting ease of a cure-all, but it makes up for it with integrity. (You want a step? Step one: Stop pretending we're all on the same staircase.) This theme is going to reappear throughout: It's not easy / It's not *supposed* to be easy / Most people make mistakes / Most people have to learn the hardest lessons more than once. If that has been your experience, the people herein will comfort you. They did me. That alone was worth the trip.

I was no expert. I had no credentials as a counselor or academic. I approached these people as merely "one of them." The events of my life had shredded any theories I used to have about how to address the question "What should I do with my life?" I had been humbled into admitting I knew nothing, and as I hit the road I was continuously humbled again by what some of these people had endured and the wisdom they seemed to radiate. I learned from them through inspiration and imitation. I also learned from the multiplicity of stories—by comparing how people talked and what language they invoked, certain patterns emerged, and I could place a story in the context of the larger picture.

I learned that it was in hard times that people usually changed the course of their life; in good times, they frequently only *talked* about change. Hard times forced them to overcome the doubts that normally gave them pause. It surprised me how often we hold ourselves back until we have no choice. So the people herein suffered layoffs, bankruptcies, divorces, evictions, illnesses, and the deaths of loved ones, and as a result they were as likely to stumble into a better life as they were to arrive there by reasoned planning. They made mistakes before summoning the courage to get it right. Their path called into question the notion that a calling is something you inherently know when you're young. Far from it. These people discovered in themselves gifts they rarely realized they had.

They spoke of fulfillment, not happiness. Very often they found fulfillment in living up to their moral responsibility to society—in finding some way to feel they were helping others, or at least connecting genuinely with others. In this sense, even though they were pursuing what they personally needed, they were learning selflessness. And while they had to fight hard to get what they loved, they also had to learn to love what they then got; while they scrapped for what was within their reach, they learned acceptance of events beyond their control. They learned that their responsibilities didn't keep them from their purpose—they were part of their purpose. (And sometimes the most important part.) They did not find some Single Perfect Answer to the question; at some point it felt right enough that they made their choice, and the energy formerly spent casting about was now devoted to making their choice fruitful for as long as it might last. In every case, they found a place that was good for them. What I mean by that is, they found something that shaped their character in a positive way. Even if they didn't succeed wildly, the pursuit brought to the surface a trait that had been neglected. They might not have discovered their calling, but they did discover a lot about themselves.

By no means have I written about only the success stories. Many of the people I included were in midtransition, searching and hoping. This presented its own challenge, because they routinely asked for my counseling. This was always an uneasy role; usually, I handled this by telling other people's stories—"Here's what this person found, in a similar situation. . . ." In a few instances, I was not so passive when I sensed that my passivity—my listening mode—was being taken inappropriately as endorsement. I didn't want to be an accomplice to a wrong turn. So I tried to guide them by reminding them of their own stated resolutions. Anyone who's counseled a friend struggling with this question knows this tension—you want to be encouraging, but you also want to be realistic. I didn't handle all these situations perfectly; I reveal these moments in the text to show my own fallibility.

People asked a great many questions that helped steer my research. Many of these questions were of the smart-aleck variety, merely intellectual/devil's advocate babble, but it was much more difficult and challenging to address those asked from the heart, by people stuck in the middle of it and honestly confused. Questions such as:

- Should I put my faith in mystical signs of destiny, or should my sense of "a right fit" be based on logical, practical reasons?
- When should I accept my lot, make peace with my ambition, and stop stressing out?
- Why do I feel guilty for thinking about this?
- Should I make money first, to fund my dream?
- How do I tell the difference between a curiosity and a passion?
- How do I weigh making myself a better person against external achievements?

- When do I need to change my situation, and when is it *me* that needs to change?
- What should I tell my parents, who worry about me?
- If I have a child, will my frustration over my work go away?
- What will it feel like when I get there? (How will I know I'm there?)

These were screamingly obvious questions, but it seemed they were almost so obvious that we hadn't publicly collected how we've learned to answer them—as if the answers should be obvious too, which they're not. Too often we're reticent about these issues. Talking about them can seem so fruitless, meanwhile inflaming anxiety and diverting us from the other things we have more control over, and can do. Yes, but it can also strengthen our resolve and shield us from distractions. I found that the biggest obstacle to answering the question this book poses is that people don't give themselves permission to take it seriously. At the risk of being fruitless, let this book be a safe place for a discussion.

This book does not research the history of its question. I don't quote experts, though I interviewed some, and I don't quote literature unless it was quoted to me by someone I wrote about. I didn't spend time in the library to write this book. Those sources of wisdom felt too abstract compared to the hard-earned record of those who actually took action, changed their life, and enjoyed or suffered the consequences.

Spending time with them affected me subtly. Afterward, I was always spent, and needed to recharge on the familiar patterns of my family, the writers' Grotto, and my soccer teams. I became hyperaware of what mattered to me and what was merely that week's noise intruding on my life. It stripped away some of the ways I had colored my past, and often I was visited by old friends in my dreams. I became more honest in person, less contrived in my writing. They helped me find my own story. They wanted to know how I'd come to be a writer, and how I'd recently become a husband (for the second time) and a father (for the first time). I'd never written about my own journey, never thought it was a story worth telling, but hearing their stories helped me tell my own in a way that it finally did have some oomph. To some it was inspiration, and to others it was kinship. *Okay, he gets it.*

My biggest surprise was how being a new dad folded into the book, and how I face this question now that I have a family. Writing hadn't come easily to me, and I've had to be very protective of my love for it. I was once so afraid that being a parent was incompatible with being a writer. The travel, the intense concentration. For years this fear had stopped me from mixing the two. Somehow, in a year in which our son, Luke, was born, and my wife, Michele, a molecular immunologist, was putting a drug through the FDA's approval process, I found the time and the room in my heart for this enormous project. I took my family with me whenever I could, which was most of the time. In his first year Luke went on seventeen trips of up to ten days in length, including weeks in London and Hong Kong, which he loved because it was hot. Now it seems like a miracle.

It's a far different book from what I originally envisioned. It reflects what I found, not what I predicted. I didn't write a single person's story until I had gotten to know two-thirds of them, and even then their meaning was just beginning to show itself. Nowhere is this more apparent than in the unconventional way I've arranged these stories. The book's not organized by industry or personality type, and it's not a travelogue. Since my method conveys how I'm implicitly suggesting we think about this question—and since figuring out how to do this didn't come easily—an explanation is probably necessary.

There are many very real stumbling blocks that prevent us from pursuing this question: *never enough money, never enough time.* We're aware of those constraints—they're right in front of us, every day. But we also have many psychological stumbling blocks that keep us from finding ourselves. Some of these are badly tangled misconceptions, some are deeply rooted fears. The two are related—like any prejudice, misconceptions get fabricated and sustained by fears. These psychological stumbling blocks are often less real than we imagine. By confronting them, we begin to see around all our obstacles, even the seemingly insurmountable ones. If you take care of these obstacles, you create an environment where the truth is invited into your life.

So this book is meant to unearth the psychological demons that haunt us. It uses people's stories to demonstrate these misconceptions and fears, and shows how people are confronting them or have gotten past them.

What are some of those fears and misconceptions?

Well, let's start with my own.

I feared I was writing a book that was mostly about an American phenomenon – the quest for identity through one's labor. This doubt hung over me like a dark thundercloud. If it were true, it significantly cheapened the whole project. I can't even explain why it cheapened it. It simply did, on its face. I'd met so many people, both at home and abroad, who had swallowed their desire to change their life because they suspected it was another foolhardy export from a country built by revolutionaries and pioneers. Americans might have bigger cars and larger grass lawns than the rest of the world, but we certainly aren't happier, or more content. On that front we're terrible role models. You'd never follow an American's prescription for happiness for the same reasons you'd never buy a snowblower that was made and tested in Jamaica.

I remember telling a visiting British magazine editor about the book over dinner. I was only a couple of months into my research. He nodded quickly, catching my drift, "I get it. I completely get it. It's a terrific book idea." My hopes lifted. "But you know –" he paused for a terribly long time "– it's mostly an American fancy, and *really*, the only vocations in which there is that fulfillment are writers, doctors, and the military." He said it with such fervor that for a good half hour I was blinded by his conviction. Of course he was right! How stupid was I! By dessert I'd regained enough of my senses to add a few other trades to his short list. I'd met an inventor of electric cars, and that was clearly his calling. Oh, and a chef. We were up to five.

After dinner I sat in my study and went over my notes. Surely there were more than five? I dug through my huge stack of correspondences. In fifteen minutes, my list of callings had over 75 entries, with no end in sight. (A month later, that magazine editor's girlfriend informed me her beau was unhappy as an editor, and longed of being a freelance writer or returning to military service.)

It's so easy to let yourself be talked out of it.

Thankfully, there were my correspondences, arguing the other side.

If it was just an American fancy, how was I to account for this letter from the London doctor who gave it up to design furniture?

Or this letter from the Dublin biotech scientist who turned out to be a lot happier as a real estate agent?

Or these long exchanges with a trader in The City, who hoped I could provide him with "the courage to find and follow what I believe in"?

Or these letters from Tel Aviv, Barbados, Singapore, Copenhagen, and New Delhi, expressing similar hope?

One theory was that we all live in the same urban global demographic, the same cultural network. This theory argued that people in Multicultural London have more in common with people in New York and Vancouver than they do with people in traditional Yorkshire. We listen to the same music, travel on similar vacations, own the same Palm 505 mobile communicator, enjoy each other's food, and all believe in freeflowing social mobility. Large immigrant populations in these cities remind us that wholesale, abrupt change is possible.

I tried that theory out for a while. It was a very seductive theory, but many of the people I was exchanging letters with didn't fit into it. They didn't listen to the same music. Some had never traveled. They weren't all well-educated. They weren't all young. Many were trapped in small towns. And nobody owned a Palm 505.

Ultimately, I recognized that just about anybody could find this question important to them, regardless of their background or age. I needed to honor that. I needed to treat them as an individual, not as a member of a class or demographic. Their stories were full of specific details, not generalizations. So I gave up trying to hang a sociological explanation on it. It doesn't matter if struggling with your identity is more popular in the U.S. than Sweden, or more popular among redheads than blondes, or more popular among waitresses than bartenders. Those analyses don't help anyone find their answer. (I'll pick up this theme again a quarter of the way into the book).

I booked three trips to the U.K., but due to a death in my family we were able to make only one of these trips. I couldn't get to Bangalore as I had hoped. As a result, only seven of the stories included here are set outside the U.S. I regret that, and I hope to correct this myopia in future editions. However, I learned enough to get over my fear that this "phenomenon" was only an American thing. That's what's important.

Their stories are organized into eight sections. In the first section, the people I interviewed are struggling with the essential paradox of trying to make a "right" decision in the absence of experience. In the second section, they're overcoming traditional class notions of where they belong. In the third, they're learning to resist the temptations that have distracted them from their true aspirations. The modern economy tends to toss us around like a hot potato, while we'd usually prefer to settle down and stay put. The people in section four have found ways to resolve that inherent conflict. In the fifth section, they're getting to know themselves as people first, then struggling with what that means for their career mission. The people in the sixth section found their right place or environment, which led in turn to greater insight. The seventh section is the longest in the book. It recognizes that we make our choices with our family in mind. The people in the final section demonstrate the virtues of patience and persistence. I include them not to admonish the young and urgent, but to respect the Big Picture. Most of us take the slow road, no shortcuts.

In addition to that macrostructure, you'll find subthemes and side conversations running story to story. They're not meant to be read out of order, though there's no harm in that. They're meant to build on each other. Ideas and terminology brought up in earlier stories are invoked in subsequent ones, and the result is meant to resemble a rolling conversation, but one in which the ideas are continually reined in by dogged reality. Like any conversation, there are times I interject and times I mostly listen.

When people heard this book's title, the most common question I'd get asked was, "So is your book about life, or about careers?" And I'd laugh, and warn them not to get trapped by semantics, and answer, "It's about people who've dared to be honest with themselves."

That Sense of "Rightness"

1 ||| An Ordinary Guy

Wouldn't it be so much easier if you got a letter in the mail when you were seventeen, signed by someone who had a direct pipeline to Ultimate Meaning, telling you exactly who you are and what your true destiny is? Then you could carry this letter around in your pocket, and when you got confused or distracted and suddenly melted down, you'd reach for your wallet and grab the letter and read it again and go, "Oh, *right.*"

Well, a friend of mine has such a letter. He's thirty-two years old and rents a bedroom from a nice lady in Phoenix near the base of Camelback Mountain. He's gray at the temples, wears Hawaiian shirts, and drives a dusty Oldsmobile that suffers from bad alignment. The car's tape player is broken, which is fine by me because I can't stand the soft rock he listens to. He loves America because friends here treat him like an ordinary person. He says being here has made him much more open-minded. He grew up in a refugee camp in southern India. When he got the letter he had just enrolled in a special school there, with the vague notion of eventually becoming a professor of Tibetan literature, though he admits he wasn't much of a student. But what else was there to do in life? No way was he going to be a farmer. Being a businessman meant having to sell, and he didn't study hard enough to ever become a doctor. He couldn't imagine sitting out his life in a government office job, filing forms. His name was Choejor Dondup, but everyone called him Ali, after the boxer, because he was big. His hair hung to his shoulders. He spent most of his time figuring out how to get into his girlfriend's pants. He played soccer. He was scared of the dark. Then one day at school he received this letter, signed by the Dalai Lama.

Ali was a big believer in the Dalai Lama.

The letter said he wasn't Choejor Dondup after all. Instead, he was the reincarnation of a warrior who, along with his five brothers, had ruled a

poor and remote region of eastern Tibet six lifetimes ago. The brothers had descended from one of Genghis Khan's grandsons. Ali's Previous One turned his back on the family's violent rule and became a monk. Over his lifetime he founded thirteen monasteries and became the great spiritual leader of this region, the Tehor. Ali's real name was Za Rinpoche, which is Tibetan for "The Dharma King."

Imagine! *You're not a dumb, lost, inexperienced seventeen-year-old! We actually have a spot picked out for you! And not just any spot!*

WANTED: Great Spiritual Leader. No experience necessary.

Nevertheless, the letter was a bit of a shock. They wanted him to attend the Drepung monastery southeast of Bombay. All Ali could think about was, "Am I going to have to cut my hair?" "Am I going to have to become a monk? *Give up sex?*" You think it would be easy if your destiny were offered on a silver platter. But Ali went around for a few days openly expressing his angst and annoying his friends by debating whether this was the right thing to do. The social pressure was so great that eventually he shut up, gave in, and went off to the monastery, keeping his doubts to himself. It took four years for the doubts to evaporate. But it's never been easy. He spent the next twelve years memorizing two-thousand-year-old ancient texts, the whole time craving the kind of understanding that comes from experience. Back in Tehor, when people are dying they hold his photograph inches from their face and stare at him, wanting him to be the last thing they ever see before they cross over into unembodied consciousness. That's how much faith they have in Rinpoche—more than he has in himself, I suspect.

I found Rinpoche like this: When my son was born, my mom cleaned out her basement and brought up my well-preserved souvenirs from my childhood, soccer trophies and warmup jackets and my high school yearbooks. In one of those yearbooks was a nice note from an upperclasswoman, Jodi, fondly remembering those long conversations we used to have during studio art classes. "What conversations?" I wanted to remember. So I tracked her down, and during another long conversation she mentioned she'd been hanging out with Rinpoche. I was curious, though not for any particular reason. Just curious. Curiosity is a raw and genuine sign from deep inside our tangled psyches, and we'd do well to follow the direction it points us in. So to Jodi I said, "I gotta meet that guy," and booked tickets to Phoenix.

What would it be like to have this certainty about your place in the world? To have it in writing from the Dalai Lama himself! Of course, my desire to understand this wasn't my only motivation. I was excited to meet a holy man. Perhaps his spiritual presence might rub off on me, and he might offer me guidance. Instead I found a friend, who, though sacred, was still utterly human and real. He was skilled at minimizing his anguish over everyday struggles, but he still faced them routinely and fought his urges like any of us. Possessing that letter had not relieved him of having to figure out where he really belonged and make some hard choices. In his mind, this question was not settled.

He and I were riding around Phoenix a little while ago, looking for some authentic Mexican food. I was joshing him about this reincarnation thing.

"Come on, you really believe it?"

"Yes."

"So, *all* of you, or just, like, your *soul?*"

He said the biggest misconception in the West, and in young Tibetans, was that mind is physical.

I said, "How do you know young Tibetans? You said you've never even been to Tibet." (China wouldn't let him into his country.)

"Like, you know, I've met many who are also in exile."

"In Phoenix?"

He said that they were mostly in New York.

"What does that even mean, 'mind is not physical'? That's so cryptic."

He tried to unpack his statement for me. Sanskrit describes five layers of self, or mind:

Physical,
feeling,
perception,
intention,
and consciousness.

———

His consciousness had been reincarnated, but his perceptions and feelings and body had not. That said, the inner layer, by itself, is no more valid or important than the outer. Self is the combination of the five.

"So on the inside you've got it figured out, but the rest of you is dragging along."

Rinpoche laughed, and it's when he laughs that he seems so wise. He learned his English in Atlanta from undergrads at Emory University, and he picked up their vocal idiosyncrasies, tossing "kind of," "like," and "you know what I mean" into every sentence. He speaks English like a teenager, but laughs like a man six lifetimes old—such a deep, merry, pure chuckle.

I asked him if Buddhists believe we all get a specific destiny.

"We don't think there's a specific place in your life to go. Everybody's destiny is to become an enlightened being and reach the everlasting state of mind."

"That's pretty easy for you to say. Your destiny arrived in the mail. What if you had to go out and get a job?"

He laughed again. "Yes, that I could not imagine."

At one of Rinpoche's "teachings" at a hospice, he described how fears hold us back from our own advancement. "Fear is like a wound within our emotions," he said. You heal a fear much like you heal a cut on your hand. If you ignore the cut, it will get infected. But it will heal itself if you pay attention to it and give it time. Same with a fear. First, recognize its existence—what kind of fear is it? Is it fear of poverty, of loneliness, of rejection? Then use common sense. Don't let the fear get infected. Often we burn 70 percent of our emotional energy on what we fear might happen (90 percent of which won't happen). By devoting our energy to our other emotions, we will heal naturally.

This didn't sink in for me right away. In the moment, my mind tagged it as "deep," and filed it away to be revisited later. Which I did. When my way of organizing this book was finally coming into focus—as stories portraying people working through their fears and misconceptions—that method rang a bell.

Rinpoche admitted to a lot of fear and reluctance. In 1998, the Dalai Lama chose him to lead a tour of monks across the United States. Rinpoche didn't want to go. He'd heard the tour required long bus rides, thirteen hours at a time. He relented when the abbot leaned on him. Rinpoche says he was a narrow-minded snob back then. Maybe a monastery sounds like a terrific place to become a deep person, but the truth was, he was sheltered and had a big ego. He didn't hang out with ordinary monks, only monks of high status.

He had no respect for other religions, and assumed anyone who wasn't a Buddhist couldn't be a nice person. He was lonely and too serious. But traveling in America did wonders for his personality. After a year, he went back to the Drepung Monastery, and everyone said, "Wow, you've changed a lot." He hung out with monks regardless of their status. He laughed all the time. He felt more grounded. His elders were so impressed they asked him to stay and teach. For once he had the balls to say, "That is not in my nature," and stick by it. He wanted to return to America, where not everyone treats him like a divine being. He wanted to understand the Western mind, how people in the West think. Exposing himself to this crazy world was making him into a better person, and that was the right path to be on.

His destiny had been decreed by a higher power, but he also hadn't quite accepted that destiny *as is*. He'd tweaked it, as a result of his experience and instincts.

I liked that he'd done so. If it were me, no matter how cool or great it would be to have a spiritual calling, and to be given this early in life, I'd still have that American notion of needing to discover things myself. I'd need independence—I'd feel controlled. I might now and then be testy about having my calling put upon me rather than arriving at it by myself. We have mixed feelings about the seductive notion of destiny. There's a persistent tension between wanting our life's purpose to be revealed to us by some higher power and wanting to scrap and fight for it against all odds—to earn it without help. We think about destiny sort of like how we feel about inheritance—we covet its fruit but it's sweeter if we earned it ourselves. And so I wasn't surprised when Rinpoche called to give me his new address and phone number.

"What happened?"

"I am not with Bodhiheart anymore." Bodhiheart was the foundation he cofounded with his sponsor—the woman in whose house he had lived until now.

"Did you get in a fight?"

"Uh, not really. Kind of. I myself am not a citizen, you know? So as my sponsor, I relied on her for legal things like this."

"Like creating the foundation."

"That is right. So I have my own foundation now." He let out a hearty laugh, his punch line coming a little quick before I could understand.

"What happened between you?"

"I felt she tried to keep people from me, control my schedule, these things, you know? Like she wanted to be the access to me. Like last time you were here? She was upset with that."

"But you're my friend!"

He sighed. "That is right. You understand."

"You don't want anyone to control you."

"That is right."

"So have you ever lived alone before?" He'd spent most of his life in a monastery with four thousand monks.

"No, never."

"Can you cook?"

"Simple things."

"Going out for burritos a lot, I bet."

"Yes, that's right."

"How big is your apartment?"

"Not too small."

"You're not still scared of the dark, are you?"

Rinpoche laughed.

"I'm glad you're learning to look out for yourself," I said.

"Yes. At this I am getting better."

Once he'd said to me, "I wish I could be ordinary sometimes." He was getting his chance.

I guess it's never easy. Even if you get a letter from the Dalai Lama, you're still going to have to disappoint some people, and have to find your own way.

This section's overall theme is how people make decisions in the absence of real experience. It's a fundamental paradox: How can you really *pick* a preference if you've never tried it, or tried it only minimally? We won't all be getting letters from the Dalai Lama instructing us. How do we know! A short interview, a brief internship, a course in the subject matter—that hardly seems like enough information to verify whether *Opportunity X* is your calling.

Thus, many ways have evolved to attack this fundamental paradox. Some methods are entirely logic-based, such as analyzing your skills for a sense of where you rightly belong. Some are mystical—seeing the guiding hand in coincidence, or even being contacted directly by spiritual guides. Sometimes a newfound sense of conviction rose from the ashes after a deeply felt tragedy or loss. Of course, some people always knew where they belonged. They just did. All these ways will be portrayed.

More specifically, the ten people in this section attacked the paradox one way, and then, once they had some actual experience, they had to adjust—not just change their life, but also change the way they constructed that sense of "rightness."

2 ||| Have You Looked Under the Bed?

IGNORING THE OBVIOUS

Noah Goldfader didn't think he was ever going to find it. He told me that since college he's had ten jobs in eight years, spread over six cities in four states on two coasts. But when I broke it down with him, employer by employer, I tallied no less than *sixteen* jobs in those eight years. He never stayed anywhere long enough to move up the ladder—everything was entry-level. Two-thirds of these jobs were in marketing and promotion. He'd given away Frappuccinos and Cuervo Gold tequila, put up placards during WNBA games and three-on-three NBA Hoop It Up tournaments, and created never-used ad campaigns for Levi's blue jeans. The highlights of his travels were pounding Coronas with Rod Stewart's band and standing on the same court with Kevin Garnett. He's thirty now. Currently unemployed. His older brother tells him to stop fucking around, thinks he's a slacker.

But Noah's no slacker. You can't fault him for not trying. My definition of a slacker is someone who thinks all jobs suck and isn't going to lift a finger. Noah would happily work sixteen-hour days if he only knew what it was he should be doing. He was all-too-desperate to find his song in life, and was panicked that there wasn't one out there for him. He didn't expect it to be easy. But he sure wanted an answer.

The night I went to meet Noah, he was living in old army housing in the Presidio in San Francisco, sharing an apartment with three roommates. We cracked a beer and sat in his tidy living room. He was thrilled I actually showed up. I think he might have vacuumed before I arrived— the air smelled of a tired electric motor. He was super-introverted, twisted up by his thoughts, but not a dungeon-dweller or a Web-geek—more goofy, maybe a little mentally lopsided; intuitive one moment, blind the next. He was a sports nut. His father was a football star for Brandeis University, then a minor league catcher in the Milwaukee Braves organization. His mom was a nurse for twenty years.

"I believe everyone has a unique gift to give the world," he agonized. "I sure as hell don't want to be one of those people who dies with the music still inside them. I wish I could find what the hell I was put on this earth to do."

He looked at me like maybe I'd pull the answer out of thin air. Long silence. I didn't know what to tell him. I wasn't exactly sure why I came here, why his story piqued my interest.

He went on. "Have you ever seen or heard Dick Vitale, the college basketball commentator? He loves what he does. You could lock him in a gym for sixteen hours a day and he'd never look at his watch. Why can't we all have a passion like that?"

I glanced over at a coffee table book on Ben Hogan. Noah grabbed the book and leafed through it. "This book makes the hairs on my arm stand up. Hogan was the ultimate. Forget Tiger. Nobody understood Hogan. Like nobody gets me. I wouldn't even know where to start when talking about Hogan. That guy had a singular fixation. I wish I had that."

Noah desperately wanted my opinion. I shot at the low-hanging fruit. "What does your brother do?"

"He's in finance down in SoCal."

"Does he love it?"

"He doesn't expect to. He's stable, has his act together, and owns his house. That's what he says matters."

"You know, some people struggle with this question, and some people just *don't*. Look for help from people who relate. Not your brother."

"I don't know. I'm starting to see his point. How many years should I spend hunting for this answer, and when should I give up and get on with my life?"

"What would 'giving up' mean?"

"It'd mean admitting there is no answer for me. Not everybody gets a passion. What do you think? What have you found? Do you think everybody gets a passion?"

"No way." Suggesting otherwise would be irresponsible. However, there was a catch—a significant catch. I was going to regret telling him this. I was almost certainly condemning him to more years of frustration. "Some people are born into their passions. Some never get them and don't care. But I think if you're *really struggling* to find it—and I think you have, I mean, you've gone all over the country to find it—it's almost certainly for a reason. I think the depth of your struggling is the sign there's some-

thing there. Something in you that's trying to get out. People who don't have passions don't struggle." I didn't know what I believed when I started my research, but I'd heard enough stories that this was coming clear. Young people often said, "I feel an urge, a vacuum. But I'm not called to anything in particular." But those who had succeeded in finding a calling remembered that feeling as the beginning of the process. "The call was muffled and vague at first. That blank urge *is* the call."

Noah nodded slowly with deep appreciation. "Wow. Yeah, my struggling *is* the sign."

"So keep looking."

"If I had something to show for these eight years, I might feel better about myself."

That was another interesting question. Are the years before you find your passion a waste? I hear that a lot. *My real life won't begin until I find my place.* That's bogus, and I told Noah so. "Sounds like in eight years you've learned a lot about promotion and marketing. Maybe those are tools you're going to need when you finally figure out what you're here for. So what if it's been Frappuccinos, Cuervo Gold, and Levi's? You're learning promotion. Maybe someday you'll need to promote what you really believe in."

Noah was listening raptly, so I launched into the story of my younger brother. He's really good with people. Always has been. For this reason he was always a natural salesperson. But he never had a passion, and he had become convinced he was not a passionate person. Our family always told him not to worry, and that when he made more money he'd feel good about what he was doing. But he did worry, and one day he gave up sales, went back to school, studied medicine, and became a nurse.

"Does he like it?" Noah asked with some urgency, his face starting to light up.

"He *loves* it. He can't wait to go to work. He talks about his patients all the time. I'm telling you this story because he took this gift with people— a gift that he'd honed in those years in sales—and he brought it to nursing. And it makes him a *great* nurse. It's the same gift, the same talent—but rather than selling insurance, or selling game meat, or selling Pennzoil, he's using it to *help people*."

Noah's face radiated enlightenment like I'd said the most insightful thing he had ever heard.

"That's what I want to do!" he blurted.

"You want to become a nurse?" I was confused.

"No, no—I want to *help people* . . ."

"Good . . ." I wasn't following, and I certainly didn't see this coming.

"I want to help people . . . *play better golf*."

Play better golf! "You do?"

"Yeah. That's what I like more than anything. I love it."

In the back of my mind, I recognized this was kind of humorous, but in the moment it felt very serious. "Wait a minute! If you love golf, why haven't you been doing that? Why have you been traveling the country, going broke, and giving yourself a hard time these eight years, when all along your passion was *golf*?"

"I never thought of it as a way to help people before. But it is. I mean, I really feel like I'm helping people when I'm giving lessons."

Probably every time in his life he brought up golf as a career, someone shot him down. He confirmed this. He mentioned his love of golf to his rabbi, and she didn't know what to make of it. Then he spent $100 an hour on two sessions with Patti Wilson, *the* guru of Silicon Valley career counselors, who is famous for helping entrepreneurs discover their dreams. Noah had high hopes and put a lot of stock in her advice. She asked him, "If you could do anything, what would you do?" He told her he wanted to make people better golfers. She dismissed this quickly, as if giving lessons on the driving range were beneath someone with a college degree. The sessions were a bust.

"You should have stuck up for yourself."

"I'm not good enough to be a club pro, anyway."

"Golf's a ten-billion-dollar industry, Noah. Surely there's a lot of jobs that don't require a scratch handicap." Noah responded like nobody had ever acted interested before.

"Can I show you something?"

"Sure." I was trying to be supportive.

He went into his bedroom, reached under his bed and pulled out two handcrafted gizmos—a swing trainer and a newfangled putter grip. Noah turned out to be an inventor. I couldn't believe it. This guy had been looking for his passion for eight years, and the whole time it was under his bed!

He said, "With a new grip like this, I can help a lot of golfers at once. It's helping people on a larger scale."

"Noah, why aren't you working at Ping or Wilson or Nike?"

He said the entry-level jobs for the manufacturers are in sales. "Would that feel good, hawking clubs to retail outlets? I don't know. I don't think I'd like it."

Ahhh, the Entry Level Problem. All entry-level jobs suck the big one. How do you get past that? "Noah, imagine for a moment you've become one of Ping's mad scientist inventors. Would that make you happy?"

"Yeah, that'd be awesome!"

"Well, twice a year you'd have to go to a Ping sales conference, at which you'd present your inventions to the Ping sales reps. These reps will be the voice of your putter grip to the stores and the pros. Your invention will live or die based on how they perceive it. Maybe you're going to be an inventor, but don't you think you'll be a more successful inventor if you've walked in a rep's shoes? If Ping called you tomorrow and hired you as an inventor, you'd probably fail miserably, because you don't know shit about distribution, or materials science, or manufacturing. If you're serious about nurturing your invention, you'll put in the years to learn the skills to protect your gift. So when the day comes, you'll be *ready*."

"Whoa, I never thought of it like that."

"People have this stupid fantasy that if you're the *creator*, or the *inventor*, or the *artist*, you hand over your creation to businessmen and cash the royalty checks. That's a fantasy. It's irresponsible to their gift. If you have a gift, you should take care of it."

"Did you do that?"

"Absolutely. During my late twenties I was attending writing school at night. I believed that someday I would write something worthwhile. So for five years, during the day, I put in my time at a small publishing house. I learned everything I could about the industry. I prepared the financials and paid the bills. I typeset books. I shipped orders. I designed jackets. I wrote press releases. I made publicity calls. You name it, I did it. I knew publishing wasn't my calling, and the pay sucked, but I was determined to have the skills to protect the books I would someday write."

"And did it make a difference?"

"When my first book came out, I did at least a half-dozen unusual things that helped my publisher get the book an audience. It made a huge difference."

"Wow."

Noah was honored that I would equate his love of golf with my love of writing. (Of course I would!) He wrote me frequently afterward, remarking how much of a relief it was to tell his story and not have someone like his brother say he was wasting his time. That's all he had ever needed. A month after we met, he jumped into entry-level golf sales, becoming a merchandise manager at a Sportmart. He also reinvented his grip prototype and sent it off to the USGA, and demonstrated it at a couple of golf expos. He was on his way. Two months later he discovered the secret of the golf swing, which had eluded him his whole life. He taught it to me at a driving range. Sometimes I feel good about my little role in his life, and other times it freaks me out that I would have said something that loosened the knot in his mind, allowing him to feel his desires without guilt.

So what about this notion? Does it really count as "helping people" to teach them the secret of the swing? Or is using that language disrespectful to the meatier contributions made by teachers, doctors, and ministers?

I've kept track of this question, and it seems that just about any profession can be performed with a confidence that it's contributing to the well-being of others—just as any profession can feel soulless and selfish. There is no official list of honorable, noble careers. The proof is in the individual's experience. You either find the pleasure of connecting with others in your daily reality or you don't—this nobility is not something that can be assigned or predetermined. Often it defies stereotypes.

In this book, you'll meet many people who devoted themselves to really helping others. But you'll also meet many like Noah Goldfader. Later in this section, you'll meet a young man who found his connection to others by baking cakes. And in the section after, you'll meet a man who stumbled into catfish farming during a tough time—it wasn't his dream, but he came to feel like a vital member of the community, part of something larger than himself.

3 ‖ Hunted by Her Cause

LEARNING FROM HARD TIMES

Janelle London always thought of herself as a cause-type person. She grew up in Austin, went to college in California, and thought she might find her cause on campus, but none quite seemed like her thing. So after graduation she used her Texas connections to join Senator Lloyd Bentsen's staff in Washington, D.C. Again, nothing stirred her heart. She thought there must be something wrong with her. "How can I be surrounded by all these lobbyists and advocates and *not* find a cause?" She had a self-described "boring" life, without any intense passion. So she went to law school—it's often what those who leave Washington do next—hoping she'd find something in law and justice that would make her come alive.

She didn't.

So she became an intellectual-property lawyer, working at a big firm in San Francisco for the next seven years. Holding on to her hope for a higher purpose was tough—she worked long hours, and she had a lot of health problems. Most of those years, she just fought to get by. Someday life would get a little easier, and then she could go looking again.

On the night of the millennium, December 31, 1999, she was thinking about the next century. All that time ahead. All that time past. Suddenly it occurred to her: *Maybe I've had my cause all along.*

Maybe I've had my cause for the past seven years, and I've been ignoring it!

Flash back to summer of 1992. Bored by work, Janelle had gone to Barcelona for a month with friends to watch the Olympics. She was getting a ton of rest, sleeping twelve hours a night or more. She was still fatigued, but figured it was the heat. It was hard keeping up with friends. She'd walk a block and need to sit down on the curb for a spell, chastising herself: "I shouldn't have had that extra croissant." Her muscles cramped,

particularly her fingers, which clenched up involuntarily. She ignored it. Seven of her ten fingers had swollen into itchy fat sausages, and she blamed the new dish detergent she'd been scrubbing the plates with.

"I don't know what I was thinking, but I kept pushing it out of my mind."

Finally, her hands were so damn itchy she walked into the ER, and the night nurses trotted her out for a laugh. "This American princess thinks itchy fingers is something to come to the hospital for!" Then they tested her and discovered her kidneys had shut down. Complete renal failure. Janelle was plucked from the shredded narrative of her old life and tossed down into this new one, unable to make sense of it. Oh shit! How is this happening to me?

She was whisked back to the United States for dialysis treatments, and was put at the bottom of the long waiting list for a kidney transplant.

Seven years later, she was still waiting. And on that night of the millennium, it was impossible to tolerate her job anymore. "I was sitting in this office, surrounded by corporate greed, doing nothing to improve this shortage." Exactly 77,589 people were awaiting an organ transplant. The previous year, 5,600 people had died while waiting for a match. What more important cause could she find!? That New Year's Eve, vowing not to be in this position another year, she gave notice. She had little money saved, but she owned a rental house in Austin, which provided enough income to cover her deductible on the dialysis treatments. She volunteered for several fund-raisers, praying it would magically evolve into full-time work.

Perhaps it was just luck, or perhaps it was karmic reward for making this

leap, but shortly later a kidney was found that matched, and she success-
fully underwent transplant surgery at Stanford Hospital.

Then more good news—after more than a year of unemployment, she
was offered a job as the executive director of the Northern California
chapter of the National Kidney Foundation. Having followed her story
for a few months, I was excited for her and we arranged to meet, finally, in
person. If possible, I like to meet people for the first time on a big day in
their life. I suggested I come by her new office on her first day of work, but
she suggested a café instead. She didn't have an ounce of fat on her; she
had recently competed in her first Transplant Olympics, and had ridden a
bicycle down the East Coast to raise money for organ-donation awareness.

For a while, our conversation centered on why she had looked everywhere for a cause but in her own experience. It now seemed ridiculous,
and the topic made her laugh at her old self.

I asked, "Is it possible that you pushed it away because you thought it
was hopeless—like, 'How can I ever really make a difference?' " I'd seen a
tendency to avoid problems that seem intractable. A lot of people like to
solve problems. Not as many are willing to *devote* themselves to problems.

"I think that was part of it," she said. "But really, I was in such a state of
denial. Three days a week I'd go to dialysis, four hours a time, and when
I'd come out of there, I would just try to pretend everything was normal.
I never talked about it with my coworkers. The last thing I wanted to do
was continue to dwell on my kidneys."

I told her that my younger brother was a transplant nurse, and he says
that patients often try very hard to forget. They want to put it behind
them.

"Like any pain," Janelle agreed. "In fact, my first year on the list, I actually had a transplant, which my body later rejected. But at the time, I
thought my problem was fixed. When I walked out of the hospital after
the surgery, I was done with this bad phase and never wanted to talk about
it again. I never went back and said 'thank you' to the nurses."

"You found your cause—but only after years of pushing it away."

"Ironically," she added, "my *mother* lost a kidney when I was in high
school. This cause has been around my whole life, waiting for me to pay
attention."

It made me wonder—how many of us have been dealt hard times in
life, suffered the blows of existence, and rather than be transformed by
it—rather than gain from it a purpose that can be so incredibly meaningful because it comes from personal experience—we simply try to get back
to normal, get past it? Most people's purpose comes from experience; it's

not something you choose out of a course catalog. But you only have a transformative experience if you're open to being changed by it.

I asked about the year of unemployment. That's a long time to be out of a job. "Did you ever think about just going back?"

"I took some piecemeal work from my old firm. It helped pay the bills, but it confirmed I really didn't want to go back. I was also volunteering at clinics and working with patients. That's what called to me. I met lots of people who worked in this field. They made this choice of life seem workable. It just took over a year to meet enough people and learn how the industry works."

I said, "Well, thank God you finally figured this out and got the job."

"Well, that's another thing. See, I turned that job down."

"You're not working?"

"No."

"Why? Janelle!"

"I don't think it's quite right for me."

It explained why we were meeting in a café, but I was dumbfounded. "You gave me a big speech about how important it is we work to increase awareness about organ donation! This job sounds like your best chance to do that! What am I missing? I don't get it."

"The job requires me to do a lot of fund-raising and budgeting."

"So?"

"My ideal job would let me be a little more involved in policy. And I'd like to have more weekly interaction with patients."

That seemed nitpicky to me, though I didn't say so. Janelle insisted she should hold out for her dream job. I suspected some deeper motive was behind it. Was she trying once again to push away memories of her trauma, memories that would be kept raw if she went to work for the National Kidney Foundation? Or had the lifestyle of unemployment made her lethargic? I'd read a statistic that people who remain unemployed for over a year commonly never go back to work again.

But it wasn't my part to protest. "Janelle, help me understand your point of view. Why not take this job and work *toward* your dream job? I mean, are you qualified for your dream job? You're a patent lawyer."

She said, "After all I've been through, I don't want to settle."

"It doesn't sound to me like running one of the biggest foundations is settling."

"Have other people you've talked to settled? Or did they hold out?"

"They usually built on what they could get, and worked towards their goal. They didn't start at the top."

She seemed unswerving in her intent. Ours was kind of an awkward hug good-bye; I'd arrived expecting to hear a success story, and instead I left with a sadness. I felt like a parent watching a child set herself up for failure by shooting too high. Dreams are kind of like children—they need time to mature before we burden them with too lofty expectations. Like the distinction between solving problems and devoting yourself to them, dreams are to be pursued, not just achieved.

A month later, I learned that my worries for her were unfounded and presumptive. Her dream job came true, incredibly, perfectly. She found the job opening on the Internet, running the patient partnership program for DaVita, the country's second-largest dialysis provider, which has forty thousand patients in five hundred centers across the United States. Not only would Janelle be supervising the program for those patients, but she would spend 30 percent of her time in D.C. lobbying and shaping policy. Exactly what she wanted. She was ecstatic. She was anxious to get started and keep me posted on how it turned out.

I apologized profusely for having doubted her motive in refusing to settle. She didn't seem to remember that I'd questioned her. In her mind, I'd been supportive, and she thought of me as an ally. That surprised me.

Over the next year, she turned into this incredibly passionate and happy person. Her new job was part of that; Janelle loved her work with patients. The other part was, she fell in love with a wonderful man named Jared, and in the next year they were married. Were the two related? Did her newfound career satisfaction put her in a better position to love someone else? She thought so, absolutely. On our last meeting, almost two years after that first one, she showed me photographs of all of her patients in the dialysis center. Then she put my hand over her left hip, where I could feel the transplanted kidney, slightly bulky, doing its work. Then she put my hand over her right hip, to feel their growing baby. There were some risks in undertaking pregnancy, but they were manageable—she'd passed all the screening tests. Besides, what was life for?

4 ||| Synchronicity or Not

Kat James had never gone to college, so she felt lucky that the long boom years carried her up into the ranks of successful professionals. She worked for a public relations agency in London. The hours were long and demanding, and she'd often wonder, "What am I after? What do I want?" Her rote answer: Someday, one of her clients would offer her a big salary and a vice presidency. She wanted to move up—or assumed she did. Didn't everyone?

The hope of getting a job like this sustained her through the many leadership changes at her agency. It was for this that she endured the two-hour commute each morning and evening, from her home in Brighton to her office in London.

A year and a half ago, at a time when many people in high-tech felt lucky to have any job at all, Kat was offered a job running the PR department at one of the hottest telecoms in the U.K. To convince her, they offered to *double* her salary. Double it!

At first she said yes, instinctively.

But the offer to double her salary had an unintended effect. It made it crystal clear that if she was to take this job, she would be doing it for the money. Not because it would be fun and interesting. For the money, plain and simple.

Over the next three weeks, she stalled. She told the telecom she was reconsidering.

She thought, *If I accept this, where will it end?*

This was not what she wanted for the rest of her life.

The thing was, Kat never really cared about money. She didn't spend much and had little desire to acquire possessions. The idea that she

needed more money to be free wasn't *her* idea, it was an ethos of the industry she worked in. She'd listened to it rather than to herself.

She told the telecom "no thanks" and instead bought tickets to go out to California. San Francisco was like Brighton, right on the ocean, without the two-hour commute to London. She wished she worked closer to the sea and nature. She didn't know what she would do when she arrived, but she'd let that work itself out.

She made her plan, but as her travel date approached, she got a sick feeling in her gut. So strong was this feeling of anxiety that she had to cancel her plans.

What was going on? What would she do?

She had one thought. She barely let herself consider it. Ever since she was six years old, Kat had said that if money was no object, and if status didn't matter, and if there was nothing in the way . . . she would be a landscape gardener.

Why not go do the thing she'd always wanted to do?

This was a laughable notion. She was not a horticultural hobbyist. She didn't even have a garden at her home! And she did not come from a family that encouraged such leaps of fancy. Her family worked in offices, not in gardens. Her mother had been employed by the same firm for thirty-two years. Her grandfather had worked for a single firm for fifty years.

A few days later, she went to a music festival, and between bands she had a tarot card reading performed, somewhat as a joke. Kat didn't believe in that stuff. Up turned goddess cards and earth cards. The tarot reader looked at these cards and pronounced, "You would be really good at tending people's gardens."

Wow! Was it that obvious, that a complete stranger could see this in her?

The next day, she recounted the amazing coincidence to a neighbor. "Are you thinking about doing it?" the neighbor asked.

"I'm thinking," Kat said.

The neighbor said she had just thrown into the trash a catalog for courses at Brighton City College. "I'll go get it," she offered.

Kat took the catalog home with her. The college offered an extensive horticulture program that awarded two-year vocational certification. The first class began the next week, and the enrollment session for the class *was that very afternoon.*

Guided by another in the string of coincidences, Kat went down to enroll immediately. She felt light and happy and excited about what she was doing.

Classes were from 9 A.M. to 5 P.M., three days a week. A third of each day was spent in the classroom, two-thirds outdoors. She loved it. There were two other former professional women in the program, so Kat didn't feel like an outsider. She rented two of the three bedrooms in her house to cover her mortgage. But what of her expenses? There was a big one-hundred-year-old nursery in Brighton that would be ideal to work for because it was only a ten-minute walk from home. She called to ask for employment. She was told they had no jobs available until Christmas season, but they suggested she stop by in person sometime. She walked over right away, and they hired her on the spot to start immediately.

More synchronicity. If she hadn't been offered that job . . . if she hadn't gone to the music festival . . . if she had waited one more day to chat with her neighbor . . . if she hadn't walked over to the nursery . . . it felt like the universe had conspired to make this new path in life easy for her, offering a vote of confidence from some mysterious force to counteract her inherent doubts.

When I arrived in Brighton a year and a half later, on an unseasonably hot day in April, it was the role of this synchronicity I most wanted to explore. Did her confidence that this was the right direction for her really depend on that alignment of good fortune? I'd heard many stories like it. If you believe in God, then believing in a guiding hand often follows. But if you're not a religious person (Kat wasn't), then how do you make sense of these beneficial strings of coincidence?

Kat's sense of this decision being right for her was still firmly intact. She loved her new life. And she still put a tiny bit of stock in that synchronicity that had guided her. "We should at least acknowledge these signs, even if we don't act on them. There's often something in them." But in the last eighteen months, the benefits of synchronicity had been replaced by the benefits of consistent hard work. Only a half hour earlier, she'd taken an exam on interior landscaping. In two months, she would earn her advanced level in garden design, and she intended to continue her training with the Royal Horticulture Society's grade 2 course next year. She was working at the nursery three days a week, and just that week she had incorporated her own design company, called Gardenscene2 (as in, "I'd like to have my garden seen to"). She had her first contract, which was to design a garden twenty by twenty meters.

She showed me her illustrations. She was turning a flat, mossy mess into a patio retreat, separated from the house by a pergola covered with aromatic climbing plants. The lawn would be returfed and an herb garden added. Numerous plants of interesting shapes, forms, and textures framed the new seating area. She was also installing solar panels to power the lighting and water heater. I was impressed by the scope. It was a significant, big-budget project that required managing contractors for the construction. I didn't even know one could earn a degree in horticulture.

This hard work had changed how she told her story. Her sense of this choice being "right" no longer hinged on a tarot reading and a timely conversation with a neighbor. After all, it wasn't just luck that had steered her to a new life. Her heart told her not to take that dream job. Her gut told her not to move to San Francisco. She'd wanted to design gardens since she was six years old. She finally listened to that desire. She would have gotten here, synchronicity or not. She now got her sense of "rightness" from the joy in her life. She was fulfilled. She was proud of her work. Every day, this "rightness" reaffirmed itself.

What then is the real role of coincidence and circumstance? It's hard to say. There's a tension there. We want to ascribe meaning to it, stitching together that vote of confidence we need. From the pattern we weave our story. The need to do this stitching comes from deep within; it's a way for our often ignored longings to communicate with our rational mind, a way to cry out. At the same time, we don't want to attribute too much to the cosmos. We prefer to be actors in our story. So like Kat, our story evolves. In its early stages, it's magic-realist. Later, when we have more to go on, we draw on actual experience.

Kat and I spent the evening walking through Old Lanes, the historic district of Brighton. I had another set of questions for her.

"You kind of dropped out of the traditional status framework," I said. "Most people need the context of a company and an industry and a title and a salary level and regular performance reviews to provide a measure of self-worth. How does one forego that, and dare go alone?"

"I've been bothered by that far less than I imagined," she said. "My life has plenty of structure and context. Between classes and the nursery and my new company, I'm very—" She paused. "I was going to say *busy,* but that's not right, because I'm not harried. I'm very *active.* I'm still pragmatic. I don't feel like a dropout."

And how was she doing financially? Did she regret not taking that doubled salary?

She said many people in her shoes would have taken the double salary in order to save up for the leap into garden design, believing that money is the path to freedom. She didn't, and she found that true freedom came from the confidence that she could live within her means, whatever those means might be. Between her hourly pay and her rented bedrooms, she made it work. More important, her sense of purpose and meaning weren't tied to her pay, because she was getting so much psychic income from her calling. It had been clarifying, releasing her from vanities.

Kat knew her *job* would change; she didn't realize how much *she* would change, being surrounded by nature rather than technology. High-tech celebrates new ideas and wants to rewrite the rule book; horticulture honors wisdom passed down for centuries. The Internet treats the world as one big global market. Horticulture respects that all gardening is local; what grows in the greenbelt of Brighton might not grow in London, et cetera. It's a very different mind-set and approach to life. Kat believes nature can teach us, nurture our souls. It makes what she does feel important.

Like one of her plants, Kat's found a bit of rich soil that nourishes her well. She's taking better care of it now.

5 ||| The Dharma Adviser

BEING VS. DOING

Here's a refrain I heard occasionally: "All this *obsession* about our careers. It's not what you *do* that's important, it's who you *are*. If people stopped *worrying* about what they do, they'd be a lot happier. Just go get a job. Enjoy your nights and weekends."

It's the Day Job philosophy, and I think it's a fine solution, if you can make it work for you. Later, there's a chapter on people who've moved to New Orleans to live in a culture that doesn't put so much emphasis on *how* you make a living. They enjoy their nights and weekends, to splendid success. And I tell the story of a woman who finally found peace and fulfillment only when she finally gave up her glamorous "dream career" and learned how to appreciate real life in all its ordinariness. Learning to love what you get—to make the best of it—is at least half the answer.

But those stories come later, and for now I'm still carrying this torch. The reality is, many people can't make that solution work for them. They have a job—but the job is eating at their soul. The job doesn't allow them enough time to spend with their kids. The job doesn't pay enough. The job requires them to act unethically. Or they just aren't any good at that job, because it requires them to be someone they aren't. I agree: Who you are is *more important than* what you do. The goal is to bring what you do in alignment with who you are, so you don't end up being someone you don't want to be.

This story expands on this conflict. Mike Blandino was focused entirely on the philosophy of *being* until real life caught up and his life got complicated. At that point, he invited me to help figure out how to get back to his quest. We corresponded for two months, and then I went to see him in Baton Rouge. I became the guide, rather than the listener.

Mike's twenty-five. As an undergrad at Louisiana State University, he

studied music, religion, and math. His grades were excellent but he never thought twice about a career; he assumed getting by would always work itself out. Those conversations were too pedestrian for him. He was absorbed with the great questions of metaphysics—"Why do we exist?" and "What is the point of the universe?" and "What's important?" His academic adviser told him he was on a quest, which was dead-on. After graduating he wandered the earth pretending to be a philosopher, following Phish on its tour through Amsterdam and Paris, popping fun drugs, reading Burroughs, and racking up debt from phone sex calls. So he came home, sorely needing a place to live and a way to eat. He held off pedestrian reality another year by ending up as the temple keeper at the Dharma Center in New Orleans, which is not in any grand temple, but a little blue house three doors off Desai Boulevard, near City Park. There he was taught that from the beginning of time everything has always been perfect and only needs to be appreciated. One night, on Ecstasy, he bumped into his old friend's ex-girlfriend, and he had a new appreciation for her. They fell in love and let nature take its course and so, of course, she got pregnant. Five months later, with her belly big as a volleyball, it dawned on her for the first time:

"Mike, one of us has to get a job. And I'm pregnant."

A job!

The quest had come to an end. Welcome to reality.

Mike figured, no problem. "I've got a BA, right?" What he didn't know about getting a job could fill a phone book. He applied for jobs that were listed, went in for interviews, and was turned down by all. Old Navy, a pharmaceutical company sales force, a fly-by-night day-trader boiler room . . . in other words, every $20K-a-year starter position. Couldn't even get hired as a security guard. He was always too smart, or too educated, or too aloof, or too naive. He applied for a job as a janitor, but didn't get it.

With nowhere else to turn, Mike went back to his alma mater in Baton Rouge and applied for a position listed in the paper. The position was offered to him—well, actually, it was offered to some other woman first, but then she had a family medical emergency, and they had to hire *right away* because the state of Louisiana was instituting a hiring freeze that very afternoon. Mike's application was sitting there, and thus he lucked into the job.

I won't tell you what his job is yet—I'm going to keep that a secret for a moment. To him, it didn't matter what type of job it was, as long as he had one. I'll say only that he sits behind a desk all day, and when we met I was sitting on the other side of that desk. He felt that his quest was severely handicapped by having a family and a job, but his way of handling this confinement was to perform his job in accordance with his Buddhist principles. This meant keeping thoughts of disappointment out by focusing on the moment. He tries to let things *be*. He doesn't complain. *The world is already perfect.*

At one point, he pulled a book from a drawer. It was a book he'd picked up at the Dharma Center, prescribing a strict Zen formula that involved breaking the workday into fifteen-minute chunks and trying, in each fifteen-minute chunk, to do only one thing and avoid distraction. This was the path to happiness it offered, and Mike had been trying to follow its suggestion. Mike asked me what I thought of the book and the philosophy.

"I think it's complete bunk," I said. "I think you should throw that away."

He was amazed. "Really? Why?"

"There's a lot of ways to find meaning in work, and that book seems ignorant of all of them." I'm normally not so blunt, but he'd asked my opinion, and I had one.

"But we can't all have a higher purpose, can we?" he asked.

"Do you like your job?"

"Very much."

"Why do you do it?" I asked.

"It pays pretty good. Nice office. Nobody bothers me."

"That's all?" Of all the ways we construct that sense of "rightness," having a nice office where nobody bothers you seemed the shallowest of all possible motives. "What about your daughter, Julia. How old is she?"

"Nine months."

"Does it feel good to provide for her and your wife? Does that fulfill you?"

"Yeah. At first it was such a relief, and now . . ." He brightened up, thinking about it, but didn't finish his sentence.

"You feel proud, right?"

"In Buddhism, pride is . . . a vice."

"I know. But that's what you *feel,* right? I mean, I can see it on your face when you talk about them."

"Yeah."

This troubled me, that he felt his religion didn't allow him to enjoy caring for others because there's a hint of ego in doing so.

We discussed the Buddhist belief that the world just needs to be appreciated—that trying to change things is often futile, and only leads to frustration. To me, this can too easily become an excuse for passivity. I shared with Mike the story of Za Rinpoche, who was an expert in maintaining a proper state of being, but nevertheless had to take control of his own life at a certain point. I argued, "Shouldn't we try to change our lives for the better?" Mike admitted that within Buddhism there was a lot of disagreement about this notion, but at his temple in New Orleans the monks taught disengagement.

"Were you always a Buddhist, Mike?"

He explained that he was from Houma, a Cajun city in the swamps south of New Orleans. His dad sold commercial insurance and his mom was an accounts receivable clerk. They're Catholics and frequently tell Mike he is going to hell. But Catholicism doesn't work for him. He used to pass out at church as a kid, because the kneeling would cut off his circulation. In those unconscious moments he would have intense visions and dreams.

"And you found Buddhism in college?" I asked.

"Yes."

"It must have been a difficult transition, with your parents not mincing words, pressuring you."

"That's right. We had a lot of fights over the wedding, too."

"But it's been necessary, sounds like."

"Yes."

"So why is it okay to search for a *church* that's right for you, but not a *pro-*

fession that's right for you? Why, when it comes to work, are we supposed to simply accept that this is just the way it is?"

This stopped him. He didn't have an answer, and he would not find one in the next two hours that we spent together.

You might be wondering why I'd criticize Mike. Why attack his views? Why not keep my thoughts to myself? Well, I might have—if Mike's job had been anything other than what it was. If he'd been a janitor, or a retail clerk, and he wanted to divide the day into fifteen-minute increments— no problem.

Here's the great irony:

Mike's job?

Career counselor!

Well, not technically. Technically, Mike's job is academic adviser. If you're one of the 1,100 students with grades good enough to be in the Honors College at LSU, a couple times a year you are supposed to walk over to the second floor of the French House and sit down with Mike for your scheduled appointment. You're supposed to tell Mike what you want to do when you grow up, and he's supposed to translate this into a list of classes you should take, which will prepare you for the life you have chosen. Until your senior year, he's the closest thing to a career counselor the school offers.

One would think that a prerequisite for giving career advice would be having had a career, or at least aspiring to one. But apparently not. Mike's never had a real job (other than this one).

Believe me, he sees the irony in this.

But it really wasn't a lack of experience that was hindering his ability to be a good career counselor. It was his devotion to his Buddhist principles of detachment. He never shared his own story with students. He doesn't try to relate to them or influence their thinking. He simply follows the es- tablished official conversation: if you want to be a doctor, take these classes; if an engineer, take these, a businessman, these.

"And what if they don't know what they want to do when they gradu- ate?" I asked.

"If they're not sure?"

"Or have no idea. What do you do then?" I asked.

"I tell them to come back when they *do* know, and I'll help them pick classes."

"You don't try to help them figure it out?"

"Not really. No. We chat a little, but that's not really my job."

I'll admit: this upset me some. I was worried Mike was neglecting his duty to those students. They *needed* him. I also thought Mike was missing out on a chance to have a very meaningful work experience. Life had dealt him this fate—why not seize it? He was wondering what to do with his life—why not make *this job* his purpose? The opportunity to do so was trickling through his fingers, like sand in an open hand.

He said, "This school is dominated by students who want to go into business and engineering. They want to make money. I don't think that way, but who am I to tell them there's more to think about?"

"You can't be telling these kids that all they should shoot for is something that pays pretty good and has a nice office where nobody bothers them."

"I don't say that."

"Your silence says it loud and clear."

He'd never thought of that. "You think I give that impression?"

"You're giving it to me."

He seemed troubled by his quandary. "What do you think I should say to them?" he asked.

"I can't put words in your mouth. Tell them what you think."

"I don't want to intrude."

I thought about it and chose my words carefully. "Mike, if a student comes in here, and she's headstrong about going into business so she can make money, I don't think you or I have a right to question that. You're absolutely right. We shouldn't intrude. But what about the students who don't show up for their appointments, or who never even call for an appointment? They're probably the ones who most need your help."

"You think I should call them?"

"Why not?"

"What would I say?"

"Encourage them to come in and talk."

"What if they think it's stupid?"

"Tell them that thinking about what they should do with their life isn't pedestrian. Tell them that if they ignore it, reality will bite them in the ass like it did you. Tell them it's modern philosophy for people who have to feed their wife and kids. Tell them it's okay not to have an answer, but it's not okay to stop looking for one. Tell them about Aristotle."

" 'What is the good life?' "

"Exactly." Aristotle spent much of his time pondering this very question.

"To so many of the students coming through here, the good life is a house with a detached garage big enough for a Land Rover that can carry their three kids to the mall."

"Not to Aristotle. The good life wasn't something you owned, it was skills you mastered. The good life wasn't to own a big home, but to aspire to being a master builder. Not to have three kids and a fluffy dog, but to aspire to be a great parent. Listen, you're a philosophy student, you probably know this stuff way better than me. Aristotle embraced strict logic a little too much for my taste. I'm just saying—until this last year you ignored what to *do* with your life because it wasn't one of the great philosophical questions. But some philosophers insist it *is*."

I was being pretty tough. At no other point in my year of interviews did I so directly challenge a subject. But Mike didn't seem to be bruised by my challenge. In fact, he responded to it. He was very interested in the possibility of reaching out to students who didn't come to him. He was naturally shy and short on words, so doing this was very scary.

"I don't have any experience," he admitted. "What do I know about the working world?"

I suggested his inexperience might help him better see the world from a student's point of view. Maybe they would relate to him, because he was young, and had sat in this very same seat not four years prior. Their angst and confusion? Mike had felt it.

"I still feel it," he admitted. "I haven't figured out much."

"You can share your mistakes," I said. "You can learn as much from mistakes as you can successes."

I think Mike knew the potential he had been sitting on. I think he was waiting for someone to make it *okay* to reach for it.

"Mike, when you were sitting here, you were told you were on a quest?"

"That's right. I really had my delusions of grandeur back then."

"Have you given up your quest?"

"It's hard to imagine ever getting back to it."

"Maybe the next phase of the quest has to be accomplished with a family and a job."

He nodded, pondering that.

I continued. "You talk like the quest is over, or on hiatus. Maybe it's not over. Maybe your quest has lead you right here. Maybe your quest has handed you this incredible opportunity to help students."

"Sometimes I've felt guilty for doing this job just to live, just to get by."

"Let it be more then. I think if you step up to it, you'll get a type of satisfaction in helping others that you've never experienced before. It'll feel good because you've been on the other side of the desk—you've been one of the confused." I wasn't telling him to go get some other job; I was telling him to attack this job differently. I was telling him not to just *be* an academic adviser. I was telling him to *do* it, and do it well.

He was going to try.

When I walked out of the French House, I noticed all the purple and gold balloons and the parents walking around with students slightly over-dressed, like everyone had been to a nice lunch. I read some of the signs on lampposts, and I realized, Oh, it's the day before graduation! Tomorrow, some five thousand students would dress in their gowns and walk through a ceremony to mark the beginning of the rest of their lives. They were young and exuberant and brimming with potential. Were they pre-pared to hang on to that feeling, when pedestrian reality would try to box them in?

6 ||| Isn't It Clear!?

Many people have this notion, or maybe it's a hope, that their calling will just come to them one day, as an epiphany, and it'll be clear. We wait for that clarity. When our notions are muddled or vague, we often don't pursue them, assuming the lack of clarity is a sign it's not our true course. If we *really* wanted to do a certain thing, the feeling would be strong, right?

Does it make sense to wait for that overpowering clarity?

Probably not. For most people I talked to, very little was clear when they began their journey. It had to unravel, slowly, over time.

Powerful epiphanies are actually very rare, and some of the most amazing ones didn't bring clarity at all.

That was the case with Debbie Brient, who had an old-fashioned religious epiphany, but didn't get that sense of clarity until two years later.

Debbie lives in San Antonio. By the date of her graduation from the University of Kansas, I'd guess she's now about fifty, but it's not always polite to ask a woman her age. Five years ago, she knew she needed something to change, but all she could think about was quitting her job and having time off. For fifteen years she had sold advertising for several Spanish-language television stations. She was a self-diagnosed workaholic, hyperactive and discombobulated, and she just wanted the treadmill to *stop*. "I was so out of touch with what I wanted," she said, "that I couldn't even order off a menu." She remembered being adventurous and willing to take risks in her youth (she had worked in Puerto Rico and Spain early in her career), and she felt that risk-taking person had been lost.

It took Debbie a year to get up the nerve to quit her job. She was afraid she'd feel lonely and unimportant. Her therapist set up a lunch for her with another professional woman who'd quit and taken a year off; the two

had lunch on Good Friday. Just meeting someone else who had done it made it okay, made it a viable option. The following Monday, Debbie told her boss she was taking a year off. The other salespeople laughed and told her she'd never make it, she'd miss it, she'd last a month.

First step: simplify. She moved from her town house into a five hundred-square-foot apartment. She got rid of all but her favorite material things, down to only what she *really needed.*

Second step: silence. The local Catholic university was affiliated with a convent in Cuernavaca, Mexico. Priests went there to plan their year ahead. She went there for two weeks. She was told not to talk to the priests; they were there to be in silence. The beds were like sleeping on cement. She felt wonderful.

Third step: travel. She'd once seen a movie about Australian Aborigines' ritual of walkabouts, completely unstructured wanderings. She dubbed her journey the "White Girl Walkabout" and headed west, alone, in her car. For a month she camped in New Mexico, Utah, and Arizona. She never stayed in hotel rooms. She never read the newspaper, never watched television, never even listened to music. She took her good experiences as omens; she felt euphoria for the first time in years.

Fourth step: go back to step one and hate yourself. A few months after getting back to San Antonio, she was tempted right back into advertising sales with a job at Telemundo that paid more than ever. She felt guilty, because she'd turned her back on what she'd hoped to do. Not surprisingly, she was more miserable than ever. She worked for Telemundo for three years, until she finally admitted that more money wasn't making her feel better.

Fifth step: repeat step three. She went on another walkabout, trying to reclaim the ground she'd lost. Before leaving, she felt heavy and defeated. The second night out, she found herself dancing with Mescalero Apache Indians around a bonfire; she took this as validation of her trip and regained her confidence.

Two weeks later, she was in Chaco Canyon, New Mexico, hiking among the historic pueblos of the Anasazi people, who lived there from 800 to 1200 A.D. It was midday; she had a backpack with water and food, and she went on a one-mile hike by herself to the pueblo of Penasco Blanco. She was mesmerized by the wonderful sound of her hiking boots crunching on the rocks underfoot. She's too wound-up a person to ever meditate; hiking is as close as she gets. She reached Penasco Blanco, and she was gazing at all the pottery shards on the ground when a voice suddenly said:

"THIS WAS YOUR HOME."

"It stopped me in my tracks," she told me. "It almost scared me. You have a normal stream of consciousness, like you're talking to yourself, and here came something else. It wasn't *my* voice."

"So did you hear it with your ear, literally?"

"No, but it was auditory, like it was inside my head but *not me.*"

"Did it have a gender?"

"The voice was very stern, very taskmaster, not gentle, and I thought of it as a man's voice, demanding my attention. And so his statement, 'THIS WAS YOUR HOME,' it was like a command, like he was telling me something, almost ordering me to do something."

"And what was he telling you?"

"Well, I didn't know. I was confused. I once lived in Albuquerque, but I didn't feel connected to New Mexico until I came here on my first walk-about. Or was he telling me I lived here in another life? Or was he telling me I ought to move back here from San Antonio? And in a way I kind of got into this mental debate with his instruction, talking back, asking, 'What do you mean?' You can imagine—I didn't want to have this incredible experience hearing this voice but not understand what he meant."

"And then what happened?"

"He said, 'ISN'T IT CLEAR!?'"

"Like it should be obvious to you?"

"Yes, and that was shocking to me because I was working hard to follow an inner voice or to do the right thing and it wasn't clear at all. So I said back, 'San Antonio's a great place, I have a great life there,' and then the voice snapped back, 'I'LL HANDLE IT!' "

" 'I'll handle it'?"

"Yes. And then that was it. It was gone."

"Did you know it was over? Was there something final in his last words?"

"I waited awhile, but that was it."

Debbie had consulted her journals right before we talked, and so she was able to reconstruct the moment.

I asked her how she felt right afterward.

"Well, I felt incredibly validated. I'd made this connection with a guide or something, and that was a reward for all the years I'd spent searching for spiritual awareness. I felt that my walkabout was justified. But I didn't feel solace. His wasn't a sympathetic voice. I felt almost scolded. He didn't say, 'Everything's going to be okay.' He insisted it should be clear, but I wasn't handed a manual. I had no idea what to do. It wasn't like, 'From here you go back to San Antonio and you do this.' There were no directions."

"Did you think your guide would handle it?"

"He said 'I'LL HANDLE IT,' and I thought, well, okay, all right—but I didn't think I could just sit back and not search for the right place or activity to dedicate my life to. I always knew I had a responsibility to continue seeking."

"Your epiphany was quite confusing."

"Absolutely."

For a while I didn't know what to make of her story. It was too mystical for my orientation. Eventually, I heard two others just like it. One woman heard a voice telling her to go to Maine. A guy named Gregory Giagnocavo was standing in the hallway of his home in Houston when he heard a voice telling him to go to Guatemala (which he couldn't have pointed to on a map). They felt guided, but as with Debbie, it was frustrating there wasn't more to the message. The voice didn't tell them what to do when they got to those places. They had to figure out the rest without any further help.

That's a significant difference from the prototypical epiphany story I learned back in high school. Saul was a Jew; he'd been commissioned by the chief priest to go to Damascus to help suppress Christianity there. As he approached Damascus on his horse, he saw a blinding light and fell off his horse and heard the voice of Jesus saying, "Why persecute thouest me?" When Saul regained his sight, it was obvious to him how he had to change. He was baptized as Paul and began preaching Christianity right away.

Clarity or not, you'd think having made that connection with her guide—even if the guide never reappeared—would help Debbie make courageous choices. You'd think she now had the spiritual strength to re-sist temptation and not fall back into her old patterns. But when she got back to San Antonio, she started looking for employment, and suddenly that daunting reality overwhelmed her again. No blissful opportunities readily emerged, and after a few months she signed on with an Internet company. The hours were long and the pay bad but she tried to rational-ize that it was a cutting-edge experience, et cetera. Her old habits sucked her back in, like the overpowering gravity of the sun. So it goes.

"Progress takes many attempts," she says now, wisely. "For me, it took three attempts and five years to end up in a place I think I am supposed to be."

Laid off a year later from the failed Internet company, she went on a trail ride in west Texas and fell in love with the land. She had trouble sleeping the first night because she was so excited to be there. The next day, she told the leader of the trail ride that she would move there if she could find work—any work. Waitressing, even. He told her that the Nature Conser-vancy of Texas had an open position for a volunteer coordinator in nearby Fort Davis. Debbie felt her gut drop. She had a moment of clarity and hunger that was completely unlike the powerful-yet-vague epiphany two years earlier. She knew: she wanted that job.

The Texas chapter of the Nature Conservancy is based in San Antonio, and on Monday morning at nine she was on the phone to the Human Re-sources Department, begging for an interview. She was told the applica-tion deadline had passed—no exceptions. And the old Debbie would have left it at that. But she wouldn't take no for an answer. She started calling friends, asking if anyone knew anybody at the Nature Conservancy. A friend of a friend of a friend later, she was sitting down with the head of the Texas chapter himself. He liked her passion but looked at her résumé and told her she wasn't suited to be the volunteer coordinator in Fort Davis.

"You've got all this sales and marketing experience," he said. "Maybe you should run Marketing and Philanthropy."

Shortly later, she was hired. And she loves it. For the first time in her life, she's working somewhere that she can imagine never leaving. Every day she goes to work for a purpose she and others find meaningful. She still works too hard, but now she's happy to do it. "I'm in the right orga-nization, in the right place. I hope to retire from here." She's having such a great experience that she feels it is nothing less than a complete miracle she made it here. She feels blessed.

I asked Debbie, "So that guide of yours—did he handle it? Or did you handle it? Because it sounded to me like *you* handled it. You wouldn't take no for an answer."

She paused. "We handled it."

I asked her to clarify. She said she deserved credit for her hustle in that critical moment. But circumstances beyond her control had to align in order to make it possible. And in those beneficial circumstances, she sees her guide's work. She even believes that in some way I was brought to her by the guide—that me telling her story was *meant to happen*.

Debbie's epiphany is one of the most important moments of her life. But here's the important catch—she notes that her epiphany didn't suddenly instill her with a desire to conserve land. She *always* had that desire—she just ignored it, at least professionally. Every time she surrounded herself with nature, she was euphoric, and every time she went back into sales, she was miserable and disconnected. "How much clearer did it have to be?" she now wonders. All the signs were there. In fact, in her journals are several statements written in the days before her epiphany, wishing she could do more to help preserve nature. So when the guide thundered "ISN'T IT CLEAR!?" he was kinda right to be indignant. Look in your journal! Look at how happy you are when around nature!

Was the voice she heard a blast from her suppressed unconscious, begging her to pay attention to her values? I don't argue with Debbie's version, but I offer that possibility for readers who balk at her spiritual account. We've all got neglected needs.

Her love of nature was *always* clear. Debbie's obstacle was not that she didn't know what made her happy. Her problem was that she never let herself imagine that what she loved could be a profession. In her mind, there were two worlds—one is the world of business, where you go to work, and the other is the world of things you care about, to be enjoyed on weekends. It's not easy to bring these worlds together (it takes hustle and training and determination), but once Debbie learned those two worlds were embodied in one organization, her mission became clear. Learning that the Nature Conservancy existed—and that they had a job open—finally opened the floodgates. Like Paul, she was on a horse at the time. But she didn't fall off her horse, and she didn't lose her sight. Her guide wasn't a spirit, he was a man who led pack trips. His words were fairly matter-of-fact—but they made it all clear.

I now tell people not to wait for epiphanies. They're great if you get one, but so often they tell you something you already know in your heart. Never underestimate our ability to ignore the obvious. So often, that's what keeps us from clarity—not a lack of desire.

7 ||| I Belong to You

Young Warren Brown wanted to somehow make the world a better place. He'd always been a Believer, though what he believed in changed over time, of course—until eighth grade it had been the Catholic Church, for which he was an altar boy. After a friend died of a bad heart, Warren felt the weight of life's seriousness and was drawn to the popular cause of the times, opposing U.S. intervention in Nicaragua. During high school he went to the Cleveland Urban League to volunteer. After college he came to Los Angeles and taught "reproductive health" (sex ed) at high schools for the state Department of Education. His course lasted one week; each week another school. He felt this work was extremely important. How many of our problems with teens are rooted in their confusion over sex? Their self-esteem, their shame. But the curriculum materials were horrendous! Depictions that omitted essential body parts! How could he teach with these! So he went to George Washington University in Washington, D.C., in order to get the credentials to speak out and revise how sex ed was taught. He earned a master's in public health and a law degree at the same time.

But he had a looming feeling that maybe this wasn't going to work out. Would he really get a job in which he felt like he was making any difference? During school he went to poverty law centers to volunteer, but they made him feel unwelcome. At parties he talked about returning to sex ed, and his fellow law students discouraged him. He hated his summer internship. His law school grades weren't that good—mostly because he wasn't sure where this was headed. Following school, he was offered a job as a litigator with the Department of Health and Human Services. It seemed like a pretty good first step. On paper, at least. One could make a logical argument that he was "well positioned," that he was "on track." But in his heart, *he knew.* Ugh.

One day, at the end of the summer, he pulled over in his car and started bawling. He felt squeezed like a sponge and out came the tears. He was worried whether he'd passed the bar; he'd broken up with his girlfriend; he'd cut his dreadlocks.

"Had HHS told you to cut them?" I asked.

"No, man. I did it to myself. I had them when I interviewed, nobody questioned them. I cut them, sort of to psyche myself up that I was going to get serious now. *I did it to myself.* Not until then did I realize how much they'd become part of my identity. It wasn't the loss of identity that upset me as much as the realization, *I'm doing this to myself.* Why? And I was driving, and thinking about this—and that Radiohead song came on, 'Let Down,' urging me to slow down, to let down, and I pulled over to the side of the road and let it out."

At HHS, he prosecuted Medicare fraud. When an HMO billed multiple times, he sued them. When an emergency room refused to treat a walk-in patient, he sued them. These were worthy cases, but common and repetitive and always quickly settled—usually for next to nothing, around $7,500, which was like handing out a parking ticket on a bank robbery. It hardly justified the work. Well, no need to complain. For someone of a different temperament, it was a worthy calling. But Warren just didn't belong.

In the last few years, Warren had become creatively fertile. In Los Angeles he had taken up oil pastels. In Washington he'd started writing poetry and sometimes sang his poems at parties. And he'd always cooked. In law school he'd held a mock "Gastronomy and the Law" course to teach fellow students how to prepare something other than tuna fish sandwiches. On the roof of his apartment he'd raised an herb garden. At that point in his life, it was hard to say—were these creative hobbies the seeds of future passions? Or were they just compensatory outlets, gasps for breath after suffocating all day at work?

In other words, he wondered, should he continue to pursue them? And if so, which one?

Among the many obstacles that might discourage a young man from choosing that direction, the biggest one was this: Wasn't it self-serving simply to indulge what you enjoy? Who does it help? How does it make any contribution? How could you justify it, on moral/philosophical terms?

"I felt really guilty about it, but I said to myself, 'You've got to work for yourself.' "

I asked, "By 'work for yourself,' you don't mean be self-employed?"

"No, I mean put myself first. I couldn't help anyone else unless I fixed my own situation. Social justice had to take a backseat. I felt bad about it, but I knew it was necessary."

"It was a strategic philosophical shift?"

"Exactly. I made a conscious decision to listen to my calls and direct myself to greatness. And once I chose to stop denying what made me happy, my life very naturally evolved."

Two moments profoundly influenced the choice he made, which was to become a cake baker and open a made-to-order bakery and café called Cakelove on U Street and 18th in Washington. He made this decision gradually, begrudgingly, reluctantly, over a year's period, slowly accepting that it was *okay* to pursue this. He moonlighted for another year, baking cakes at night before leaving his job at HHS. The retail shop didn't open for another year and a half after that. It was, as transformations go, not very *decisive*, which is completely typical—it's usually a much slower process than anyone expects. Nevertheless, he did it, and he pointed to two moments that nudged him over that moral/philosophical hurdle. The first gave him Emotional Clarity; the second Mental Clarity.

The first: Late one Friday night, he was frosting a cake for one of the senior managers in his office. Trying to make it look extra nice, he spread the butter-cream frosting in a spiral pattern, and then unconsciously decorated the top with candied naval-orange segments in a similar spiral-star pattern. He realized, "Hey, that's the same spiral-star pattern that filled the background of those family portraits I used to paint back in Los Angeles." Suddenly, in that moment, he experienced an epiphany. Not a voice like Debbie's, but a similar spiritual charge. He was overtaken with emotion and a sense of connectedness to his past. He had a friend, Luke, who had died when Warren was fourteen; Luke had looked out for Warren when he was a boy, teaching him to play basketball and how to talk to girls. Ever since, Warren had an occasional feeling that Luke was still looking out for him, and in that moment with the spiral star on the cake, it was like the Angel of Luke was touching his shoulder, connecting his head to his heart to his soul.

"That star pattern was so common, always reappearing. It *tied my life together*," he remembered. "The feeling I had—it's hard to explain—it was like the cake was saying, 'I *belong* to you, Warren.' "

I belong to you. I am not a frivolous escape. I am part of you. Stop denying it.

The second moment occurred a few months later: He'd recently told his family that he was thinking of leaving law to pursue his passion for culinary arts. They'd been supportive ("I think their exact words were 'Do it!' ") and of course they wanted to know what that meant. Open a restaurant? Become a cook? His analytical legal brain was warning him: The restaurant market is oversaturated. He flew to New York to visit his aunt. It was early Saturday morning. He was carrying a "funky-looking grandma cake," as he described it. "Nothing special, not presentable, not finished." Without a cake box to store it in, he covered it with blue plastic wrap. It looked quite ugly, frankly. But as he walked through the airport and held it in his lap on the plane, everyone had a friendly comment. The cake excited them. They invoked the birthdays of their lovers as reasons for him to give them the cake. He arrived at Kennedy and was sitting outside baggage claim waiting for his aunt to arrive, and he was overtaken with a clearheaded revelation: Cakes got people excited, even ugly grandma cakes. Cakes made people think of each other, their lovers and family. Cakes meant good times. Cakes were part of the celebration of life. People love to talk about cakes. Cakes were the highest profit margin product in any bakery. The most time-consuming step in cake-making was putting a smooth finish on frosting, but this cake proved that a cake could look homemade and still trigger the drool reflex. He smelled opportunity.

That afternoon, sitting on a boat, he told his aunt, "It's going to be cakes. Just cakes."

Your brain can think through every detail, but that's like leading a horse to water. Sometimes the obvious wells up, swelling with emotion, until it bursts forth as a revelation. And only then can your brain really be put to good use—making it happen in the smartest way possible.

Two weeks later, Warren was sitting in a community business class. He analyzed the bakeries in Washington, and then he did the same in six other cities. He held cake parties, first at his apartment and then at a local art gallery. He gave up his Friday nights out. He tweaked recipes. He was selling about fifteen cakes a week, mostly to friends (and their friends). Still, he was unsure whether to jump to full-time, and so he kept his day job. Then, on a seemingly random Tuesday morning, he woke up and discovered he couldn't move his limbs. Nor could he control his breathing. With intense concentration, he managed to pick up the phone. First call: his parents (his father was a pulmonologist). Second call: his neighbor, who got him to the emergency room, where they kept him under observation for a few hours. "You're suffering from exhaustion," the doctor told him. "Slow down." Until then he didn't know that exhaustion could manifest itself as near paralysis. He assumed a young man could run on empty forever. It was time to choose.

More fear: what would he do for money until the bakery started breaking even? Would complete strangers love his cakes as much as his friends did? Were his friends just being kind? Warren was feeling very raw; he found himself overcome by social issues of the day, listening to many politicians. Was he ever going to tackle those issues in his life? He realized he needed to wage a campaign of his own—he needed to be *that* prepared.

He asked for a three-month leave. His boss had tasted Warren's cakes and wanted him to succeed. Taking a leave rather than quitting offered a safety net that both men hoped wouldn't be needed. Warren charged $6,700 to his credit card to purchase a twenty-quart mixer, an electric oven with ten baking racks, and a double-door refrigerator. He rented a commercial kitchen. Nine cafés in the District stocked his cakes, and he accepted orders by phone. He earned just enough to pay his apartment rent and utilities, and make small payments on his credit card. One day he went back to HHS and cleaned out his desk. His plans for a retail front were continually pushed back, spring to fall, fall to spring. Finally, he hired his staff of twelve, and Cakelove opened its doors on March 30, 2002.

And a funny thing happened on the way to simply doing what he enjoyed: *everyone thanked him.* As if he had helped them! They thanked him for his luscious cakes. They thanked him for bringing a little more life to U Street. They thanked him for inspiring them to keep their own dreams alive. Crowds formed outside the doors! Crowds! Crowds, for a tiny little fifteen-by-twenty-foot working bakery with no standing room! Cakelove symbolized something undefined by words but felt by all. It filled a need in the neighborhood and a need in the soul. After a decade of spin and image control and hype, there was a society-wide hunger for anything genuine and authentic. His scratch-made "grandma" cakes hit the spot.

Friends in D.C. began writing me about Warren from the day Cakelove opened. He fostered a sense of community.

I went to see the new Love Café that had just opened across the street from the bakery. "A place for the crowd to at least sit down," Warren said, smiling. His staff was growing. His banker had come on as his business manager. He would turn thirty-three in a week. That, and the success of his venture, made him think about what was next. In his activities, he's a naturally creative person, but in conversation he is most interested in talking about what society needs. Society needs more people lit by passion, and fewer simply able to do what they're told. Society needs an educational system that properly equips people with the tools they need to pursue what they believe in. The educational system needs to teach teens about sex so they don't get hung up on it, don't bottle it up, and can invest their energy in productive desires. Warren hadn't forgotten about that.

"Do you still put yourself first?" I asked.

He answered by talking about a difficult personnel situation in the bakery—an attitude-challenged employee reluctant to learn new skills. "Another owner might fire him. I don't think that way. My purpose is to work with him, you know? Coach him, grow him. Same with our location—another owner might use the success to move to a fancier neighborhood. *This* is my neighborhood; I want to be a part of making it nicer." He was serving his community. He was the kind of person who needed that. Most people do, they just don't know it.

I asked, "Are you special?"

"The only thing special about me is I just decided to say 'F it.' " Then he clarified, sharing again the story of his epiphany, in which, for a moment, he felt special. Touched. "Most people don't want to accept their potential. It hints of an accompanying responsibility to live up to that potential. Acknowledging my potential required accepting that I could be different, that I could deserve the attention of others, that I might be special—or at least unique. Acknowledging your potential is setting yourself up to be criticized for being willing to stand out, and nobody wants to be laughed at. That fear held me back for some time."

"You went to law school and you were a lawyer, albeit briefly. That helped you when it came to launching this business, right?"

"It did. In law school, you're trained to analyze, to really think it through, and you learn to trust your conclusions. I was not *that* rigorous a thinker before law school."

"So, for people who read about your story—even though you *quit* the law, left it behind, followed your passion—even though you consider the law a *diversion* from your true path—you can imagine how they would take away a very different message than *trust your passion*. They might naturally think, 'I've got to go to law school or business school first. It'll help me.' "

This was a new and interesting thought for him. "I would never want to say to someone else, 'Don't take the path I took.' But I do wish I had done this sooner, and if I feel I made missteps, it's natural to point them out to people when they ask me for advice. The world would be a better place if more people let themselves be energized by their natural enthusiasms."

8 ⫼ The Brain Candy Generation

Well, what if you haven't had a transformative experience, like Janelle London, and you don't harbor a secret dream, like Kat James? Can you analyze your way to a solution that feels "right"? Can you think your way to an answer?

Lori Gottlieb took that route. She decided there was nothing more important than answering this once and for all. She considered her years as a junior production executive in Hollywood a big mistake. She grew up in L.A., used her college alumni network to score summer internships, and those internships led to job offers, which she took because what else was there to do? She became successful but felt like a fraud. Who was she to tell these writers how to write? Unplugging herself from that realm was so painful and embarrassing, she never wanted to have to go through that again. Her biggest fear was that she would make another mistake and waste more of her precious life. She didn't want to be a person who simply stumbled into her life. She wanted to get this right. So she gave herself three years to sort it out.

Lori attacked the question like nobody ever had. She dug out her diaries from her childhood. She rejected the model of her father, who ground it out as a stockbroker. Fifty years with the same firm, his motto was "work is a four-letter word." She gave herself permission to dream. She investigated every dream. Astronaut. Corporate spy. Ballet dancer. Scientist. She took classes through UCLA Extension in photography and figure drawing. She interviewed others who had left Hollywood. She broke every job down by skill set and laid that over a grid of her innate talents. She filled out every exercise in the *What Color Is Your Parachute?* books. She distilled every job down to its essence, to its inherent brain candy. Bottom line, her answer had to keep her brain firing at high gear. She was Phi Beta Kappa at Yale, and couldn't let her brain gather moss. She realized what her mind really loved was solving puzzles. Well, okay, who solves puzzles for a living? Doctors! A patient presents symptoms, and the doctor has to figure out what's wrong. Day and night, doctors are solving puzzles! So Lori did her homework. She called up brain surgeons and oncologists and invited herself to observe them on their rounds. She enrolled in premed classes at Pepperdine.

Organic chemistry was a wet dream! Endorphins flooded her bloodstream. She felt more alert, more alive, than she ever had in her years of Hollywood story meetings. This was it! This was what she'd always been looking for! Her med-school application was so persuasive that every school wanted her. And why not? Finally a student who was in it because she loved it, not just because she wanted the status, or her parents pushed, or she didn't know what else to do. Lori chose Stanford's program, which throws students right into the clinic, face-time with patients, real-life problems to be solved. Lori was so convinced, she was interviewed by a national magazine about her journey. The article became an inspiration to lost souls everywhere. (Later, I met people who'd clipped and saved the article.) The woman who loved solving puzzles had solved the biggest puzzle of all: where she belonged.

Can you see where this is headed?

Lori dropped out of Stanford Medical School after only two and a half months.

Lori's a tiny, anxious woman. Of course, I'd be anxious too if I had to account for this goof. She wore her dark chocolate hair in a tight bun and hid behind dark chocolate sunglasses. She lived near campus in a painfully generic dank duplex, what she called her "refugee camp." She was ashamed to let me in. Most days she didn't shower until the afternoon. It'd been a year and a half since she dropped out, though she frequently reminded me that, technically, she was "on leave," and could go back. In other words, technically, she wasn't lying when she still told people she was a Stanford medical student. Her ego was a little bruised, and affiliating herself with Stanford helped when people wondered what she was doing with her life.

"But are you even thinking of going back?" I asked.

"No. That life's not for me." She seemed dead certain.

"So what happened? What went wrong?"

"Well, I forgot that I was going to have to deal with sick people. Sick and old. Most patients are over sixty, with arthritis and diabetes. I didn't want to spend my days like that."

What? "How could you have forgotten that? I mean, when you're sick, you go see the doctor. Doctors attend sick people."

"Of course I knew that but I didn't think about what kind of environment it would create. I'm sensitive to my environment, and I don't want to hang around sick people all day."

We talked some more and she seemed to think it was that simple. Dropped a variable in the equation. Left an ingredient out of the recipe. But if it were that simple, she could plug that factor back into her formula, redo her grids and matrices, and spit out another answer. She'd be earning her Ph.D. in chemistry (which she loved), on her way to being a scientist. Scientists hang out with other scientists and mice. No sick people.

Instead, Lori had bogged down in a nowhere zone. She briefly jumped aboard a dot-com, because they seemed to be having so much fun. She did a little of this and a little of that to get by. Her ambition still went unquenched, and she was too competitive by nature to be happy for long as an eclectic free radical, where she couldn't measure herself against others.

So what happened?

I've thought about her a lot. We stayed in touch, and over time her story has suggested a meaning for me.

Organic chemistry is predictable; if you know the rules, you can anticipate the results with great accuracy. And while organic chemistry is the basis of all life, it's a huge mistake to think humans are as predictable as the equations in a classroom. Solving the puzzle of our ill health requires trial and error, some hope, some faith, and some guesswork. The same goes for figuring out your place in life. It's not a puzzle that can be figured out on paper. You have to try something, see if it works, and learn from it.

Lori was always saying she understood my book and its topic, and really related to it. But she always got the title wrong, no matter how many times I corrected her. Even in e-mails months later, she kept calling it my *What Do I Want to Be When I Grow Up?* book. I think that's a notably different question. It lacks the "Should," which hints at a moral or aspirational imperative, and it overemphasizes "Want," as in I want I want I want. . . .

Our wants are fleeting. They are also indulgent. Every philosophy draws a hard line between what you want and what you need. When Lori defined her relevant question as What do I want? she went hunting for brain candy when she should have highlighted experiences she related to emotionally, and deeply.

Lori wanted her work to be "a twenty-four-hour-a-day high." Friends scolded her for being naive, spoiled, and idealistic. "If I ever agree with that, I will cease to be alive, metaphorically." At first I took her side. I actually underlined her "twenty-four-hour high" quote three times in my notebook and threw some exclamation marks in the margins for good measure. When I started this book, I too thought what would make us happy was Exciting!/Challenging!/Brainwork! In one of my novels, I had written, "What young people wanted more than anything else . . . was a place to go during the day where their brain wasn't wasted."

But my research wasn't backing this up. Those who've found their place weren't reporting twenty-four-hour highs. They're not jazzed all the time. They still complain about annoying administrivia randomly puncturing their concentration. Their language invoked a different troika: meaningful/significant/fulfilling. And they rarely ever talk about their work without interweaving some of their personal history, explaining how the two are related.

Brain candy! A lot of jobs can give you the quick rush—ER physician, currency trader, start-up junkie, concert promoter, grill cook—anything with a lot of risk or a furious amount of activity. But before you can label it your calling, it has to take on personal significance and be woven into the story of your life.

The conclusion that brain candy is not enough is probably the most threatening to our generation's belief system. In this belief system, the world is a battle between the Boring and the Stimulating. We channel-surf through jobs and relationships, pushing the button at the first hint of slowing down. Like Lori, we've rejected the compromises of our parents' generation, who sought safety and security. Anyone who comes along and murmurs that "stimulation is not everything" is quickly tuned out, because we don't want to hear it anymore.

But there's a difference between something that stimulates you for a year and something you can be passionate about for ten years. What is the difference? One thing is not ten times more stimulating than the other. *The difference is whether your heart's in it.* You don't find your purpose above the neck. If you use your brain to solve this problem, you'll usually end up with an answer that only makes your brain happy. I struggled with this myself, but not until I began this project and listened to hundreds of others did the pattern make itself shockingly clear.

Lori's heart was not in being a doctor. It didn't matter how many puzzles she solved.

The traditional search for a career begins with the question "What am I good at?" But that's often not the right starting point for finding a calling. You can get good at what you need to serve what you believe in. You can learn Spanish, you can learn budgets, you can learn to listen. The true search is for what you believe in. When your heart's engaged, the inevitable headaches and daily annoyances become tolerable and don't derail your commitment. Let your brain be your heart's soldier.

So what happened to Lori? Well, think back to the dilemma that kicked off her journey. She felt like an imposter as a studio executive, telling writers how to change their scripts. She had no training as a writer; she'd never written scripts herself. She *was* an imposter.

But did she really need to quit Hollywood entirely, and throw away her past?

After her elaborate detour, which she now jokingly refers to as her quarter-life crisis, Lori's gone back to Hollywood and is trying to make it as a screenwriter. She's pitching the studios now, like the writers who used to pitch her. Partly this was a matter of survival; she knows that industry best, and her family is there. But it feels right, because it's a more accurate solution to her original problem. She's treating scripts with a humility and respect she didn't as an executive. It's not her ultimate purpose, not the perfect answer she sought, but it makes her feel whole. She's turning her weakness into a strength. There's something meaningful in that mission. She doesn't feel like an imposter anymore.

Sometimes, what you're *not* good at is the place to start. Learning to do it, and do it well, might fix the problem.

9 ||| Parasite Entrepreneurism

Spending time with these subjects has made me look back and think about when I was that kid coming out of college, trying to hang on to my exuberance.

It's not an era I'm accustomed to pondering. It was not easy to become a writer, and most of my twenties have been packed down into that frozen iceberg of all things forgotten. The story of those years is too confusing, too random. There's too many pieces, too many jobs I held down. It's been easiest just to think of it all as *Before*. I made it through them. I don't want to go back.

But the subjects I interview frequently ask me about those years, and some stories are starting to bubble up.

I was told in high school that I couldn't write, that my ideas were unintelligible. My teachers weren't being mean. They were being honest. At the time, they were right. I was better at math. I was *great* at math. I scored nearly perfect on every math aptitude test, and competed in the Washington State Math Championships held every year at Central Washington University. Too bad I couldn't see the point of math. I could solve for the relationship between X and Y, but the relationship of math to society completely eluded me. It was my gift, but I didn't want it.

In college I avoided English classes, because I'd recognized how they dragged down my GPA.

I majored in economics, the practical thing. But I wrote one personal essay that was published in the school newspaper. It was about "being versus doing," and back then I took the side of being. As a senior, everyone asks you what you'll be *doing* next year. My answer: "*Being Po* is what I'll be doing a year from now." That quote was enlarged and turned into the essay's title. Many students told me how much it calmed their fear of being boxed in by a job description.

But what was I going to do, actually, after I graduated? I didn't know. I'd been working since seventh grade. Busboy, cafeteria manager, line cook, cement factory janitor, sports medicine intern, assembly line technician manufacturing bus lifts, kitchen manager, aerobics instructor, bookkeeper. It was an impossible list to sort out. In contrast, the feedback I got on that one essay had hatched this curiosity that I might be a writer, despite what my teachers had always said.

The summer after college, I followed my girlfriend to New York, where she had a job. We slept on her sister's couch. I had all this free time and absolutely no money to spend. So I decided to attempt a novel. How else could I discern if I had talent? I wrote longhand into spiral-bound notebooks. At the end of the summer, I borrowed a neighbor's typewriter and began to translate my scratch into a legible form. Rereading my novel, one thing was clear: *It was so incredibly bad.* Even *I* couldn't stand reading it. After a hundred pages of laborious typing, I stopped cold with boredom. Clearly I had no talent after all. My teachers were right.

It was time to face the truth, grow up, buy a suit, and go get a real job. My girlfriend was transferred to San Francisco, and so I followed her.

Playing up my economics degree, I got a real job.

Every morning I slipped into a navy wool suit and rode the bus downtown, saluted the chipper security guard, rode up to the twenty-second floor, strolled past the window offices, and eventually took my seat in the back row in a gray windowless room of twelve young professionals my age. My employer was a litigation consulting firm—supposedly a blend of the best of law and the best of management consulting. It was the perfect setup job for law school or business school. That wasn't my plan (I don't think I had a plan), but it suggests the high reputation this firm had.

The image that had lured me was not the reality inside its doors.

Our client was a large utility, which was suing the state of California for reimbursement of the $5 billion it spent building two nuclear reactors in San Luis Obispo. The reactors were budgeted at a billion each, and our client blamed inflation for most of the $3 billion overage. So our firm created enormous spreadsheets, each hundreds of pages long, detailing every expense over ten years, factoring out inflation. That wasn't my job, though. Oh no. That would have been the job I would get to do in two years if I was good at my job.

My job was to use a ten-key manual calculator and add up columns of numbers on the spreadsheets to make sure the computer hadn't made a rounding error. If the computer was correct, we put a little red check mark on the bottom of the column. Then, with that same column, we'd do it again. Every column needed to be checked twice. That, and only that, was all I ever got to do. Ten or eleven hours a day, six days a week. I was being paid $12 an hour and being billed out at $75 an hour to our client (which was in turn passing the cost on to the lawsuit). All twelve of us in that windowless room were doing this. I was in the back row, staring at the backs of heads, entertained only by the occasional ghost of a bra strap or a bare Achilles. The crazy thing was, at least ten of my associates were competitive about being the fastest spreadsheet checker. They'd been brainwashed to believe rounding errors were as dangerous as the Ebola virus, and our spreadsheets had to be clean! It might occur to you that we were printing money for the firm by racking up billable hours like monkeys hidden behind a door, but it didn't occur to us.

I'd had grueling and mind-numbing jobs before (janitor, assembly line), but we always acknowledged we were mere shit shovelers. Here, everyone pretended what we were doing was somehow important, somehow relevant. The pretending was the worst part.

I wanted out by the second day—they'd misrepresented themselves— but I had $42,000 in student loans to pay off versus less than a month's worth of savings. Besides, I couldn't quit. Years of competitive sports and my natural stubbornness made me hold quitting in such low regard that it was simply unacceptable. I was sure nobody would hire a quitter. So I made the best of it. "It's just a day job," I tried to persuade myself, even though my days usually stretched well into the night.

After a couple weeks I began crying into my pillow at night. My girlfriend would hold me and offer solace. I fantasized about someday getting Saturdays off. I felt like my soul was withering away. Every dollar I spent was extending my prison time that much longer. So I ate rice and cabbage at night. Cornflakes with powdered milk for breakfast. I doctored my bus transfers to use them for the ride home. On my family's birthdays, I'd save the dollar a greeting card cost and draw my own on a scrap of paper. One day I went swimming at the YMCA. The entrance to the pool was through the showers, and at the entrance to the showers there was a scale to weigh yourself. So I stepped on the base and set the weights at 157 pounds, because 157 pounds is what I'd weighed ever since high school. The lever arm fell hard. Hmm . . . I must have lost some weight. So I slid the one-pound weight to the left, tap, tap, tap, waiting for that lever arm to rise.

Then I moved the fifty-pound weight one notch over, and resumed tapping, tapping . . . tapping. The lever arm finally lifted up to balance.

One hundred thirty-two pounds.

I wasn't metaphorically withering away, I was *literally* withering away. For several months I'd avoided spending five dollars on lunch by raiding the coffee room. Along with coffee and tea, the firm offered Carnation sugar-free instant cocoa mix, in single-serving packets. I would dump four or five packets in a Styrofoam cup, add enough water to stir the powder into a pudding, and spoon down the calories. I'd get invited to lunch, and all I could think about was that five dollars I'd never see again. "Oh, I brought mine today," I'd say, and beg out. Five dollars today, five dollars tomorrow, that's $125 a month (six-day workweek), that's $2,400 a year I could save by skipping lunch. The crazy thing is, until I discovered I was vanishing, I was secretly proud of my ingenious technique for saving money. I'd walk around with my cup of cocoa and nobody was the wiser. I thought I'd found a secret loophole in the code of ordinary human behavior. I was always looking for loopholes—things that people did unconsciously, out of custom, that were unnecessary.

I got a performance review and mentioned to my reviewer that I wasn't happy. He said that was normal. In two years I could go to business school and put it behind me. I didn't tell him that at the rate I was losing body mass, in two years I'd weigh seven pounds.

I dragged out that college essay I'd written a year earlier. "*Being Po* is what I'll be doing a year from now," I had naïvely predicted. Boy, did I ever get it wrong. I didn't feel like myself at all. What I was *doing* was killing me.

I daydreamed about every escapist fantasy imaginable. One of those daydreams was that I'd magically grow rich designing greeting cards. So my girlfriend and I began to secretly design and draw an imaginary line of absurdist cartoon greeting cards—to have something to hope for! That would have been it for me—I didn't want to dare risk destroying this fantasy by subjecting it to reality—but my girlfriend was more practical than I was, and she started to think it was stupid we'd done these drawings and were going to let them sit idle. She went to greeting card stores and asked some questions, introduced herself to some sales reps, attended a gift conference—how hard could it be?—and suddenly our fantasy, this vessel of hope, had a little more room to grow. A month later we'd raised ten thousand dollars, five hundred at a time, and I was running a greeting card company out of the back of that windowless room at the litigation consulting firm.

I'd come in early as ever, take my seat in the back row, lay out my spreadsheets as if I were working, and start to make phone calls to my sales reps around the country. All day long I'd talk to stores, talk to the printer, order boxes and paper, et cetera. I used the firm's computers and copiers to do the accounting and print invoices. We had forty-eight card designs and were on sale in about two hundred stores in twenty states. The whole room knew what I was doing, but three of them had invested $500 each in the company—they needed hope too—and the others were so flabbergasted at my complete and utter disregard for propriety that they didn't know what to say. At lunch I'd walk around to the greeting card stores downtown to make sure our cards were displayed. At the end of the day, I'd scratch a couple red check marks at the bottom of the spreadsheet columns and turn in my work.

It was a new type of small company incubation—I called it parasite entrepreneurism. When I'd gained the weight back, and my confidence was brimming, and I'd gone through a full order cycle with the cards, I quit the firm to do the cards full-time. Funny thing was, the greeting cards didn't last long—like a parasite and its host, there was something essential in the symbiosis between my fondness for greeting cards and my hatred of spreadsheets. Once I was out on my own, I really didn't have the dynamism anymore. It wasn't nearly as much fun to run a greeting card company as it was to run a greeting card company out of the back of a suffocating law/consulting firm, leeching off their infrastructure. After six months, the card company died for lack of effort. That was okay; I thought it was my dream but once I gave myself to it, it clearly wasn't. I got another job, as a bond salesman, then as an editor of a political newsletter, then as a high school teacher, and then in small-press book publishing.

If you met me in the years after, and asked me what I did or what I'd done, I wouldn't have mentioned my year in that windowless room. I rarely mentioned the greeting card company. I didn't want to reveal weakness or revisit my shame at having lost people's money, albeit a small amount. What was the point? I was looking forward for answers, not backward.

For a long time, the shame of a wasted year kept me from being open about it. Now, having put it on paper, I look back, and I see nothing to be ashamed of. I see in my own character a gem of reinvention—an ability to create and improvise out of a bad situation.

When I began this book, I was looking for courage in the stories of others. I now realize: I've always had it, right here, in my own story.

There's always a tension between what's really happened and what we think our stories are *supposed* to sound like.

As a writer, I'm learning not to bend the truth too much. It's too easy to accidentally erase the really good stuff.

For the longest time, I didn't think I had a story. But meaningful events and turning points have been there all along, churning down in my psyche, waiting for me to recognize them. In accepting my past—in not asking it to be more dramatic that it was—in not asking it to compare with other people's stories—I can finally wake up to how it's shaped me, and embrace where it's steering me.

Similarly, we all have passions if we choose to see them. But we have to look backward even more than forward, and we have to chase away our preconceptions of what we think our passion is supposed to be, or not supposed to be.

10 ||| Lacking an Off Switch

So, all these diverse ways of puzzling for a right fit—do they share anything in common?

Certainly, and here it is: Initial guesses might have been guided by palm readers or aptitude tests or well-reasoned hypotheses, but the real wisdom was in the experience.

In fact, if anything, people too often ignored the strong message of their experience. They failed to embrace it because they believed their calling was to be figured out intellectually. Think again of Noah looking everywhere but under his bed . . . Janelle looking everywhere but in her illness . . . Mike chopping the day into fifteen-minute increments . . . Debbie not seeing her cause in her own journal . . . Lori solving the puzzle with her brain . . . me pretending I could survive in a "real" job.

People say they have no idea where to start, but so often, even as they say that, there's some insight waiting for them in the experiences they've already had.

The corollary is also worth noting: If you feel you haven't had enough experience, don't burden yourself with the expectation that you should be able to "know" what's right. Find ways to give yourself a taste. Interests evolve into hobbies or volunteer work, which grow into passions. It takes time, more time than anyone imagines.

In other words, don't be distracted by those rare birds who always seemed to know what they wanted to do. It's common to envy them, and to assume they have it easy. But they often have the hardest time of all when it doesn't work out. Such as Jessica Grossman.

I found Jessica when scouting for doctors who had left medicine. She was twenty-eight. She'd been an ob-gyn at Thomas Jefferson University Hospital in Philadelphia until four months ago. We arranged to meet the first time at a Starbucks, which became awkward quickly, because she needed to pause often while she wiped tears from her eyes, smudging her mascara and eyeshadow. Twice she sobbed and curled up into a ball in her chair.

Jessica had a glamorous aura and dressed chic in a navy sweater, checkered slacks, boots with a swooping high heel, and plenty of well-considered accessories. Her hair fell in long strawberry-blond curls. She fantasized about going into fashion, and had brainstormed about it with a friend who was a designer for Gap. "But my parents would kill me," she said. For money, she was working as a consultant to a surgical robotics company. The work was more interesting than she expected, but she thought of it only as a place marker to buy time. She felt like a total failure.

"Every moment of my life, from when I was a little girl, all I'd ever wanted to do, and all I'd ever prepared for, was to practice medicine," she said, welling up with tears again. "Can you understand this? I'd been working sixteen-hour days for years. I had no personal life. I never could go to a gym. I never got my nails done. Never went on a date. So when I left, I didn't leave my job. I left my life. I left everything. I left my soul."

She kept asking if I'd interviewed women who had to leave their child—that's how deeply she felt about it.

Growing up, Jessica's dad was a famous cardiologist at Harvard's Brigham Hospital. He never pressured her to become a physician (she swears). But he was such a fabulous role model, because he had a palpable passion for his work. Passion is infectious—so few people have it for their work that when you do glimpse it, it makes an indelible impression. As a little girl, whenever it snowed and the schools were closed, Jessica's father would bring her to the hospital and let her hang out in a break room in the basement, among the clicking steam pipes. There was colored chalk to play with, and she'd eat her pack lunch and never be bored. By junior high, her father's pupils would sometimes eat lunch with her, and she saw their reverence for her dad. In high school, she followed him on rounds, blending in with his entourage of students. He had a miraculous ability to tune this entourage out when with a patient. He would sit on the edge of his patients' bed, hold their hand, look them in the eye, and be 100 percent there. Jessica prayed for snow.

After four years of med school at Thomas Jefferson, Jessica chose obstetrics and gynecology. She liked working alongside strong women and having women doctors as role models. From her experience one summer in a lab in which she performed a lot of operations on animals, she knew she had a surgeon's mentality ("let's just get in there and cut the thing out"), as opposed to a medicine mentality, which tries to figure out what could be causing the problem before doing anything one might regret. She liked blood and guts. She knew the hours would be bad, because babies arrive on their own schedule, and she didn't think that would be a problem. She knew ob-gyns get sued a lot, but that didn't seem like a reason not to follow her heart. Jessica belonged on the labor and delivery ward. It was an exciting environment, punctuated by intense joy and relief. Every day she felt a surge of adrenaline.

Within a year, Jessica's resolve and conviction wore down under the 130-hour workweeks, which was to be expected for any doctor going through his or her internship. Misery and exhaustion were part of the deal. What she didn't anticipate was what she gradually learned about herself over the next two years.

"I don't have an 'off' switch," Jessica said. "It turns out that doctors not only have to be very good at giving of themselves to their patients—they have to be even better at drawing the line, and protecting themselves. I don't have that ability. The others did. My dad did. I don't have it, and I couldn't learn it."

For instance, Jessica commonly cried with and for her patients. She also gave her patients her home phone number, even though the hospital had a rule against that. Jessica regularly took the shifts that nobody else wanted to work, and on major holidays the other interns knew they could hit her up to take their shifts because she couldn't say no. Whatever her work asked, she gave, far too unselfishly.

One day a nurse was kicked in the belly by the mother during a particularly difficult delivery, when the baby's shoulder was stuck behind the pubic bone, and they had to climb on top of this mother and fold her up like a pretzel. The baby came out dead, but Jessica resuscitated the baby, and all was fine until the nurse told Jessica she'd been kicked. Blood trickled down the inside of the nurse's leg. She was four months pregnant. She didn't lose her baby, but she easily could have, and it scared the hell out of Jessica, who walked into the stairwell and burst into tears.

One day last September, Jessica almost peed on herself after many hours during which she wouldn't even let herself go to the bathroom. "Is this what it's come to?" she thought. It was time for a vacation. So she went to London for a few days, and she went to Harrods and bought nice gifts for the other five interns. Jessica loved these girls; they were her peers and the only regular people in her life. When she came home, she wrapped the gifts in nice paper and put them in the call room for the other girls. . . .

Jessica couldn't finish the story.

"What happened?" I asked.

She sucked it up for a moment. "Nobody ever said 'thank you.' Not one of them."

"That's terrible!"

"They were so busy. Most of them forgot it a second after opening it."

New Year's Eve was her last day. She was working because, of course, nobody else wanted to. She knew it was her last day, and so she was kind of happy. Her father called—he wasn't handling her departure very well. He told her he loved her and whatever she needed was fine . . . "But what about not doing the obstetrics and just doing gynecology?" he suggested. She didn't need him to solve her problems. She needed him to understand.

"Dad, I'm leaving tomorrow."

The next morning she walked out of the hospital for the last time. She felt like a plucked chicken.

"Some people can do it," she said. "I can't. I failed at it."

She either had to learn to draw boundaries, or she had to find work that didn't ask too much from her. She was shooting for the latter because the former seemed unacceptable.

"I don't want to be a person who cares only so much, who has to communicate to people, 'Okay, you've used up your five minutes of love.' No. That's not the kind of person I want to be."

Jessica was brand-new to wondering who she was and how she fit in. "I'm going to miss thinking I had a destiny. I'm going to miss that certainty."

On paper, Jessica's life was typical for a twenty-eight-year-old. You might wonder, what was her problem? She had a job, she was dating, she could go to the gym and get her nails done whenever she wanted. It was a better life, but it lacked the focus and single-mindedness she was used to. She couldn't see the purpose of it. And that left a big psychological hole. The need to understand your story is primal. People accustomed to doubt and uncertainty have learned how to incorporate that into their story. Jessica's brain had never been wired that way.

Jessica asked, "So you've talked to people who thought they had a certain destiny and discovered they belonged somewhere else?"

"Sure."

"How do they manage not to feel like that first part of their life was anything but a complete waste of time? If the genuine part of their life came later, what of this early part? How does it fit in?"

"Well, they learn from it. As long as they are able to transform it into a lesson which they can now apply."

"But what if there is no lesson? What if it all feels like a waste?"

"Is it a waste?" I asked. "If the purpose of your life was to be as great a doctor as your father, then you might have stalled. But if the purpose of life is to be true to yourself, when you walked out of that hospital, you passed your first big test."

For a moment, this way of telling her story helped her find value in those abandoned years. But the sense of failure came back quickly, and haunted her for a while. She kept her job at the surgical robotics company—it was a pretty good job—but it wasn't what she had gone to school all those years to do. That she stumbled into it in a pinch seemed so haphazard, not a proper story. Random. She never doubted that her decision to leave medicine was the right one, but at no time in the next two years was she able to duplicate that sense of belonging she had at the hospital.

In Another
Class

11 ||| The Ungrateful Soldier

The night I came home from seeing Tim Bratcher, I told my wife, "He worked himself into a really intense, dark mood. I'm not sure it was good for him to talk to me."

"I'm sure you were supportive."

"I tried. He kept saying, 'Please don't be disappointed in me.' Having me there was holding a mirror up to the ways he's neglected his potential. Maybe this was the wrong day to meet."

Tim had finished the three-day California bar exam that afternoon, then met me at his apartment shortly afterward. He was convinced he'd failed the exam—that some unhappy, bottled-up piece of his soul had sabotaged his test-taking to keep him from being a lawyer in California.

Tim's towering. He stands six-seven. He was a skinny freak in high school, and wore black fingernail polish and Goth clothes and long hair to exaggerate his outsiderness. But now, in his early thirties, he's filled out and handsome and clean-cut—courtesy of two years stationed in Panama with the U.S. Army. He's incredibly polite and conscientious. It took me a while to get him to stop calling me "sir." When ladies meet him, they ask if he's somebody famous, or maybe a politician. His accent is pure Kentucky. He never forgets that his parents were barely high school grads. Dad grew up in a place called Hoodoo Holler, which just about suggests it all: outhouses, bare feet, scant pavement.

"What the heck is a hick like me doing in Silicon Valley, huh?" he said when we met.

His apartment was depressing. Maybe I have bad associations with these multilevel bachelor-pad complexes: low ceilings, pale manila spackled walls, old carpet, track lights. Where divorced men go to disappear. I

sat by the sliding glass pane doors, clinging to my view of the fountain. Tim sat in the dark, chewing Skoal.

"Po, I honestly believe in my heart that I'm capable of great things. But the life's draining out of me. Hell, it's being sucked out of me. If I don't do something soon—but I'm such a shit. Why haven't I done something? I should have done something long ago."

No sooner had he said these words than he double-backed, chastising himself for brooding. "How ungrateful am I!"

Half of Tim wanted there to be more to his life than being a corporate lawyer. But the other half of him couldn't let go of that status, because he'd fought so damn hard to earn it—had to prove so many doubters wrong:

1. He'd been a screwup in his first try at college, Western Kentucky University, and caused so much trouble he was asked to leave after his sophomore year. The military instilled in him a moral compass, and he came back to the University of Louisville to finish with seven semesters of perfect 4.0 grades.

2. However, his stellar transcript had been blemished when the Student Affairs Office attached a letter of reprimand to his permanent file. Acting alone, Tim had torn down the posters at a rally protesting the military buildup in the Persian Gulf. Student Affairs charged him with violating the protesters' rights to protest. They held the hearing without him present—he was called for active duty at Fort Knox. He cried unfair, no due process, but was not allowed to defend himself. Right then he vowed to become a lawyer. He showed me the letter of reprimand, dated November 12, 1991. It still makes him livid. His perfect transcript—ruined! He

stayed at Louisville for law school and graduated fifth in his class. He was hired by Stites & Harbison, which recruits from only Harvard and Yale. In Louisville, dropping that name will most definitely impress Louisville's genteel old landed families. At Stites & Harbison, Tim was named the heir apparent to T. Kennedy Helm III. He was even invited to the Warners' Christmas party. Look at me, Dad! From Hoodoo Holler to the Warners' Christmas party in only two generations! He was a ladies' man. He drove a Toyota Avalon, which is a pretty fancy car in Louisville. He felt invincible. So invincible that he took a risk—

3. He came to Silicon Valley and got his butt kicked. He was hired by Cooley Godward, one of the Valley's more prestigious firms. Law firm salary is based on years worked, and Cooley Godward deducted two years off his résumé—the small town discount. Tim never got over this dis. He was convinced he was an outcast, the subject of an invisible prejudice against his funny accent and non–Ivy League credentials. He was lonely, he made no friends, and the quality of his work sucked. He didn't last a year. Three months ago he was asked to leave the firm. Now he was interviewing with research labs to be their general counsel. As much as he wanted to go home, he couldn't—he had to prove Cooley wrong.

"Why was your work suddenly so poor?" I asked.

"I don't know!"

"Maybe it was because you were here for the wrong reasons."

"Like what?"

"You tell me. Why did you come here?"

"When I got here, I thought I'd arrived. I remember driving up Interstate 280, cruising along, taking in the view of those beautiful mountains and sweeping vistas. Filter's song came on, 'Take a Picture.' So in my mind's eye, I did. I was on top of the world. 'Hey, Dad, what do you think of your son now?' "

"Sounds like you came to impress people back home."

"I know! Dammit, I know! But I can't turn it off! I don't know why I'm doing it! I'm in a walking slumber."

Tim was never going to open up to his own gifts until he was able to turn off his need to prove his worth by other people's yardstick. I told him about a financier I had recently interviewed. He quit and tried to choose a more meaningful path. He went about it like an MBA, scoring his choices against five metrics he'd decided were important. He could never pull the trigger. Then he read C. S. Lewis's article on the fallacy of the Inner Ring—people think they're important by belonging to an inner circle.

One night he had a dream that his girlfriend was walking down the side-walk arm in arm with an old B-school friend of his. He realized his inner circle was a dinner he'd had one night with other young B-school grads shortly after they got out of school. That night, he'd been the Stud. It had been two years, but in his mind he was still jockeying for status in that circle. Everything was filtered through their eyes.

"Was he ever able to defuse that urge?" Tim asked, intrigued.

"No. He went back to the financial world, humbled."

"Damn! I don't want that to happen to me! I don't want to be some grain of sand catching a slow ride in the desert on the devil's breath."

"Who's at the table in your inner circle, Tim? Your dad?"

"My dad wants me to be happy. He's proud of me no matter what."

"T. Kennedy Helm the Third?"

"And always will be. He took me under his wing. I owe him to do well."

"The adjudicator of your Student Affairs hearing?"

"All those people! And Cooley Godward too! But what good is it if I can't let them go?"

"Tim, why did you become a corporate lawyer when your heart was clearly in civil rights law? Why did you abandon that?"

"I don't know. I was stupid. I got sucked in. It felt good to be wanted and to be praised."

"But somehow that praise isn't quite enough for you."

"And that's why I'm so twisted up! Why can't that be enough for me!?"

"For some people it's not."

"You think I should be a civil rights lawyer?"

"Don't look to me for answers."

"I respect your opinion and would like to hear it."

"I'm afraid to tell you. I don't want you to try to prove yourself to me. I don't want to be at your inner table."

"I shared my life in hopes you'd have some perspective. That's why I've done this, opened up the Bratchelor Pad, opened up my heart—so you would tell me what you think."

He made it clear he would feel cheated, and maybe even used, if I didn't share my honest assessment.

"Friend to friend, then," I insisted. "I'm not an expert, and I've screwed up my own life a few times."

"I'd like to hear it."

"All right. If you're stuck on impressing people, at least impress people you like and admire, rather than people you hate. Which means get out of here. You can't sort out the real you in this environment. Maybe that's because you got off on the wrong foot, but the way you talk about it—you despise everything about Silicon Valley. Leave. Take the first step. Then, maybe what you need will be easier to sort out."

"Damn, when you say it like that it sounds so easy and so obvious. So what does it say about me, if I lack the nerve to do such a simple thing?"

"What does it say?"

"That I'm full of shit. I can't believe you're even listening to me. I can't believe I'm wasting your time."

"I actually find your despair kind of gripping."

C. S. Lewis's "The Inner Ring" was actually a speech delivered, in 1944, at King's College at the University of London. Lewis was unapologetically middle-aged; his audience was young and primed to play a part in the postwar reconstruction of Europe. But Lewis believed most of the students would not live up to that calling. They would be finding jobs, getting married, and acquiring facts. Lewis asserted that the strongest of all human drives is the desire to belong to an Inner Ring, an imaginary circle of the important. He warned the students, though, that this ring is an illusion. No sooner do you crack one ring than you are soon obsessed with joining the even-more-exclusive ring inside that one. Status is like an onion, comprised of endless layers, and no matter how many rings you cracked, you were still on the outside. "If you follow that desire, you will reach no inside that is worth reaching," he insisted. It took conscious and continuous effort not to be an "inner ringer," someone distracted by this game. The true road lies in quite another direction.

When Tim was out to prove his detractors wrong, he focused all his strength on that target. Once he'd proven his merit, he was lost for what to do.

I liked Tim a great deal. He was so honest with me. I never got a good read on his first screwup, when he was asked to leave Western Kentucky. The university had censored an acerbic comic strip he'd been drawing for a school paper, and in reaction he'd stopped taking art or English classes. Did it start there? I was afraid to cause more confusion by digging too deep. He'd also had a near-death experience in Panama, when he contracted an unknown tropical disease that put him in a coma for a week. When he came to, the attending nurse was crying. They'd thought he was dead, and suddenly—still in his sleep—he screamed for his mother. A dead man screaming "Mother! Mother! Mother!" Tim couldn't say if or how that experience had changed him.

A month later, he called to say he had accepted a position with a Very Big Law Firm in Atlanta. They were not dinging any years off his résumé.

He felt at home during the recruiting visit, with the soothing sound of southern accents in his ears. And his ease had shown; they were enchanted with Tim. Nevertheless, he felt like a bit of a coward for taking the job, and asked me not to be disappointed in him. He was still afraid he was sleeping on his potential. I told him only to worry when he forgets about his potential. He was leaving in a week and looking forward to the long drive from Vegas through Moab to Denver.

Atlanta wasn't his salvation, but it was a better place to sort out the next steps. We wrote each other often, and his letters were thoughtful and eloquent. He had an easy time meeting women. He went to concerts and had a social life. He worked on the thirty-fourth floor of the SunTrust building, and traded up from his Avalon to a Sequoia, dropping some serious bucks on a custom stereo. He was still trying to impress people, clocking thirteen-hour days, but the people he was impressing were ones he liked and respected. His boss was funny and even-keeled. He still described a "weight around my soul," but his inherent doubt and misery settled down to a tolerable level. His edginess came back and then retreated, like the bite of the seasons. He started teaching community-education seminars, which he loved, and was loved by the lawyers in his class. For the first time, he could see a feasible path to fulfillment, perhaps an adjunct position at a law school, then a faculty position.

I see a pattern in his story now, with the benefit of many other interviews, that I didn't see in the moment. In a way, there are two Tims. The Working Class Tim, and the Educated Class Tim. The Working Class Tim is the college dropout military man from barefoot Hoodoo Holler who clawed his way up to Louisville's most prestigious law firm. There's plenty of meaning and fulfillment in having proven his detractors wrong. That's enough accomplishment for one life.

The Educated Class Tim is the 4.0 student, top law firm associate, and survivor of a near-death experience who knows life is precious. (He didn't grow up in Hoodoo Holler—his father did.) Having benefited from a strong family and great schools, he now wants to give back to society, or to assume a leadership role—to make a difference. He knows there's more to life than being invited to the Warners' Christmas party.

These two Tims—these two class views—were at war with each other. So when the Educated Class Tim expresses an urge to find a career more vital to society, the Working Class Tim sees that urge *not as admirable but as selfish*. It's an insult to Working Class Tim, implying his accomplishment was not enough. So Working Class Tim plays the trump card—"You're educated, you came from a good family, you're privileged—*you're not enti-*

tled to unhappiness." And there's nothing the Educated Tim can say in re-turn. He must take his lashing. And Tim feels struck with guilt, triggering his cannon shot, "How ungrateful am I!"

The nine stories in this section illustrate the way class influences how we answer the question of what to do with our lives. More specifically, these stories challenge some of those class stereotypes. Some are stories of working class individuals who woke up to the importance of finding meaningful work—challenging the convention that it's a desire only of the educated class. Then there are stories of very educated people who chose to live among the working class—for all who fear that you can't fit in, or life won't be interesting enough, surrounded by people who aren't like you.

The stories in this section also will be a lot muddier than those in the last—these people's journeys are complicated by poverty, raising children, business corruption, layoffs, depression, and hospitalization for illness. As a result, they rarely *chose* their current situation, as if off a menu. Rather, they stumbled into it, improvising, taking advantage of the few slim scraps thrown their way.

12 ||| The Umbrella of Freedom

ANYONE CAN FIND THIS IMPORTANT

Of all the psychological stumbling blocks that keep people from finding themselves, the most common problem is that people feel guilty for simply taking the question seriously.

I'd come to Miami chasing this intellectual thread. So many people I interviewed around the country felt guilty for obsessing about what kind of work they should do. It felt self-indulgent. They would say things like, "Poor people, they don't get to choose. And they're still happy. New immigrants, they're ecstatic to have any job at all. You don't see any of them stressing out about who they are. They want to do well." There was something terribly perverse with this mental logic: We should live like poor people? Why? Poor people sure don't want to live like poor people—shouldn't we take their word for it? Besides, I wasn't even sure this oft-repeated assertion was true. Immigrants go through an enormous challenge to their identity, and the biggest blow to their esteem is in getting knocked down several rungs on the career ladder. Yes, most simply want to do well—anything that makes them money is fine with them—but not all. Some care. Deeply.

So I thought Miami was the right place to explore these questions. A study had come out that said Cubans are the most successful first-generation immigrants ever in the United States.

I met Ana Miyares at a luncheon put on by Florida International University's School of Entrepreneurship, which was held to honor two inductees into their hall of fame. This seemed a good place to meet Cuban Americans who had rebuilt their lives after having them stripped away by Castro, or by immigrating, or by having to learn English. I chatted with a lot of attendees, hoping to find a lead. Ana was short and stocky. She

looked like a nun. She told me she was recently teaching a résumé-writing class for new immigrants.

"I asked them to stand up and tell me what work they did in Cuba," she recounted. "So they stand. 'I was an electrical engineer.' 'I was a broadcast journalist.' They go on like this until I interrupt. I told them, 'No. You *are* an engineer. You *are* a journalist. You are still that person. You do not lose that identity when you get here.' "

I wanted to hear more of her perspective, so I told her about my book. Could we spend some time together, and would she tell me about her life?

"Yes, I would very much like to talk with you," she rasped. "But you have to know: I am not a dollar bill."

"What does that mean, 'I am not a dollar bill'?"

"Everyone loves a dollar bill," she said. "Not everyone loves Ana."

Ana's story is tainted with a dark cloud of sadness. On the second day, the cloud opened up and poured everywhere. In less than an hour the streets were flooded, cars were stalling everywhere, the city was shut down. Ana kept coaxing her little VW bug on, talking slowly in her raspy voice. The sadness was over a foot deep everywhere. We sought refuge in Little Havana. She had this place where she had done some of her best and most important organizing. A nondescript two-story community center off SW First Avenue. She was a hero to many here. I saw the sign, CARE PLUS. I started to get out of the car.

"No, we cannot go in," she said. "I'm showing it to you."

"It's a building, Ana."

"Well, there it is."

"Why can't we go in?"

"I can't talk about that."

"You won't, or you can't?"

"It is too hard for me."

I looked at her. I wasn't buying it. She was tougher than that. She'd already told me about her divorce, her estrangement from her family, misunderstandings between her and her daughter, and how much money was in her bank account (or not). She restarted the car and circled the block.

She said, "I am persona non grata in there right now."

"I thought you were a hero."

"Yes, that is true."

"I'm not following."

"Perhaps since it is raining we should talk about umbrellas."

"Okay—umbrellas."

Ana was an executive at a bank for a long time, then quit to do social work, with which she has had a love/hate thing going for several years. She's been struggling to find the in-between. Umbrellas can explain her opinion of both professions. A banker wants to give you an umbrella when it's not raining, and then when it starts to rain, gets nervous and wants to take it back. A social worker writes a grant to get the umbrellas, but people don't get the umbrellas because the social worker has to write a grant explaining why some people get umbrellas and others don't.

I tried to interpolate from her cryptic allegory. "So, are you saying that back in that building, there are a whole lot of . . . umbrellas, for lack of a better word, that nobody is getting?"

She answered, "In literature, the wolf is dressed up as a grandmother."

The warmer I got, the more cryptic she became. I knew Ana's first project as a social worker was at a facility in Little Havana—it had to be this one. She established a program called Time Dollars, a sort of volunteering bank in which people deposit (give) an hour of their expertise and then can withdraw an hour of someone else's expertise. House painters and tax preparers and day care providers and grunt laborers participate. It's a remarkably beautiful alternative economy that runs itself and costs nothing. An hour for an hour. On a starting grant of only $12,000, Ana recruited 3,500 people into the network, who exchanged 12,000 hours of time a month. I let my imagination paint in how this might have gone so awry that Ana couldn't even show her face in the building. Perhaps Care Plus had fallen under the control of a dictatorial executive director? Perhaps that dictator took advantage of people's free labor time to inflate her budget, or to make it balance? Did Ana try to blow the whistle? I didn't know, but these were my suspicions.

I felt Ana's vast loneliness.

"I'm lonely but I'm happy," Ana warned.

On the Lost versus Found Spectrum, Ana should be a Found—she quit to go where her heart told her to go. She's *found* in the sense that she knows herself. But it has brought no peace. The tug-of-war never ends.

To respect Ana's story, you have to understand how Cuban-American culture views social work, and how it views family. Social work is highly distrusted. There is nothing wrong with it, but as a system, it is easily corrupted. It hints of Castro. It is not regarded as a noble calling. Family, on the other hand, is more important than God. Your family is with you at all times. I don't mean that metaphorically—you go to the airport, family goes with you. You go to your soccer game, family goes with you. You go to a barbecue, family goes with you. You go to be inducted into Florida International University's hall of fame, you buy three tables—one for your employees, two for your family.

Ana descended from a line of prominent bankers in Cuba who lost everything to Castro. One morning Ana was a ten-year-old girl in a protected household with servants. Forty-five minutes later she was a ten-year-old adult in a Cuban camp down in Homestead, taking care of her seven-year-old sister. It was years before she saw her parents again, but she carried their hopes to rebuild what the family had lost. As a teenager she began working in the microfiche department of a branch of United Jersey Bank. Filer, teller, branch manager, she slowly worked her way out of the branch and into its headquarters, in Elizabeth, New Jersey. In Cuban culture, there is intense pressure to be successful, to rise up. Ana wanted to be a vice president, like everyone else. She became an auditor. Then a lending officer. By her mid-thirties, she was senior vice president, and in line to one day run the bank. She was the pride of her family. But she wasn't happy.

Behind her eyes, she led a secret life. On Sunday nights, she got tired knowing she had to go to work the next day. Her friends were social workers. Civil servants at Health and Human Services, or therapists at hospitals, welfare case workers. She admired what they did. Ana was always looking to volunteer, and she found ways to do so on weekends. But she could never do it full-time. She was too afraid of her family's disapproval, too afraid to let them down.

One of her friends told her about a grassroots redevelopment program that was looking for a director. Ana longed to go for it, but feared how her family would react. "Please tell them I'm not interested," Ana said to her friend.

"No, I'm sick of listening to you. It's always, you want to, but you can't. If you are not interested, then you go tell them yourself."

So Ana went to tell them she wasn't interested, and walked out having promised them she'd do it for a year. The job paid $25,000—$17,000 after taxes.

She went home, and she asked her mother if they could move to a smaller, less expensive apartment.

"Why?" her mother asked.

"Because I want to give myself a chance to see if I can be happy before I die. I have ninety-eight thousand dollars in the bank. Please don't stop me."

Her mother couldn't understand it, but she didn't refuse. The rest of her family wasn't so kind. One day Ana was in the kitchen and she heard her two aunts talking about having her mother committed. Ana couldn't believe it—her mother was old but still lucid. Then Ana realized they weren't talking about her mother—they were talking about *her*. It was Ana they wanted committed.

Another time, her cousin invited her to a party. "You can come, Ana, but only if you won't tell people what you do."

"Why not?"

"Because I am embarrassed for you. They will think you are crazy."

The only reason she stayed in contact with her family was for her daughter, who needed to spend time with her *tías* and *tíos*. To this day, they continually bug Ana, "When are you going to settle down, get married—you're not getting any younger." Most of Ana's family has since moved across the state, and recently her daughter chose to leave Ana and join them, now that she is about to start her own family.

Ana sums it up this way: "Back in Cuba, they would say of me, 'Ana is a light, but one that projects outside the house, not inside.' That is still true. That is me. Happiness comes at the expense of ones we love."

Social work didn't make her happy, though. From one nonprofit to another, from city contracts to federal agencies, she kept running into the same systemic problems. "Nonprofits require you to sell your soul to the politicians. You have to fight for money against other agencies," she said bitterly. "Then I find there is backstabbing everywhere. And they don't really care about the people. Keeping them poor is their business. As long as they keep them poor, they keep getting more grants or bigger budgets. Then, there are the volunteers. The message implicit in volunteering is, 'You need me, I'm good, I'm better than you, you have nothing to give.' "

Within a few years the $98,000 was gone. Her life's savings. She didn't want to go back to banking. "So I went to church. And I'm sitting in church, and I asked God, 'Where do I belong? Where do I go? How do I make a living?' "

Shortly after, she met Edgar Kahn, the founder of the Time Dollars movement. Time Dollars seemed to be the answer to her prayers—she could work in the impoverished communities, but teach them to help each other, rather than to be helped by the government. She told Kahn, "I will not write you a single grant. I will not come to Washington to shake hands. I will not be an employee of Time Dollars, because I do not want to be dependent on you. I will work contract by contract, getting Time Dollars programs started."

Kahn said okay, and Ana has been much more resolved about her place in life ever since. She's incredibly proud of Time Dollars. "All people really need is to be treated with respect. We need someone else to help us see inside ourselves, until you can see how beautiful you are. That's what Time Dollars does. So-called poor communities are rich in assets and resources. Time Dollars helps people in those communities remember in what ways they are rich." She's started programs in Miami, Baltimore, Phoenix, St. Louis, Japan, and England.

That said, Ana is still wary. The theme of her life is the continuous fight for her freedom—Castro, family, husbands, jobs, enemies, all tried to make her into somebody she's not. She seems unable to put her whole trust in Time Dollars. She takes other projects on the side—teaching in a housing project in Homestead, or hurricane relief—simply because she doesn't want to be dependent, like a jilted lover, unable to ever commit again. And she sees money as a danger too. "If you don't need money," she said, "it can't control you." Most of her friends now are new refugees; they're learning to have everything while Ana's learning to have nothing. If they go to dinner, they ask for a doggie bag and put half the plate's food in it before they eat. (They'll eat the rest tomorrow.) They save plastic grocery bags for a million uses. Ana teaches them the importance of opening a checking account and getting a credit card. They're afraid of the credit card but Ana pushes them to use it and build credit. One friend had saved $2,000 and was going to buy a used car with it. Ana persuaded her to use it as a down payment on a brand-new car. These lessons are reproduced and exchanged in her classrooms and in her work. At these fringes, an economy takes root.

In that classic Joseph Conrad way, Ana's going native. Meaning she's adopting the customs and habits of those she leads. I've continued to stay in touch with her, but it hasn't been easy. I'll leave messages at her home, in Washington with Time Dollars, at the motel she sometimes stays at, on her cell phone, and on her pager—and I usually don't hear back. Sometimes I'll get her if it's between 10 and 11 P.M. The rest of the time she's out there somewhere, beyond reach, doing her work, helping the people she considers her real family.

This would be such a happier story if I could say that Ana found her in-between in Time Dollars, and now her life is happy and she's reunited with her family, and she makes a decent, modest living, and she even has a new boyfriend. Plenty of people who do the kind of work that Ana does have that sort of picturesque life. (My older brother, for example—a former bank lending officer, he runs microcredit programs in several countries for Project Hope, a large nonprofit, and lives in the suburbs of Northern Virginia with his family.) But I came to Miami and I found Ana, and I can't hide what I saw. I'm aware that when I mention she's getting by on less than twenty-five grand a year, I kill any chance that someone else will choose to follow the path she's blazed. Ana's story becomes the story of a saint—maybe a curmudgeonly saint, or a flawed saint—but a saint nonetheless, because who but a saint would find her security in getting by on less and less every year? The only thing I can do about how her story turns out is perhaps say it doesn't have to be that way. That's Ana. She's a bit of a slave to her ideals—freedom, independence. Or, I should say, she's a bit of a slave to idealism—any kind of idealism. Her mother sent Ana to America because she believed that there was something in Ana's character that was going to make her a big Communist. Only ten, Ana was already in love with Castro. He was such an idealist! Ana was the kind of person who would want to be a martyr. Today Ana has different ideals—capitalism for all, capitalism will rescue the poor—and she will probably die in her boots, forever devoted to it.

Back to my original query that brought me to Miami: How are we to handle the *privilege* of being able to author our own life? Should we renounce our privilege, and live like others, finding meaning in family, in God, in providing, and in country? Or should we revel in this privilege, because we live in countries where we are free to choose friends over family, choose from many religions, and choose how we provide?

"Americans take this country for granted," Ana said, when we were out having dinner with her friends. "Too many neglect the opportunity they are given. This is the land of dreams."

What is freedom for, if not to live where nobody can tell you who to be, and who not to be? What is freedom for, if not the chance to define for yourself who you are?

13 ||| A College Man

Even though she was an immigrant, Ana was from the Cuban upper class, and class is often more enduring than country. Whether it takes one generation or two, immigrants from educated, professional classes usually climb their way back up to their former class in the United States.

So, what about working-class people from hard-scrap beginnings—do they laugh at the notion that it's important to find our "right" place? Is pondering "What should I do with my life?" a luxury only for those whose mortgages are automatically deducted from fat bank accounts on the first of the month, and whose children attend schools that don't balk at the cost of textbooks, and who pay to have their house cleaned? I assumed that was the case when I started the book, but the next few stories are among many that taught me that assumption isn't true, or fair. Ultimately, I found that just about anybody could find this question important to them, regardless of their background.

Stephen Lyons is a big man with white hair and a trim beard, glacier sunglasses and a cowboy hat. Stephen was from a family of blue-collar tradesmen, none of whom had attended college. He trained as an electrician, but dreamed of being an architect, and used a coast guard scholarship to get into college. But the stipend barely covered meals, and his first wife wanted things, so she pushed him to drop out and be an electrician. They had children, and suddenly he needed every penny just to get by. But that marriage didn't last, and for many years after, Stephen wondered what he could have been had he gone to college. Electrical work paid fine, though, and the Bay Area was growing, so for many years he had regular work wiring the vast suburbs of the East Bay and South Bay. But when the recession of the early 1990s hit, construction halted and there was suddenly no work. He'd recently married Camille, an English as a Second Language teacher who saw in him an untapped intellect. She encouraged him to dream of more, but then she lost her job too, and reality scorched their aspirations. They couldn't make the payments on their little house in Castro Valley, a middle-class city in the East Bay. Within months the bank foreclosed and the sheriff posted an eviction notice on their door. The locks were changed and the house was sold at auction. For a man who builds houses, losing his own was a crippling blow.

They rented a tiny apartment in Marin City, which is a poorer town in Marin County, and began to hunt for work. Nobody needed an electrician. There was no construction going on.

Stephen was desperate. He heard that Dominican College had a cranky HVAC air-conditioning system prone to breaking down. So he showed up, cornered the facilities manager, and offered to maintain the system. He learned that the college had budgeted a half million dollars for repairs (it was a big system, and it's hot in Marin), and was about to contract the job out to a big firm. Stephen pressed. They had nothing to lose by giving him a crack at it for a month. He offered to work for free, for a month, give him a shot.

A month later he was on the payroll, and over the next few years he kept the campus cool. Was this his dream? God, no. But he needed a job. Then he found out that as a college employee, he was entitled to free tuition. It was a chance at the college classes he'd always wanted. Of all the things he learned in college, one of the most important lessons was that other people really weren't any smarter than he was. He earned a business degree attending classes at night and started to read *The Wall Street Journal*, getting a little of that can-do hop back in his step. For his final class, he submitted a business plan for a solar energy company. He was changing, developing an inner focus. When he walked around campus, other students thought he was a professor. He'd developed that aura. He could work seven days a week and not get tired. He made drawings for a small dream house he would someday build if he ever found the money for the land.

Now he speaks in the phrases of a self-determinist. "I realized I had it in me to be successful. I was tired of struggling—tired of thinking that life was a struggle. So I decided to be successful. Why not? Why not me?"

He kept his day job while becoming a certified installer of solar equipment. He put in a few small jobs by himself. Made payments on the tools he needed. Kept modifying his business plan. The catch is, solar power systems pay for themselves over thirty years. Only a small number of peo-

ple have thirty grand to outfit their house and the patience to wait thirty years before that investment is in the black. Jumping into the solar energy business doesn't make economic sense. Or, I should say, being in the solar business means counting on a supply of clients who willingly disregard the bottom line. Stephen knew that, and he was in no position to fight those economics.

When the California energy crisis struck, he thought this was his chance. Rolling blackouts left neighborhoods without electricity, and gasoline prices shot up fifty cents a gallon. Independent service operators were asked to testify before Congress. News of the crisis dominated the front pages. The public was suddenly interested in alternative energy sources.

The numbers tilted a little in his direction. The public hatred for PG&E was so intense that he figured there were homeowners out there who didn't want to be dependent on PG&E for power. Stephen wasn't a risk taker by nature, but he was pretty sure California would reinstate solar rebates and tax credits that would cut the cost of solar systems in half. If he ever wanted to start his company, he had to do it *now,* and hope that a toehold in the market would lead to a boom once the rebates were signed into law. Stephen did some creative visualization, then quit his job and took a gripless open-handed jump into the void.

I spent a day with Stephen and one of his crews on a job site, installing roof mounts and PV cells on a residential house in northern Marin. In addition to installing the equipment, Stephen applied for the permits, secured neighborhood approval, and coordinated inspections by PG&E. Stephen is a perfect example of a guy evolving up the labor food chain, in seven years transforming from a blue-collar guy barely able to survive, slowly learning what he believed in, then putting it together by creating work that he believed in.

I told him I was worried about how much to encourage people. I didn't want to spawn false hopes.

He gave that some thought, and then scoffed dryly. "It's a shame if people neglect what they can become."

"Do you think other people can do what you've done?"

He gave this even more thought. "If you're going to hold me up as a role model, the important thing to emphasize is, I'm not just some electrician-for-hire who now works for himself. I got divorced, I lost my house, I went through a lot, and that shaped my character. I understand now it's a matter of character. Getting my degree shaped my character, taught me how to think. If you think starting a business is like winning the Lotto, something that you gamble on and luck into, and *whoopee,* then Lotto odds are about your odds. But if you develop the character—then yeah, the odds are pretty darn good you'll succeed."

On our next break, I asked him how important renewable energy was to him. Was that a big part of his job satisfaction? He said that it was, but probably just as important was that the product of his labor was up on people's roofs, for all to see. In the public eye. "Electricians don't normally get that kind of visibility. Our work is hidden. You only think about it if it's broke. This is different, and it's a kind of pride I didn't anticipate. This is our fourth job, and I love being able to look up and say, *I did that.*"

I tried to ask him about the creative visualization he mentioned.

"You'll have to ask my wife about that," he said. He seemed uncomfortable talking about it. He gave me her phone number. I called her and drove up to San Rafael to meet her.

Stephen's wife, Camille, took over the story. She and Stephen met and befriended a young Chinese man who was training to become an artist. The young man's career choice was devastating and embarrassing to his father, who was a famous banker in Taiwan. They fought and fought, and the young man felt guilty; he couldn't become an artist because he saw his paintings through his dad's eyes. So the young man taught himself inner peace and nonjudgment. Only then could he release his paintings.

"So what about creative visualization?" I asked.

"That's what Stephen calls it because he doesn't know what to call it. They were really friends who felt safe with each other in talking about their dreams."

The right kind of friends.

A month later, Governor Gray Davis increased funding for the rebate program, and another month after that, the tax credits passed into law. The phone started to ring off the hook at Stephen's office. He had more business than he could handle. He hired his brother, and his son, and then his son-in-law, and then every good hardworking kid he could find. But he still wasn't done until he found a quarter-acre of land in Santa Rosa that he thought suited him, took out a mortgage, and broke ground on his dream house.

NEITHER FIGHT NOR FLIGHT

Anthony Anderson makes mincemeat of class distinctions. He was a high school dropout from Chicago's roughest schools whose life was saved by joining the navy. But he wasn't raised in poverty by uneducated parents—his relatives worked for the Board of Education in Chicago. His mother was an accountant with Blue Cross who loved math and drilled it into Anthony. By age four he could add and subtract, and was considered so smart he started first grade a year early.

He now lives in West Seattle. He owns a nice starter home with his partner, Shelbi. They drive a Land Rover (with a rear compartment big enough for their two Great Danes) and eat protein-heavy diets and can talk about all the new restaurants and books—like any other bourgeois bohemian couple. Very up-and-coming middle-class.

Anthony's job, however, is in the marine construction business. He works the night shift on the retrofit for the Tacoma Narrows Bridge. He is a commercial diver, one of the few black divers in the country. He puts on a dry suit and a huge helmet and descends 150 feet to the bottom of Puget Sound for four hours at a time, where he operates an underwater blowtorch on the new footings for the suspension bridge while battling the currents. For such dangerous, specialized work, the money is very good. It's far more than his job—it's his calling, his passion, his dream come true, and it didn't come easily.

Just three years ago, he was drifting, unemployed. He lived out of a Chevy Suburban parked on the street. Then he slept on a mattress in a guy's garage over on Pigeon Hill. Even then, he knew what his calling was. He'd been to dive school in Seattle. He'd done his two-year apprenticeship down in Louisiana working on oil rigs. But he couldn't break into union work in the Northwest. Knowing your calling is not to be confused with succeeding at it. The last three years, he's learned what it takes to get from the former to the latter. He can't quite put it into words, like Stephen Lyons—or can he?

Tentatively, he summarized, "It's about confidence. With me, it's always been about confidence. When I approach a situation with confidence, I lean in, I figure it out, I succeed. When I lack confidence, I pull back and withdraw. My confidence was taken away from me when I was a boy." Sadness flashed across his eyes. A haunting memory. He said, "I remember myself being studious and inventive as a kid. Then it was snuffed out."

His aunt was a secretary for Reverend Jesse Jackson's PUSH Coalition. Anthony's elders had devoted themselves to changing the system, but in the meantime they mostly complained about it. It had an undesirable effect on young Anthony. It taught him to imitate their outrage, their finger-pointing. They tried to mold him with tough love; they tried to teach him to endure any situation, such as in ninth grade, when his mom moved in with her father and Anthony enrolled in a new high school. It was a very rough, bad school. Being new *and* a year younger, Anthony was repeatedly bullied and beaten up by the older students. His mom met twice with the school counselor to discuss her son's discipline problems, but she wouldn't transfer him to another school. "You've got to learn to stick it out," she told him.

Instead, the message he got was, *she simply doesn't care about me.*

He skipped school the next week, hoping to avoid another beating. He got one anyway, when his mom found out he was hiding at home rather than sitting in class. His grandfather and aunt disciplined him physically, to teach him the most important lesson they could—*you can't skip school.* He remembers sitting by the window, watching them come up the walkway, knowing what he was in for. (I'm sparing you the details.)

"That was my giving-up-on-them point," Anthony said. "In a way, it was liberating. When suddenly my grandfather was in on it, for the first time I understood why my mom and aunt were always disciplining me that way. Because he *taught* it to them. And it had been taught to him, generation down to generation, certainly all the way back since slavery. I couldn't forgive them, but it helped to have this understanding."

Six years in the navy gave him more perspective. Teamed with guys from all over the country, with a skinny white guy from Texas as his bunk-mate, Anthony learned that the way he was raised was only one way, not the only way. "It broke down the untruths I grew up with," he said. They traveled to Japan, Italy, Cuba, and throughout the United States.

Is the contribution the armed services make by broadening young peo-

ple's horizons underappreciated? It certainly was by me when I started this book. My father was a marine, but when he enrolled at eighteen he had other choices. A lot of young people don't have those other choices. If they're not going to college, there's really no other way out—no other way to transcend their circumstances. My interviews and correspondence with a dozen grateful young soldiers made this clear. Didn't they complain about the low pay and regimented bureaucracy? Absolutely. But they were still grateful. As Anthony said, "If I didn't go into the military, I would have been a broke, homeless pothead."

One day two navy divers came to Anthony's unit and talked about what they did. Days later he caught a special on the Discovery Channel about deep-sea diving, and he could see what those two guys had described. From that day on, Anthony was hooked. He requested to become a navy diver. He was still a bit of a troublemaker; his request was denied repeatedly, fueling bitterness until he finally accepted that his disobedience and unruliness had consequences. When his tour ended, he moved to Seattle for dive school.

"What most appealed to you about it?" I asked.

"The total concentration required. The one-hundred-percent-total-focus, can't-slip-up carefulness. That has always been its appeal and still is. When I focus I feel clear-minded. When I don't focus, I've always been haunted by a dark, shadowy blur."

"A dark, shadowy blur?"

"Yeah."

"Is it something in particular?"

"No, just a feeling, like just outside your vision."

After dive school he spent two years training on oil rigs in Louisiana, a right-to-work state. When he came back to Seattle, he got a job dockside but the old boys' network wouldn't let him into the water.

"For a long time, I believed it was racism, just as I did when the navy denied my requests. I had been taught in my youth to see racism everywhere, including in situations where that isn't at all what was going on. Marine construction really is an old boys' network. It's kind of a hazing process, but race has nothing to do with it. So much of diving can't be taught in school. You have to earn the trust of older divers before they'll share their know-how. So I felt shut out. Occasionally they would test me—send me down into the currents in the dark with a torch. If you resent being tested, as I did—my attitude gave me no chance. Eventually I was laid off, and I started my downward spiral."

In his twenty-nine years, Anthony had never learned to earn a thing rather than wait in line for it. He'd blamed everyone but himself. When he ended up unemployed and unable to afford a place to live, an odd kind of clarity came to him. "I need to go through this," he told himself. "I need to figure this out." With a friend, he went kayaking on the Methow River in central Washington. He told his friend, "Just leave me out here." He spent the next six weeks living in the woods. It wasn't a contemplative, restorative time. He was there out of sheer stubbornness. The inclement weather drove him back to Seattle, where he slept in the Suburban and then that guy's garage. Finally, when all the evidence was in, and obstinacy and umbrage had proven to be of no use at all, he spoke his first humble words ever:

"I've got to get some help."

Anthony went to the local Veterans Administration Hospital. They suggested that he was using alcohol and pot to deaden his senses. He didn't deny it. He joined a group. When not there, he went to the library for shelter. There, among the endless shelves of books, a very unexpected thing happened. That bright little boy, studious and inventive, was still alive inside him, ready to come back out. Underneath all those cloaks of trained helplessness was a smart kid who loved to read. First he read everything there was to know about the science of childhood development. He read book after book on psychology, depression, and attention deficit/hyperactivity disorder.

Then he read everything that might help him in diving. "I studied it like a college course." He put himself through a course on steel—on all the mechanical properties of different alloys, understanding for the first time what kind of steel was appropriate for what kind of job. Then he taught himself civil engineering. Then land erosion and oceanography, because some diving work requires surveying erosion damage on beachheads. He also taught himself plumbing.

"For the first time I was knowledgeable. When I went back to work, I was prepared. Having all that information in my mind—it gave me confidence."

His attitude was the biggest difference. "I used to have this fight-or-flight response to any conflict. Neither option served me well. Stuck on a barge, you can't run anywhere. I learned to silence that instinct, and resolve just to work it out."

For example, there is a kind of class stereotyping in the trade. Some of the guys have been to college, but around the barge they slip back into a blue-collar dialect. In order to be accepted as one of them, Anthony had to pretend he was the kind of Southern boy they all met down in the Gulf when doing their apprenticeships. He had to stoop to ghetto talk, *yo, brother,* when he'd *never* talked that way in his life and wasn't very good at it. He hated doing it, but it broke the ice and now they are getting to know the real Anthony.

Another example has been his relationship with Shelbi, his partner. Fight-or-flight would only destroy the good thing they've created. "There are nights I just need to go for a drive," he admits. "But they're far more infrequent." Finding each other began a new life for both of them. Shelbi married young and divorced young. Her past seems like a bad dream she once had. They've been given a second chance; they treasure it.

I get it now. I get what Anthony is trying to teach me. There is no fight-or-flight at the bottom of the sea. When problems arise, they are dealt with as challenges, addressed with total concentration. Down at the bottom of the sea, Anthony is honing his coping mechanisms, honing his ability to deal with life's frustrations. So that he can succeed as a diver, yes, but also so he can hang on to his relationship, this second chance.

You might have in your memory banks an image of the Tacoma Narrows suspension bridge. It's one of the most famous disaster films ever. Taken in 1940, the grainy black-and-white footage captures the concrete road of the Narrows snapping like a whip in a windstorm and twisting into a semihelix before falling into Puget Sound. The wreckage of the old bridge is apparently still down there. The bridge was rebuilt and now, sixty years later, Anthony is part of the retrofit team that makes sure the Narrows can withstand the awesome destructive forces of nature. Just as he and Shelbi are a team learning to withstand the dark, shadowy blur that would tear apart any relationship, or destroy any spirit.

Now when I want to run from my problems, I think about Anthony, hanging on with one hand at the bottom of the sea.

Hang on, hang on.

15 ⫶ Building a Cathedral

I met Bart Handford in a diner near his apartment in the Adams Morgan neighborhood of Washington, D.C. He hadn't yet shaved that morning, but he would do so before he went over to the community center where he volunteered. He was thickset and wore a T-shirt that draped over his big shoulders. His brown eyes were sensitive, and his Arkansas accent was slight. He was thirty-nine, and he had been out of a job for six months. Even in his worst-case scenario, he thought he'd have a job by now, doing logistics or scheduling again, though he really wanted a policy position overseeing rural development, which is sort of what he had been doing before he and everyone else in the Clinton-Gore administration were relieved of work.

He stayed away from other Clinton alumni. Nobody was working, and it quickly got depressing to dwell on it. His girlfriend was the communications director for an Illinois senator, so he went out with her friends, most of whom were employed.

In late December, the White House Liaison Office had asked everyone in the administration to submit a letter of resignation, forward-dated to 12:00 noon on Saturday, January 20. Supposedly Washington is great at absorbing the party out of power, but that hadn't happened when I was there. The District of Columbia holds standing-room-only seminars on unemployment in the Canon Caucus Room. *This is how you fill out the Blue Sheet to receive your benefits. . . .*

Nobody's sure how many people are out of a job; the Government Printing Office puts out a Plum Book, which lists all the Schedule C appointed positions—there's maybe 3,500 in there, according to one of my sources. But there's 22,000 administration alumni—and I know that's a good figure, because I got it from the woman who runs the alumni asso-

ciation, and she got it from someone inside the DNC. That's one of the ways you learn to talk in D.C.—since everyone is in the business of crafting a message, every number and statistic is only as good as the source it comes from. People litter their sentences with footnotes. Except for Bart Handford—maybe because of his background, he's much more plainspoken. Another thing they talk about in D.C. is "point of view." Many young people are drawn to politics for the weightiness and the sniff of power, and they're just in it for the gamesmanship until the day (or the campaign) when they finally develop their point of view. Most people could tell me exactly which events led to their suddenly getting a point of view—the Anita Hill/Clarence Thomas hearings, for instance. Well, Bart Handford's always had a point of view. The Democrats are traditionally the party of the common worker, but most of the staffers have never met one. Bart doesn't have that problem, because a year before he joined the Clintons, he was working the night shift at the ConAgra chicken fingers plant in Batesville, Arkansas, as part of the cleaning crew.

He'd tried college, but didn't last long and didn't really see the point. He drove a newspaper delivery truck, and then he worked his way up at a florist from delivery boy to store manager, which he felt served him very well because he was dealing with people at the most emotional times of their lives—deaths, weddings, holidays, Valentine's Day. Then he killed a year in the Kimberly-Clark baby wipes plant. But the ConAgra job sent him back to college. At night the plant was over 120 degrees, and he'd stand there cleaning the chicken fryers, drenched with sweat, which ran down into his rubber boots. Every couple hours, he had to take his boots off and dump the sweat out. After a year, he started to see the benefit of getting a degree.

He enrolled at Arkansas State and signed up for classes in political science. One of his strongest memories was of watching the Watergate hearings during the summer of '74, when he was ten years old. He knew it wasn't practical to major in poli sci, but he wasn't planning to go into politics—he just needed a bachelor's degree to qualify him for a desk job and keep him off the assembly lines.

Bart didn't make it through the first semester. One night driving home in his Delta 88, he was crossing a railroad track and was struck by a freight train on the driver's side. Not all the crossings are protected by signal gates, and in the dark the freight train couldn't be seen. Bart woke up three days later in a hospital in Little Rock. His spleen was ruptured, his lung punctured, and his ribs, clavicle, and arms were broken in multiple places. But his head and his legs were okay. He was told that he'd lost so much blood in the ambulance that he had basically died by the time he reached the hospital, but somehow he wasn't dead.

Six weeks later they wheeled him out of the hospital and put him in a bedroom in his parents' house. It took most of a year to rehabilitate. He figured college and all it might lead to were now out of the question. When he could work again, he was hired as a manager at a Little Caesars pizza restaurant. With all the medical bills, he needed a second job, and so he went over to the Clinton campaign headquarters in the old *Arkansas Gazette* building and put his résumé in. When Clinton won the nomination at the Democratic convention, all the senior operatives moved back to Little Rock. They called Bart in to the second floor. It was complete chaos. There were ten phone lines, and whenever one rang, someone screamed out over the floor. They asked Bart why he wanted a job. He said he'd always voted for the governor, ever since his first campaign. When he was a newspaper delivery driver, Clinton had come into the back room where the boys roll the papers to shake some hands. Bart's hands were black with ink, but Clinton didn't hesitate. Ever since then, he'd always respected the governor.

He got the job answering phones, and soon the floor was filled with volunteers from all over the country.

I asked, "Was it just another job? A second income?"

"In my heart I was hoping it would be something *more*—"

"And was it?"

He said, "More than I had ever imagined. I'd worked very hard before, doing menial work. I never complained that it was grunt work, but I always hoped that one day my labor would contribute to something I believed in, something meaningful. Suddenly I was surrounded by all these other volunteers, most of them five years younger than me, from schools I could never dream of attending, and they were doing nothing but grunt work eighteen hours a day, seven days a week, and doing it gladly, because they all believed in it."

"That was a new feeling?"

"It's like that old story: three guys laying bricks are asked why they're doing it. The first guy says, 'I'm doing it for the wages.' The second guy says, 'I'm doing it to support my family.' The third guy says, 'I'm helping to build a cathedral.' For the first time in my life I was helping to build a cathedral. I felt like I'd found my home, and I'd found my people. On that campaign, I discovered what I really liked to do."

"Had you been looking for your cathedral? Over the years, all those menial jobs, did you just focus on getting paid, or were you jockeying between jobs, trying to find happiness, trying to find something more cathedral-like?"

"It probably sounds silly to you when I list out the jobs I had, but for stretches I hoped I'd find my cathedral. I lost track of that ambition when I started working in the plants, but with all that free time after the accident, I rekindled that hope. Was working at Little Caesars it? No, and I never thought it would be. But I had hope."

When Clinton won the presidency, Bart was offered a position as office manager of the Office of Scheduling and Advance for the White House. He was flattered just to be included. They asked him how much he needed to be paid. The White House budget is scrutinized heavily, so they asked him to not pad his figure. He thought about it, and then asked for $28,000, which would have gone a long way in Arkansas, but resulted in a huge sticker shock when he got to Washington and discovered what an apartment costs to rent, and how much people drop on drinks, and how expensive it is to catch a cab across town. He was stuck with his meager pay. Bart borrowed money from his folks to get by. It didn't matter. He had his passion.

Everyone has to pay his dues in politics. Scheduling and Advance is thankless work, and Bart was only noticed if something went wrong— someone didn't get told that their meeting with the president had been changed, et cetera. But those who are paying their dues aren't miserable, and they have a kind of religious fervor about it. Because the president's schedule is so intense, the advance team lives on adrenaline, panicking to make sure every public appearance comes off smoothly. Bart flew to Northern Ireland and South Africa on trips with the president, places he never would have seen in his lifetime if his career hadn't taken this amazing turn. Everybody in politics travels a lot. That's one of the standard perks. And it's a type of travel that is more memorable than, say, business travel—even though they work sixteen-hour days when traveling, they do it with a team of compatriots, and always seem to come back with stories of crazy things that happened late in the night, after the bars had closed.

After two and a half years, Bart couldn't live on $28,000 anymore, and he was ready to be rewarded for his devotion. It was time to transition away from political skills and develop a policy specialty. He was appointed to the Department of Agriculture as regional coordinator for rural development in the Midwest. The agency ran a program that brought clean water to rural people by lending money for the construction of aqueducts and wells. Bart's job wasn't to run that program—the actual implementation of programs is done by entrenched civil servants. Political appointees set the agenda for the agency. The Republicans in Congress had just slashed the program's budget by 35 percent, so Bart's mission was to generate publicity, and get the word out that this was a program worth not only saving, but funding back to full levels.

Bart had a cause to fight for. He flew down to Mountain View, Arkansas, which wasn't far from his hometown. He found five hundred people living in the Ozarks drinking water that was so cloudy and muddy it was revolting—when they had any water at all. He went down to border shantytowns in Texas, where crop workers were getting water from irrigation ditches contaminated with pesticides. Bart found out that over a million people in America didn't have drinking water in their homes at all. The amazing thing was, the loan program wasn't actually costing the government any money. Even though they were loaning to the poorest counties in America, the default rate was less than one-tenth of 1 percent. Bart came back to Washington and made his case to the representatives from the districts he had visited. He was fighting for their attention against every other issue (which somebody else like him believed in with equal conviction), but by the next year's budget, the program's full funding had been restored. It was a great triumph.

Bart was reinvigorated. He saw where his future might lie. Last year, he earned his college degree by attending night classes at the University of Maryland. He wasn't upset about being laid off in January—he'd campaigned for Gore on weekends, but he would have had to resign his USDA post anyway and hope for a new appointment. So he was always expecting a hiatus—

"—Just not for this long," he added.

"And you want to get back into policy?"

"Deeper into it. I'd like to be running a program, not just putting the right spin on it. It's a quantum leap, from political hack to the world of policy and business."

"There aren't positions to apply for?"

"There are, but I'm going to need an MBA to qualify."

"So did you apply to grad schools?" Quickly I did the calendar math in my head—he was laid off in January, but knew it was coming . . . applications are due in early winter. . . .

He paused. Ahh, *the pause.* There's a point in almost every interaction where the subjects stop presenting themselves as willful architects of their own destiny, and downshift into admitting sometimes they can't seem to control their own hands and feet. There's always this *pause.*

"Po, I didn't send in my applications."

"Why not?"

"I took the GMAT in September, and then I requested the applications . . ."

"What are you not saying?"

"I'm embarrassed, Po. I had never applied to schools of this caliber before. I had no idea how *complicated* it was. Recommendations, essays, financials—I didn't know all this had to get done."

"You had nothing but free time."

"I didn't like any of my essays. I would be writing and thinking, 'These people are never going to let a hick like me into their school.' The application process reminded me exactly where I'd come from, and how little I really knew. I've been intimidated. From the moment I came to Washington, I've been surrounded by the smartest people from the best schools, and they seem to know something I don't know, like they've all been taught a secret language. And they *have*—the language of applications. They've all been through it before. To get into Arkansas State, I just waved my high school diploma. I've got to learn the language. I decided to take the year to perfect my applications, and apply next year. I didn't realize it would be so hard to get work in the interim. Now I see I made a mistake."

"Bart, you've been in this community for eight years. You don't feel you belong?"

He said, "I've got to get over my inferiority complex."

"Or use common sense to tune it out. You worked for the White House, for god's sake. That's pretty impressive."

"It is?"

"Yeah."

"The honor of it is easy to forget, in a town like this."

We ate our breakfast and went through too many cups of coffee. I kept thinking about all the poli sci undergrads who never had the resolve to pay their dues in politics, so they went off to Wall Street or law school. I admired Bart for how far he'd come, and it pained me to see him now paralyzed to go the rest of the way.

Bart spent much of the next year working part time for a Maryland abortion rights league and as a volunteer teaching adult education for Academy of Hope. Those essays percolated in his mind. In October, he took an intense Outward Bound course in Mexico, where he confronted some of his preconceptions. Did he really want to learn economic development? Yes. Did he really have to earn an MBA to run a development program? Maybe. Did he have to *run* a program, versus work his way up? No. And with that, his paralysis released. He took a job with the New Israel Fund, which finances economic-development projects in Israel. He traveled to Jerusalem regularly. He found it very satisfying.

IT'S SUPPOSED TO BE HARD

So do we need our work to be meaningful because we no longer go to church? Could this "meaning gap" be easily solved with a little more scripture and prayer? This was suggested to me by a number of people, and it seemed apparent—most of my friends who consider themselves Jewish or Catholic or Hindu rarely practice the rituals they reminisce so fondly about. The concept of one's "calling" has been distorted from a religious call to a career imperative. Maybe it needs to be distorted back.

However, it's not true. At least I didn't find it to be true. Half the people in this book are devout, and not once did that insulate them from struggling with the question of what to do with their life. Most of them sat down with their rector/pastor/father/guru and asked for guidance. Rarely did that bring them peace or settle their mind. Many spoke of how helpless their religious adviser seemed. One of those people was Barry Brown, who lived in the county seat down in the boot of southeastern Indiana. It's a rural and depressed place. The high mark of population in the county was the 1880 census, when they hit fourteen thousand residents. "I'm one of those people who doesn't really count," was how Barry first described himself. He has a BA in English from IU-Bloomington, but never built on his education and never thought of work as anything but a way to get by. He sold Kubota tractors, then was a shipping clerk, then found work at the state mental hospital. He'd been in the army. He was an Episcopalian, and that's where he got his meaning. "What should I do with my life?" was not a question that had ever plagued him. But lately, he'd been rotating in the security department of the riverboat casinos that were licensed six years ago in hopes of juicing the economy, and it was making him question everything.

Barry rotated among stations at one of the casinos, the *Belterra*. Most of the time he stood on his feet doing nothing useful. His job was merely to observe and count. When one of the slot machines paid out a jackpot, Barry did the count, and then the floor attendant counted, to make sure the denominations pouring from the machine jibed with the paperwork. Occasionally he delivered chips to the blackjack tables. The first time he did that, his knees got weak. He was carrying $60,000. He'd never seen so much money. Barry couldn't understand the fascination of gambling. He tried it once and found it about as much fun as weeding an onion row.

Every evening, buses arrive from Cleveland and Dayton and Indianapolis and Louisville, dumping out hordes of people with hard-earned money to lose. They enter the babel of illusion, deceived by the music and moving lights into feeling like they're doing something interesting. They lose track of time in the permanent indoor twilight, unsure whether it's night or day in the real world. They come to be numbed to their feelings and problems. The corrupting influence of this floating den of iniquity works its magic. Slowly their inhibitions relax. They see their neighbors as marks.

When you understand how the environment of casinos work, you understand how the whole economy works.

Welcome! Welcome to the nonstop spending machine! You won't feel a thing!

I found Barry by the same happenstance that brought me to so many others: an e-mail I sent out to a few friends was forwarded along, eventually reaching people in places where I didn't know a soul.

The night he received my e-mail, Barry had been standing duty. He heard his coworkers laughing. They were watching this little old man lose his money. Down to his last few chips, the man had started to cry. Tears were falling from his eyes as the last of his chips disappeared into the slot. He was bawling. Barry had seen that happen many times before, but he couldn't believe his coworkers were laughing at the poor man's expense.

"Go back to Dayton, old man," they teased.

"He's not a tourist," Barry intervened. "I've seen him before, at the YMCA and at Goodwill. He can't afford to lose that money."

"Boo hoo."

"When did you get so callous?"

"Shut up, bleeding heart." Now they were laughing at Barry.

Now the tears came to Barry's eyes. Embarrassed, he ran from the pavilion out onto the deck and stood at the rail over the dark Ohio River and cried.

Years worth of tears fell from Barry as big thoughts came to him. What am I doing here? What is this place doing to me? He could see into his future, and in that future he had become as callous as his coworkers, picking on poor old men. He didn't want to be that way. But the babel of illusion would work on him. Every day he'd accept a little more, until one day he'd think it was normal. Barry fought to keep a grip on reality. *This* is *not* reality, he told himself.

One of Barry's earliest memories came back to him. He couldn't have been more than four. The top of the pew couldn't have been much below his eye level. Reverend Wright's baritone boomed from the pulpit. His barrel chest lifted his Geneva gown. Reverend Wright was an old-time Calvinist, very formal—crisp white shirt, black tie, black shoes, his dark wavy hair combed back. Most sermons are sales pitches, but his weren't. His sermon was inspired by the first question in the old catechism, "Why were we created?" Worshiping God was not enough, Reverend Wright insisted. You must also offer up to God your skills and your honest labor. You must find your place.

Standing on the deck of the *Belterra,* Barry was struck with guilt. His ancestors had come over here from Scotland and Switzerland with high ideals, and here he was securing the process by which people parted with their hard-earned cash. He had done nothing to live up to the ideals expressed in Wright's sermon.

When he went home that night, Barry was unable to sleep. In the middle of the night he went online and, out of the blue, my random e-mail arrived, solace at a time when his friends felt like strangers. The next day, he was still so ashamed he stayed home from work. We talked by phone. "I don't feel worthy of God's love," he said. "Or anyone else's, for that matter."

"Why?"

"Reverend Wright had it right. Sorting out your vocation is a serious matter. I've ignored it, because it's too hard. Well, of course it's hard! Serious things *are* hard!"

I told him most people have the opposite reaction. They find it really hard, and they feel guilty because they think it's supposed to be a lot easier than it is.

"No! That's the lie of our culture. That everything's supposed to be fun and easy. Even our religions make it fun and easy to be religious. They waffle, they don't make a clear statement. The old-time religions have unraveled. They had it right. It's not supposed to be easy."

"So what are you going to do? Are you going to quit?"

"I don't know. I have an obligation not to eat up my savings. But I've seen what those casinos do to people, and I don't want it to happen to me."

"You feel trapped?"

"Yeah."

I guessed that he didn't have too many options in such a depressed county. "Barry, I'm fishing here, but—what have you thought would be *too hard* to do?"

"It'd be too hard to commute to Columbus or Cincinnati. Also, a couple years ago, I was going to study for the Microsoft A+ certification exam, but I stopped."

"Because it was too hard?"

"I might look into it again."

A month later, Barry said to me, "I never thought you'd be interested in the story of someone like me."

I told him I'd been cut short by a publicist in Manhattan, who said the topic of my book wasn't for the Wal-Mart crowd. It was a common assumption that this concern was phantom angst that only afflicts overeducated happiness chasers who need a cold slap in the face and a dose of "get with it" reality.

This disturbed Barry. "So they don't think someone like me cares about my place in the world?"

"I think it's that your economic situation is so marginal, you don't have a choice."

"Maybe I don't have much choice. But I still care."

Some of that care had been redirected to his garden. He was planting more than he had in years, even though the humidity in the Ohio River Valley was so bad he had trouble breathing. He kept working at the casinos, simply because he had to. He'd asked his rector for advice, and the rector had been sympathetic but unhelpful—he told Barry to keep a grip on himself and not lose it, and eventually find something else to do. A few weeks later Barry went to his doctor for the flu. The doc read him like a book, bluntly putting it to him, "You're depressed." Barry explained why. "Don't blame yourself for those casinos," the doctor advised. He prescribed Celexa, which has helped Barry's mood but stimulated wild dreams—one night he dreamt he was in the pavilion at *Belterra,* and John Calvin rode through on a horse, followed by the Marx Brothers.

His religious conscience continued to burst back into his awareness, and twice the line between his dreams and his reality was blurred.

He was working one busy night at the *Belterra* when he had what in earlier times would have been called a vision, but that he recognized now was a hallucination. He looked up, and there was John Calvin himself, holding a chalice, looking down on the babel. Angrily, Calvin pronounced, "I don't give you the cup of blessing but the curse!" and he threw down the chalice, which burst into flame.

"I really lost it," Barry admitted. His adrenaline was pumping and he took it out on his uniform, tearing it off his body and then into shreds.

The casino put him on a short medical leave. "My coworkers thought I was crazy, but they didn't really mind. They think it's quaint that I have these old-fashioned ethical values."

Then, he added, "If I had to spend the next ten years working for the *Belterra,* I won't make it, honestly."

He traveled to Ireland to assist with the Ulster Project, in which Catholic and Protestant teenagers are brought together to learn tolerance and trust of each other. Barry is both very devout and, in particular, extremely sensitive to divisiveness. So while the hallucination happened at work (always at the casinos, never while gardening), Barry didn't believe his work dilemma was his only trigger. At the time of that first hallucination, Barry was preoccupied by the military buildup leading to the war in Iraq. And his next hallucination came eight months later, when the Episcopal Church was divided by a debate over whether to confirm the first openly gay bishop. This time he held on during the hallucination and didn't lose it. He recognized it as not real, as a chemical event.

Barry kept his post at the *Belterra,* but he began to work on a plan that would turn his hobby, gardening, into a side business as a perennial nursery. His brother—who sold Kubotas—had a customer in the landscaping business who needed more plants that were adaptable to the local climate. Barry got some tutoring in Latin in order to understand botanical terminology. He hooked up with a high school classmate, now a retired banker, who taught at the Venture Out Business Center. Barry built a propagation unit for rootings and cuttings, one for holly and one for another type of heavy-leafed privet. He ordered these cuttings from Pennsylvania, father north, so they'd be heartier. That was the rule of thumb—down in the boot of Indiana, they needed heartier hibiscus, heartier azaleas, shrub roses. His brother offered to let Barry buy a Kubota at cost, which would allow him to increase his volume. Barry didn't pull the trigger on that— he was going to grow this slowly. He had something to hope for, and it was sweet just to have that feeling back.

17 ||| Lady Reads the News

A GOOD DAY JOB

"Lady J," as she goes by on the radio, wasn't sure whether she wanted me to use her story. She likes hiding behind her throaty voice and kittenish byline, letting the rest be an ageless/faceless mystery. Who is she? Whoever the listener imagines her to be. "Oh, you go right ahead, do whatever you want," she decided, but I sensed that wouldn't be the last time she'd change her mind.

So I'll stick with Lady J. When I take her picture (while riding in a bus) I suggest she bun her hair and shy from my lens. Mystery intact.

Her radio work is what one might call her sideline, her hobby, but that would be measuring it only by the amount of time she spends doing it. She can be heard on one of the local Minneapolis rock stations for a total of seven and a half minutes per morning. Each half hour from 6 A.M. to 8 A.M., the music breaks as Lady J reads the ninety-second news segment live. She leaves the station and arrives at her regular day job before nine. Reading the news allows scant chance to let her personality out, but that's okay. It pays almost nothing, and that's okay too. It's radio. A little goes a long way. It's her lifeline.

"Some days, it seems to make everything else bearable—you know what I mean? It's just always been there."

Growing up in St. Louis, she had three brothers. Her father wouldn't let her play with them because he didn't want her to turn into a tomboy. She was also very heavy, at fifteen weighing sixty pounds more than she does now. The kids at school teased her about her weight and her voice, which was very deep. "Ooh! She's got a boy's voice! She likes girls!"

"The radio became my best friend," she said. She loved to spin the dial and be transported. She managed to lose all the weight and as a senior was voted prom queen. Her favorite station also held a contest—not a beauty

contest, but an aspirational contest to win an internship, sort of "What do you want to do with your life?" She was crowned Miss KEZK, and was interviewed on the air for ten minutes.

"When I heard my voice? Oh, man, that was it. I fell in love with that feeling."

She attended college in Indiana. On the university station she went by "Lady New York" because she had cousins there and it sounded more cosmopolitan than being from the Midwest. Her father didn't approve of studying broadcasting; he wanted her to take computer science, which would "give her options." She took some business courses to please him, got her degree in psychology, and begged to be given a chance to try radio.

After college, she gave herself five years. She found gigs in Syracuse and Birmingham. She knew she couldn't indulge this forever, so she set goals. She wanted to be in a major market, and she wanted to cover a major news event. In 1991, she moved to Minneapolis ("major enough") and covered the Persian Gulf War (not that she went to Dubai with the press corps, but the station devoted a larger portion of every hour to news during the war). She'd met her goals—enough to look herself in the mirror with pride and say, "I did it." Her five years were up. It was time to move on, find something respectable, get on with her life.

Lady J became an auditor for a big accounting firm—one of those that's no longer around. It's been merged, and then the merged firm eventually imploded after a string of ethical improprieties was revealed. She never witnessed that numbers-fudging. Back before the merger, she respected her work and the firm.

Mergers so often change things. It's the number one complaint I hear, the generic version of which goes like this: "I was fine with it. It wasn't my dream but I liked my work. Then the company was sold, and the culture changed. They were squeezing more money out of our customers, and I was on the front line, making excuses, hocking for a firm I no longer believed in."

Lady J had been there seven years prior to the merger. One day she had a new boss, and the fun seemed to evaporate. After a year of it, Lady J needed an outlet. She started moonlighting in radio again. A little Sunday-afternoon gig, then the morning news. Her boss at the accounting firm seemed to resent it but couldn't do anything about it.

"Why'd she care what you did with your free time?" I asked.

"Simply put? Because she was a bitch. She resented anyone who seemed to be having more fun than her. She considered it disloyal. She said I should be putting that energy into my firm work."

"Did she discriminate against you because of it?"

"I noticed I wasn't being sent to the most prestigious clients. But I was unhappier anyway, so my enthusiasm wasn't what it once was. So I don't know if you could call it discrimination."

As auditors, they spent most of their time at client work sites. They kept careful time sheets, and it was considered treason not to be on time and well dressed every single day. Had to represent the firm! One morning the radio station asked Lady J to record the daily entertainment report. It aired later—at 9:30 A.M.—but it sounded live. Lady J was on-site with a client, the University of Minnesota. Someone heard it, mistook it for a live report, and called Lady J's boss, who immediately called the regional headquarters to start her termination. Lady J went about her workday with no idea this was happening. The next morning she stopped by the office for a meeting. The regional manager heard she was there, pulled her out of the meeting, and told her she was history.

For what!?

"For cheating the company."

What!?

It should have been a simple misunderstanding. When the University of Minnesota sent a certified letter testifying Lady J was on-site at the alleged time, her job should have been restored. When the radio station sent a certified letter stating the entertainment report was taped, not live, she should have been reinstated. Instead, she had to hire an employment attorney, who assured her that he could get her job back. It was a slam-dunk case.

But did she really want to go back? They'd shown their true character. Maybe her boss was a bad egg, but the firm had backed her up despite evidence otherwise. The firm hadn't been the same since the merger, and all the other accounting firms were being gobbled up.

"I was disappointed with their utter lack of humanity. I didn't want to go back to a cancerous environment. I wanted to be where people appreciated my talents. That experience *convicted* me about what was really going on."

How easy it was to label her passion "that thing I used to do when I was young"! Not until someone tried to take it away did she realize she would never give it up again.

She had just signed an agreement to purchase a condominium. Unlikely anytime soon to have a comfortable salary, she forfeited her escrow payment.

"That hurt. Oh, that *really* hurt. I was mad, and my anger helped me. You can survive on nothing when you're mad."

She rented in a much cheaper neighborhood, begged for a night shift at the radio station, and went back to school. Picking up on her psychology degree, she studied full-time toward a master's in social work, which she earned eighteen months ago. She is now a licensed therapist at the Hennepin County Medical Center, working with at-risk teens, mostly sixteen- to eighteen-year-old girls on welfare. (We were headed there on the bus from the radio station.)

"I miss the nice salary. I can't lie about that." She paused, remembering fondly her old lifestyle, then her mind moved on to another thought. "I'm not sure where I belong. I went to college, I come from a good family, I am supposed to be a professional, right? I have never been near a welfare line. Growing up middle-class, you are very aware and very proud not to be lower-class. But these girls are teens. They're easy to *want* to help, though not easy *to* help. Bottom line? It doesn't pay a lot, but it allows me to do what I love."

"So it's really a day job?"

She shot me a look. *Don't disrespect me.* "It's a *good* day job. It's my contribution. I'm doing *good*. The radio is my fun. If I had to choose?" She paused. "Well, I guess I *don't*. That's the point."

At the hospital, I wasn't allowed into the one-on-one sessions, but there were already two girls waiting in the lobby for Lady J, or Mrs. ——, as they called her. They called me "lumberjack" and "Paul Bunyan." One had brought her eight-week-old daughter to show Lady J; she was proud and wanted Lady J to know she was doing good. The other begged Lady J for her stylish clothes. "You ever going to throw that away, Mrs. ——? You can give it to me first." They idolized her.

"The main way I rub off on them is as a role model," she admitted. "I don't see them enough to make a big difference with the problems they face. I teach them enough to learn that such-and-such, like him hitting you, it's wrong, it's not normal. But not enough to get him to stop. Some girls want to see me more, but as their mentor, not as their therapist. I don't pretend otherwise. That's kinda the deal."

"I heard you this morning, *Lady J*," the first girl teased.

"Really? What did I say, then?"

"I don't remember. But I *heard* you."

Lady J sneaked me a smile.

18 ||| Getting Oily, Then Even

Over the course of my research, I met dozens of people who were morally troubled by their work. They felt they were screwing society, not improving it. No matter how unpalatable their work became, those feelings of shame and loathing were almost never enough, by themselves, to spur them to finally take action and quit. An accumulating social cost only set the stage for the moment of drama, which came when it got personal—when it was not society being screwed, but the individual. Something personal had to be at stake. These next two stories flush this out.

Bryce needed someone to tell his story to, and he found me. He'd been through a hard year and come out the other end a new man; though the worst of it was over he was afraid of backsliding. For three months, I heard from him twice a week. Sometimes his missives had little to do with his story—he'd rant about the Dallas Mavericks, for which he held season tickets, or share an embarrassing anecdote from the previous night's blind date. When I was in Dallas we'd tear into some game meat at Matt's No Place, then cruise around in Bryce's truck on a tour of local toxic cleanup sites, using the cover of night to avoid suspicion. I think he needed me there to legitimize the choice he'd made, and to help him stick by it. When his work situation finally settled down, and he found the peace he'd always wanted, Bryce no longer needed to talk. He didn't regret talking—not at all—he wanted to preserve his privacy. He asked that I not use his real name. I didn't like it but I had no choice. "Bryce" is a pseudonym. He also asked that I not name the big oil company that used to sign his paycheck, so I'll call them Big & Oily, or maybe just B.O.

Bryce is a throwback to the Burt Reynolds genre of masculinity. Mustache. Swept-back curls. Gleaming teeth. Mischievous eyes. In the movie version of his life, he's handsome enough to play himself. He grew up on a cotton farm in West Texas, back when his dad was paid by the federal government not to grow cotton.

Bryce is a geologist. When he called me, he'd just taken a job as the enforcer of environmental regulations for Collin County, and he was proud of it. His primary task was forcing oil companies to stop gasoline leakage from their underground storage tanks into groundwater wells. He worked in a county office alongside a food inspector, a building permit inspector, a septic system inspector, and a hazardous materials emergency response coordinator. The pay was less than half what he earned at Big & Oily, which clearly bothered him. He was wary of government bureaucracies, the turtle's pace of their work culture. I had a sense that his commitment to this job would last only as long as his need to get revenge. And Big & Oily was doing everything it could to weaken his resolve.

He whipped out his cell phone and played a message his answering machine recorded that afternoon. The call was from an old compatriot at Big & Oily: *"Hey, Bryce, what's going on, man? I'm in town and I've got the company's credit card tonight. Thought we might take you out and get you in trouble."*

"Did you call him back?" I asked.

Silence = yes.

"Are you going out with him?"

"Why do you think you're here with me?"

I could tell that Bryce liked the notion of being a Force for Good, and he loved bringing Big & Oily to its knees at the negotiating table, but he was adjusting to the loneliness of it. He wasn't part of a tight community, and that made him vulnerable.

"Can I make an observation?" I asked.

"Sure."

"When you talk about that partying you used to do—you still honor it with a frat house relish. The more hammered you got, the more glory to the story."

"That's how everyone talks."

"Not everyone."

"Everyone in Texas."

"Sounds like you miss it."

"Naw."

"Would you go back?"

"Never."

But my concern was well founded. Over the next month, Bryce kept being enticed to return to the warm and cozy embrace of Big & Oily.

I told him to watch out. "They're trying to get you off their back in Collin County."

"Of course they are."

"What if they're lying to you? They lied to you before."

"I'd make them put it in writing."

"I can't believe you'd even consider doing business with them again."

"This is probably no good for the pretty picture in your book, huh?"

"No, believe me, I appreciate the realism." I wasn't drawn to saints. We can worship saints, but we can't emulate them. I would rather hear how the weak of will end up doing some good. The hesitant, all-too-human.

"I'm just thinking about it," he said. "That's all it is. A man can't help but think about these things."

A week later he called to say he was going to give notice with the county unless they increased his salary. All along, he was bugging me to join him for a Mavericks playoff game. I thought it was time I went, and made plans for Game 6 at Reunion Arena. But the Mavericks were eliminated by the Spurs in Game 5. He had even less to root for now. I stayed in San Francisco, and Bryce went off to his high school reunion in West Texas.

When Bryce was at UT Austin in the early 1980s, oil was still gushing at forty dollars a barrel. He got a summer job making a hundred bucks a day as a roustabout on the drill rigs. He was told if he earned a geology degree, the money would get a lot better. They needed geologists to examine drill cuttings to determine if there was oil below. It was fun, it was outdoors, and it was good science. Plus he'd get an equity percentage in any wells that hit. He had visions of kicking back and living off the royalties. But shortly after he graduated, the price of oil crashed, hard, and didn't bottom out until it hit nine dollars a barrel. The oil exploration industry in Texas was dead. Not kind of dead, like the computer industry, or almost dead, like the dot-com industry. There was no pretending. The laments of software engineers coming out of universities today have nothing on Bryce. In six months he was selling used cars off a lot in Lubbock, wondering, *what happened?*

Cut to: 1989. The *Exxon Valdez* spilled eleven million gallons of heavy crude into Prince William Sound, Alaska, and in its wake a tiny new industry boomed: Environmental Consulting. Nobody trusted Big Oil to clean up its own mess. In most states, new laws forced oil companies to pay independent consulting firms to monitor their toxic land, and, when determined necessary, to oversee the cleanup. When that law was passed in Texas, Bryce was hailed off the car lot for a phone call. It was his best friend from college.

"You gotta come to Dallas, Bryce. You can get a job in a heartbeat."

"With who?"

"The oil companies are panicked about the bad press. They're throwing money around like you wouldn't believe. They need geologists to clean up their land."

"You're shitting me."

"I'm not. Get back here. *Now.*"

It didn't take long for Bryce to decide. *Getting paid big bucks to clean up the environment?* How good does that sound?

Too good to be true, he discovered. The so-called independent firm he joined was nursing from Big & Oily's titty. They called it "the game," and it was played like this: The boys at Big & Oily who controlled the lucrative contracts let it be known they had a weakness for golf and strip clubs. Bryce would reserve a tee time, plunk down the course fees, load the cooler, and make sure his wallet was stuffed with cash in case the day became a long night, which it frequently did. The next day, Bryce would get a call: "We're going to throw you a few more sites, Bryce." These sites numbered in the thousands. Every underground storage tank that leaked a little gasoline or benzene had to be evaluated for whether it was contaminating groundwater aquifers. Bryce would drill a monitoring well and file reports with the local regulatory agencies, recommending that no action needed to be taken. B.O. made it absolutely clear: his job was to keep them out of trouble. They instituted an incentive plan, where his bonus was inversely proportional to how much they spent on cleanup. The regulatory agencies in each county were undertrained and overwhelmed. They'd haul B.O. in for a meeting to review these sites. B.O. would trot out Bryce as their "independent" consultant. Bryce stalled, distracted, buried facts, argued, protested, and defended. Some of these regulators didn't mind a round of golf now and then.

Bryce became a legend around Big & Oily for his escapades on a night he doesn't even remember, but has been told it involved him spinning donuts in his 300ZX on the eighteenth fairway at Rancho Luna. The Z ended up in a reservoir drainage ditch. There was also something about Bryce in a golf cart with a Dallas Mavericks cheerleader. All Bryce remembered was waking up covered in mud and grass burrs.

"That was the night I became part of the family," he told me.

He used "family" to describe the culture around Big & Oily. Sometimes he used the phrase "country club." Or "fraternity." He always described himself as Golden Boy.

"You knew what you were doing was wrong?"

"I avoided thinking about it."

"Pretty tough to avoid, I'd think."

"The money was intoxicating. Drinking was a big part of it, too. I'm sure I was drinking to forget. Then it was the culture. They were my friends. We got a laugh out of stalling the agencies. We took pride in doing it well. I judged myself by how much money I made."

I recognized it's a lot easier to get sucked in if you grew up on a cotton farm and your last job was selling used cars.

"Did you think of leaving?" I asked.

"All the time. But to do what? My contacts and my friends were in the game."

"Did you think you'd play the game forever?"

"I hoped not. I left one consulting firm and founded a new one with four friends. We had some hope that we might get bought out, and could quit with a decent lump sum."

So when did his redemption come?

Did it come when he woke up in a motel room with a skull-cracking hangover, finding himself a divorced man?

It did not.

Did it come when Big & Oily began to squeeze its consultants, and the free-flowing cash began to dry up?

It did not.

Did it come when Collin County filed a multimillion-dollar lawsuit against Big & Oily over twenty-one sites Bryce had stalled on?

It did not.

Did it come when it was discovered that MTBE (a gasoline additive) escaped even newer, government-approved, "leakproof" storage tanks?

It did not.

He could always say of the family, "these are a great group of guys," and firmly believe it. There is a bond between men, and as long as one never breaks that bond, men will ignore other sins. They had always been good to Bryce. Always paid him on time, always thanked him when he did a good job, always sent a Christmas card, always called when he was sick.

It was in the eleventh year that the family finally revealed its true character. Bryce was cut out of the game by one of his business partners, whom he calls "Person X" because merely invoking his name spins Bryce into fits of anger. They had been buddies for years. One afternoon, Bryce learned that Person X had drained their consulting firm's annual profits. The money had been paid out for suspicious expenses. Bryce drove over to his house that night and confronted him. The next morning, Big &

Oily canceled its contracts with Bryce and awarded them to Person X, who had formed a new firm.

"That was a dark day," he said.

Bryce was in shock for a week. He couldn't understand why he was made an outcast—and still doesn't. At forty, he figured he was too old to find another field to work in, but that was the surface problem. That job had been the justification for his whole personality. At work he'd learned to be evasive, to employ white lies and errors of omission, and now he recognized that was how he treated everyone. Over the next ten months, he coached himself to be direct and answer questions plainly. He stopped drinking, which was the easier part for him—he didn't know where to go at night if he wasn't going to drink. So he read constantly, killing time, waiting for he didn't know what. He played pickup basketball at the gym. Lost thirty pounds. As a practical matter he sold his house and managed to get by on a lot less money, but much more disturbing was that his sense of humor was scrambled. He didn't know what was funny. Everything that used to be funny was no longer funny. Those eleven years of moral compromise ran deeper than he'd ever realized.

Big & Oily offered Bryce a small number of other sites, but he couldn't stomach working for them. He started thinking about naval base cleanup, and sat on one committee, but found the cacophony of those bureaucracies intolerable. Then a friend told him about the county oversight position.

For all those who were morally troubled by their work, it surprised me how few ever considered simply switching sides. What better way to make use of what you've witnessed? But it's a culture shock, as Bryce found out. A chance to get even might sound like the perfect gig, but it required a whole different mindset. For instance, with this county job, what did it lead to? It wasn't what you'd call a dead-end job, but it was an end in itself. It wasn't a path to something else. Every other job Bryce had had was rimmed with possibilities of something else—sometimes the unknown, but it kept hope alive. The finality of the county job was a little suffocating. He could do this, but could he do it *forever?*

His first week, he shocked Big & Oily when he showed up wearing the county badge. He sat down across the table from their new Golden Boy and growled, "Get to know what it feels like to be a kept man. They own you now." He turned to Big & Oily and warned, "I know your every tactic. Those days are over in this county." It felt great, really great, until one of them quipped back, "What are you driving these days, Bryce?" and they laughed.

Money!

It was going to bring him down. In the root of his mind, the boys at Big & Oily were still his inner circle.

Every time they saw Bryce, they asked what he was driving, where he was living, which restaurants he'd been to, which golf courses he'd played at. Every question was a dig. Then he'd go back to his county office and sit at his desk, alone, eating his $2.99 cellophane-wrapped turkey breast sandwich.

The hardest thing about doing the right thing for yourself is you usually have to do it alone.

Bryce was on the fence when he took off for his high school reunion in West Texas. He ran into his high school sweetheart, Charline. She looked fantastic! She was single again too. He told Charline what he was up to, and because he wanted her to think he had some money, he added that he'd be leaving the county soon for this much better-paying job with Big & Oily. Her face soured as he described the job, and she said, "That doesn't sound like the Bryce I remember."

That stopped him cold.

When he thought back to high school, he always thought of himself as pupalike, unformed, clueless about real life. But Charline insisted not. "You were a thoughtful guy. You were conscientious. Maybe you didn't know what you wanted to be when you grew up, but you knew your *values*. You weren't a jerk like some others."

They spent much of that weekend together. They weren't trying to recapture the past, but it is likely that we fall in love with people who bring out the part of ourselves we want to see more of. In Bryce's case, he wanted to bring back the character he'd lost. The next week he called to say the county had agreed to give him a raise, and he wasn't going anywhere. He sounded a lot more upbeat. I asked him about the money, and he said, "Ahh, you spend what you earn."

A month later I heard from Bryce. He and Charline were planning their marriage. He went to a barbecue with the other inspectors, and he saw that his county job wasn't a dead end, it could lead to a state job or into research at a federal lab. He'd acclimated. Both his work life and his love life had come full circle, and that had a sweet resonance, a sense of fit, the feeling of no longer being lost, no longer chasing the wind.

THE FEAR THAT OUR CHOICES ARE IRREVERSIBLE

Here's another thought that stops people, one I hinted at in Bryce's story: there are a lot of possibilities that sound exciting—but you're not sure you'd want to do them forever. And because of their quirky nature, they're résumé killers—they slam a lot of doors shut. Sure, it'd be a fun ride, but where do you go from there?

Well, imagine you were a Harvard MBA, then an investment banker with First Boston at the vice president level. At that point, if you had the guts, you could jump to about anywhere white-collar and respectable, or you could stay put and get rich. Instead, imagine you went off and did something crazy like this:

> 1990–present   CATFISH FARMER (Indianola, Mississippi)
> Managed 8,000 acres of row crops and 1,500 water acres of catfish (5.5 million head). $16 million annual sales. Side businesses wholly or partially owned include cotton gin, flying service for pesticide spraying, feed mill, fish processing plant, and adult extended care facility.

That's what Don Linn's résumé looks like, and that's about all I knew of his story when I went to see him. But my curiosity was raging. What would his life be like? Would the foolish originality of this path be worth its stubborn irreversibility? Was it, indeed, a one-way ticket? Could daily life in the third-poorest county in the poorest state in the union possibly be *interesting* enough to keep his Ivy League mind engaged?

To get to Indianola, you fly to Memphis, drive down past Graceland, and keep going in that direction for half a day. Once you get to Indianola, to find Don Linn's office, take a right at the four-way stop sign and then take a left where the church used to be and it'll be a quarter mile ahead.

Where the church used to be?

How would I know where the church *used to be?* But that's the way you get directions in the mid-South. Don grew up in South Carolina and Tennessee, and then spent the go-go eighties in Dallas, but a southern accent ain't the beginning of how they talk here. You never say it rained. You might say "we got ourselves a little private rain, inch and a tenth," or, "it was a real packing rain," meaning the clay soil glued itself into a crust that the cotton sprouts have a hard time busting through, or, if the rain was heavy, you'd say "we done got thundered on." When the catfish tastes good, it's "on flavor." The foreman is called the straw boss, and if he's off drinking you're told, "he got the Jack attack." And when you go looking for him and run into one of the farmhands, the conversation might transact like this:

"How you been?"

"I been good."

"Where you been?"

"I been around."

"So when you figure he be around then?"

"He be here ten minutes or so."

Eleven thousand people live here. Unemployment is 12 percent, not bad. Cash advance shops outnumber bank branches. A trenchant crack problem plagues the neighborhood on the other side of the railroad tracks. You can't get any men to work during bow hunting season. Conversations focus on hunting, football, and who's screwing who. The local weekly newspaper lists *every* traffic fine and charge brought by the local police. Most of the jobs listed are for drivers. A truck driver takes home $8.50 an hour, the women at the catfish processing plant a little less, and the seining crew, which dredges the ponds, earns minimum wage. A straw boss earns anywhere from $40,000 to $100,000.

Don gets up at 4 A.M. every morning to read. Almost every day, a shipment arrives from Amazon.com with more brain food. Don misses New England's intellectual culture, but he's insistent on one point, which took him a year to wake up to: "It'd be easy to mistake these people's ways for lack of intelligence, but most of them are as smart as you and me. They've never been out in the world. Some are uneducated, but they know their business better than I know mine."

This part of the state doesn't have a long history. It was swamp and bayou until the levees were constructed along the Mississippi in the 1920s. The hardwood forests of mangrove, pecan, and walnut were cleared to get rid of mosquitoes and stop the spread of malaria. The drained land was so heavy with clay, they named it "gumbo." It wouldn't seep. Only the old high spots could grow corn, so with the rest they farmed rice, but rice is prohibitively expensive. Two decades ago someone dug a five-foot pond in the gumbo and tried raising catfish. This made a certain economic sense. Catfish are nature's most efficient animal in turning feed into protein (twice as efficient as chickens, for instance). Catfish are the hogs of aquaculture—they'll eat anything. Fish pick up their flavor from their environment. Catfish acquire their legendary aroma by scarfing off the bottom, where fish rot. A decade ago, someone started feeding catfish a puffed cereal that had been aerated and thus floated. The filets from young catfish that eat off the water's surface are as flaky and light as any freshwater whitefish. It used to take three days to net a fish, truck it to the plant, get it fileted and frozen. Now it takes thirty minutes. Boom! The catfish industry exploded, and this part of the country finally had the means to sustain itself and a reason to be proud.

That's about when Don arrived. He's six feet even, thick sideswept auburn hair, too-pink skin for these parts, and has let his gut go a little. He hasn't changed much what he wears: pleated khakis, pink polo shirts, deck shoes. Don's here as a businessman. His wife talks a lot about a "sense of place," and if you enjoy being close to nature, rolling the sleeves up, there's psychic income galore. But Don isn't one of those people. He didn't come to Mississippi with the sentiment that farming was particularly noble. Back in Dallas, he didn't own a cabin out in lake country. He carries a rifle in case he encounters a water moccasin, but that's all it's used for. The adrenaline he gets, that charge that makes it all worthwhile, comes entirely from the risks and rewards of running a big complex operation.

His first day on the job, a flock of Canadian geese arrived by truck—that sounds weird, I know, but the geese had been purchased, with the intent that they'd populate the bayou that ran through their land. The geese were thrown into a cabin and had their way with the place. Don had to go in there with pruning shears and clip their wings. Quickly covered in goose shit and blood, Don was wondering what he'd got himself into.

A few nights later, the phone rang at 2 A.M. Don couldn't sleep anyway, it was so hot.

"Get on out to the ponds," the voice said.

Don drove out to the ponds, each of which is about the size of a football field. There was a froth on the water. Something had driven those fish crazy, and a lot of them were turning belly up.

"They can't breathe," Don was told. "They're coming to the surface to get a gulp of air."

Why would fish be breathing air? It didn't make any sense. Slowly he figured it out. There's ten thousand head of fish to every acre—unbelievably thick with fish, and they're burning oxygen to digest their food. During the day, sunlight triggers photosynthesis in the algae, keeping the water oxygenated. On a hot night, with the water evaporating, the oxygen runs out. Don put a paddle wheel on the water to stir air into it, but it was too late. For the next month, Don rode around the ponds at night, monitoring the oxygen levels with a measuring device on a long pole, trying to keep his fish alive by allocating paddle wheels where the situation was desperate.

Don found that other farmers wouldn't return his phone calls. He wondered if he'd done something to insult them. Then he found out that it was insulting to use the phone. They like to chat in person, down at the café or by the side of the road.

I make it sound like his MBA ain't worth a lick here, and I don't mean to. Farming is a famously tough business. It's as risky as biotech and it pays out no better than T-bills. (That's including the aid income from the government, which is more than half of the total income on most farms.) The difference between making 2 percent profit a year and losing your shirt is in maximizing the efficiency of resources. Catfish fingerlings cost five cents per, and by the time a fish is big enough to harvest, with twelve ounces of meat on its bones, Don has spent fifty-five cents on every fish. He sells them for about seventy cents a pound. You can't harvest the fish when it's too hot, or they won't be on flavor. If the fish get too big while you're waiting for their flavor to clean out, they become too tough.

Grow crops are even more weather-dependent. Corn goes in mid-

March, then some early soybeans. Wait for another cold snap, then plant the cotton. It costs $325 to raise and pick an acre of cotton. Most of that money used to go into pesticides. But now there's worm-resistant seed, which can get by with little pesticide—except the seed is expensive, which means Don's bet is already in the ground. If the sprouts get hailed on or can't get a stand through the crust, he loses his bet. Last summer, it was so hot that Don's plants couldn't pollinate. Back at his office, Don has computer programs generating wall charts that map out every penny spent on every acre. He spends two hours every day watching the commodities exchanges and hedging his risk by buying or selling in the futures market. In the language of an MBA, it's a classic resource optimization problem. In the language of a farmer, it's just life.

Late his first year, Don earned the respect of the other farmers in the valley. Five big farms share ownership in a catfish processing cooperative, Delta Pride. Don got a call at midnight from the co-op's bookkeeper. The bookkeeper had been ordered by two executives to make fictional entries inflating sales. On behalf of the co-op, Don went in the next morning and fired them on the spot. He discovered the co-op was in bad financial shape. None of the farms could afford to lose their investment. Don decided to step in and run it himself for a year. He nursed the business back to strength and won over the locals. He saved a couple hundred jobs.

The next year, Don learned that good people were having to leave Indianola for Jackson, where they could get care for their elderly parents. So Don created an elder-care facility, sort of like day care for parents. It was so successful he now has three centers.

Don's dedication and resourcefulness have paid off. Despite the deteriorating agricultural economy countrywide, Don's business has grown—at rates even his business school mates would admire. Revenue has tripled and profits have quadrupled.

I rode with Don on his rounds. He's calm and thoughtful. Nothing I asked him caught him off guard or forced him to contemplate something he hasn't already considered on his own. That said, he was hungry to talk with me and to show me the good and bad of his life. He didn't leave anything out.

Most of Don's days are spent shuttling about in his Suburban, making sure everything's getting done. The rule of thumb for farming is, "go wherever you're spending or making the most money at that moment." This morning a seining crew was harvesting the catfish in pond 9. They'd stretched a huge net across the water, dragging each end with a tractor.

Two men in chest waders walked along the pond bottom, one foot on the net to keep it from floating to the surface. Don doesn't have to say too much. His presence is a motivator. If his hires don't think they're being monitored, they'll slack off. That's the work culture here, so that's the essential nature of his role, and it's hard for that not to have its erosive effect—he has to be slightly watchful, just about all the time. Don didn't learn this lesson quickly, and it's not in his basic nature. On Wall Street everybody's income was tied to their performance, and that was all the motivation anyone needed. Supervision was nil. So when Don came to Mississippi, he tried to vest his employees with back-end incentives and empower them with autonomy, et cetera, but the traditional culture was too entrenched to overcome.

I asked Don why he left First Boston.

"I started out at Paine Webber," he said. "We were drilled and drilled that if we gave good advice we'd get business. Clients would come to us. And I was so successful doing that in Boston that the firm asked me to run their Dallas office. This was 1987, the height of the fever. Investment banking changed, it became predatory. Six months into it, First Boston made me an offer to move my team over to their firm. They were more prestigious, so I went ahead."

The way investment banking works, every couple years someone invents a new kind of financing deal. If it flies, and everyone makes money, they reproduce this deal on every other company they can sell it to—whether it fits them or not. In the late 1990s, this deal was the IPO. A few dynamic start-ups went public and became huge successes. So banks jumped in and took a couple hundred other start-ups public, even though few were worthy. In the mideighties, the equivalent deal was the LBO, the leveraged buyout. First Boston performed a headline-grabbing multibillion-dollar leveraged buyout for Federated Stores, and earned huge fees in the process. In the following two years, First Boston ordered all of its corporate financiers to sell lookalike deals to their clients. That's the nature of the beast. It's no different from Hollywood cranking out the *Matrix* sequels, or the record industry churning out boy bands.

I know this because at the time, I was an assistant bond salesman at First Boston; I sold the Federated Stores debt and everything else behind it.

"So you understand this then," Don said.

"I think I was too young to understand it at the time, but since then, in seeing the pattern repeated with IPOs, I slowly realized how the business works."

"Well, I was old enough to know I didn't want to do business that way, and I told my bosses as much. I told them I'd only generate business I was comfortable with. I became passive-aggressive, dragging my feet, not calling my clients. Then I had one particular client, and I was ordered to push an LBO on him. I knew the numbers wouldn't work—if he did the deal, he'd never be able to pay off the bonds—but we were supposed to be long gone by then. I was embarrassed to put together the proposal. That night, I thought hard about it. I knew I couldn't do it. My father was a high school principal. My role model was a professor of finance at Vanderbilt. They never compromised their ethics."

"So what'd you do?"

"Well, around this same time, my baby boy was walking but not yet talking. He'd entered that phase when he was developing separation anxiety. Part of that is he'd cry if he was ever picked up by strangers. And you remember how it was—I was gone five or six days a week. I was flying to New York twice a week. All week I'd stare at his picture, and I loved him so much it practically made me cry with joy to think about him. He was becoming a little person. All week long I wanted nothing more than to be able to come home and hold him. Pick him up in my arms and play with him."

"And he didn't recognize you?"

"I was a stranger. He'd cry if his mother walked out of the room, but he'd cry if I walked *in* the room. That was when it finally hit me. No more."

Don's story fit the same pattern as Bryce's—unethical business alone wasn't enough to impel a change. It had to get personal. For Bryce, that point came when his best friend betrayed him. For me, churning billable hours didn't get me to quit—it was realizing how much weight I'd lost. If you need to summon the will to make a change, don't debate ethics. Get personal. If you don't believe in the integrity of your profession, you can debate the ethics of it forever and never do anything. But if you define the personal toll it's taking, it hits a lot closer to home.

"So did you quit?" I asked. I had memories of bankers who quit or were fired; they were ushered from the building by security guards in minutes.

"Not exactly. I came to an agreement with the firm that after the bonus cycle, I wouldn't re-up for another round. I had about thirty days to figure out what to do next."

"You didn't have savings?"

"Well, I had some, but with a mortgage and two kids . . ." He wasn't going to let himself hang out for months waiting for a vision.

"So, of all the things you could have done, how in the world did you end up a catfish farmer? Particularly if you didn't think it was noble, and you weren't an outdoorsman itching to get back to the land?"

"It wasn't like I chose catfish farmer off a long list of possibilities. It was the only opportunity that presented itself."

This farm had been passed down in his wife's family since the Depression, but her generation had run for the cities and wanted nothing to do with farming. If they couldn't find somebody to manage the operation, the family would have to sell the land. During this thirty-day period, Don's father-in-law paid them a visit, described his problem, and Don—who'd never in his wildest dreams considered something like this—volunteered for the job. It wasn't a well-analyzed decision. He saw an out. And he thought it would be good for his kids to run in trees and fields and sky.

"Weren't you afraid?"

"I sure was."

"Of?"

"Of how it would look. Not then, but later. I was aware it would look like a step down to my old business school classmates. Would anyone ever hire me, after I'd done this crazy thing? I didn't think so. This would be it. The last stop. I expected to be buried in the backyard." He meant this literally—there was a burial plot behind the house.

"Was that feeling of being able to see the rest of your life, knowing it wouldn't change much—was that comfortable or uncomfortable?"

"Both."

Farming may be just a business to Don, but it's had a different effect on him from investment banking, just as the catfish changed when it started feeding from cleaner water. Success here doesn't come at someone else's expense. Don isn't trying to steal another farm's business. He can't outbid them or charge more than the market will bear, and there's no chance for excessive profits. It encourages him to be steady, to take it slow, and to ride out the crises.

I took the chance to bring up the irreversibility question. Was he going to do this forever? Did he even have a choice?

He said, "Those soybeans we watched going in—those are the last soybeans we'll ever plant."

"What are you going to grow instead?"

"Nothing. We're selling the farm."

"Why? You can't make any money?"

"No, we're doing fine. We've had some tough years, but the farm's well capitalized. The family wants their money out." If his wife's older relatives died, the estate tax would be triggered, and the next generation would have to cough up far more cash than they had. "My job's up in September," he added.

This was a bit of a shock. I'd only been there two days, but I could tell I'd have memories of this place forever.

"Why don't you buy it?" I asked.

"Can't afford it."

"How long have you known?"

"Since the end of last season."

"How's it make you feel?"

"Scared of the uncertainty."

"I bet."

"I'll be all right, though."

"What are you thinking of doing?"

"Well, I would have thought that nobody in the world wants to hire a former banker turned farmer. But, as it turns out, I've become a bit of an expert on transgenic foodstuffs. I've seen firsthand the good it can do. I put us into a program for experimental farms. The summer nights here were too hot to grow corn until Monsanto invented a strain for the mid-South. Our seeds are engineered to be worm resistant. Some aren't genetic hybrids—they have one gene scratched out. There's a new catfish cereal that has fish meal protein mixed in, though we've held back on using that yet. I've been reading all the research as these and other products came to market. So, it's a little premature—I haven't been hired yet—but there's some biotech start-ups who are interested in the diversity of my background. I'm talking to headhunters and flying out for interviews."

"Wow."

"Yeah."

"Who would have thought taking such a crazy leap would turn out to be the perfect stepping-stone to get in on the next new thing?"

"Not me."

"What part of the country?"

"Big cities. Bay Area, Boston, Maryland, Research Triangle."

"Intellectual havens."

"Yup. And I won't be swatting mosquitoes in November."

I was really heartened to know it was going to work out for Don—that this wasn't irreversible—and we talked about it a lot. As he said, "You close one door behind you, and inevitably another opens up in front." In these start-ups, they need a business manager who understands what farmers want and why they're wary of newfangled products. It's a lot easier to imagine them buying seed from Don, who's walked in their shoes, than from some bioengineer who's never set foot on a farm.

In fact, when we get back to the office, Don has a phoner with a head-hunter. Don's done more than read the research—he's flown to meet with many of the researchers in person, for his own education. He visited a lab in Boston where they were splicing salmon genes into catfish DNA, with the hopes their supercatfish would get the magical ice water gene.

Don told me this upcoming passage felt different from the one he made a decade ago. He's not trying to play it down, minimize the change it will surely bring. "*Transition*'s not the right word—it'll require a transforma-tion." Last October, he went to a continuing education retreat at Harvard, taught by a sociology professor named Shoshana Zuboff. Her course was called "Odyssey," and it was mostly attended by businesspeople looking for the next thing in life. She had Don write his autobiography, then helped him expand on it, write more and more into it, picking out themes, adding layers. She built her course around the metaphor of an oyster shell; the outside layer, the formative layer, is fragile and vulnerable, but the old layers are hard and strong. Don figures he's got enough layers on him now to hold out no matter how hard it gets in the next year. He's looking for-ward to not merely "changing hats," but changing heads. Did you ever hear businessmen brag about all the "hats" they wore? As if wearing the hat were enough, rather than the whole uniform, or more—embodying the whole point of view.

At some point, we have to give up the habit of measuring ourselves against our peers. Don did that long ago. But to prepare for this upcoming passage, he's been tracking down his old friends and reestablishing con-tact. Ironically, his life compares well. Most of Don's classmates who chose investment banking because it would be a bridge to some other yet-unknown destination never ended up crossing the bridge. They were trained to be bankers, they got good at it, they never left its domain. Most have turned out to be sad guys with gray lives, bankers at accounting firms, brokers at Schwab, earning half what they did a decade ago—the good times couldn't last forever. Don's come to think the strategy of keep-ing your doors open is mostly an illusion, or a trap.

A month after my visit, I called for Don to find out if his conversations with that headhunter had led to a job yet, and/or if he might be coming to San Francisco to interview.

"Oh, he's not here," Don's secretary said.

"When will he be back?"

"Well, he went out into the country to set a pile of stumps on fire."

"Mmmm. How long you figure that take?"

"Could be right quick, but if those stumps are slow to catch, he could be a while."

"Well you tell him I said hi."

"I sure will."

Don e-mailed me that night. He'd come upon the final words Raymond Carver ever wrote, which spoke to him mightily:

> And did you get what
> You wanted from this life even so?
> I did.

That was classic Don. Ying-yanging between piles of stumps by day, Carver's verse by night.

Temptations
vs.
Aspirations

20 ⫴ A Billion Is Chump Change

There's a part of my story I can't make sense of.

I loved selling bonds. I was a sales assistant, meaning I sold on behalf of my two bosses to their clients, mostly banks and savings and loans. I sat right between both of them, clearing their trades, hearing every whisper of every call, missing nothing, and handling everything they didn't have time for. Their clients learned to trust me. My math gift made it easy to find the story in a pattern of numbers, spot anomalies, and exploit them. As a budding writer, I enjoyed translating that story into words, lending it a bit of drama, making the pitch zing. It was clear to all I had a rare talent for the markets, and when I was twenty-four, after I'd been on the mortgage desk for eighteen months, the firm offered me a position as full salesman, with projected first-year commissions of $300,000. The two guys I worked for earned two to four times this amount, so I knew it was no joke. I could reach their level within a few years. But for some reason, I turned the firm down, and walked away with nothing.

I didn't say no right away. I wasn't good at saying no to anybody's face. So I said that sounded good, can we talk about it later? And I'd go home with my stomach in knots, dreading having to make a decision. The firm kept bringing it up, and I strung them along for a couple months, until they finally realized I wasn't biting.

My ability to understand how I resisted that temptation only gets foggier over time. How could I be so stupid! It wasn't my dream, but so what? Why not do it a couple years and sock away a nest egg? I honestly don't know. I probably had a handful of reasons at the time, but in retrospect none outweigh the reasons to have a half million dollars in my savings account. I'm too embarrassed to tell you my reasons, for it will clearly reveal I am perhaps the stupidest person of all time. Even though it worked out, and anyone would say I made the right decision, I still second-guess it.

I was drawn to the sales floor from the moment I walked the edge of its trenches. A friend had passed around my résumé, and I was called in for an interview. I didn't know what the job was. It didn't matter—I was already sold. Men and women were running around, hollering at each other, gesturing with their arms, cracking jokes. Their sleeves were rolled up and their ties loosened and they were eating at their desks or throwing phones or barking into the squawk box. They called each other by nicknames—Q, Mayo, Doll, Dan-O, Crash. I didn't know what a bond was, or the difference between a bid and an offer, but coming from that suffocating windowless room at the litigation firm, this looked like a blast. It had an egalitarian ethic; titles meant nothing and management was thin to none. The gig paid about 35K. I should have bargained for more—they probably wanted me to counter—but I would have hung out on that sales floor for less.

I thrived in that environment. It was so loose, so unpoliced, that I felt incredibly free to be myself. After a year, the firm brought in a distinguished elderly Chinese gentleman, Mr. Bob Chang, to cover the pipeline of high net worth investors moving to the states from Hong Kong. The firm warned me to rein in my eccentricity around Mr. Chang, be a little more proper. But in two weeks I had Mr. Chang standing on an imaginary pitching mound in the middle of the sales floor, throwing fastballs of wadded paper down the aisle into my catcher's glove. During peak trading hours. Nobody said a word to me about it. As long as Mr. Chang was happy, I was untouchable.

This was in San Francisco, not New York. So we had to be at the office by 5 A.M. It was punishing to drag myself down there at that wee hour, when the streets were empty and the sky was dark, but in some way this added to its luster—I wasn't one of the faceless drones who filled the sidewalks at 8:56 every morning, hurrying to clock in my face time. I didn't feel so anonymous, so indistinguishable, so unnoticed by the eye of history.

But after eighteen months, I was itching for a new environment. And I'm not good at not scratching my itches. That environment had taught me what it could.

Example 1: I went in there with a terrible fear of picking up the phone. I was the kind of guy who put off for a week calling the hardware store to see if they carried a certain brand of paint. Calling people for job interviews was way out of my league. But my desk at First Boston had over two hundred direct phone lines to the firm's accounts, all at a push of a button, and on an average day I would have to make (or answer) a couple hundred phone calls, to pitch a trade or quote a price or confirm a settlement. I had to make those calls or I was fired. It pushed me. I got over my fear. Gone forever.

Example 2: I learned an attitude, a cavalierness around money—how to show no fear and keep my wits when the sums get big. From the first day, I had nearly a billion dollars a day pass through my hands. Does that sound like a lot? It sure did to me. The first time I processed a trade for $300 million, I could barely stand, I was so afraid I'd somehow screw it up. But anybody who's worked in the debt markets knows that a $300 million trade in overnight repos is actually meaningless slop. It's a doggie bag, scraps left over from whatever the banks didn't get properly invested that day. The commissions on it are barely enough to buy a shoe shine and a taxi ride home. A billion dollars a day is chump change, if it's only one day at a time. So it's that kind of attitude I learned—that a billion dollars can be mere chump change, nothing to get impressed about. Nobody ever taught me this directly or said it aloud—it was the flavor of the room, and like a catfish I soaked it up. I carry that attitude with me to this day. I'm so easily unimpressed by the dollar signs.

So maybe that's why I didn't stay two more years. Maybe the environment made me immune to its temptations. It vaccinated me. The firm offered me three hundred grand, and I was callous about it. *Three hundred isn't really that much money,* I would say. *It's not enough to retire on. It's enough to get habit forming. And that's a pretty expensive habit.* It was like play money. What would I possibly need that money for?

"Well, money is freedom," my dad said.

"I'm already free," I shot back.

"It's a different kind of freedom that you'll learn to appreciate later in life."

"Then I'll deal with it then."

That makes it sound like my dad was some Paternal Quote Generator, but in fact he'd recently rebuilt his life after putting his company through bankruptcy—he *knew* the feeling of independence one has when making money, and he *knew,* way too intimately, the loss of control one feels under insurmountable debt—he learned it the hard way. But I ignored that, and wrote off his words as typical Mr. Cleaver Dad stuff. I had no idea how to listen.

I couldn't take it seriously. If I was financially independent, I would never have to take work I didn't want to do. But to become financially independent, I had to take work I didn't want to do. Two years would lead to five years, and then I'd be like one of Don Linn's old friends. Why waste years trying to game the system? Why fabricate excuses for why I should stick at a job that wasn't, ultimately, the real me? There had to be a more straightforward way.

I had found myself writing at night again, and around the same time as I was waffling on their job offer, I took my first night writing class at San Francisco State. It wasn't actually a "class"; this was during the summer session, and I met three times one-on-one with my professor, Michael Rubin. Each session lasted an hour. Professor Rubin sat at his gunmetal gray desk in a small office and patiently dissected my sentences line by line. He was dying of AIDS—we didn't talk about it, but it was obvious. I kept thinking, "This guy's *dying,* and he's choosing to spend three of his last hours on earth with *me,* a total stranger, a clumsy beginning writer." Whether it was his love of writing or his love of teaching that kept him there, I didn't know. But that was humbling, to see a man care so much.

By contrast, at work I was surrounded by men and women who were only trying to score big and cash out. They were a few more years away from never having to worry about money again. I might have stayed if one of them had put his arm around my shoulder and said, "This is my calling. This is my natural environment. Let me tell you how I'm making a life out of it." That didn't happen.

Still, I was leaning toward taking their offer. How could I resist? They insisted that as part of the deal, I would attend night school at Golden Gate University (near the office) and work toward my MBA. It would be purely for show—they liked being able to say that every salesperson in the firm had an MBA. "Go get C's if you want, we don't care," they said. "It'll be a breeze for a guy like you."

Just drop the writing class, enroll in a business class.

Just drop the writing class. . . .

Like Lady J with her precious seven minutes of radio time, only then did I recognize how important my writing was to me.

I enrolled in another writing class for fall, and gave the firm a reluctant good-bye.

Oddly, they are all still in the business thirteen years later, all but two at different firms. Some are rich, some aren't, but none left the life behind. They learned that having been at one of the best firms on Wall Street is a currency, it means something, but it only means something on Wall Street. Take that title off Wall Street, and it gets devalued fast. You can't trade it into a position in other industries and make anywhere near the kind of money. Wall Street teaches that money is the only unbiased and objective measure of a person. Trading out of the business is a stupid trade that few make.

Failure's hard, but success is far more dangerous. If you're successful at the wrong thing, the mix of praise and money and opportunity can lock you in forever. It is so, so much harder to leave a good thing.

21 ||| That Magical Thing

How many times do you really face a choice in life? How many times will you get the benefit of arriving at a crossroads, where you don't have to fight the tug of rolling inertia, and your choice isn't going to hurt someone you love?

Not many.

Make them count. They *will* define you.

When I left First Boston, I joined my girlfriend managing and writing a subscription-only newsletter on San Francisco politics. I was earning about one thousand dollars a month. At night I took my classes at San Francisco State, a lonely commuter school of mostly part-time students. I continued to wedge one class a week into my schedule for the next seven years. You might think that I had an obvious topic to write about, bringing to school my incredible front-row perspective on the unique macho culture of global finance. But I went five years before it even occurred to me I could use that setting in fiction.

That wasn't what *serious* fiction writers wrote about, and I wanted to impress my teachers. The writers and books they held up as role models didn't go near the workplace. Minimalism was in vogue. Nobody wanted to read about the jobs we so wanted to escape from. Writing school was a window to leave that dull numbness behind. We were encouraged to find our material in our childhood, and in our family heritage, and in our travels abroad, and in our rocky love lives. My writing was decent, but it was severely handicapped by lack of material, because I didn't have a rocky love life and I'd never traveled anywhere. I eked out some stories that later made it into anthologies and literary journals, but the going was slow. I didn't know it was slow at the time. I thought that was the deal. Years passed.

I'd reached the upper-level MFA workshops, and I had a story due in two days. I had nothing to turn in. I didn't have anything to write about because I'd spent my entire adult life hauling my ass off to one job after another. With deadline looming, I stubbornly decided I would write about that—about hauling my ass off to work at 4 A.M. Something magical happened. I wrote a story in about twelve hours. I didn't need sleep. And it wasn't a straightforward confessional memoir story; it incorporated for the first time the wilder writing styles I loved—magical realism, absurdism, satire. These were forms that until then I'd never been able to control. But I found my voice in a topic I finally had something to say about. When I submitted it to the workshop, I was dead certain everybody would hate it and find it inappropriate. It was everything serious writing wasn't supposed to be—funny, bloated with overwritten sentences, and set entirely on the bond sales floor. These deficiencies were pointed out to me in class, but in the hallways later, classmates admitted they liked it anyway. It was different in a good way, they said.

The next few months presented me with the biggest crossroads of my writing career. This is the pattern of my life, both professional and personal: every time I am about to follow my heart, I am offered enormous temptation. At this point, I'd been a graduate student for five years and dreamed of nothing but getting a collection of my short stories published. I'd been talking frequently to my friend's agent, and she agreed to represent me when I had enough stories together. I sent her this new story I was so proud of . . . and she never got back to me. No matter, because one of my earlier stories that had been published in a literary journal made it into the hands of an editor at a new imprint, Harper SF. He took me out for lunch at Zuni Café and intimated he wanted to publish my stories as soon as he got his imprint's budget authorized by the parent conglomerate. With great excitement I presented this new story on top of my others . . . and two weeks later he told me he loved them all except this new one. I was confused about how to handle it. Publishers had been rejecting my stories for eight years; finally one was interested, but not in the writing I was most jazzed by.

"I'm still waiting on my budget," he said. "Hang in there. It won't be much money but we'll get it done soon."

"I'd still like to include this story," I said.

"We'll talk about it," he said, meaning *not likely*.

A couple nights later, I ran into that agent at a party. I cornered her and asked what she thought of that new story I sent her.

"I didn't get it," she said.

"You didn't receive it?"

"No, I received it, and I read it, but I didn't *get* it. I didn't understand it. I wasn't engaged."

"Really? I was so excited about it. I was thinking of making it into a novel."

Seeing I was on the verge of making a big mistake, she tried to set me right. "It was one of the least interesting stories you've sent me."

I did want to make it into a novel. I'd scratched the surface with that story and I thought I could do a lot with the premise. My plan was to work on the novel while the short stories were getting published. But nobody else liked that plan. I sent the story to two other notable writers whose advice and encouragement thus far had been invaluable to me. I hung on their every word. They saw merits in the story but didn't think I should go in that direction.

I think back and am so grateful the promised contract for the short stories never arrived. He never resolved his budget fight and a different editor took over the imprint. I'd resisted the temptation of a $300,000 salary, but I don't think I was strong enough to resist having those stories I'd slaved over for five years get published. The minor ensuing praise would have locked me into that track forever. My writing would have gone in a different direction (but a well-traveled one).

Everybody I respected told me to drop the novel, but I couldn't. All I had to go on was my memory of those magical twelve hours in which writing was no longer so painful, no longer so exhausting, no longer insubstantial. Would it happen again the next time I sat down to write? There was only one way to find out.

So I found a new agent, and with his encouragement I set to work on the novel. I anticipated the writing would take a couple years.

I was done in four months.

That magical thing kept happening.

My agent sent the novel to the one editor he believed would like it. He read it that night and bought it the next day. Then the Brits bought it, and the Germans, and the Japanese, and the Koreans, the Russians, the Italians, the Greeks, the Danes, Dutch, Spaniards, Portuguese, and Chinese.

The success I've enjoyed since then has never resolved this underlying shame I carry that I've been writing books about topics that serious writers don't touch. I have never quite gotten over that stigma. Most of my fan mail begins, "Dear Po, I never thought I'd want to read a book set in the business world, but I was at the bookstore and read a few pages and the next thing you know, I'm writing you."

But that's the material life dealt me, and I was never going to be successful until I accepted it and worked with it.

Let me bring this full circle. I've found that a lot of people have the same stigma about the "What should I do with my life?" question as I had writing a novel about bond salesmen. They fear it's not a *serious* question, because it's mostly about the job, not the heart, not character, not love, not issues that matter.

But it is about those things. That's what I hope these stories reveal. "What should I do with my life?" is the modern, secular version of the great timeless questions about our identity, such as "Who am I?" and "Where do I belong?" We ask it in this new way simply because constant disruption in our society *forces* us to—every time we graduate, or get downsized, or move to a new city, we're confronted with *this version* of the question. It's a little more pragmatic than its philosophical and religious antecedents, reflecting the bottom-line reality that we can search for our identity only so long without making ends meet. Asking the question aspires to end the conflict between who you are and what you do. Answering the question is the way to protect yourself from being lathed into someone you're not.

22 ⦀ The Lockbox Fantasy

Couldn't I have published those short stories, and *then* published the novel? Couldn't I have spent two more years at First Boston, then gone to writing school?

Why not get rich, then do your dream?

When I started this book, I assumed I'd find numerous examples of that path. Surely, among all the young millionaires who left Wall Street or Silicon Valley, I'd find some who used their money to bankroll a successful run at the dream they always harbored.

But I didn't find any.

I found tons of rich guys who were now giving a lot away to charity, or who were traveling the world on a big yacht. I found plenty who only discovered their purpose *after* they made some money. Plenty who always wanted to own an island, and now they do, or who always wanted to own a plane, and now they do. But that's not what I'm talking about.

I'm talking about the garden-variety fantasy—put your dream in a lockbox, go out and make Fuck You money, then come back to the lockbox and pick up where you left off.

I met plenty who tried, but none who succeeded.

I found Wall Streeters who went off to the finest art schools, but never made a splash.

I found dot-commers who went down to Hollywood to write movies, but never met with success.

I'm sure they're out there, but compared with how prevalent the fantasy is, examples of the strategy succeeding should be easier to find. Shouldn't they? Particularly for someone like me, since I know thousands of people who got rich in those industries.

What about Mark Cuban, who made $3 billion in the Internet, then bought the Dallas Mavericks? Well, he doesn't count. He didn't put his dream in a lockbox. He loved sports, so he built a sports radio site to listen to his beloved Chicago Cubs games, and the next thing he knew he had $3 billion. He followed his passion, he didn't lock it away.

I've seen lots of people get rich. It takes twice as long as anyone plans for. It's more work than anyone expects. It requires more sacrifices, more changes—you don't come away from that the same person who went in. And you end up so emotionally invested in that world—and psychologically adapted to that world—that you don't *really* want to ditch it, take the money and run. In the battle to succeed, you develop a respect for its difficulty. You adopt values. And even though you might have plenty of money to pump into, say, a nightclub, you can't get pride out of owning a money-loser.

I met some rich guys who bought nightclubs. But they sold them. I know lots more guys who *invested* in nightclubs. It's just a cool thing in their portfolio.

Let me describe the kind of person I was much more likely to meet. I met people like this in droves. I didn't go looking for them—they came to me. They were twenty-eight, or thirty-five, or forty-six, or fifty-two, and they'd gotten accustomed to making "very good" bank. Filthy rich? No. But did they have enough to quit and change their life? Sure. They wanted to. Ten times a day they'd fantasize about doing it. But they couldn't. Couldn't seem to cut off that pipeline of cash. They'd come to me because they'd heard I walked away from money. They want to know how I did that. They want the golden key to unlock their golden handcuffs. No matter how much they earned, it was never quite enough to free them. Similar to the way ethical objections rarely triggered a change by themselves, having enough money to change rarely triggered the change by itself. It had to get personal. Something else had to pull the trigger.

Going in, everyone thinks they'll be strong enough to resist the golden handcuffs and the glowing praise.

I'll do this for a few years. . . .

Wait! Wait! What about those Microsoft millionaires?

Again, I found plenty who found something worthwhile to do *after* they made their money. But when they were twenty-four, and starting at Microsoft, they didn't say to themselves, "I really want to own a stonemason company and build marquee fireplaces with rare Italian rock. But that's going to cost a lot of money, so I'd better work here for ten years." I met another who always wanted to import exotic fabrics from southern India; she put some money into that dream, and probably could have afforded to lose money on it for years, but she didn't respect it unless it existed on its own merits. She didn't want a hobby.

Toy stores, organic farms, same thing.

Okay, it happens. I know it does.

Dream. Lockbox. Fuck You money. Lockbox. Dream.

That cold, calculated formula.

Rarer than I ever imagined.

I'm not advocating giving up your day jobs to chase pipe dreams. But don't put your dreams in lockboxes, and don't invest years of your life in a day job for the wad you expect to have at the end. Believe in that myth at your own peril.

So if those formulaic stories don't exist, let's look at those that do. The stories in this section portray people overcoming temptation and reawakening to their aspirations. Temptation takes many forms. The temptation of money is prominent here, sure, but so is the appeal of being well respected, the ache to be loved, and the desire to fulfill other people's ideals. All can manifest themselves outwardly as "ambition." Then there's the temptations that sap our strength: the seduction of convenience, and the sedative of tranquillity. You'll see there's no formula; you'll see they're not always successful; you'll see that having money might make it possible, but doesn't make it easy.

23 ||| A Tour of the Country

When he was twenty-two and graduating from Trinity College, Cambridge, Anthony Wilson faced a choice. His first instinct was to become a schoolteacher, which he'd worked as one summer in a Palestinian community in Israel. So he applied to teach in the public school system. But Anthony also had an "in" with the British Foreign Office. One of his college friends' fathers was a diplomat. There is nothing more prestigious than the Foreign Office, and its gravitational pull is hard to resist unless you have a clear idea of your alternative. So Anthony joined the Foreign Office, mostly just to keep his family off his back, reasoning that he could always return to teaching—"I'll do this, *then* that."

For the next eight years, he felt like he'd made a profitable choice. Only thirty years old, he was on the fast track to becoming an ambassador. What was not to like? He traveled, met with local politicians, and wrote reports about the ever evolving, often delicate situation abroad. He'd been stationed in Cyprus and with the U.K. delegation to the United Nations in New York. He was now in his fourth year in Bangkok, Thailand. He found it very stimulating. But turning thirty made him ask, "Do I want to be doing this at sixty?" Every additional year in the Foreign Office made it that more difficult to eventually extricate himself.

Then he developed a series of strange infections. He felt a pain under his ribs and found it hard to breathe walking up a flight of stairs. Malaise set in. His lethargy was made worse by insomnia. His doctor diagnosed him with the Epstein-Barr virus, more commonly called infectious mononucleosis, which is more serious in adults than in children, but it's not a virus that wins the patient much sympathy. It stays dormant in the blood forever, occasionally reactivating in times of stress. Anthony was ordered to rest or risk rupturing his spleen. He felt almost well enough to

carry on, but resting didn't seem to make it better. He lay flat on his back in bed, submitting to periodic blood draws, suffering the hot and muggy climate, waiting for the doctor to pronounce him well.

Being ill made Anthony not take his life for granted. He'd always had a sense that life was vulnerable, a precious opportunity not to be misspent. He'd lost his father in a shooting accident at fifteen; his father liked to hunt their land, and one day tripped while crossing a field. He'd also lost his best college friend; at eighteen, an accident had left him a quadriplegic, and at twenty-two he died of a resulting complication, a chest infection.

The memory of these misfortunes pushed Anthony to ask himself a simple question: "If I were to make an early exit from this world, what will I feel worst about *not* getting done?" That phrase, expressed just so, rang with poignancy and cut through his layers of confusion. Not "What will I be most proud of?" nor "What will be my legacy?" but "*What will I feel worst about* not *getting done?*" It questioned the logic of his plan "do this, then that." Time might be too short for *that.*

He started thinking again about the public school system back home. He'd heard they were so desperate for teachers that they were importing them from Australia, New Zealand, and Canada. That seemed a tragedy. Anthony had befriended many diplomats from the Canadian Foreign Office. He always admired one part of their training: before going abroad to represent their country, they spent months touring their own country. For how could they speak for Canada if they hadn't experienced Canada firsthand?

Anthony didn't feel right representing Britain abroad. In college, he'd spent one summer volunteering in Nicaragua. Had he ever considered helping out back home? What did he know about his country? He'd only known the most exclusive echelon of society. His father had been an old-fashioned, tweed-wearing English gentleman landowner who liked to hunt and fish his five hundred acres in Worcestershire. When Anthony was born, his father was already fifty and his mother forty-eight. At an early age Anthony had been sent to his father's boarding school, then continued in his legacy to Eton and Cambridge.

After six months in bed, Anthony was finally pronounced well enough to resume his life. He took a flight home—the end of this, the beginning of that.

Five years later, I came to London to see Anthony. He was teaching at a public secondary school in Walthamstow, a district at the end of the Victoria line infamous for its dog-racing track and street crime. It's fair to say that the school where Anthony taught is not a school where parents want their children. It ranks in the bottom 1 or 2 percent nationally. These kids are so hard on teachers that the prior year, one-third of the teachers didn't come back. Despite the difficult circumstances, Anthony enjoyed working with the children and was proud of every one of their accomplishments. He was teaching drama and English; he'd found that drama was a passable outlet for students' boisterous energy, and a good way to get them interested in literature.

I arrived at a climactic point. He'd been teaching many of these sixteen-year-olds since they were eleven. Tomorrow, Anthony's students would go before the national examiners and be judged. Today, they were conducting their final rehearsals. Anthony had worked eighty hours the last two weeks, causing him so much stress that he was suffering flashbacks of his mononucleosis—a funny rash was reappearing on his throat, and that mysterious pressure under his rib cage had returned.

I watched their rehearsal. Several of the students had clearly responded well to Anthony's five years of coaching, while others clearly had not, and the sad, frustrating thing was that both types were onstage at the same time. Anthony barked out, "Focus!" to the actors and "Silence!" to the spectators. His voice was deep and commanding; he'd undoubtedly spent many years onstage during his own schooling.

Afterward, he critiqued their spotty effort. "You have a *great* deal of work remaining to be put in, and only one day in which to do so."

Was there any way this train wouldn't derail?

Was there any way that his best students of five years wouldn't be dragged back into the gutter by their classmates?

I thought of how my cabbie had described Walthamstow—"Those who grow up here never leave."

Anthony and I retreated to a local pub. He was overdue for a pint and an hour of repose.

He agreed to be profiled and talked openly, but he was concerned that he not be portrayed as a role model.

"My experience is simply not applicable to others," he said. "I would never expect others to make the same choice I did. What I'm doing is not *that* 'noble.' I work among these people, but at night I retreat to the leisure of my house and girlfriend. I've kept my old friends, I go with them to trendy restaurants and on weekend jaunts. You must understand—I have other *means*. I own four apartments, of which I rent three for income." He felt that this disqualified him from being an example for his generation.

I insisted that his choice was admirable, hero or not. He insisted that free will—choosing your path—was an incredible luxury. I didn't know if this observation stemmed from his wealthy upbringing, or from his five years of witnessing students rarely rise above their Walthamstow surroundings. Anthony said he was always primed to question life, because the world of his father was disappearing anyway. Anthony could follow his father to Eton and Cambridge, but he could never become a gentleman farmer. That lifestyle had died with his father. Anthony always knew he'd need to find a new life.

Again I disagreed. "You don't think most kids today don't feel the same way—that the life their parents lead isn't an option anymore? The social contract that bound husband to wife and worker to employer is long gone." Besides, I told him most readers would be relieved to know that he had hung on to his friends and enjoyed a regular social life after hours, that being a schoolteacher hadn't swallowed his entire life.

I asked what his mother thought of him becoming a schoolteacher at one of the poorest-performing schools in the country.

"Mom is disgraced." He laughed.

When he had first started teaching, he didn't have a strong conviction. He'd told himself he was just looking, and he could go back to the Foreign Office. "I was in an anonymous state for some time," he said.

So would he keep doing it?

He would. Next year he would pursue a master's in education. After final exams, he intended to take six months off, making his way from Seattle down the west coast of the Americas, eventually ending up in Santiago, Chile. Along the way, he hoped to decide between educational psychology and educational policy—the former a path back into the schools, working directly with students, the latter a path into administration, contributing to reforming the school system.

His students ended up doing fine in their final exams. They focused their effort, and the examiners said some very nice things. Half the group obtained A grades. About ten of his forty-five students would go on to take a performing arts course, and the others would continue their studies in some fashion. They might leave Walthamstow after all.

A few months later, Anthony and I were able to spend a couple days together in San Francisco as he traveled south. His hair cropped and his feet sandaled, Anthony was the embodiment of relaxed traveler. He wrote again soon from San Cristóbal de Las Casas, Mexico.

He wouldn't like me to extract wisdom from his story, but I have the benefit of hearing many stories like his. What distinguishes people like Anthony is that their motivation comes from the heart, rather than the head. Life is not a dress rehearsal, it's the real thing. It's that one chance in front of the examiners. It's precious and vulnerable. And those who feel this are willing to make hard choices.

The intellectually motivated person might read Anthony's story while thinking, That would be a good thing to do, but imagine all the bureaucratic crap he has to put up with! I considered writing about the bureaucrap he has to fight—curriculum auditors had turned the school upside down the week prior to my visit—but why indulge that conversation? The right question is not "What's the Crap Factor?" The right question is "How can I find something that moves my heart, so that the inevitable crap storm is bearable?"

Lately, I've found myself talking about what I call the Brilliant Masses. The Brilliant Masses are composed of nothing less than the many great people of our generation, the bright, the talented, the intelligent, the resourceful, and the creative—far too many of whom are operating at quarter speed, unsure of their place in the world, contributing far too little to the productive engine of modern civilization, still feeling like observers, all feeling like they haven't come close to living up to their potential. The Brilliant Masses are mostly intellectually motivated, so if they cross over and get involved, their commitment is conditioned on being respected, and on a minimum of unnecessary idiocy, and on winning/succeeding. They like being cerebral. In their tribes, it's cool.

Being guided by the heart is almost never something an intellectually motivated person *chooses* to do. It's something that happens to him—usually something painful. Anthony chose to tour his own country and devote himself to its improvement after he spent six months flat on his back.

So where is his generation?

Waiting to learn it has only one life to give.

24 ⫴ After a Brief Period of Experimentation

FEAR OF SAYING NO

I start a lot of books but don't finish them, and I don't watch a ton of movies, because I don't want to water down or drown out the few that really mean a lot to me.

One of those few was a movie that came out in 1985, the year before I graduated from college—*St. Elmo's Fire.* It was an ensemble piece about seven friends and the unexpected turns their lives took in the first year after they graduated from Georgetown. Watching it, I thought, Hey, that's me up there. Along with *The Breakfast Club,* which showcased many of the same actors, it launched the Brat Pack—they were going to be *my generation's* actors. Rob Lowe played a drunk who tries and fails at about a half dozen jobs before finally going off to New York to chase his dream, playing the saxophone. Andrew McCarthy played a frustrated hack reporter who wanted to write about the meaning of life for a change—something deep. Something real.

The screenplay had been penned by Carl Kurlander, with lots of help from the director, Joel Schumacher. Carl was twenty-four at the time, and the movie was based on a short story he had written during his senior year at Duke. Carl wasn't enrolled in creative writing classes when he wrote the story—he'd been taking premed classes because all of his mom's husbands had been gastroenterologists, and he was probably looking for her approval. He was rescued from that fate when his short story fell into the hands of an English professor, and the next thing Carl knew, he had won an internship to come out to Hollywood for a year. During the filming of the movie, he went out for sushi with Andie MacDowell, and then drove her up to Mulholland Drive in his Volkswagen Rabbit, where he parked in the dirt and showed her the view of Los Angeles at night. Carl was already sensing that Hollywood was going to betray his artistic integrity. Drunk

on sake, he promised Andie that when the shooting wrapped he was moving home to Pittsburgh, where he had grown up, to write short stories
about their generation, stories from the heart, something deep, something
real.

Carl didn't live up to his promise.

I know this not because I am a student of the movie, but because Carl
Kurlander was one of the first people who contacted me out of the blue
when I spread the word I was writing this book. I didn't recognize his
name and had never heard of him, but he was happy to explain it because
my topic fascinated him. It had been seventeen years since he'd made that
promise to Andie. Partly he was writing me out of concern that Hollywood would do to me what it did to him. He was living above Sunset
Plaza in a house designed by the architect Robert Byrd, with David
Schwimmer as one neighbor and Richard Simmons as the other. He
drove a Land Rover with the vanity plate CK LANDER. C. K. Lander was the
pen name he used for that first short story—he had created it to protect his
identity and integrity. The pen name was to be a kind of temple, used only
for *real* writing. What was once a temple had become a vanity plate!—what
had he done? "I'd become an unlikeable narrator in my own story," he told
me with self-disgust. "I've become Holden Caulfield's older brother, the
phony, who wrote one good short story and went to Hollywood and never
wrote anything else worth a damn." Carl had written a lucrative sitcom for
teens, *Saved by the Bell.* He sometimes wasn't proud of this. By most people's measure, he was a success—he was well off, and he was well known
in his industry. But by his own measure, Carl had turned his back on his
purpose in life.

Carl reiterated to me that it was always his fantasy to move back to
Pittsburgh and regain the writing voice he'd lost along the way. I treated
him kindly and promised if he ever did it, I would come see him—but I
sort of blew him off, because I thought, Fat chance. Carl got the hint, and
after a while our correspondence fell off. Seven months later, he copied
me in on a mass e-mailing, giving his new coordinates. The area code and
the address were in Pittsburgh. The guy had finally done it! And I had to
go see him. I waited three months, until some of the novelty had worn off.
I was dying to know what had pushed him to finally take the improbable
leap. I was also wondering if he really needed to be in a different city to
find his voice—why couldn't he write his stories from Beverly Hills?

I should make clear that Carl wouldn't tell his story the way I'm telling
it. He can't seem to keep endless movie references out of his sentences—
as if his own real life is too muddled to make sense of without allusions to

popular culture. ("It's like that scene in ____, or, "It's the same arc that was done in ____.") That's part of the bad habit he needed to shake. He also can't seem to avoid talking about a woman he long ago had an irrational crush on. She's intersected his life a few times since, but in a circumstantial way only, not in a meaningful way, and I'm not going to mention her again. Carl's been married a long time, and he has a two-year-old daughter.

Sometimes I just wanted to hug him and say, *This is* your *story, Carl, not the sequel to some movie, and not some girl's.*

There is a building on the campus of the University of Pittsburgh that is so tall it can be seen from almost anywhere in the city. It is called the Cathedral of Learning, and at 535 feet, it is the second-tallest educational structure in the world. It was built in 1937, contains forty floors of offices and classrooms, and is truly a *cathedral*—the ground-floor chamber vaults up in classic Gothic architecture, with a labyrinth of chapels and belfries separated by equilateral arches. If you grow up in Pittsburgh, this building becomes an indelible symbol of all things academic and pure.

Carl had come here to teach for the year. His office and his classes were in this building, and he rarely left it during the day. "To me, this building is as glamorous as a studio lot," he said. "I wanted to bathe in something altruistic and clean, and I think it's having the desired effect. For years I told people in Hollywood I wanted to come back here, and they always said, 'Being in a different place isn't going to make you any happier.' But it *has*. I'm happy. I like the feel of the city. When it rains here, I'm even happier. Maybe it'll wear off, but I'm reveling in the genuineness of what I feel here, and the power of my memories."

He was realizing his real journey had just started. Would he really be able to regain his voice? What would he do when the year was out? If he moved back to Hollywood, would he ever write movies about the meaning of life? Carl was panicked and obsessed with these concerns. He looks like a blond, curly-haired version of *Seinfeld*'s George Costanza, and he talks like Woody Allen, rambling, repeating himself, zigzagging with his doubts. That's his natural vocal style, and he wants to see himself writing in that voice again. Movies don't get to ramble anymore. But his students love his digressions, and every hour he spends on his feet in front of his class is like an hour of voice workshop, *this is your voice.* . . . He loves his creative writing class in particular, and like so many rookie teachers who aren't yet burned out, he has an incredible gift of raw energy for the students. He's fresh meat. They call him by his first name, and they all laugh at his jokes, and when he asked what they did over the Thanksgiving weekend, they let out with some incredibly honest and idiosyncratic stories. Real life! Carl's loving it. Pitt is no Harvard; many of his students are the first generation in their family to go to college, which means Carl feels needed—these are students for whom he can make a difference.

That's the bright side. Undergrads. But the Cathedral of Learning has twenty floors of graduate students and professors who belong to the canon of Academia, one of the only cultures with a higher bullshit quotient than Hollywood. It turns out that since Carl went to college, academia has come up with something called the Freytag Triangle, by which all short fiction can be diagrammed and piece by piece leached of all mystery. It's very important that the Freytag Triangle be drawn on the chalkboard a few times during every class. It resembles a regular old three-sided triangle in many ways, but apparently it requires a PhD to tell the difference.

One night Carl had to deliver a colloquium for the graduate students in the film studies program. On the way over, he kept wondering aloud, "What's a colloquium? How does it differ from a lecture?" To make fun of academicians' manner of over-titling, he'd billed his speech as "An Anecdotal Analysis Inside a Post-Classical, Increasingly Globalized Hollywood, 1982–2001." Nobody got the joke. He tried to conform to their conventions, following an outline and draining his analysis of any personal stories, but eventually he couldn't help it and busted out the old scrapbook for some show 'n' tell. Carl would tell a funny story, and the graduate students would nod knowingly with recognition that Carl had clearly never been to graduate school.

His speech was interesting, though. Carl's thesis was that he was able to make *St. Elmo's Fire* because he arrived in Hollywood during a brief period of experimentation. Studio executives had put out some expensive bombs, and it would be two years before the studios would figure out how to quadruple their revenue by exploiting soundtracks, video, foreign markets, and product tie-ins. Hollywood's studio system today is not broken; it books more revenue than ever, and that's the standard it measures everything by. Box office. It doesn't need writers to experiment.

"How'd I do?" Carl asked, as we were walking out. It was a load off his shoulders to have it done. Somewhere during the hour, he and I both figured out that the difference between a colloquium and a lecture is that you deliver a lecture to just students, but in a colloquium other professors show up and sit in judgment.

When we reached the car, I asked, "Aren't you afraid you're going to swap Hollywood's voice for Academia's voice? The Three-Act Structure replaced by the Freytag Triangle? Trying to impress lesbian erotic poets rather than studio executives?"

He paused, and took his response in a different direction. "See, how can you do that? Somehow you cannot idolize a place like this. How come I can't? You've been here one day, and you can see into the shadows better than I do after three months."

"I just don't want you to lose track of why you came here."

"God, I wish I had your sincerity. Really. You're like Gary Cooper."

"Don't idolize *me* now."

Another pause. "How do I do it?" he asked.

"Not lose track?"

"Yes."

"Don't live for their approval. Don't live for anyone's approval."

"Everyone wants approval."

"That's just argumentative."

"They do!"

"Sure they do. But you can take a break from it. Not forever, but a while."

I told him about a recent year, in which I was trying to heal after my divorce. Remorse and guilt had nearly paralyzed me. I realized one of my problems was my parents were viewing my divorce through the lens of their own. Both thought I should handle mine the way they had handled theirs. So for a year, I insisted my parents not express any judgment—approval or disapproval. About *anything*. I wanted them to know me, not to fix me. It was exceedingly difficult to get the habit of, but I found I wanted to share with them a lot more. I shared out of desire, not responsibility. Because one of my books came out during this same year, I didn't read any of its reviews. This had nothing to do with hostility toward reviewers, and nothing to do with that book. I needed a year where I could listen to my own inner voices and rediscover who I was.

Carl found this experiment inconceivable. But he understood the concept. He said back in Hollywood he would sit by the phone, waiting for it to ring with business. If it rang a lot, it meant he was wanted and needed. If it didn't ring, he would start to feel like nobody loved him anymore.

Carl said, "The phone doesn't ring much here. But that doesn't scare me anymore."

Carl and I were uniquely uncensored with each other. His story didn't reveal itself to me like a mystery, one clue at a time. Because of his rambling style, the whole story jumped out from our first minutes together. Time was flattened; events that occurred twenty-one years ago were as immediate as his hunger for lunch today. Long sentences would connect his parent-child relationship with director Joel Schumacher to his mother's multiple absent husbands to the rarity of long-lasting marriages in Hollywood to the way he's raising his daughter today. Since I'd had a bit of a broken childhood too, he viewed me as his alter ego, and said so often. He was eager to read the stories I'd written of my childhood. "Where are the novels in which carpools appear?" he lamented. "Why is nobody writing about this stuff?" (Of course, plenty of writers *are* writing about that stuff, and so his rant feels like a call to himself—*Why have I not been writing about that stuff?*)

We went out for some Chinese cuisine with his daughter and his wife, Natalie, who had indulged Carl's need to return to Pittsburgh with grace, but she let it be known that one year here was more than enough for her.

"Somehow, forty thousand dollars in Pittsburgh feels like four hundred thousand dollars does in Beverly Hills," Carl said, after he paid for our dinner with a twenty-dollar bill.

"Not to me it doesn't," Natalie offered. "I miss cable."

"We just have to adjust our expectations," Carl suggested.

"I know. It's good for us."

It was like he'd dragged his family camping.

Later, Carl and I went out into the neighborhood. It was quiet and dark and peaceful. The rain had stopped. A few houses had already strung Christmas lights along their windows. The feeling was timeless. It could have been any November night in the last thirty years. We were high schoolers out looking to score beer. We were grade schoolers out past our bedtime. We were parents looking for our kids. His rental house overlooked the elementary school playground where he used to get beat up by schoolyard bullies. Not far away was the apartment over a garage that he moved into with his mom and little brother after she got divorced (the first time).

"She would send me out to the bar around the corner at night to buy her a pack of smokes," he said.

We went around the corner, and there was the bar, now a storefront.

"You were?"

"Twelve. . . . You?"

"Twelve."

"See! You understand."

"Tell me anyway."

"It was another time of experimentation. The institution of the nuclear family was breaking down just as the working-class economy in Pittsburgh was breaking down. People thought, 'Hey, let's get divorced.' They had no idea about the consequences, they were just trying something different. In Pittsburgh, we were like the *first*. It was scandalous, for a prominent doctor to get divorced. *Nobody* lived in an apartment."

And a few blocks later stood the house where they moved a couple years later.

"When I was fifteen, I walked home from school one day and there was a moving van in the driveway."

"You were moving again?"

"No. My *mom* told us she was running away to New York to be an actress."

"Out of the blue?"

"Yes."

"Without you?"

"She enrolled my little brother and me in Shady Side Academy, a prestigious boarding school outside of town, real old-world conservative, the place where the Heinzes and the Carnegies all sent their kids." He got distracted for a moment talking about the school. They have a three-million-dollar ice hockey rink, but no stage theater, which tells you where their priorities were.

I'd heard about Shady Side Academy on my way in from the airport, and learned it didn't board on weekends. I asked Carl where they went on Fridays through Mondays.

"Mom had signed me up to be the baby-sitter for the kids of a wealthy Arab man in town. He looked out for us. And in the summers, he took us to Chautauqua, a couple hours away, where he owned the St. Elmo's Hotel. I worked as a bellhop. I developed the most abnormal-sized crush on a waitress. That was the basis for the short story I wrote at Duke that won me the internship in Hollywood." Again he started to ramble about his years at Duke, his Marxist phase, going to Washington to protest . . . but I kept cutting him off, because I thought this stuff about his mother running away was too important, and it explained a lot of why he could never leave Hollywood, which placated him with its artificial affection. So we went back to his office over his garage, and he dug out his boxes of photos and mementos from his years in Hollywood. Carl had spent years of his life idolizing that waitress, and it was obvious to me that this self-generated illusion came from a deep longing created by the absence of his mother.

In Hollywood, that void was filled by Joel Schumacher, who became both the mother-figure and father-figure Carl needed. "We can't be a minute late!" Joel would order him, hustling him out the door. Then in the car, Joel would offer inspiration: "Nobody writes as good as you, Carl." While writing *St. Elmo's Fire,* Carl was living in the laundry room of the Anarchists' Collective. The pledge he made to Andie MacDowell was not the only one of its kind—many times he told Joel that as soon as he'd made $50,000, he was moving back to Pittsburgh. He told everyone who asked, and many who didn't, that he wasn't going to stay in Hollywood. When the filming of *St. Elmo's Fire* wrapped, Carl's agent brought him a project that some studio wanted him to write. It was about a man who thinks he knows what babies are thinking. Carl had no interest. He was going to write the stories of his generation!

"Tell them I'm going back to Pittsburgh," he instructed his agent.

"Well, this is how we say *no* in Hollywood," the agent explained. "We ask for *too much money.* You get the same result, but you don't insult anyone about the integrity of their project." Hollywood has developed elaborate customs by which nobody ever quite has to say *no* or *yes.* Nobody wants to offend someone who might end up winning an Oscar or running a studio. The unfortunate result is people have a terrible time being direct. When new writers arrive in Hollywood, they get the impression their career is about to really take off, because it seems that *everyone loves me!* This partly explains why box office results have become the measure of success—all other forms of praise have lost their currency. Praise is cheap and plentiful.

So Carl's agent asked for too much money, and the studio said okay, and paid him. Carl was on the hook for writing a movie about a man who could read babies' minds.

"How much was too much money?" I asked.

"A hundred thousand. That *was* a lot of money back then."

"Don't be so hard on yourself, Carl. No young writer could say no to that."

"You could."

"No way! Are you kidding? At twenty-four?"

"But you turned down a *lot* more than that."

"To be a salesman! Not to *write!*"

Hearing this from me seemed to alleviate some of his guilt.

Carl began writing the talking baby movie. He soon learned that getting hired to write a movie is still a huge leap away from that movie getting made. It was suggested that he might improve his movie's chances if he did his "research" by hanging out with the babies of important studio executives. So C. K. Lander, great writer of his generation, became a babysitter again, schmoozing eight-month-olds and newborns, hoping they might put in a good word with Daddy or Mommy. All this did was humiliate Carl and destroy his self-respect; the project was shelved.

But there were other producers who wanted to hire Carl, other people eager to tell him how much they loved his work. Pittsburgh wasn't going anywhere. Hollywood creates insecurity at a slightly higher rate than it fills the void with money and love. For every movie shot, there are fifty in development that don't get made, and for every two new television shows there are seventy writer-teams getting paid to write pilots that will never make it. It's not just *possible* to make a decent living in Hollywood without ever having a movie in a theater or a TV show on the air—it's commonplace. Writers are cut off from the feedback of the audience; they rarely get exposed to what real people think of their work. Well-paid writers like Carl end up starving for recognition and have to live off the crumbs of flattery from executives, who tell them repeatedly that what gets their movie made is having stars attached to the project. So the writers are asked to rewrite their scripts with a certain famous actor in mind.

"I got really good at imitating the voices of the stars," Carl explained. "We chase success. We write in the style of last year's Oscar winner. I could write in everybody's voice but my own."

As Carl described all this, I started to understand why he had to move away from Hollywood to regain his voice. My curiosity swung to wondering how he'd ever managed to leave.

"How'd you do it, Carl?"

"I'm not sure," he said. "It still amazes me."

"What do you think was the first trigger?"

"Yahoo!"

"Yahoo!?"

"I was writing a script about Silicon Valley, *The Great Gatsby* reset in Sunnyvale, and I was allowed into Yahoo! for a couple days to research the project."

He arrived expecting to see an incredible ostentatious display of wealth. At the time, a full three-quarters of the employees were millionaires. "But they were still working in cubicles. Even the founders! And they were so nice!" One moment that stood out: an assistant had to get lunch for David Filo and Jerry Yang. She grabbed two premade turkey sandwiches from the cafeteria and threw them on the table in the conference room. Carl couldn't believe she hadn't asked them what they wanted, or let them customize their orders. When Carl was her age, he had to get lunch one day for Joel Schumacher and another executive. Joel ordered gazpacho with no croutons, no sour cream, and chopped egg on the side. The other executive ordered a hamburger with grilled onions on the side. But the burger came by accident with the onions *on* the burger. The executive refused to eat it, and chewed Carl out for not checking the order to make sure it was accurate before presenting it.

"My few days at Yahoo! really put Hollywood's absurd values in perspective," Carl said. "I'd assumed wealth ruined *everybody,* but it wasn't everybody. They were all millionaires, and still had their values."

That script died a slow death like all his others, but he became hypersensitive to his life in Beverly Hills. "That's when I realized what I'd become. Like the vanity license plate—I suddenly wanted it off my car."

He reached into a file drawer and pulled out the culprit, CK LANDER. He said, "I used to think this was so cool. Now it embarrasses me."

Around the time Carl first contacted me, the Writer's Guild appeared determined to strike. It was narrowly avoided, but in the approaching months, every writer in Hollywood was facing the possibility of not working for a while. Carl pined for Pittsburgh. As he does every year, Carl filled out the card from his old high school that requested donations. He put down his credit card number beside a donation amount and mailed it off. Right after that, he lost his credit card. So he e-mailed Shady Side to provide his new credit card number, and after a woman there dug out his card and learned he worked in Hollywood, he wrote that he always had this fantasy he would come back there and teach. She e-mailed back that one of their English teachers was going on sabbatical—they needed a teacher for the year. She also knew the head of the department at Pitt, who invited Carl to visit and meet with some of the faculty.

"When we sold the house and moved here, I thought that was it, fade out, end of story. Man overcomes temptation, moves home, roll credits. I thought we would get here, and it would all click, and the rest would be easy. I never thought through what I'd do once I finally got here. But now I'm really aware that moving was only the first step. I'm kind of embarrassed. It took me seventeen years to take the *first step*."

"Are you going to stay?"

"I have no idea. What do you think?"

"About what?"

"About what's going to happen to me."

"Have you been writing?"

"I just started something."

"A story or a script?"

"Uh, it's a memoir."

"Great! Good for you."

"But it's not *my* memoir."

"What do you mean?"

"Do you know Louie Anderson?"

"The comedian? The host of *Family Feud?*"

"Yeah, but he also wrote that book, *Dear Dad*. The publisher wants the prequel, all the rich stuff about his childhood. A lot of amazing stuff happened to him."

"So what the hell does this have to do with you?"

"He's a close friend, and he asked me to write the book for him."

I suddenly understood, and I was simultaneously deeply disappointed and frustrated and sorry for Carl. "You're writing Louie Anderson's memoirs," I repeated in a hushed, astonished tone.

"It won't take me more than a few months," he said. "Right?"

"That's pretty optimistic. Usually you get sucked into the editing cycle and it consumes twice the time you anticipated."

"I was afraid of that."

"Carl, why do it at all? Why give even three months to someone else's story when you sold your house and moved across the country to write your own story? Any other writer, I'd say sure, take the work, it's a paycheck. But you don't need the money. You only have a year here. It's not why you came."

His wife had joined us, and I got the feeling she had made the same obvious point several times.

"I couldn't turn him down," Carl said. "He needed me."

"Tell him you can't do it," I insisted. "What kind of friend asks you to write *his* book when everyone knows you need to write *your* book? If you were an alcoholic, I'd call him an enabler."

Carl admitted he'd grown scared about whether he could really write his own story, and he thought this might be a good bridge—it would be a book, not another script, and it would be about early family material, which Carl also wanted to mine in his own story. Carl kept insisting he could write the book quickly.

I said, "I don't know what to tell you, Carl. Since I write books, I find it kind of insulting that you believe you can just dash one off for a friend, not recognizing the amount of work that will be involved."

This was a hard moment, because until that time, I was implicitly giving Carl my approval. I'd flown across the country, and we were fast becoming friends, and I could see this meant a *lot* to him. None of his friends in Hollywood had come to see him, and few probably would. Suddenly I was the Voice of Disapproval. In the moment, I just wanted to brush it away and be friends again, but in the back of my mind I was trying to remember, "This is the guy who wrote *St. Elmo's Fire!* This is the guy who inspired me! Look out for him! Help him regain his courage!"

But how? I didn't want to insult him. I told him the stories of others who had put their nose right up to their destiny, only to get sidetracked by last-minute temptation, or in Carl's lexicon, the Third Act Complication. We are our own worst enemies. I grew weary quickly, and I had to call it a night. I could have taken his extra bedroom, but I went to a hotel, where I proceeded to stare at the ceiling for about three hours. Why was I so worked up about this? Why did it matter? I don't know. The stories of others had been brainwashing me, surely. I had been surrounding myself with acts of courage. Was I pushing Carl when really I needed to do something for myself? Had I betrayed my own artistic integrity? I lay there, working through the choices I'd made the last nine years. I'd resisted a lot of offers, but not always. I still had a long way to go. I woke up in my clothes late the next morning, wondering whether I should walk over to the Cathedral of Learning for another day. My sadness was gone. Carl had mentioned several times he would have lots of time for me today, because his students would be filling out teacher evaluations and grading him. I suddenly thought, it's his Day of Judgment! And I knew what his students thought of him would matter a little too much to Carl. I called him at home, let it ring a few times, and then wavered and hung up.

A moment later my phone rang.

"Hello?"

"Po."

"I just called you."

"I know. I star-sixty-nined you."

"I just wanted to say—" What was I trying to say? "—It means so much to me how you've let me into your life, Carl. Into your classes, into your marriage, into your past, into your house. I wasn't sure if I should even say this, because I don't want you to care what I think. But I think your story will mean something to people. You have a good story. Your story—I think it's important."

"I always thought it was meaningful."

"It is, Carl, whether you write it or I. And . . ."

"And?"

Now I was rambling. "And I want you to know that what those students think of you doesn't matter, Carl. You're a good teacher, I've seen it. You keep doing what you're doing, it'll be all right."

"Oh, I don't care what those kids think."

"You don't?"

"Naw."

"Oh. Well, good."

I promised to come back to Pittsburgh with my wife and son that summer. Carl promised not to spend much time on Louie Anderson's book. And in this way, our future was again bound tight in our hopes for it. It wasn't wise to make these promises—they would be hard to live up to—but we seemed unable not to swear to them.

25 ||| There's More to Motherhood than Baking Cookies

NEVER GIVE UP

When Mary Ann Clark graduated from college in 1960, she wanted to save the world—from poverty, birth defects, and malnutrition. "But if I had anything to give, I thought I should give it to my children first." Twenty years and four children later, on the verge of starting the career she'd looked forward to for so long, she unexpectedly got pregnant again, and gave birth in her early forties to a fifth child. The second phase of her life turned out to be the same as her first. Many moms awe me with their patience, but Mary Ann laps them all. She and I corresponded for several months, and I went to see her the day after her sixty-fifth birthday—an age when many consider retiring, like her husband, Hal, who was making plans. But retirement didn't interest her at all. "I've just started working!" She smiled. "And I'd like to continue!" She is the field interviewer for a large research study of childhood leukemia. She travels all over Northern California. "This is exciting for me! I've got to make a contribution!"

I insert her story here for several reasons:

1. This rolling conversation is badly in need of a mother's story;
2. the last couple stories suggest it's *okay*, it's *normal*, to take many years before pursuing your calling, and Mary Ann's story is here to ring it louder—yes, yes!;
3. you can have more than one purpose in life, and you can do them together or do them sequentially—it doesn't matter, so long as you are pursuing them and not some other, unimportant thing.

"I'm from the 'Because I Said So' generation," she remarked. That's not how she raised her kids—that's how she was raised, in urban Philadelphia. She was one of six children. Her mother gave birth to three before the

war, and to three more after the war. Mary Ann's grandmother had passed away in between, and so her mother had little help in raising the second crop. Mothering was hard enough without a second hand, and young Mary Ann took note of this. She took note of the grudge her mother seemed to bear. She took note of the counterexample—one of her father's sisters. This aunt was unmarried, and an accountant, and traveled frequently, and always had a story to tell. So did her father, who was a biochemist and always interested in diet and nutrition. At the dinner table, he always had something in his day to recount, while her mother didn't. He seemed to have more fun. On Saturdays, when he worked a half day, he would often bring the children to his lab. This made an impression on Mary Ann. She had a brain and wanted to use it. Housework didn't appeal to her. She never *assumed* she would get married. Carrying on in the vein of her father, she studied food and nutrition and minored in science, graduating with a BS in home economics from LaSalle. The summer prior, she had worked as a dietician at Fitzgerald Mercy Hospital. She'd loved it and planned to return. The job was waiting for her.

But Hal wanted to get married. He campaigned hard. Hal had gone to high school with her brothers, while she was at Little Flower. They didn't date then, but "he was the Boy of My Dreams and the dream never died," Mary Ann explained. He came back into her life in college. Mary Ann was torn. "I made the right choice, but for the wrong reasons," she admitted. "I thought I could marry Hal and still do whatever I wanted. I liked the idea of independence." She had little intention of giving it up, but soon discovered the necessary compromises of partnership. Mercy Hospital was on the other side of Philly, an hour-and-a-half bus ride each way. Working there was impractical. Anyway, she got pregnant quickly.

"Back then, that's just the way it was. I was a Catholic schoolgirl of the fifties. My classmates and friends were doing the same. I thought I had so much to offer society. We had a do-gooder attitude. But first, I wanted to give it to my children. Whatever you can give your children—*it's free*. If I didn't give them language, culture, attitudes, they'd have to start from scratch. My first responsibility was to them. In the first ten years, there was never a time that I wasn't either pregnant or nursing a baby. There was plenty of time in the future to have a career. But I didn't at all feel like I had dropped out. I still had that sense of worth—*I'd gone to college!* That was special. We had so much optimism and energy."

Hal was offered a job with IBM, and they soon moved to Hopewell Junction, New York (pop. 4,000). Mary Ann ferried her kids to swim practice and planned Girl Scout meetings and drove the elderly ladies next door to the store. She tended an organic garden and built a solar addition. And still had more energy to give.

"It was around the early seventies that women began the mantra 'There's more to life than baking cookies,' and I couldn't have agreed more."

She played the organ at church and served on the Women in Church Committee for the Archdiocese of New York. She was on the local conservation commission. In the early seventies, she began substitute teaching at the junior high, her youngest girl in tow. Most of her friends were doing the same, working their schedules around their children. By law, Mary Ann was limited to substituting eighty days a year unless she had a teaching credential or master's degree. So when Route 84 opened to Danbury, Mary Ann started taking one class a semester at night at Western Connecticut University. She was patient, so patient. By the time her youngest was in junior high school, most of Mary Ann's friends were well entrenched in the job market as nurses or dieticians or teachers. Money was tight for the Clarks; the padding in their budget went straight to college tuition. They needed a second income. In December of 1979, she completed her course work for her master's degree in general education. Her youngest, Karen, would start high school the next fall. Mary Ann would begin teaching health education full-time.

Finally, the payoff for her patience!

But in February, she discovered she was pregnant. Mimi, their fifth child, was born on Thanksgiving 1980.

"One must deal with the cards they are dealt," Mary Ann insisted. Then, "I can't say it wasn't without a lot of frustration. I'm better with babies than I am with pregnancies. I had my moments." Then, back to her optimism: "Of all the things that could have happened to us, relatively, a baby was easy to deal with. We had friends with cancer and MS and heart disease." Mary Ann described her ambiguity of feeling as a cross between Walter Mitty and Eeyore. "I have spent most of my life planning a vision of what I would do after my family was grown."

I'm not doing this story justice. I think Mary Ann felt the same way when she was telling it to me. I think so many mothers feel that way, period. Mother stories are very hard to tell. There's a tendency—a gravitational pull—to deliver them in the same cadence as we tell career stories. We list projects and achievements that don't have anything to do with nurturing our children. So twenty years of Mary Ann's mothering is described by naming the committees she served on. The truth is, all those side projects were not nearly as much work as the daily attention required in raising four children.

One mother I interviewed was adamant that this book should include not just mothers but stay-at-home moms. I agreed, and asked her to share her story. She then wrote me several thousand words of description, ten pages long, at the end of which she realized, "I've told you every detail about my various projects [among them, getting a local school built], and yet I've told you absolutely nothing about my kids! I haven't even told you their names!" This shocked her. She'd intended to do the opposite, but once she began writing, she succumbed to the usual story conventions, leading with vocational accomplishments.

Why is it so hard to tell a mother's story?

I put this question to many mothers, and a few answers came back again and again: 1) A culture that celebrates careers more than parenting doesn't pick up on the subtlety inherent in a mother's story. The subtle triumphs of a baby finally going to sleep, or a child learning a new letter, get drowned out by the noise of a big career advancement. 2) Mothers' lives are fractured. They don't have one single project that makes for a simple, strong story line. They're involved in their children's lives, in their communities, in their schools, in their extended families. Mary Ann compared it to the painter Georges Seurat's famous pointillist work *A Sunday Afternoon on the Island of La Grande Jatte*. "It's laid down one dot at a time. Rarely does anyone else recognize the meaning of that one dot." In other words, a mother's life makes a great painting, but not a linear story. 3) Parenting is so personal; there's a religious righteousness when parents talk about their philosophies. Talking about them out loud usually offends someone. 4) A good mother doesn't own her accomplishments. Her children do.

And since children can thrive and fail independent of good parenting, it's hard to tease out what a mother's contribution really is. You can't give all the credit to the mom.

It's with this in mind that Mary Ann's story has special merit. That she waited forty-plus years to begin her career is marvelous (nice! terrific!)— but her real purpose, her first purpose, was to help her kids survive and thrive. With her fifth child, that wasn't easy.

In Mary Ann's accounting of her life, in her column of regrets, perhaps at the very top you'd find this inconspicuous entry: being a Thanksgiving baby, her daughter Mimi could enter kindergarten at five or at six—she had the option of waiting a year. And because Mimi weighed a mere thirty-two pounds at the time, Mary Ann held her back, to grow a little. It was a well-meaning decision, but one that's been reconsidered a million times. Eight years later, Mimi was thirteen when Hal was laid off with many other IBM engineers. His friends simply retired, but the Clarks needed tuition for Mimi's schooling. In the middle of the year, Hal was offered a job across the country, in Scotts Valley, near Santa Cruz. Mimi had a year and a half of junior high remaining.

The memory brought pain to Mary Ann's voice. "If I'd enrolled her in kindergarten at five, she would have been fourteen by then. And we just would have let Hal move to California. I would have stayed with Mimi to finish junior high. As it was, we moved her, in the middle of the year, at a precious time in her development."

Mimi had a strong emotional attachment to their home in Hopewell Junction. The friends she'd grown up with were all still there. She wrote a letter to her pastor insisting she wasn't moving.

Mary Ann's tone suggested this story was leading somewhere painful. Offering a peremptory excuse, she explained, "We always gave the kids a say, but in this decision there really was no choice. It couldn't be changed."

At the airport, there was a storm, and the planes were late. In order to make their Chicago connection, the airline said they couldn't take Mimi's bunny. Mary Ann stood by her daughter. "I was not getting on the plane without that rabbit." Hal went ahead. They took a plane the next day.

The California schools were on a semester system and didn't insist on Mimi entering classes until the second semester. So every day, for the first two weeks, Mary Ann and Mimi would go down to the beach in Santa Cruz.

Mary Ann paused, sighed, looked into space.

"And one day, Mimi refused to go down to the beach."

"Had something happened there the day before?"

"No, not that. Nothing like that. She was protesting. She just refused to go. And wouldn't go anymore."

I couldn't yet grasp what she was implying. Her daughter wouldn't go to the beach? So what? But the beach was the start of far more to come, so that nontrip to the beach was loaded with all the emotion and regret. Mary Ann recounted the rest of it with fairly good cheer, her voice implying, *These are just the kinds of challenges a mother might get, and that's just the way it is.*

"She wouldn't eat anything I cooked. She wouldn't eat at the dinner table. I tried everything, it didn't matter. She would stand at the counter over there and refuse to join us. If I'd cooked it, she would ignore it. And she wouldn't talk to us at all."

"Wouldn't talk?"

"She lived in the house with us, but she wanted nothing to do with us. She wouldn't go to counseling. She wouldn't talk to us, would just ignore us. For the next nine years."

"Nine years!"

"Yes, nine years. She was sweet and nice to everyone else. I never gave up. It was very painful, as you can imagine. But you never give up on a child."

Mary Ann had planned to start her career when Mimi began high school. And when Mimi chose to attend Santa Catalina, down in Monterey, forty-eight miles away, maybe that was for the best. Santa Catalina was a boarding school. But then Mimi decided she didn't want to board. There was a bus service, but Mimi didn't like the bus. So every afternoon, for four years, Mary Ann drove down to Monterey to pick her daughter and friends up from school. (One of their fathers took the morning leg). Ninety-six miles a day, trapped in the same car with a daughter who refused to talk to her. Mimi also hated it when Mary Ann talked to her friends. The career would wait until Mimi went to college.

"Those years, I didn't feel like I belonged here in California. I didn't have a way to connect with others. I tried working part-time, in food service, but after six months realized that wasn't my taste. I was committed to doing the driving, though. Mimi's academics improved, and that seemed the most important thing. It was *okay*."

Mimi went to college at Loyola Marymount in Los Angeles. She'd been excited to attend. Then, something happened. "We really don't know *what* happened." Mary Ann learned that Mimi had run away. Her older sister went down to L.A. and found her at a friend's house. She hadn't been going to class and had told friends she was sick.

"She came home to live with us again. She was really a vegetable. She walked in the front door, dropped her suitcases, and went to her room. The suitcases sat in the front hallway for months, until I finally said to her, 'If you put them away, I'll let you get a cat.' Mimi signed up for community college courses, but never went to any classes. She talked to nobody. She was very reclusive."

"This was how long ago?"

"Three years. It's really so much better now. We have our Mimi back. It's like night and day."

"What happened?"

"First, some friends asked her to be their baby boy's nanny. She was always so good with little kids. The kids on this block always loved her. He's going to kindergarten now. She really responded to him. Then recently, just these last few months, she shined that light on the rest of us. She started taking classes at the Academy of Art College, in San Francisco— even though she's living here—and she loves it. All that time, she was really just looking for something to love. And then the day after Thanksgiving, she said to me, 'Let's go out and go shopping.' I hadn't been out with her for years and years. Over Christmas, Mimi bonded with my son Frankie's wife, Audrey, who's an interior designer. Somehow, that just clicked for Mimi. She finally felt like part of this family. And one day she came out of her room and said, 'Hi, mom!' very friendly. And that was it. At last, it was over. We don't really know what happened, but it's gone. She became herself again. Her boyfriend eats here with us often."

"You must have felt helpless. For years."

"Oh yes. But I still have so many fond memories of when she was young, and new memories recently. I never gave up."

Indeed. Two years ago, she spotted a classified ad in the newspaper. "It said something about 'knowledge of nutrition,' which made me think I could apply." She was hired as a research interviewer for a large, significant study on the possible environmental and genetic factors that contribute to childhood leukemia. The study has been in progress since 1995, involves nine hospitals, and has been sponsored by the Northern California Cancer Center and UC-Berkeley. Mary Ann's work is sorta like mine: she drives around and interviews mothers and their children for a couple hours. She takes dust samples and learns family-illness histories and records what household products are stored in the home.

"It's very rewarding work," she said, with significant satisfaction. "Illness crosses every barrier. No one seems to escape. I've still got my save-the-world attitude. I've got lots of energy, good health. I don't feel unusual. In today's economy, many don't retire at my age."

She's proud to have watched society evolve. "In my day, if a woman was pregnant, it looked bad for a corporation to expect her to work. It was considered cruel to let a pregnant woman work. We used to be afraid of a diverse workforce—my father was angrily criticized for hiring black people in his lab—but now we're proud to be part of a diverse workforce. Diversity is admirable. We no longer impose so many standards on people. They have choices. Women can work or stay home. It's important that they have that choice, and that we let people become whatever they're called to become." She summed it up this way: "I waited a long time to work. And from my perspective, regardless of the unemployment rate, it's really a fairly good time to be working."

26 ||| The Chemical Engineer
Who Lacked a Chemical

WHAT'S REAL?

When I told Julia Meriwether that I'd like to come to San Antonio, preferably on a day when her feelings would be on the surface, she suggested I hang out the weekend of her wedding to Patrick Harrigan. I knew that weekend wouldn't allow us much chance to talk in private, so we talked by phone until then. We discussed some things she hadn't really talked about with anyone, not her dad, not her best friends, not even Patrick, and so I had to be a little careful, not wanting to get her on a who-am-I? jag before the big day. But her mind was dwelling on that question already, and she appreciated having someone to talk to about it. She was going to be starting her life over, in a way. Patrick was a protocol officer in the air force, and he was being restationed to Robins Air Force Base in Georgia. They were moving after the honeymoon.

So when I showed up for the weekend's festivities, I was in the unusual position of having spent less time with her than anyone else in attendance, but knowing more of her real story than some of her oldest friends.

Her oldest friends were the nine other geeks from the honors science classes at MacArthur High School, class of 1985. Four women and five men. Though graduate schools and careers had dispersed them over the country, they were still a tight group, stayed in touch regularly, and used each other's weddings as an excuse to see each other. I found them remarkably refreshing. Not one was a computer geek; they had gone into hard sciences, from genetic engineering to astrophysics. They were the type who laugh too easily, and too hard, at the slightest bit of physical humor. They were also the kind of people who might walk up at a wedding reception and say, without provocation, "I was thinking more about how on the moon there can be places which get constant sunlight within a few kilometers of places in constant darkness near absolute zero. . . ."

Julia had been the only one in the group to leave scientific research. She earned her BS in chemical engineering, then joined Du Pont's prestigious Field Program. She studied superconductivity for two years and synthetic plastics for another two. Du Pont bent over backward to make her happy, but Julia grew depressed, sank into a scary black mood, and finally quit. Engineering wasn't for her. She came back to San Antonio, and to avoid becoming a waitress, she started substitute teaching sixth-grade science. She was offered a permanent job, took it, and spent seven happy years at Alamo Heights Junior High.

None of her family or friends thought there was much more to it than that—almost everyone in Julia's large family was a late bloomer. Her parents encouraged their children to travel. One of her sisters had taken a year off school to pack salmon in Alaska. Her older sister followed her father into family medicine, but not until she was in her thirties. Her five siblings had waited until their thirties to get married and have children. So Julia's story fit the pattern. *Of course* Julia would toy around in engineering before finding happiness as a teacher right here in San Antonio. *Of course* she wouldn't get married until she was thirty-three. All the Meriwethers were like that.

San Antonio is the seventh-largest city in the United States, but it is not a highly competitive urban metropolis with a wealthy upper class whose sons and daughters go off to the Ivy League expecting to run the world in ten years. The wealthy in San Antonio wouldn't be wealthy in many other cities. Nothing is made here that's sold elsewhere, except for Pace salsa. But nothing like airplanes, computers, medicine, or movies. Its local industries are tourism and military bases. A third of the population seems to be military retirees who have fond memories of green hills and sunshine from when they were stationed here. They reenter the workforce in their mid-forties and depress the overall wages because they're willing to work for little, since they already receive a full-pay military pension. You can't earn a lot here unless you're a developer, and even that line doesn't generate a fat margin. Modest houses in the best neighborhoods of Alamo Heights and Terrell Hills sell for as low as $140,000. All of this means that San Antonio is a little bit sleepy, and its best and brightest don't think outside of Texas. They graduate from public high schools and enroll at UT, Rice, A&M, Baylor, et cetera. By the time they're thirty, on average they're less likely to be riddled with angst over whether they've lived up to their potential. But by the time they were thirty-three, as Julia and her friends were, they'd discovered they're as smart as anyone else out there, and they were feeling a latent urge to aim higher, and to expect more from themselves.

So on Friday night, as her friends caught up with each other, it seemed everybody was facing a decision about whether to make some personal sacrifices in order to fulfill these growing ambitions. The astrophysicist had to decide by Monday whether to leave his tenured position at the University of Oklahoma, where he ran the national weather forecast system, for a private-sector job in Colorado that would allow him to study advanced space travel, which was always his dream. "Meteorology is interesting, but space travel is cool," he said. Two other guys chipped in with their opinion. One had designed the space shuttle's global positioning satellite system at NASA. (He invited me to come see him at NASA Goddard when I was in D.C., and I took him up on that two months later.) The other worked for Jet Propulsion Laboratory, and he'd driven up from Houston, having spent the last twenty-four hours fixing the computer systems on the international space station *Alpha*'s fifty-eight-foot robot arm. I had no doubt that on Monday the meteorologist would be headed to Colorado.

They wondered aloud why they hadn't been raised to aspire to more. They knew they were smart—they'd been National Merit Scholars. But only one had even applied to a college outside Texas. I blamed it on rampant Texas boasting. Texans are raised to believe everything in Texas is bigger and better than its equivalent outside the state. Harvard is the Rice of the north. Austin's music scene is better than Nashville's. Dallas's gay community is better than San Francisco's. San Antonio's Sea World is the best Sea World. The Silicon Hills is a better place to do business than Silicon Valley. Bigger and better. That's all you ever hear in Texas, and though it's always expressed slightly in jest, I can imagine if I were eighteen I'd think it was taboo to be curious about the rest of the world.

The wedding was at a local Presbyterian church. I went looking for a toilet and ended up accidentally in Julia's dressing room, where I shouldn't have been. She wasn't a bit nervous. Julia looks a lot like her mother, who is from Hong Kong and part Asian. Julia also has lots of freckles. She wore a traditional white gown, snug on top, billowing at the legs, decked with little white flower petals of satin, and a long veil flipped back behind her pinned dark hair.

Patrick's uncle is a pastor and performed the service; his father was best man. The reception was at Julia's parents' house in Alamo Heights. It was a sweet and unembarrassing wedding by Texas standards. Julia was completely herself, holding court, laughing, happy and in love, untouched by the usual stress over whether the event would come off, whether family would get along, and whether someone's ex-husband would get drunk and end up in the pool. The band didn't have to stoop to playing "YMCA" and "Celebrate" to get people dancing. The caterers didn't run out of sushi before everyone had their turn at the buffet. None of this is really relevant to Julia's story, but I describe it to make clear that her confusion about the rest of her life didn't bleed over into her love life. In that she felt secure.

Julia's doubts about who she was were triggered last Thanksgiving, when her medical insurer notified her they would no longer cover her antidepressant, and she had to switch over to one they would. This required her to taper off her old antidepressant, and for the first time in a long time her blood system was free of meds. Julia always believed that her real self was her medicated self; the antidepressants simply made her feel normal. She never noticed any side effects. She told herself, *I just have a medical condition.*

Sure enough, in those two weeks after Thanksgiving, before the new meds kicked in, Julia felt that old urge to tear her life apart, to make a change. She wanted to quit teaching. She became recalcitrant and snippy and withdrawn. But she told herself, "This depression is not because my brain lacks a chemical. I have good reason to be unhappy." The principal of her school was an asshole; four of the nine science teachers had resigned because of run-ins with this principal. Julia had had run-ins too, but the medication had suppressed her desire to fight back. The medication had a scary side effect after all—it turned off the instinct to protect herself. Riding a surge of willpower to reclaim herself, and afraid that the new drugs would restore her complacency, she quit her teaching position midsemester, with no notice, leaving the school in the lurch; her students had to finish the term with substitutes. She told her friends that she'd burned out on teaching and wanted to take it easy before the wedding; few knew she'd ever been on medication, let alone that she'd recently gone off it.

Julia started to seriously question the accepted version of her adult life. Were these past seven years of steady happiness real? She was certain the last year and a half had been a fraud, ever since this principal took over her school. But what about the five years before that? She couldn't trust her feelings so she wrote down the facts. The facts were:

- She never *wanted* to become a teacher.
- Even after her first year as a substitute, she didn't apply for a teaching post—the district recruited her.
- She took the job because the school was only a mile from her parents' house, where she was living. It was convenient and offered summers off.
- At the time, she *wanted* to go to a Native American reservation in South Dakota and help out any way she could, even if it was to drive a school bus.

It really bugged her that she hadn't gone to that reservation seven years ago. Whatever happened to that idealistic streak? Her engineering classes were mostly in environmental courses. Her minor had been Latin American politics. When interviewing for jobs her senior year, she always asked her potential future employer if their company did business with the Pinochet regime in Chile, and if they didn't know the answer or said yes, she refused to consider an offer from them. What had happened to *that* Julia? Had she grown into a realist, as most people do as they get older, or had the drugs turned her idealism off? She simply didn't know.

Thankfully she wasn't on the right drugs while she was at Du Pont, or she might still be trapped there. Boy, those days were awful. Julia blamed them for triggering her first real severe depression.

It hadn't started out bad. Du Pont's Field Program groomed engineers to become managers. Every year, 120 chem E's are chosen from thousands of applicants. They congregate for an annual management camp, are given lots of special training, and have their own yearbook with everyone's photo inside. The program allowed Julia to rotate every couple years through Du Pont's diverse divisions until she found one worth choosing as her permanent specialty. It's a remarkably enlightened program, because it doesn't force its engineers to choose before they're ready to.

After her first two years in superconductivity research, Julia considered quitting. Du Pont convinced her to try something else. She warned them she wouldn't work on weapons or environmental poisons, so they suggested a plastics and rubber division in Beaumont, Texas, which would be close to home.

Beaumont turned out to be a hellhole. She was fine for three months, high off that first hit of newness, and then her Quarter System Alarm Clock went off. The only thing that smells worse than a fish processing plant is a paper pulp mill. And the only thing that smells worse than a paper mill is burning plastic. Julia was surrounded by all three in Beaumont. If the wind blew from the south, the rotting fish got her. If it came from the north, the paper mill stink soaked into her clothes. If the wind was still, she worked in a cloud of burning plastic.

The plant was a maze the size of several shopping malls. Outdoor walkways on three levels ran between the buildings. Julia got lost repeatedly. She rode a bicycle around the plant and whenever something broke, she went to interview the line workers to learn why it might have broken.

After nine months Julia was assigned to a team creating the roofing material for the Alamodome. To manufacture this stuff required a great deal of chlorine gas, and Julia was made responsible for the process hazard review on the chlorine gas. She thought this was irresponsible. She didn't have enough experience to do it. She was freaked out that she might gas the town and kill hundreds. She felt as if she were impersonating an engineer, and lacked confidence in her abilities. She recognized she was unhappy, but the only thing she could control was her job, so she assumed she had to leave engineering. She started to break out in tears at work. A friend of hers would poke her head into the hallway, glance left and right, and when the coast was clear rush Julia out to her car and send her home.

Julia went on medication, but it wasn't making any difference. She started to have daydreams of committing suicide. On her drives home she'd have the urge to plough her car into a cement freeway pylon. *If I turn right now* . . . Instead she finally turned herself in. This wasn't right. She resigned and went home to San Antonio to live with her parents.

The crazy thing was, when she left Du Pont her department threw her a going-away party, and everyone was really happy for her. "I envy you," they said. "I wish I could just quit." "Congratulations." It was the first time Julia realized they weren't happy either, and were only doing it to make their mortgages.

So now, seven years later, Julia doesn't know if what made her so unhappy was engineering, Beaumont, or her condition. There's plenty of evidence to blame her condition, and plenty of evidence to blame Beaumont, but almost no evidence to blame engineering.

"I wonder if I threw the baby out with the bathwater," she said.

Only recently she remembered that when she left Beaumont and sought medical help in San Antonio, she was given different medication. So maybe Beaumont wasn't really as bad as she remembered—maybe she was on the wrong medication. Julia Meriwether is the chemical engineer who left engineering because her brain lacked the right chemical.

"I always loved engineering," she said. "You've met my friends. I was one of them."

She's also learned, from a seminar at UT, that feeling like an unqualified imposter at work is common. So common that it has a name: Imposter syndrome. It's particularly common among women thrust into lots of responsibility in a male-dominated work culture, where the men make it taboo to ask questions because they don't want to appear uninformed or unintelligent. In other words, Julia learned that feeling like an imposter *wasn't* a sign that she didn't belong there. It was a sign that she had to ask more questions.

Most of all, she feels in retrospect that she *fled* engineering, more out of fear than out of wisdom.

"Did I leave it behind because I was so afraid of my depression?" she asked.

So Julia is left with these shards of memories and impressions, while trying, like her friends, not to sell her potential short. She knows that her happiness or unhappiness isn't dependent on her job. But her job is the one thing she can change.

Looming on her horizon is the fact that she wants to have kids, but she's not supposed to be pregnant on these meds. What will she do? She doesn't know. Will she be happy when her baby is born, or will she be depressed?

At her wedding, I got only a brief moment alone with her. I asked her what she was thinking of doing when she and Patrick moved to Georgia. Was she going to have kids right away? Was she going back to work? She'd decided she needed to figure this out, even if it meant backtracking seven years. She was applying for engineering jobs on the base. She'd sent in her résumé for a position overseeing an electroplating operation and managing hazardous waste byproducts. She might like it, or she might hate it, but she needed to find out for her own peace of mind. I thought this was brave.

"I need to know what's real," she said.

We kissed and hugged good-bye. I felt like I had to ask her why I was privy to her story. Why had she told me what she hadn't told her oldest friends?

"Because you're the only one who really asked," she said.

Considering all she felt had happened, she was surprised those who loved her most hadn't pried into her moods or made her justify her decision to abandon engineering. They'd always given her carte-blanche support—"whatever you need is fine, no matter whatever it is you need"—but consequently left her in a vacuum to figure this out by herself. Time and again, she was told by her family, "Let me know when you make a decision." Now she wishes they'd intervened, and made her explain why she left engineering wholesale.

I heard this echoed more than I ever expected by the people I met while writing this book. The stereotype is that domineering parents push their kids to succeed, killing their children's love for whatever they're studying. But the opposite was far more common—young people who were given too much leeway by parents afraid of being overbearing, when their children really needed help in identifying what was important to them. It's difficult terrain, no doubt. If Julia had come to me, in the middle of her Beaumont depression, I would have been willing to butt in, but I would have given her bad advice. I would have told her to quit and find something else entirely. I would have suspected she went into engineering only because all her best friends did it.

I'm not sure there are right answers, which means we have to let it be okay that we make what appear, in hindsight, to have been mistakes. We shouldn't beat ourselves up about it. As I told Carl Kurlander, very few people get it right without missteps. It's normal to have gotten off track for long periods.

It took a few months, but Julia found work at Robins Air Force Base as an industrial engineer.

Destination vs. Journey?

27 ||| Guidance, Navigation, and Control

THREE LESSONS FROM ONE WHO'S STAYED PUT

The aerospace engineer who invited me to NASA Goddard was Russell Carpenter, and he was an amazing oddity in today's times. I decided to spend the day with him several months later not only to goof around in the flight dynamics center, but because Russell had confessed an astonishing fact that I needed to understand. When he told it to me, I didn't realize right away how extraordinary it was, but as I heard hundreds and hundreds of people's stories, it stood out.

Get this: Russell Carpenter, thirty-five, has had only one employer his entire adult life.

Having a single employer was commonplace in our parents' generation, even as the social contract was torn up in the 1970s. So we don't think of it as a weird thing. But consider it for a moment—how many thirty-five-year-olds do you know who've had only one employer? It's rare. I could count the ones I know personally on a single hand—they went to work for Microsoft during college, and have had yet-to-vest stock options chaining them to the company whenever temptation lurked. But Russell is a GS-14, stuck to government pay scales—the money is *okay,* but never the reason to stay. He's watched fellow engineers peel away to join dot-coms and the human genome project, but the glitz and moola have never rocked his conviction that NASA is his place. Lately, private space exploration has garnered the buzz, but Russell's had no trouble staying put. So without money to keep him, and without sizzle to keep him, why has he stayed?

What might we learn from a guy who has never compromised—from a guy whose work doesn't shoot for the moon, but shoots way past the moon?

Russell works in a NASA division called Spacecraft GNC: Guidance, Navigation, and Control. Or, in NASA slang—

"Where am I?"

"Where do I want to go?"

and "How will I get there?"

—which is a nice metaphor for the purposeful manner in which Russell has boldly navigated life. He did not drift aimlessly in space, was not tugged off track by the gravitational pull of other worlds.

"Where am I?" *I'm a kid in junior high, watching* Cosmos *and Carl Sagan, thinking it's the coolest thing I've ever seen.*

"Where do I want to go?" *I want to go work for NASA on space exploration.*

"How will I get there?" *Well, I'm not astronaut material, so I'll be an engineer.*

UT Austin has a program with NASA that's similar to ROTC. NASA pays your tuition if you work your summers and two years after school. Russell took advantage of this, and when he was done they offered to send him back to UT for his PhD. Until 1998, he was at Johnson Space Center working on the space shuttle. At that point he moved to Goddard, outside the beltway of Washington, D.C., in order to work on satellites. The space shuttle was an incredible team environment, and he got to work directly with the astronauts, but the cutting edge in GNC has moved to satellites. NASA builds a shuttle every five years or so, while Goddard builds a couple satellites every couple years. In order to implement the newest rage in guidance systems, Russell jumped to satellites.

This newest rage is not like the rages that swept through the high-tech sector the last few years. Engineers don't hype it, and it's still several years away from implementation. The halls and offices at NASA are quiet. They're content with slowly pushing toward a solution. Which I took as Extractable Lesson #1: Time Frame. In most companies, goals and objectives are set quarterly. These goals are highly measurable, and tied to compensation, but they're awfully short-term. Is it any wonder people jump from job to job in such a culture? Can anything really great be accomplished in ninety days? Russell watched so many Internet engineers compromise their science in order to patch something together for a quarterly milestone. "I never thought what they were doing was cool. It was so clear they were creating problems for themselves down the road. We would never do it that way." The opposite of the corporate culture is the government culture, which slugs away at problems that seem intractable. People have a natural tendency not to work on problems where they can't make a difference. As a result, bureaucracies form and become bogged down with fatigue. At NASA, Russell has found an intermediate time frame, where he can accomplish the high-minded objectives GNC is charged with, but not today, and not tomorrow, and not ninety days from now.

The objective NASA was charged with was to measure some things in space that would require a telescope aperture a mile wide. Well, you might be able to build a mile-wide mirror, but you couldn't get it into space. The Hubble telescope was the biggest telescope NASA could build and get into orbit. So someone thought of creating a flying network of semiautonomous drone satellites, like a swarm of flies, that would fly up to a mile apart, each taking readings. This created a huge challenge for GNC, because now each drone satellite needs its own guidance system, and it's infinitely more complicated because they have to know where the other drones are too. Not just to fly in formation, but to take accurate measurements. Global positioning is easy if you're on Earth, but it's a lot trickier when Earth is two years away. What are your zero coordinates? Where's the center?

This is the problem Russell works on. He was test-driving some software he'd written. He'd hypnotized two computers into thinking they were up in space, and he instructed them to measure the thickness of Iceland's ice cap with laser altimeters. Depending on their fictional positions in space, their readings would vary, and Russell had a way to combine them accurately. Don't ask me.

"But basically, the end product of what we do is black boxes," Russell explained. "We build a small piece of computer hardware and software that gets riveted onto the satellite."

He escorted me into the enormous bays where a satellite was being built. One of these black boxes was being installed onto the frame that very minute. Then we went into his computer lab, where he assembles and tests the black boxes. This is unlike any computer lab I'd seen. Their black boxes must work under incredible heat, radiation, cold, g-forces, electric pulse, and vibration. They had everything but the Samsonite gorilla to beat up their components. They had a kiln to cook the chips in, a radiation oven of some sort, a centrifugal whirly spinner, a superfreezer, a vacuum to re-create zero gravity, a blowtorch to toast hard drives like marshmallows. Every black box that emerges from this testing can take a beating. Aerospace engineers are obsessed with redundancy and backup systems. They know that metals give, that gears slip, that motors overheat, and they plan for this in their designs. Not everything has to go right for it to work.

This obsession shows up in every aspect of their lives. Later, Russell gave me driving instructions to his condo about six different ways. There was the left-left-right variety, but also the miles and minutes permutations, in case I preferred to measure distance either way, and the signpost/monument version, and then, in case I missed any of these turns, he had various contingency directions to either get back on track or take a different route, when that was locally optimal. This is how NASA engineers are trained to think. Which I took as Extractable Lesson #2: Russell hasn't let minor setbacks get in his way. His backup plans do not lead to different destinations, such as "If I don't get into business school, I'll be a schoolteacher." His backup plans lead to the same destination, and if you have to arrive late by the back road, that's fine. Not everything has to go right. His hopes are not pinned to a single turning point.

You want to put a mile-wide mirror into orbit?

It *is* possible.

Russell made it clear he was no genius. He introduced me to a genius inventor he works with, but Russell's your ordinary aerospace PhD. His method is his secret, but it's no secret.

I drove to his house because I wanted to attend that night's Bowie Baysox game with him. The Baysox are a AA minor league baseball team, and their stadium is in the woods behind Russell's condo. Russell goes often. The tickets are cheap, every seat is close to the field, and the beers are good. They draw about nine thousand fans a game. It was a great summer night, and the Baysox won in the bottom of the ninth when a little-used catcher hit a grand slam. The game had looked as if it were over ten minutes earlier, with the Baysox down three runs with two outs. I suggested we skip out and not get stuck in the parking lot, but Russell wanted to watch to the end. Which I took as Extractable Lesson #3: Russell leads a balanced life. He does not let himself get burned out. He is not in a rush. He takes advantage of his after-hours. He had bought a town house in Alexandria, Virginia, with his girlfriend, and was going to move in as soon as it was completed. If he reads something stupid in the newspaper, he has the time to write a letter to the editor. NASA sponsors a variety of clubs and gives each club a trailer on the back grounds. Russell was a member of the flying club, and with about fourteen other guys bought a Cessna 172, which they kept at a small private airport ten minutes down the road. Most of the other guys have families and a little less time, so Russell has use of the plane whenever he wants. On weekends, Russell often flies up to Teterborough or down to the Outer Banks, in North Carolina. He has a good life. But he's very humble about it. He wasn't selling me on anything. He didn't take me to the Baysox to show me how great his life was—he wanted to see the game.

"Do you realize that having had only one employer makes you pretty uncommon?" I asked.

"I never really thought about it," he said. "I guess you're right. It's not a point of pride with me. I always wanted to work on cool things. But not what the media thinks is cool—what I think is cool. If something else really cool came along, and it meant leaving NASA, I wouldn't have trouble doing it."

"But you're not a cool chaser, Russell. I've met a million cool chasers. Cool is usually a thing of the moment. The way you think, it's different. It is."

"I suppose you're right."

I told him I had to get back to Washington.

"Do you want to go out the front way or back way?"

"I think I'll go out the way I came in."

"The back way is quicker."

"Okay."

"Now if you miss it . . ."

Most stories in this book portray people who've made their life better by making significant changes. So you might think I'm an advocate for changing your life. But I would never pretend it's that simple. Russell's story demonstrates the other side of the coin—it's equally important to be able to make the most of your situation, whether that situation lasts three years or a lifetime. Those in this book who succeeded in their quest have all learned this lesson. Yes, they made changes, but then they dug in and worked tenaciously to make the best of their new life.

The four stories of this section mine the tension between embracing change and sticking it out, between pursuing and accepting. Heidi Olson has changed her life many times, and fully intends to continue doing so—but in each situation, she's invested the time to make a significant impact. She's a good role model for people who want to have many careers. Leela de Souza's early career was devoted to a sole passion—dance. She then went through a period of embracing change and jumping around a lot. Recently, she realized her true character fit the former method more than the latter, but it's required a significant shift in attitude. Like Leela, Wendy Jones already got to live a dream life. But she considers the nine years since then a more important accomplishment—as she's learned to love the simple pleasures of an ordinary life.

28 ||| The Boom Wrangler Has
Many Reasons to Live

CHANGE, FOR SOME, KEEPS THEM ALIVE

Heidi Olson's job, currently, is to rebuild the Cantor Fitzgerald brokerage firm after it lost seven hundred employees in the World Trade Center attacks. I spent some time with her on the twenty-ninth floor of a Park Avenue building, where she had leased temporary headquarters until a new one is built in Shrewsbury, New Jersey. I watched seventy-two traders bark orders and bicker over which one of them had just bought a certain stock. Heidi said it is not a sad place to work, that now and then a wave of grief clobbers someone and they need a hug. There is also a steady sense of fulfillment, to be here, and to be around so much emotion. A window-washer was on a scaffold outside, cleaning the glass. As he was lowering himself, his scaffold rubbed against the glass, a weird scratching sound and vibration from an unexpected place, and Heidi flinched, hard, looking over her shoulder as her heart raced.

Until this chance, she thought of her career as a cliché. Every newsworthy trend, she'd been a part of. She's what I would have called a Boom Wrangler. The Summer of Leveraged Buyouts. Art in the eighties. The tech gold rush and the IPO rage. She was there. Now she's part of the most newsworthy event of this young century, and her past is no longer a cliché. It was, she now sees, training for *this* moment, this incredible and unforeseeable crisis. The ultimate rebuild.

"It seems this was my destiny, to be available when the call came. I'm the perfect person for this. Everything else I've done prepared me for this job."

The thing about Heidi, though, is that she's never been looking for a destiny. She's never asked the universe to send her one. She was content to chase the heat and excitement of whatever her generation found hot and exciting. She fully expected that every half-decade or so, she would grow bored and need to find something new to challenge her. Being a Boom Wrangler's fine with her.

So Heidi's retelling of her story, in light of the tragedy, only goes so far. She's not suddenly a "destiny" person. She fully expects that the intense phase of this job will be over in a year, and it will mature into a fairly normal blah-job, which she will eventually leave. She does not believe that the emotional enormity of what's going on here will change her basic pattern. This surprised me. I thought, maybe an event like this can be *so* intense with pain and significance that it becomes a thing one would never leave. It would be too important to one's psyche to simply flip for, say, a flashier challenge that had no psychological import. Coming to work was never a more conscious decision than in the days after September 11, 2001. Just getting in that elevator and sitting down at one's desk was deeply meaningful. It symbolized moving on with life, or showing strength, or it was a humiliation (if it was the last place one wanted to be) that ignited the will to make some changes.

Heidi did not just ride the elevator and sit down at her desk. For the firm that was most devastated by the attacks, she had to find a new building, and make sure the elevators were working, and bring in new desks for the traders to sit at. And phone lines, and computers, and market data . . . they needed grief counseling, and funeral planning, and increased security . . . an endless list. Three hundred employees of Cantor Fitzgerald did not die in the attacks, and an amazing 289 of them decided that the best way to deal with their grief was to come back to work for the firm. For Heidi, wouldn't this add up to something that would last forever? Wouldn't those who came back to work be so bonded together as the Cantor "family" that walking away would no longer be possible?

Heidi says no.

I find Heidi's story fascinating. It's rare to find a Boom Wrangler whose philosophy has been truly challenged. Boom Wranglers usually avoid the kinds of emotional crises that other people in the book have gone through. With change as their mantra, they always have an out. It's hard to find one who's had a reason to think, "Maybe I should stay put." Heidi has, but won't. I'll fill in the details.

Heidi is about five-five, blond hair in a bob, rimless eyeglasses, efficient, no-nonsense, no reason for nonsense anymore, lets it out fast. Her husband is an architect who travels a lot; her son is eight and her daughter, who is adopted from Ecuador, is two. Her cell phone is never turned off, because Howard might need her. Howard is Howard Lutnick, founder of Cantor Fitzgerald; the two went to Haverford College with a friend of mine, which is how I met her. During Wall Street's go-go years, she was at Yale getting her master's degree in public and private management. She's walked that line between nonprofits and for-profits her whole career. When leveraged buyouts dominated the headlines, she worked at J. P. Morgan, but that was too far astray from the line she liked, so she then joined up with Tom Krens, the dynamic and controversial director of the Guggenheim Foundation, then newly hired.

It was a cool time. During the 1980s, all this Wall Street new money needed somewhere to go, and a good amount of it went toward art. But the old-money syndicates that surrounded the traditional-minded museums shut the new money out. The few museums that were open to the new money, like the Guggenheim, created a different kind of art culture, less stodgy, more entrepreneurial. Art emerged as a serious professional job for the first time. Heidi Olson worked for Krens for five years, doing a lot of everything—driving donors around, meeting with artists, writing grants, talking to the press, and running the membership department. It was a start-up atmosphere. Krens had dozens of ideas and was always coming up with more. They renovated and expanded the Guggenheim, opened the Guggenheim Soho, and began plans for what became MASS MoCA, a museum of contemporary art in Massachusetts. While most museums refused to tinker with their traditions, Krens embraced change. He instilled in Heidi (if she didn't have it already) the belief that change keeps any institution, and any individual, full of life. Heidi became his director of budget and planning, floated a bond issue for the Guggenheim's plans, and then took Krens's words to heart. Even though Bilbao was in the works, it wasn't enough to keep Heidi there. It would be more of the same.

"There was no reason to keep doing it," she said.

For the next two years, she was the director of finance for Orbis, a flying eye hospital. They had a DC 8 (and later a DC 10) outfitted with high-tech microscopes and modern ophthalmology technology. They flew around the third world teaching local doctors how to treat and prevent blindness.

Then she came to Cantor Fitzgerald, and in the past few years she's run various projects—always at the forefront of how the firm was changing. She was the CFO for technology, building up the company's technology business, then built eSpeed, a division that was spun off and taken public. But running eSpeed, even with its growth rate, was too pedestrian. She didn't want to be a bean counter. So she did business development, acquiring new firms for Cantor, and she became the person who got newly acquired companies plugged in to the rest of the company.

The reason Heidi Olson is not dead is because she was laid off last April. With the market's downturn, the deal flow dried up and the company consolidated. There was no rapid growth for her to manage. Heidi understood the reasons for being laid off, but it wasn't handled well.

"I had issues with it, but the people I had issues with are now all dead."

Heidi went through some soul-searching last summer. What was she looking for? There had never been a job description that fit her. "I do best in organizations in flux," she realized. "If they're undergoing rapid change, need to be reinvented or fixed, a cleanup or a new build, I'll do great. I'm not right for a regular job." With that criterion in mind, Heidi looked at jobs in many industries, but didn't find anything quite for her.

On September 13, Howard Lutnick called and gave her this enormous job. He needed someone capable of building a company, fast—but also someone who knew him, could deal with his personality, and knew Cantor. Someone he trusted. Heidi was the only person on earth left who fit that description.

"There had to be someone for Howard to call," she said. "It was the ultimate challenge. I suppose I'm fatalistic about it."

Her new title was chief administrative officer, equities group. It's five or six jobs at any other firm. Volunteers reached out to help continually. The traders here were amazingly patient. They're a breed of people who want everything fixed *now*. But not one has yelled at her. For a while, every morning men would cry in the elevator. To show your emotion is now to show you're human. It's a good thing.

I asked her how she dealt with the fact that she would have been dead if she wasn't laid off.

"There but for the grace of God go I," she said, tossing her hands to the sky.

Had it affected how she thought of her life?

"No," she said. "It is unprocessable. It's too absurd. To lose one or two friends—that's all our generation has ever had to deal with before. We are not prepared to watch our coworkers die in a combat zone. We lost more than two out of every three. The coping goes on in a different part of my mind. Every day I open the newspaper, and I know dead people." *The New York Times* had been running obituaries for two months. "Every day I know at least one person who died and another person as an acquaintance of friends. How absurd is that?"

And had it changed what mattered to her?

"I don't care if my son wants to wear a shirt with a hole in it anymore. If I'm late, it doesn't cause me any stress anymore. I'll get there when I get there. There's no anxiety in the little things. My family matters more to me, but ironically, I worked four days a week for eight years to spend more time with my kids. Now I'm needed here at least sixty hours a week."

I was amazed that being so needed didn't translate into a long-term vision for Heidi. But it simply didn't. She didn't need her life to be a complete circle, or to run along a consistent theme. She didn't need it all to add up.

"After college, I worked for a year at an insurance company. I decided to go to Oxford for a year, because, well, it was Oxford. I told the other women at work, and one said, 'I wish I could just up and go to Oxford.' So I asked, 'Why don't you?' She said, 'I would, but I bought a couch.' I always remembered that moment, and I never wanted to be that woman. I never wanted to be trapped by my belongings, my past, my commitments."

The Boom Wrangler buys lots of couches, but never lets herself be trapped by that commitment.

The Boom Wrangler makes her way through life by sniffing out the next big opportunity. The Boom Wrangler doesn't really care what it is that's booming, because the adrenaline comes from the rapid pace of change itself—having to rewrite org charts and business plans, appease personalities, raise money, and compete against equally nimble rivals. The Boom Wrangler enjoys the spotlight. Financial reward is often involved, but it's not as essential as the excitement. Intensity is her passion. She works hard and plays hard. The Boom Wrangler learns from each ride, but the kinds of things she learns are modern carpentry—how to write a press release, pitch a venture capitalist, run a meeting, negotiate a lease. When a boom tails off, and she is faced with the question "Well, now what?" the operating principle that drives her decision is *Where's the next boom? What will be exciting?*

I've met a lot of Boom Wranglers. They often don't live up to their résumés; they were *there* during the boom, but never really made a mark. I chose Heidi's story to tell because she represents the better half of Boom Wrangling. She's hopped through five careers, but she gave each of them the time to pay off. She got heavily involved. She functionally ran many of the organizations, even though she was never the figurehead. Her commitment lasted an average of four years at each stage. She made a difference—made an impact—before moving on.

I think that's key. Fulfillment rarely is found in breezy encounters.

Boom Wranglers were only one species in the wide-ranging genus that might best be described as "Those Who Change a Lot." This grouping doesn't include the many who are forced to change by layoffs, or by having to move. It's people who *choose* to jump around. Maybe a need to stay in motion isn't a problem—maybe it's the solution. Constant reinvention. Why not? Why does there have to be an ultimate destination? What's wrong with being permanently restless? Changing careers is a modern form of wandering. It's how we expose ourselves to more of the world without ditching our responsibilities or draining our savings. I met many who'd given up the expectation that their passions should stay lit for long. "Life is a great opportunity to try out all the things I'm interested in," one wrote. Their only constant was wanderlust. "It took me a while to realize that I was born to wonder what to do with my life," wrote another. "And in the wondering, experience constant metamorphosis."

I call these people Change Artists, and when it's honest, it's a wonderful life strategy. True Change Artists are able to have many powerfully intense passions. Change on the horizon is not an excuse to avoid getting emotionally involved in the present. And that's the test. There are many who would fail it. There are many like the Bay Area woman who wrote, "I just can't seem to develop a passion for anything I have done." Or the guy in New England who confessed, "Sometimes I think I'm one of those people who will find a reason to be dissatisfied under any circumstances. I have managed to tear through several careers and even more short-lived relationships in the search for something I can't name or identify." A woman in Nebraska hoped I'd recognize the distinction between "explorers" and "runners"—"I imagine you'll find there are many people attempting to escape their own selves in the guise of challenging the unknown."

In other words, it's easy to pretend you're a Change Artist when you're more of a Change Junkie. This became clear to me when I was interviewing a young woman who'd had five distinct careers by her early thirties. Every career had started out great, then fell off a cliff. She felt an incredible itch to move on, find something else. She would run at the first sign of boredom. Considering yet another major life transition, she finally started wondering if the problem was *her,* not her job. Had she ever really given any of her choices a chance? There was always a voice in her head pitching fantasies of a better life elsewhere.

Eventually she realized this came from her childhood. Her mother had married four times; she moved around a lot as a kid, boomeranging from one financial extreme to the other. With her birth father they lived on food stamps. With one of her stepfathers, they lived in a mansion on the beach and had every luxury they could desire. She summed it up this way: "I got used to lots of change. Change was normal. And when change wasn't under way, I'd feel stagnant. I'll never feel secure standing still. I'm uncomfortable without chaos." She vowed to stop looking for new things until she could overcome this itch to tear her life up. She challenged herself to be truly involved in what she was doing then, and look for ways to improve her situation rather than chuck it.

Most of us have grown up with a lot of change in our lives. Of the nine hundred people I talked to, Russell Carpenter was the only one who had the same employer his entire adult life. Consider that for a second. We all know it's a different world out there, but do we recognize how different it is? In his seminal book, *Working,* Studs Terkel found admirable people who were content to stay put.

I found people dizzy from change and upheaval.

Most people still crave a place where they can be content, grow roots a little, make an impact. In order to find it, we might need to ask whether our opposing itch to bounce around is genuine, or whether it's rooted in a past we didn't ask for.

These next two stories present variations on this theme. Both women moved around a lot—Leela through many jobs, Wendy by having a career that kept her traveling—but only when they stopped running did they find the fulfillment they'd been craving.

BE YOUR OWN AUDIENCE

In the end, it worked out for Leela de Souza. After a year-and-a-half of unemployment, she finally gave up looking for that Perfect Job that was going to fit her abundant talents best, and she realized she needed to devote herself to something she really believed in—and then accept the regular entry point into that field. "I'm willing to start from scratch at a good company," she said. "I don't care how junior I am. You have to get satisfaction from being part of the mission." This was a new way of making a decision for her; if this had been two or four years earlier, it's unlikely she would have taken the job she did, as a salesperson. But the company was the biotech leader Genentech, and the product she'd be selling was Rituxan, which is used to treat non-Hodgkin's lymphoma. She'd decided that saving lives was a mission she could believe in. She hoped she would be part of this mission for a long time.

Through regular interviews over two years, I watched Leela learn, eventually, to make a decision this way. At the beginning of that time, she made decisions very differently. She was riding a streak of very prestigious jobs that challenged her with "vertical learning curves" (a buzzword at the time). She routinely scouted for the next exciting opportunity. Among her business school classmates, it was generally accepted that to stay fresh, to keep learning, you needed a new job in a new field every couple years. Leela de Souza was making decisions very much like the Boom Wrangler Heidi Olson. Her story is about how she realized that way of life wasn't for her.

Leela's father was from a family of many doctors in India. Upon coming to America, he found work in medical sales. Her mother trained as a flautist with the Chicago Symphony. Leela was bright, but she excelled

only in classes that required her to memorize, like math and science. Her father paid her a hundred dollars for every A on her report card, which perhaps undermined any inherent joy in learning for learning's sake. She rarely read and never wrote, didn't have critical thinking skills. Leela was also tall, slender, and a graceful athlete. She studied ballet from the age of four. Diving. Gymnastics. Tennis.

Leela had photographic memories of two turning points in her life. *It was 1983. My cast had been removed, my broken ankle healed but tender. During my time off, I'd decided to stop being a generalist and become "The Ace of One Thing." I remember those words, that phrase. My mother found out where the Hubbard Street studios were and took me to watch, hoping it would inspire me with my ankle rehab. I watched, and I was absolutely transformed. This was contemporary ballet, not classical. More athletic. Perfect for me. I thought, "This is it." I had a deep sense of passion at a very young age. Complete clarity. I was fifteen.*

Leela won a scholarship with Hubbard Street, studying under Mark Morris that summer. She danced seven hours a day, six days a week. She worked her way up through the corps, turned professional out of high school, became a soloist, and was promoted to principal when two dancers retired. She made very little, only about $28,000 a year, but money was irrelevant in her world. She had fame and acclaim. Four months a year, she toured internationally. She imprinted on that rush of performing for a packed opera house.

Leela always knew she would "someday" go to college. She had met too many formerly great dancers who at thirty-five were uneducated and unemployed. Fearing she'd end up in that plight, she retired in her mid-twenties with several good years left on her legs. She took the SAT and applied to college. She did well on the test by memorizing math and vocabulary.

It was 1989. I had been accepted to many universities. I couldn't decide which to attend. I walked down to the mailbox carrying two yes/no letters, both checked "yes." One was to Princeton, one to Chicago. I stood over the mailbox. Princeton is a great education, but one where I could still cheat my potential by taking classes that relied on memorization. Chicago is renowned for its classical method—100 percent critical thinking, writing papers every week on Antigone *and other Great Books. At Chicago, I'll have to face my intellect. I remember the moment perfectly. I mailed the one to Chicago.*

She had something to prove to herself, so she never skipped or transferred out of a class because it was too hard or she didn't like it. By the time she graduated she'd perfected her mind like she'd once honed ballet poses. She knew how to ask questions and how to think. The education cost $100,000, which she scratched together with the help of some scholarships and debt, with no assistance from her parents. Leela wanted ownership of her education, wanted it to be something she gave herself. She'd gone to college not for what it could lead to, not for what it could get her, not to trigger a long chain of events leading to prestige and security, but simply to have an adept mind.

But now what? What to do with this mind?

Over the next seven years, Leela made seemingly smart decisions, but never got any closer to making a choice. She was exposed to the highest echelons of society, and it all interested her, yet nothing grabbed her, nothing made her think, "This is it."

Her training included a year in Spain, Stanford Business School, consulting with McKinsey & Company, a White House Fellowship, and public relations with Burson Marsteller.

Each of these exposed her to more choices, but as she described them to me, I couldn't help feeling like they added up to an endless tour ride through Foreignland, Businessland, Policyland, and Technologyland. She never jumped off the tour bus and rolled up her shirtsleeves and got down in the dirt. She never got involved. She had cases. She had clients. She met with diplomats. She gave advice but did not put herself in a position to take action. There was a real difference between Leela de Souza and Heidi Olson; Heidi's jobs lasted an average of four years, enough time to get heavily involved and be a leader. Leela's jobs, by comparison, were tentative and noncommittal; her tenures averaged fewer than two years. She was always in search mode. She stayed on that tour bus, and soon she was no longer the young prodigy.

Leela was working in public relations when I first interviewed her. After the initial three-month adrenaline high, this had regressed into a mere day job, and she was casting about for what her next great opportunity might be. She had jumped into PR after a friend in the business spoke passionately about the work she was doing for clients. Leela made the mistake of assuming that PR work is inherently passion-inducing, when passion is really a complex organic chemistry between an individual and her job that isn't replicable or mass-produceable.

Leela had racked up seven years of experience, yet she was as completely uncertain of what to do with her life as she'd been the day she graduated from the University of Chicago.

I have this term I use now and then: Phi Beta Slacker. If a traditional slacker hops between temping, waitressing, working at record stores, telemarketing, and more temping, Phi Beta Slackers hop between esteemed grad schools, fat corporate gigs, and prestigious fellowships, looking like they have their act together but really having no more clue where they're headed than anyone else. And while slackers are not lazy by nature—they actually want to work, just not at the wrong thing or for the wrong reason—Phi Beta Slackers have a great gift for the world, if they can figure out what it is, or defuse whatever is holding them back.

I hoped Leela would find that gift and get off the tour bus. Cursed as she is with infinite abilities and choices, her dilemma is not a very sympathetic one. But I kept listening, checking in with her regularly. I considered her a proxy for Phi Beta Slackers everywhere. They could make such a difference in the world if they could only stop trying to impress each other, stop trying to prove themselves. There comes a point in life when one has to face the question, "Okay, I've proven I'm smart. Now, what am I going to *do* with my smarts? How am I going to contribute?" Leela had imprinted on the roar of a packed opera house. She was accustomed to acclaim and an intense performance high. So she kept looking for that same kind of acclaim and stimulation in her series of jobs. Phi Beta Slackers all share this dynamic; they all have their equivalent of that packed opera house. Top grades. Awards. Prestigious jobs.

Getting off the tour bus means going without that applause for a while.

Two months after our first meeting, Leela's firm laid off another round of people. She accepted a buyout and joined the unemployed. It was for the best; she imagined this would be the chance to finally figure out where she really belonged. She promised that she would write me at the end of the summer and explain what she'd figured out. I didn't ask her to make this promise. I didn't think she had a chance of figuring it out in three months. But she made the promise out of some need to look like she was the master of her destiny.

In late September, after I left several messages, wondering how she was doing, an e-mail finally arrived.

I must admit I have been feeling unusually empty in the attempt to send you a written update. I've been staring at what feels like a blank canvas depicting my unconventional journey with no words to make sense of my current crossroads. Ironic that others find my journey "extraordinary," yet right now I'm at a loss for how to put it all together. I wish there was a stronger lexical thread between the paragraphs of my life. Or at least one more visible to me now as I search for that dream job. I dream of work that would put it all together and allow me to wake up every morning totally jazzed about what I'm doing. Ugh . . . how I wish it would fall into my lap. Perhaps I could then write you an update that would fit neatly into your storyline, which I'm assuming believed that this unconventional road is, in fact, the high road.

We met for lunch a few days later. "Why do you think I wanted a neat story line?" I asked.

"Well, if you're going to write it, it has to hang together, doesn't it? It can't just be a crazy scrabble."

"I think I'll find some themes in your crazy scrabble."

I told her that I thought of her e-mail as a huge breakthrough. She'd given up the need to come across looking brilliant. That's not easy, and once it's done, it's very liberating.

She found her search very difficult. "It's one of the few things in life where being smarter doesn't give you any advantage in finding your answer." She was afraid she'd never find such an answer. "I've definitely felt a level of anxiety and depression I've never had in my life, ever."

She was no longer comfortable with the serial nature of her life.

"I now look at people who've been in one industry for ten or fifteen years, and I look at them with great envy," she said. "I miss that, I yearn for it, and my life feels rootless because I don't have that. More than ever I'm looking for the feeling I had when I danced for eighteen years, and I learned to do something very well and be very dedicated to it. Because that's what gives life stability and meaning, and it's not this hopping around."

One of the things that had led her to hop around was this need for constant stimulation.

"Maybe I shouldn't be looking for highs," she admitted. "Ever since I left Chicago, I've been looking to replace that feeling of being on stage. Maybe I've been looking for the wrong thing."

She was beginning to adapt to the more pedestrian gratifications of life off stage. She had no choice.

Six months later, she'd grown wiser about her search. After a frantic series of informational interviews with people from various careers—which had only increased her anxiety—she stopped expecting the answer to be *out there*. "I finally stopped looking around externally," she said. "I was looking everywhere but inside myself. It really scared me to go there. So much of what I've done has been for recognition or achievement, not really from within."

Leela used to be the kind of person who chased highs. It turned out that it was this low point that changed her, more than any high. She was more grateful and appreciated life's preciousness. She was able to rule out a lot of choices that she couldn't before.

She was starting to see that good chemistry would require not just the right opportunity, but a different attitude on her part.

"You end up searching for something that's not out there," she said. "You have to realize you have to select something and make it work for you. I can't just keep looking for that perfect job—there isn't a perfect job that's going to marry these things I've done and make me happy. That's too *outside* myself. It's going to come from me, *inside,* and from committing to something. I didn't start out on that stage—I worked myself there, I started with the poses and pliés. I've got to start again with the pliés."

Rather than asking "What can I do *next*?" or even "What will make me happy?" she was starting to see the relevant question as "To what can I devote my life?"

She spent more time with a family in East Palo Alto that she mentored. She produced a benefit for a nonprofit that celebrated the partnership between Bay Area artists and business leaders. To make money, she took on piecemeal consulting jobs—kind of like high-level temp work.

One of those short consulting jobs was with Genentech. With her foot in their door, she met people from the marketing department. Medicine had always had a certain gravitas in her worldview. She had very little experience with illness or genomics, but biotech felt weighty and real. Important. Why not make a choice of this, and put her energy into it? She hustled, met with the appropriate people, waited, hoped, crossed her fingers, et cetera, and a couple months later they decided to hire her, as part of an initiative for some "out of the box" hires.

The money didn't compare to what she had earned before. That didn't matter. She was grateful for a paycheck. Besides, she'd long ago learned that money was an arbitrary measure of worth. "The high point of my life, the thing that brought me fame and acclaim, the thing I was by far the best at, paid less than thirty thousand dollars. Then I spend only two years studying business, and suddenly the marketplace says I'm qualified to earn $120,000 a year. Four times as much! Without a drop of business experience! Was I really that different a person? It's absolutely wrong to think money is an objective measure of a person. There's a lot of things you can't put a price tag on."

For years she'd craved a place to carve out as her own. She didn't so much find her choice as finally grow to accept it. It simply had to work itself out, and it did. Many times I wanted to speed the process up, but it really can't be speeded up. The wait was worth it.

BACK TO REALITY

Her first, angry e-mail was only four lines long. Following a subject line that testified "corporate life is not so bad," she took issue with a short rant she had found on my website. "You make it sound like a day job is a cop-out," she chastised. "I have a day job but I'm proud that I made the leap from my dream to reality. I can actually pay my bills, and you know what?—most days that feels good." She gave no specifics, not even her name, and no clues as to where in the country she lived. Something in my gut sensed there was a story here, if I could get its author to reveal more.

We corresponded occasionally for a couple weeks. Slowly came her gender, and then her first initial, W. She wrote generally about corporate life and dream life, without any identifying details. The lack of specificity kept me intrigued. There was a reason for her secrecy: "The path my life took *after* living my dream made me a much happier, more interesting person. But people only want to hear about the early years. They're not interested in my life now. So I hide the early years, so people can discover the real me."

Slowly she trusted my sincerity of interest in the "real" her. She agreed to be profiled if it might help bring this point of view to the book. Her name was Wendy Jones. I wouldn't have to get on a plane to come see her—a drive across the Golden Gate Bridge would get me there. She worked in Marin and lived in Sonoma. She was forty-two.

She grew up in Albuquerque. Her father was a secret service agent, her mother a schoolteacher who earned $30,000 a year. They've been married fifty years. Wendy was one of four children. In high school, her dream was to travel. She wanted to be a flight attendant, but back then there were height requirements, and Wendy was too tall: five ten. All her friends and boyfriends were shorter, so she stooped and slouched. Her parents sent her to a finishing school to improve her posture. The series of classes ended with a trip to New York for a modeling convention and competition at the Waldorf-Astoria hotel. She had put up with the classes because she wanted to see New York.

Out of thousands of teens at the convention, Wendy won. The prize was to be a modeling contract with the Ford agency. Instead, Wendy snuck out to head down to the fashion district. She wanted to see the building at 550 Seventh Avenue; all the famous clothes designers had their studios inside. She was standing in the building's lobby, soaking up the atmosphere, when the lobby guard asked, "Are you here for the go-see?" Unsure what a "go-see" was, she nodded. He sent her up. On the elevator was a very distinguished-looking man. He too asked her, "Are you here for the go-see?"

"Yes," she said.

"What agency are you with?"

"Ford," she tried.

"Ford doesn't have runway models," he said doubtfully.

He got off at her floor and went through a door. She went to the receptionist.

"Name?"

"Wendy Jones."

"You're not on the list."

The receptionist's phone rang. She listened, hung up. "Go through that door."

She entered a showroom. Another man told her to get dressed. She changed into a dress and shoes.

"Walk!" boomed a voice. It was the man from the elevator.

She walked. Clumsily. Terribly.

"No! Follow me! Like this!" He demonstrated, she followed.

"Okay then," he said after a moment. "We're hiring you. Here's the booker at Zoli." Zoli was the agency for runway models. "It only pays two thousand a week." He told the other girls to leave.

Wendy didn't know what she was hired for. It turned out that she had been hired as an in-house model, and that the man on the elevator was Oscar de la Renta. She was only eighteen. That was the beginning of a fifteen-year career as a show model, working continuously in New York, Europe, and Japan.

She wasn't gorgeous, and she couldn't walk, but those things could be fixed with training and makeup. She was tall and slender, the perfect size, able to wear any designer's clothes off the rack. She was that size naturally, without any dieting or exercise. And for the first five years of her career, that was the reason she stayed busy. "They just wanted girls that could fit in the clothes," she said.

Her dream came true suddenly, and too easily, and without any hard work at all on her part. For that reason, she never felt that she deserved her success. It was a fluke, determined entirely by her genes, and not an accomplishment.

Very often we don't value the things that come easiest to us. It's the things we work for, the things we earn, that we treasure most.

Her life had almost no similarities to a conventional life. She never owned a car. She didn't keep an apartment in New York. Everything was taken care of for her. Her agents in different markets arranged her travel and bookings. She lived entirely in hotel rooms and studios owned by designers. Maids cleaned up. She never had to cook for herself. It was impossible to have genuine relationships because she was constantly leaving town. She learned to be a loner. She traveled light, without any belongings. Modeling wasn't her dream (traveling was), but she got caught up in the lifestyle and the narrow world of fashion.

"I met amazing people and thought I was more important than I actually was," she said.

Eventually she learned to manage some of her career rather than cede control to others. She wasn't the genius in the family, but she'd managed to squeeze in four quarters of college. She saved a fair amount of her money. She watched models do drugs and behave badly, but never fell into that hole. Some of her success she earned simply by not making bad choices when everyone else did. She was dependable, and became sought-after by designers.

Wendy told me all this in a very matter-of-fact tone, without any of the self-indulgence that signals someone living in their past. She wasn't overly proud and wasn't hoping any of this would impress me. We were having lunch after spending the morning at her office. I waited for her to talk about how she left that life behind, and then prodded her to do so.

"You don't want to ask me more about those years?" she asked.

"Is there something you think is important you didn't tell me?"

"No, just—" She looked at me again. Maybe I was for real. "Usually people want to hear, you know, all the dirt. What designers I worked for, what they were like, did I sleep with any of them. Or what such-and-such famous model was like. Who took drugs. What hotels we stayed in. All the sleazy glamorous stuff. And then people assume I made a lot more money than I did, and so they figure something must have happened that I'm not rich and retired now."

"Were you famous?"

"Not like runway models today are famous, and never like print models are famous, but yes. Enough to be recognized on the street occasionally."

I watched her. I was trying to sense what lingering effect all those years had. "Are you still a loner?" I asked.

"I'm trying not to be, but yes."

"Do you have a boyfriend?"

"I want to, but no. I'm dating."

"Is it hard to have a genuine relationship now? Like, do you push away, need to be by yourself?"

"Maybe a little. But I'm aware of it. My parents are my role model, and I often feel that no relationship in my life can compare to theirs. Half a century together and they're still on their honeymoon."

"What about money? Have you adjusted to the value of a dollar?"

"I've adjusted to paying my own way, which I didn't have to do before. But I never lost touch with the value of a dollar. My mother was a schoolteacher."

She talked a lot about her family, including her brainiac sister and younger brother, who was a police officer in Dallas when he was killed on the job. He was twenty-five. Wendy was thirty-one and in Europe at the time. She'd wanted to leave modeling for a while, having recognized that it wasn't fun anymore, but she was afraid to leave because she had no skills. She couldn't even type. What would she do? When her brother was killed, she quit immediately and moved back to New York, where she was closer to her family. She had many offers to come back to work, but wasn't interested. Modeling had kept her from spending time with her brother. It was tainted in that way. She couldn't be around it. Unsure what else to do, she said yes when a friend of hers, a photographer, asked her to represent his work. Soon she agented several photographers to catalogs.

After a year, not feeling better, she finally started seeing a grief counselor. To help her get on with her life, she left New York, which was too steeped in the modeling business. She moved to the West Coast, and then, because catalogs and photographers were still a connection to her past, she left them behind to be a recruiter. She worked on commission for different "chop houses," cold-calling workers. She worked her way up to respectable placement agencies. Two years ago, she was hired into the human resources department at Restoration Hardware, where she is now the director of recruiting for their corporate division. She had offers from other companies for up to $20,000 more in salary, but wanted to work here.

"It was my very first 'real' job," she said. "And I was forty years old." She was completely unready for the office politics and the weird corporate rituals, like performance reviews. "I'm here every day, working beside my boss, and suddenly one day we have to turn and look at each other in judgment. When you're not used to it, it's very demeaning." She got over it. Her boss has become her true mentor and friend.

"I've never been happier than in the last two years," she said.

Wendy gave me an extensive tour of Restoration Hardware's headquarters. Every product they sell really appeals to the nesting instinct. But it's more than that. Plato believed in Forms, these categorical ideals that exist in our head. Any chair we sit in is compared by our minds to what we mean by "chair," or what we mean by "bedspread," which in combination come to represent what we mean by "home." Restoration Hardware's products are straight out of our Platonic ideal of home. They're timeless. They conjure home. The more I soaked in, the more I saw Wendy's company as a temple of domesticity. It was not surprising that after fifteen years of never having an apartment or a car or a steady relationship, she had chosen this place of worship to immerse herself in, as a sort of training course in the simple pleasures of home.

As director of recruiting, she doesn't look for people whose dream is to work for Restoration Hardware. "Most people fall into things," she said. She's looking for the right fit, not credentials. "Degrees are small-minded," she insists, reminding me she doesn't have one. She hires from other industries. One of the reasons her work is so meaningful is she's sort of rescuing drifting souls like the one she used to be and giving them a home. Or at least a work home.

"Do people here know who you were?" I asked.

"Not at first. I was afraid of not being taken seriously. On my résumé, and in conversation, I would tell people that I traveled internationally on behalf of Bill Blass, Calvin Klein, and other designers. Most people assumed that was a fancy way of saying I was a sales rep. Three months into this job, I was outed. A banker was meeting with the CEO, and he saw me in the halls. He was shocked to see me, asked why I'd left modeling. Right in front of the CEO and CFO. Everyone in the company knew within half an hour."

I said, "And now you've got the guts to let me out you publicly."

"It's not something I want you to do, but I recognize it's part of doing this with you."

"What's changed?"

"I'm proud that I've made it back to reality. Most models work until they stop getting bookings and their only option is to marry some wealthy man."

Last December she was in Union Square when one of the women handing out perfume samples asked, "Are you Wendy Jones?" Wendy realized they used to model together. The look in the woman's face was one of deep shame and embarrassment; she tried to pretend she wasn't really just a perfume model, considered the lowest form of modeling. "I'm just doing this as a favor to a friend," she said. Soon the word spread, and Wendy got calls at her office from out-of-work models hoping for a job. They had no skills, not even résumés. They were unhireable.

"It was a defining moment for me," Wendy said. "I'm a very happy person. I wish I could say that they seem happy. I was proud of myself, maybe for the first time in my life. That was the first time I feel I really accomplished something in all these intervening years."

Among the many models she worked with, she knows of only two others who have gone on to successful second careers. One's a writer and the other an antiques dealer.

Wendy's been in her place in Sonoma for twenty-five months straight, which is a new record for her, by four months. "I still have that itch for the gypsy lifestyle," she admits. For the last nine years, she's been hauling around a bunch of taped-up boxes. They're full of old portfolios and mementos of her brother. She avoided opening them for so long that she came to think of them as Pandora's boxes.

"Six weeks ago, I finally unpacked."

"How's it feel?"

She answered by repeating words that came to her last weekend, when she bumped into the photographer she used to work with. "What happened to you?" he asked. "You just disappeared." She explained her transition and added, "As a model I was always just existing day to day. Now I'm truly living my life."

To me, she added, "That's really how I feel. I'm truly living my life."

"What did your old photographer friend think of that?"

"We went out for drinks. We laughed about old times. At the end of the night he said, 'It's great to see you've cracked the code.' "

Her past is resurfacing all around her. Talking to me is a way to confront it and no longer hide. We'd come a long way in a few weeks from her first e-mail.

"You were really mad at me when you wrote that, weren't you?"

"I felt like you were bashing my choice of lifestyle on your website."

"I'm going to soften that rant," I said. "Rewrite it a little. I think you were right to call me on it."

The subtext to our conversations was the question, "When should I make peace with my ambition and settle down?" The one feeling everyone in this book has experienced is of missing out on life. For some people, this recognition leads them to pursue a dream; for others, it leads them to let the dream go. Sometimes that's the wisest choice. I'm not just paying those words lip service—I've seen both sides of chasing dreams.

I mentioned earlier that my father had put his company through bankruptcy. He had grown up in the insurance industry, but in the late seventies he got the entrepreneurial bug, borrowed from a bank at 20 percent interest, and purchased a thirty-employee light-industrial company that refurbished telephones. He ran it well and loved it, but after a few years the Justice Department succeeded in breaking apart AT&T. AT&T, in turn, broke all of its subcontractor contracts. My dad no longer had a contract with his biggest customer, and his company plunged into bankruptcy, a long and arduous process that almost took our house and car. Could he have jumped back on the entrepreneurial horse again? Sure. But should he? He didn't like the feeling of total loss of control. He didn't like the temper that rose up in him. He didn't like not being able to sleep at night. He hated the feeling that he couldn't provide for his sons. He recognized that his psychological makeup was not a good fit for failing. We all must ask this test question if we are considering chasing a dream: Am I the kind of person who will find fulfillment even if I fail? It's easy to be a magnanimous guy if the coin lands on heads. But to play a game of chance means you have to be capable of handling tails. Going to court that summer was such a terrible experience for my father. He saved himself by using his afternoons to do something his heart told him to do. He took a Coast Guard training course and earned his skipper's license. At the end of the summer, he skippered a ninety-six-foot-long, 1929-built wooden passenger vessel all the way up to Alaska. It was his salvation. He eventually decided, I think rightly, to go back to selling commercial insurance. He'd always been a great insurance broker, and he learned in this time of crisis that he probably wasn't cut out for managing more than small teams of people. In any big firm, if you're good at doing the work, you get promoted and don't do the work anymore. My dad liked being the one who did the work. He told his firm that was where he fit. He had the awareness to recognize where he was most productive. And now, in his retirement to horse ranching, he's found in himself a sweetness and thoughtfulness that he never expected.

Know Thyself

31 ||| New Person, Same Job?

A DIFFERENT KIND OF HARD WORK

Her Volvo wagon swung to the curb in front of the Louisville Public Library's main branch. I got in, and she drove toward Cherokee Park. A summer rain threatened. She wore sandals, khakis, a striped prep shirt, and a silver choker necklace. On the backseat rested that week's reading: library hardcover editions of Frank Owen's *Clubland* and Mary Roach's *Stiff*. She devoured a couple books a week during her two years of soul-searching. She'd also spent many hours with a therapist, who had been incredibly helpful in getting her to let her real self out. The therapist at one point suggested she try to express herself through art. In the back of the Volvo she'd brought along her most significant self-portrait: on black chalkboard, actual sized, the white-dashed outline of a person—like from a murder scene, *the body fell here.* Her arms were crossed above her head, and bloodied nails held her wrists to the spot. Twine then circled the board, knotted in small bow ties around the bloodied nails, invoking several possibilities.

I asked, "Why the dotted line?"

"To me, it suggests she doesn't know where her boundaries are. It begs the question 'Who belongs here?' "

"Sometimes twine is used to wrap presents in that way. She's being offered, even as she's being crucified."

This complexity appealed to her, though she wouldn't reveal if she had intended it.

Complexity had replaced simplicity, and in that ambiguity there was an outlet for whatever bubbled up. She enjoyed being open to interpretation.

Last week, her therapist said, "You don't have to come back anymore. Things are going well for you."

"It was like I graduated," she told me, finding it kind of funny.

Her two years of netherworld—of purgatory, of in between—were about to end.

In Cherokee Park, we walked out to a shelter overlooking the forest.

"Did you get the call?" I asked.

"Yeah, I got the call about an hour ago. I got the job. I start in three weeks."

"Congratulations."

"Thank you."

It seemed important to be in Louisville the day she got the job. But this moment didn't live up to that expectation. The mood wasn't celebratory. We knew it was sort of a gamble to go back to her former employer, one she had nicknamed "Corporate America." She'd been there for several years and proved herself a fabulously successful corporate warrior. But that bottom-line mind-set was no longer her mind-set. That go-getter culture of long workdays and hitting the bars every night with her coworkers had robbed her of something important. Or maybe she had only herself to blame. Sometimes, people use their work addiction to avoid genuine emotion. Work becomes a dam, holding back what wants to naturally flow. If you're afraid of what might come out, you work harder to beat it back, same as people who drink to forget.

She'd assumed that her period of self-examination would culminate in a major career change. She figured she'd turn into a social worker or therapist. (To pay bills during the past two years, she'd held several day jobs in which her ego and identity were uninvolved.) Then, over the last couple months, her intuition had steered her back to the place she'd left. Knowing herself was its own reward, she'd realized, and didn't have to be reflected in a new occupation.

Like the dark clouds that rumbled overhead, one question hung over the afternoon: When she returned to that corporate culture, could she still be herself?

Her name is Evan Hambrick. She was thirty.

She surveyed the clouds. Unintimidated, she asked, "Should we take a walk?"

In Corporate America, she had been a financial auditor and internal consultant, squeezing divisions for more profit. She bossed people around, acting like the expert. She transferred between divisions, including stints in New York and Hong Kong for two years, before settling in Cincinnati so she could be closer to home.

One day she made plans to attend her younger brother's dress rehearsal for an upcoming play. He was a senior down in Lexington. The play didn't start until 8 P.M. She would finish work early, drive down, and make it in time. At 5 P.M., she was summoned to a conference call. The call droned on endlessly. Evan watched the clock, panicking, suffocating. She snuck out.

Her brother and fellow students had adapted a book to the stage. The book was Frank X. Walker's *Affrilachia,* about the African-American experience in the Appalachian mountains of Kentucky. The students danced, had a good time, improvised. Evan had never seen her brother's work before. How talented he was!

"They seemed so free, so spirited and happy. I wanted a taste of it. And that was it. My eyes were opened. Seeing him, I knew I couldn't do this kind of work anymore. I went in and quit the very next day. With no prospects or plans for the future."

I asked, "Did you really just quit? Cold?" I'd found that people used this phrase when it was often more complicated.

"I told them I had some personal issues going on. They told me if I went to therapy, I could take a leave of absence. I had no intention of going back. But I thought the therapy would be good for me."

Evan was aware that she'd mistook her career for her life. So in Louisville she built a life with plenty of room—room to read, room to socialize, room for love (there'd never been time for love!), room to learn about her roots from her parents, room to build a tighter bond with her parents, room for complexity and ambiguity, room to exercise regularly. Room to take classes in art, psychology, and writing. Most of all, it was a life with room for emotional closeness and introspection. The kind of life in which her career was going absolutely nowhere, the kind of life that

MBAs often sneer at, the kind of life that might provoke the comment "You want to find yourself? Look in the mirror! Now get back to work!"

Her father had been devastated when she left Corporate America. He often woke her mother in the night, confused, worried for their daughter. He was from Alabama in the Jim Crow era. He'd left college and become a railroad machinist, building axles for railcars. He coached his daughter to choose activities not because they're fun, but because they make sense. Get a degree in business, not political science. You will not fail, there is no alternative. He drilled into her, "People will always be looking at you. So you have to stand up and be a good example *at all times,* or you will confirm their suspicions. We have to work twice as hard." She felt she owed it to her race; she owed it to a long line of people who had sacrificed, a line beginning with her parents and stretching a long way back. She fulfilled their hopes, but in proving the corporate world should (and could) be color blind, she'd blinded herself to all the parts of life that didn't contribute to the bottom line.

So maybe Corporate America wasn't to blame? The job might have crowded out the rest of life, but maybe she let it do that. Maybe she'd *wanted* it to do that. A demanding job is sometimes the safest place to hide from your true feelings. She'd always worked as a way of suppressing anger, worked so as to feel needed, worked so as to feel accepted. Maybe she'd created her own experience at Corporate America. Maybe it wasn't her boss, it wasn't her coworkers.

Sometimes people don't need a new profession, they just need a better life outside work. So often, we use the demands of our job as an excuse for not having that life. The truth is, we're afraid of rejection from would-be friends, our relationships with our family are strained, we don't feel cool enough, we don't think we quite belong. Meanwhile, our work is always happy to have us. It's easy, emotionally, even as we take pride in how supposedly "hard" we have to work. It's far more threatening to slow down and listen to needs that have been ignored.

If you ask the wrong question, you'll get the wrong answer. Leela de Souza found fulfillment when she stopped asking what would make her happy and instead asked, "To what could I devote my life?" Evan Hambrick stopped looking for her needs to be met entirely by her career and realized the answers she'd been looking for were in her personal life.

Two months ago, she began interviewing at various companies. Her litmus test was how they responded to the two-year gap in her résumé. If they accepted it and looked past it, then that was cool. If they couldn't understand why a person would need some time off, forget them. Several companies failed the test. One interviewer at an accounting firm was so upset by the gap that he called her at home that night, trying to get her to justify what she'd done with her time. His tone was accusatory, as if he was offended. "Why, again, would you do this?" he asked repeatedly. Evan was so disheartened, she gave up, and wrote me that she wasn't going back to the corporate world. She was going back to school . . . she was going to figure out where she really belonged, once and for all. . . .

When I got her letter, I worried that in some way I was an influence, a breeze of wind, inspiring this vow of new direction. I hadn't said anything overtly, but was my presence in her life (albeit only as a pen pal) *implicitly* encouraging her to leave the corporate life? I reread our four months of letters. If anything, I had leaned the other way: I had repeatedly suggested that it was perfectly okay to reenter corporate life. My letters had been intentionally bland, apolitical. Careful only to follow, never lead. So I was honestly relieved when she wrote back a couple weeks later and admitted she'd simply panicked. Other interviews had gone much better, particularly one with her old employer.

In the lobby, she almost turned around and walked out. Then she went upstairs. "I met people, and it was a lot more diverse than I remembered it," she recounted. "There were a lot of people I hoped could be my friends—people I would have looked right past two years ago. They didn't have a problem with my time off. They accepted my explanation and moved on. I know it's still going to be a challenge; the hours are long. But they're a lot more tolerant than I used to believe. I'm going to be a lot more tolerant myself. I feel like I can return to Corporate America as a kinder, gentler, more self-aware individual."

She'd put the need to reinvent her career behind her. "I guess I believed that only people who risk it all and do a career one-eighty have real stories to tell. Yet, over time, I've realized that my real goals are modest: to buy a home like the ones I run and drive past every day, find a partner with whom I can share my life, and work at a job that challenges my mind without destroying my soul. These wishes seem so *ordinary*. Perhaps that's okay."

It certainly was. But would it be okay with her employer? Were they going to tolerate her intention to live a real life? During her interview, she'd been asked if she could handle the inevitable long hours.

"And how did you respond?" I asked.

"I told them, 'I'm used to it.' "

"You told them what they wanted to hear."

"Enough to make it a nonissue."

"Are you scared that's going to be a problem?"

"My mother is."

Who wasn't? I wanted her wish to be fulfilled. I wanted her return to Corporate America as the prodigal daughter to be the end of the story. I tried to ignore the obvious question: *Why had she chosen a job (again!) that clearly didn't want her to have a personal life?* Maybe she believed she could change the culture.

Evan described her first three weeks back on the job as some of the most frustrating weeks of her life. Though she clocked sixty hours a week, it wasn't enough for her boss, who demanded her staff ask permission before going to lunch, and who complained when Evan left at 6 P.M. to meet friends for dinner. The old Evan would have simply accepted these rules. But the new Evan couldn't be silent. The tension culminated in a shouting match with her boss, and then a few days later, Evan went to human resources. In the mornings, in the shower, it was hard not to cry. She wrote, "I want my life and my happy demeanor back!" Yet she recognized that part of her just didn't want to grow up.

She hung in there, and the situation improved. It didn't seem like it would—she second-guessed herself several times—but over the next three months she made it work. She didn't change the culture, but she made it clear she wasn't going to drink the Kool-Aid again. She found a comfort level, even with her manager. She liked being "the alternative one" among the business conservatives. She would never say "This is where I belong," but she was okay with that. On her list of Things to Worry About Constantly, her professional situation no longer ranked high.

The theme for this section is exactly Evan's conundrum. The four people whose stories follow are all practical people—or maybe the better way to say it is, like Evan, they all began as practical people yet dared to look inward, into the murky terrain of their own psyches. They then struggled over what to do with their newfound understanding—was an attitude change enough, or was a life change necessary?

32 ||| My New Start-Up

When the New Economy imploded, it took more than six months for the stubborn deniers to admit their hoped-for quick rebound was nowhere in sight. The techies were starting to acknowledge the solution to their problem was not to retreat from rocky start-ups to sturdy Ciscos, or to climb up the food chain from founding companies to funding them, or to hop from dot-coms to telecoms. No sector was immune. It was not all going to be fine. Friends of mine had to can their friends, and then they were canned too.

If they were lucky enough to score a new job, it was no longer dressed up in this hubbub about changing the world, or taking down evil Microsoft, or whupping the Fortune 500. It was a paycheck. Employed or not, rich or poor, winner or loser—how they defined themselves and what gave their life meaning was going to have to change.

They weren't well equipped for this turn inward. Accustomed to being able to conquer challenges quickly, they discovered that making this change was a lot harder than they had anticipated. I have a lot of stories to share, but none portrays this drama better than George Milano's. The Internet boom was in his past, but the way it had taught him to think was harder to shake.

George is thirty-eight, with curly Mediterranean black hair, purposeful in his mannerisms, polite. He's having one meaningful conversation a day, and in his determination to fulfill that goal, he was willing to risk his pride and image by admitting to me his concerns. He's been reading Francis Fukuyama's *Trust* and Robert D. Putnam's *Bowling Alone*. He was concerned about community, which he feared had been lost in the last three decades, or maybe in the last three years, a time during which he'd also lost his one romantic love and his closest friend and a good deal of money. It had humbled him. He didn't know where to turn.

George shares a two-bedroom rented apartment on the tiptop of Potrero Hill. It's spotlessly clean and uncluttered by the usual knickknacks one accumulates. From the couch tucked into the bay window of the living room, he looks down on the South of Market industrial neighborhood that was home to so many dot-coms, with the skyline of old money downtown rising up behind it. He can see right into the baseball park's center field, and he can tell if Bay Bridge traffic is backed up. The view pans from Antioch in the north to Fremont in the south. Fantastic perspective, and it was perspective George needed when he settled into this couch after leaving start-ups forever. For two weeks straight he hung out in his pajamas reading Stephen Ambrose's *Citizen Soldiers* and watching the ten-segment World War II documentary *The World at War*. It was the only thing he could relate to. Battle.

I'm not sure the war analogy is deserved, but it was customary for dot-commers to borrow the heavy-handed language of timeless dramas to describe how intensely they felt about their business machinations. "The last year was hell," George said, as if he might roll up his leg and show me a napalm burn. "I saw an ugliness in human character that destroyed my faith in my common man." It was a raging bonfire of greed, a sick and disgusting chase to get rich and get out. All propriety had been tossed aside as his employees sensed this was their last chance to score big before the inevitable crash. The start-up George founded, Statement, was tearing itself apart faster than it could build itself up. George hired an office manager; after six weeks she demanded a promotion, and wanted it effective *that day*. The week some very interested venture capitalists came in for a demonstration, his vice president of engineering effectively cut bait and ran to a competing start-up, taking ten members of his engineering staff with him. The VCs backed out of the deal. George hired a new engineering VP, but he was no better. Several times he blackmailed George and kept the code hostage. He refused to finish the programming for a major milestone unless he was given some of George's equity. It seemed like every high-level employee was gunning to bump George off and take the CEO spot. George was so frustrated that he decided to sell the company.

The bonfire didn't burn out; it only intensified. George found a buyer, a company called Digital Insight. They put an offer on the table. The offer was dependent on the engineering staff staying on board for two-and-a-half years. One of these key engineers was a young Russian immigrant, Vlad. He was set to make $800,000 in the sale. You would think a Russian immigrant would think $800,000 was a lot of money and be grateful. God bless America. But that wasn't enough for him. He threatened to bad-mouth the software in due diligence if he didn't receive a bigger cut.

"But you're going to make $800,000!" George argued. "Aren't you happy with that? Isn't that enough?"

Vlad blew him off. He said, "For only eight hundred grand, I can't get motivated."

"Can't get motivated!"

"On the free market I'd earn $150 an hour. That's $22,000 a month. In two and a half years, $660,000. So $800,000 doesn't impress me. You have to do better."

The one gratifying thing about building Statement was George's relationship with his close friend, Jason. They'd known each other since working at a previous start-up. They'd gone to Mardi Gras together. Jason was in his early twenties, and he was going to make $2 million in the sale. He wanted more. He wanted some of George's shares. In the final month of closing, George lost a third of his shares in order to get the deal done. But Digital Insight's shares were dropping in value too, and the lost time was costing everyone. In the months between initial offer and closing, the purchase price dropped by half. On the last day, after the paperwork was signed, Jason told George, "I never want to see your face again."

George's father had founded a home medical supply business in Pittsburgh with roughly one hundred employees—big enough to be stable, but small enough that George's father knew everybody by name, knew their kids, loaned them money, took care of his people. His father was a patriarch at that company and in the city. When he went out on the town, his father would run into customers he had helped, people he had given medical supplies on credit. When his customers died, George's father always attended their funerals. George started cleaning shelves in the warehouse at the age of nine for twenty-five cents an hour. He drove delivery trucks in high school, and made sales at doctors' offices nights and summers until he graduated from Stanford. His father wanted George to take over, but George didn't want the benefits of nepotism. He wanted to make a name for himself. He had entrepreneurism in his blood. Statement was George's third company; though neither of the others were big successes, it didn't matter. Start-ups allowed a kind of open-book collectivism, a chance to work with your friends and share a passion. His first two start-ups had that feeling. But at Statement, all that had been good turned bad.

Nevertheless, George had walked away from the sale with $9 million. He knew he deserved no sympathy. He never had to work again. After two weeks on the couch, it was time to buck up and get on with his life. But do what? Start another company? He couldn't stomach it. Besides, that's all he had ever done. It was time to do something different.

So he thought, "Well, I should do some good in the world. I know how to get things done and to motivate people. Maybe I can apply what I've learned."

For a couple years, George had mentored his housecleaner's son and occasionally gone to his high school as his "parent or guardian" when his mother couldn't. George had always been aghast at the poor quality of the boy's education but never lifted a finger to change it. Why not? Sometimes the call comes as anger.

He went down to Eastside Preparatory School, a successful charter school in East Palo Alto. They had an entrepreneurship club extending from their economics class. George volunteered to help the club. The school asked him to fund-raise instead. Okay. George had the best of intentions, but the culture shock was severe. Internet culture taught him to find inefficiency repulsive, but nonprofits do not exist to maximize efficiency. Every time a meeting was unnecessarily canceled, or dragged on too long, George got frustrated. The executive director of the school, Chris Bischof, was a charismatic leader who raised money wherever he spoke. George revered Bischof, but couldn't put him in a PowerPoint presentation. Without Bischof the pitch was unarticulated. In the language of the Internet, Bischof didn't *scale*. One of the Internet axioms was, "It's easier to raise $100 million than it is $10 million." People want to believe and invest in big ideas. Why not a whole chain of Eastside Preps, doing good throughout the country's inner cities? But charter schools are busy saving the world one kid at a time. They ignored George's input. He had never been treated this way.

George wasn't famous on the Internet scene, but he was well enough known that at every party someone recognized him. He had earned notoriety and respect, which translated into people listening to him and getting done what he wanted done.

"I was spoiled by my recognition, my power, my ability to make things happen," George said.

He realized nobody in education reform was going to listen to him unless he met them halfway. For half a decade he'd been looking at the world through Internet glasses. While he held those values dear, he reluctantly had to shake them.

To begin this conversion, George decided to discover his roots. George's grandmother had come to Pittsburgh from Italy when his mother was young, and they had never been back. George decided to meet his long-lost cousins and aunts, who lived in the small impoverished city of Eboli, down near Naples.

George spoke some Italian from studying in Siena a few years earlier. So he called a cousin out of the blue and told him he would arrive at the train station on such and such day and time. George made a hotel reservation too, thinking, These people don't even know who I am. He didn't want to impose. He flew over there, took the train, and was met at the station by the cousin. And another cousin. The cousins fought over who got to drive George around. In the next three days, he was introduced to twenty-five households. He'd go from one house to another without a break. Never made it to his hotel. They fought over whose house he ate in, who he sat next to at the table, and whose bed he slept in. George had never seen such an incredible outpouring, such love, simply because he was *family*. The only thing he had in common with these people was their genes. Many of them were only semiliterate. George thought he knew what family meant—but he found it impossible to comprehend the depth and power of the family bond in his relatives.

In San Francisco, a man was measured by his ability to raise millions of dollars. Eboli was still recovering from an earthquake that struck in 1980, so nobody had any money. In Eboli, a man is measured by how dutiful he is to his mother. In Italy, 50 percent of the men live within one kilometer of their mothers. One of a man's duties is to give his mother grandchildren. So on the doorstep of every household, George would be introduced with a snicker:

"This is your long-lost American cousin, grandson of Consulata Manzione. He is thirty-six, *unmarried!*—and lives *five thousand* kilometers from his mother."

What a different way of looking at the world!

On the way back from Eboli, George spent some more time in Siena. He was fascinated with the Palio, a medieval horse race that's reenacted every spring in Siena. George wanted to buy a big house on the parade route as a family vacation home. He had the money, he was ready to make an offer. But you know how Italians are! *Come on over, we'll have some espresso and talk it over.* And George would go over for coffee and they'd chat and never get around to the paperwork. *Hey, meet my friends!* George was ready to wire the money, but he finally gave up.

So . . . being a do-gooder didn't work out, and his relatives thought he was a freak . . . what else could he do? The words of his cousins kept ringing in his ears: *never been married.* It was worse than that. George had never been in love. Not really. Girlfriends sure, but never truly, madly in love. He would love to be married and have kids.

So last February, George bought a personal ad on Match.com. Met a venture capitalist right away, and they fell madly in love. Inexperienced with these powerful feelings, George figured he was a quick learner. But love isn't like that. Nine women can't have a baby in one month.

Well, George's gut instinct was that she was the one for him. George told her, "You're my new start-up." I know that sounds terribly unromantic, but she was a VC, she knew what he meant: he was going to devote himself to their relationship, 24/7/365. It would be his focus, his passion, the thing he wanted to perfect. She found it endearing. Secretly, he figured they'd be married in less than a year. Tops. Six months wouldn't surprise him.

And?

"I think I scared her off."

"No duh. Why did you ever believe you could come on so strong?"

"She liked it. At first."

"Absolutely. But it takes time to reconcile this new intense lovey-dovey lifestyle with who you were before you fell in love. You have to let that happen naturally. You can't force it."

"That's sort of what she said."

I got a chance to meet her only in passing. They were friends now, and as friends they got to know each other better. Now they realize they were never right for each other. I can't tell if George's heart was broken. I figured it had to be, but he talked about it somewhat matter-of-factly without revealing any emotion.

George had not worked in a year. He'd made valiant first tries at community service, discovering his roots, and falling in love, but I wasn't sure how much he'd really learned. His internet values still lingered. He told me that it was hard to focus on more than one thing, that he was happiest in attack-and-conquer mode. He also said, "I'm a big disbeliever in balance." To him, a balanced life suggested mediocrity. When a friend tells him she's living a more balanced life now, George suspects she simply hasn't found anything she cares enough about to embrace wholly.

He said, "It's hard for me to think about limits."

And a moment later, "I have an appetite for big goals. Reading this stack of books is nice, planning a trip to Kauai is fine, but as goals go, they're too small. I need something meatier."

Even though he vowed never to start another company, he itched for it. Badly. Compared with start-ups, real life felt so *bland*. I thought about how so many other people changed only because they absolutely had to—they saved themselves only when pushed to the brink. George seemed cursed by his nine million dollars. He didn't *have* to change. He had nine million dollars of padding to insulate him from pain.

So what now? He was building on the little he'd learned. His trip to Italy had really affected him. The tightness of their bonds there made him aware of how tenuous our bonds are here. He wanted to do something about the loss of community in our culture. But he couldn't pin down what that something should be. In the meantime, "my goal is to have one meaningful conversation every day," he said.

The next time I went up to Potrero Hill, George was packing for another trip to Eboli. His flight was in the morning. This time he was taking his mother and his sister and her five young children. Friends told him he was crazy to travel all that way with five kids. What a nightmare! Did he have any idea how hard it would be to corral them? Five feeding schedules. Five nap schedules. San Francisco to Pittsburgh. Pittsburgh to Rome. Rome to Naples. Naples to Eboli by train. Shuttles, double taxis. Impossible! They advised him to take two kids now, and bring the other three on his next trip. But George found pride in its difficulty. He wanted to be a dad, he wanted his own family. He would be the father figure on this trip. He would learn what it was like. Anyway, that was the plan.

George got rid of his Internet glasses somewhere on that second trip to Italy. Maybe it was some combination of seeing how Italians view the world and simultaneously how little children see the world that helped him realize his old way of seeing the world was not the only way, or even the best way. He was finally ready to begin the rest of his life. Shortly after he got back, he bought a house a few blocks away from the one he had rented, and he put down his roots. He met another woman and fell in love again, this time for keeps. They live together now.

On the day of September 11, between replays of that morning's tragedy, George read Diane Ravitch's *Left Back: A Century of Failed School Reforms.* TV Screen. Book. TV Screen. Book. That night, his past finally faded away, and George decided to make a career change into education reform. He recognized that this would not be a thing he could solve, rather a problem to devote himself to. He volunteered again at two charter schools in San Francisco and Oakland, and got certified as a high-school-level social studies teacher. He's now at Stanford, earning his master's in education and getting some classroom experience. He hopes to help start charter schools when he graduates.

I tell George's story a lot, and it's usually when I want to push people to be aware what kind of glasses they're wearing. Our surroundings may have changed, but our perspective lags. We all have our ways of looking at the world, and we have to ask, "Am I looking through my own eyes, or am I looking through glasses I don't even realize are there?"

33 ||| Dropping the Watermelon

THE PRACTICAL WAY TO PURSUE THE IMPRACTICAL

Marcela Widrig's blueprint for her life always included best-case scenarios and backup plans. She was a realist. Her passion might have been cultural studies, but she didn't pretend—the jobs were in business, and the entry-level jobs were in sales. So she earned a business degree, but studied languages too, becoming fluent in Spanish, Italian, and French. When it came time for her MBA, she attended Bocconi University in Milan. She honed herself for international sales, and when she graduated she was hired by a big modem manufacturer as their sales director for southern Europe. She loved it. She was based in Barcelona and traveled everywhere. Lisbon! Johannesburg! Prague! She had no pulse for modems, but she was interacting with these cultures, learning each country's style of negotiation, whether they talk business first and then drink, or drink first and then talk business. The pace of business was serene. It allowed her time to really know her clients. Talk always veered to politics or family. She told her friends this was her dream job, what she'd always wanted. She stayed in Barcelona for five years. Then she got a promotion. She was doing so well the company wanted her to cover Asia and Brazil as well. Great! More cultures to learn, more intriguing people to meet.

The catch was, the company needed her to be based in the United States. So Marcela chose San Francisco, which had always struck her as European in its ways. Ha ha.

The culture shock was far worse than when she'd moved to Italy. Most of her frustration was attributable to the Inevitable Cocktail Party Question: "What do you *do*?" She'd been away long enough to forget about this disgusting American custom. She found it degrading and reductive and mercenary. In Europe, nobody asked that question, but here they blasted it at her constantly. It became her "fingernails on the chalkboard." She felt compartmentalized and judged according to how she answered. Sure, she had a cool job, but if she described it poorly, she was pigeonholed. Even if they were impressed, that tainted it, as if she'd learned these languages and studied abroad so she could impress peers at networking events. It drove her crazy.

I think that Marcela was so frustrated by the Inevitable Cocktail Party Question because it confronted her with her choices. She didn't like being challenged because she'd been burying her dissatisfaction, until it drove her to make changes. When I started this book, I thought the Question was a scourge on our society, a contagious mental virus transmitted via verbal exchanges. But I'm starting to see that the Question serves a valuable role. The Question is how we hold ourselves accountable to the opportunity we're given. We live in a rich country, so rich that we're blessed with the ultimate privilege: to be true to our individual nature. Our economy is so vast that we don't have to grind it out forever at jobs we hate. For the most part, we get to choose. And so a status system has evolved that values being unique and true even more than it values being financially successful.

In other words, if you don't like the Question, maybe it's partly because you don't like your answer.

Well, Marcela was able to get away from the question on her travels. But the Internet economy was quickly changing how business was transacted around the world. Its ethos was speed. Forget local color and custom. Get the deal done in a day, fly to another city, do another deal. Or, forget even showing up in person for a meeting—e-mail makes it so easy! All the human contact was gone. The global economy was blurring the world into an impersonalized monoculture. It wasn't interesting anymore.

Marcela didn't recognize this right away. What she noticed was constant fatigue during the day and insomnia at night. Then frequent migraines. Back in Barcelona she'd occasionally gone to this yoga studio, and mixed in with the classes was some Israeli guru's notions about how the body stores unhappiness or fear and manifests it as physical pain. She'd always found that interesting. Marcela knew she was not in sync.

One day she buzzed into Hong Kong and grabbed an express lunch with a client, and then he was shuttling her back to the airport, the whole while droning on about how she should give him exclusive distributorship of the province, yakking too fast, nothing but price, best price, me, me, fast, too fast. He let her off at the curb and she boarded another plane and took her window seat and stared out the porthole at the tarmac and realized what was wrong. "That's it. I cannot sell one more modem," she vowed. But do what? She knew what she wanted: She missed human contact. She wanted to touch people. She thought of that Israeli guru, Grinberg. He had an institute in Switzerland. Wouldn't it be great to study with him? Marcela was too practical, too businesslike, to do anything rash. It was a nice fantasy, but awfully hokey. She kept her job.

Meanwhile, she let the fantasy mature into a hobby. She earned a massage certificate taking classes on weekends. Six months went by before she let friends know what she was up to. Everyone in San Francisco was jumping on the Internet bandwagon and she longed to venture in the other direction, to get physical rather than virtual. Consistent with her character, she planned it out meticulously. On her vacations, she studied at the institute in Switzerland. The classes cost more than an Ivy League graduate degree and required a ton of studying, which helped Marcela feel like she wasn't doing something frivolous, or dropping out for an easy life. She always came back jazzed. She kept promising herself that when she socked away another thousand dollars, she'd quit her job. But she was afraid. She'd always provided for herself. Financial stability was her baseline. Could she really make a living doing bodywork? So she'd save another thousand, and another; she was like a hamster in a wheel. It might never have happened if the guiding hand of fate hadn't intervened. The day after she got back from one of her Switzerland trips, she was laid off. Her company went under. She was thirty-two.

This was her chance to at least *try.* She printed up business cards. She photocopied flyers and tacked them to bulletin boards. She set up a table at the Whole Foods market. She gave away ten-minute freebies, but the customers could tell something wasn't right. Marcela was so scared her stomach hurt, and they could sense it. None of those freebies were turning into paying clients.

She had prepared exactly for this circumstance. This is going to sound like a game of semantics, but the Grinberg method teaches people to *embrace* their fears rather than *avoid* them. American culture coaxes people into states of denial by always saying, "Look on the bright side," or "Don't feel sad." When we put on the happy face, we swallow our fears. This becomes an energy whorl trapped in our bodies, continually pushed down. How the combination of massage and philosophy works to fix that, I'm not really sure. It made perfect sense to me when Marcela explained it, but

I haven't been able to put it back into words without making it sound like I live on an ashram, channeling the spirit of honeybees. In fact, I'm embarrassed even to be telling you this story right now, and I'm afraid you're going to put the book down before it gets too precious. But I'll risk it: Embracing your fears means letting yourself be sad when you're sad, and so the massage is not supposed to make the customer feel better, it's supposed to make the customer feel sad/pain/fear. Does that make sense? I think it's like sad music, which can be wonderful to listen to, and bring about a nice zone of melancholy in which you stop pushing yourself to be perfect.

Let me try again. Carrying this negative energy around is like carrying a twenty-pound watermelon—you can't give a good hug when you've got a watermelon in your arms. It blocks your connections to others. So Marcela needed to let go of her watermelon.

Marcela acknowledged this pain in her gut and this terrible dread that possessed her, and she said back to it, "Oh no, you're not going to stop me." She wasn't going to grant her fears that kind of power over her. She refused to live in fear of the unknown. When she went back to the Whole Foods some weeks later, the clients started rolling in. The watermelon was gone. It took about a year to drop the business suit persona and truly embrace her new profession.

So here's what I wanted to know: Does a solo career in bodywork put you on a downward slide to loosey-goosey-land? That'd be my fear. In fact, I might as well admit that's why I'm telling this story: to confront my own watermelon. My last three books were set in the world of *business,* and suddenly I'm writing about bodyworkers and high lamas? What's my dad going to think? Will *The Wall Street Journal* ever talk to me again? Well, I think we have to cop to that fear, and recognize that finding our calling might get a little internal, but that doesn't mean we're going to wig out.

As for Marcela, her practical side was fully intact. She was drawing up business plans and raising capital for a big studio. She saved a lot of her money, and she kept backup plans in case this didn't work out.

"Do you ever feel isolated?" I asked. "Working alone? I mean, you used to travel the world."

"I get a far more powerful and genuine connection to people now. That's what I *always* wanted—to connect with unusual and interesting people."

"You used to get a sense of importance from being a moneymaker within a big company. Where do you get that now, without a structure around you?"

"I used to need that. I was proud of being the top salesperson and I got satisfaction from succeeding. But when I could see that need was actually hurting me, leading me toward depression, it was no longer so important to be successful in that highly visible and external way."

I asked Marcela if the Inevitable Cocktail Party Question still bothers her today.

"Maybe it's only recently stopped causing me stress."

"What do you tell people when they ask now?"

"I've been doing bodywork for a year and a half now, and only recently have I been able to say that. 'I do bodywork.' "

"Sounds like you're comfortable with that answer."

"I love what I do, and I think it comes across. Now it seems as though I could be nowhere else than right where I am."

"You've always been practical, so are you a different person now? Or are you really the same person, now just doing something different?"

"If you'd come to see me three years ago, you would have met a very different person. I used to be a victim of my circumstances. Most of the time, I thought I had no choice, I had to do what the situation called for, keep going. My pace has slowed down enough now that I see choices, and I make them consciously. That's how you begin to feel like you are in command of your life again—you start making choices consciously, expecting the consequences, not being afraid of them."

I'm often asked some form of this question: "Should I jump into my dream, or should I nurture it slowly, on the side?"

For instance, if pursuing a dream required going back to school, you might wonder whether to quit your job and enroll in school full-time, or take the slow road and attend an occasional night class.

But when I tried to map this general question to the real life stories of those I'd interviewed, the stories didn't work as examples of one strategy or another. Marcela found the practical way to do the impractical thing: she nurtured it slowly for years. But then came the point where she was forced to finally jump. Almost every story had this duality. Which is to say, the question's a bit of a mirage. You'll have to nurture it, *and* you'll have to jump on its back. It takes time. If you want to give yourself a fair chance to succeed, never expect too much too soon.

THE RÉSUMÉ "ME" VS. THE WORK-IN-PROGRESS "ME"

When Nicole Heinrich began writing me, she gave the Official Version of her story, suitable for public distribution. Nicole had lived several of the entrepreneurial adventures young people commonly fantasize about. After graduating from the University of Wisconsin, she flew to Tokyo, Japan, and became a translator for high-powered Japanese executives from the electronics industry. When she'd milked that for all it was worth, she journeyed to Nice, France (her parents were French immigrants), and founded a successful bed-and-breakfast for American tourists called the Cultural Oasis. A few years later, Nicole felt the call for something new, so she returned to Chicago and looked around for a good idea. She saw an opportunity in printer toner, seized it, and cofounded one of the fastest-growing companies in the Midwest. Nicole became known in the industry and around Chicago as "The Toner Queen." She was a regular at all the young society events, like the Shark Ball and the Green Tie Ball.

But that was the Official Version. There was also a real version, waiting to be told.

Nicole began e-mailing me in the spring, and by my own metrics she seemed like a good candidate to profile. She was young (thirty-three) and intrepid and culturally worldly—she was a great role model, wasn't she? But I couldn't get interested. I had a hard time saying why—I guess I couldn't find the hook in her story. I was interested in people who had overcome their weaknesses, and Nicole gave the impression of being a natural-born risk taker.

I challenged her on this, so she kept sending more details of her life, which didn't alter my first impression. Her story was always laced with upbeat philosophizing, as if all one had to do to succeed was never let anything wipe that smile off your face.

Her correspondence had an odd formality. Her very first e-mail had referred me to her bio on her company website, which made her sound like Superwoman. When I asked her to share some stories about the bed-and-breakfast in Nice, she sent back an indented list of the seven positives and the five negatives, but not a single anecdote. I felt like she had trouble communicating her emotions. By then I'd already decided she wasn't going to make it into the book, and I even went to Chicago to visit some other people and didn't call her.

I kept conversing out of basic politeness. I was also curious—why had she contacted me in the first place? Eventually she mentioned she wanted to leave her company to do something else, but she was really unclear about what direction to take. This had been hard for her to admit, because she was classifying herself not as a role model but as a case-in-progress. But I didn't have any answers, and her veneer was too thick for me to see what was really going on, so I let it be.

A couple months later, she wrote me again, conveying that she felt rejected. (That was her first sign of honest emotion.) She wanted to know why I'd decided not to use her story in my book. I'd told her all along why. But in the months of silence I'd started to see real value, not so much in her story, but in how she was learning to tell her story, learning to open up. In the late nineties, there was such pressure to define ourselves by our external accomplishments. What we learned about ourselves got drowned out. How do we tell our story so that it reflects our full depth? I sensed that if Nicole was looking for direction, the clues to build on weren't in the Official Version of her story. They were in the unspoken version.

So at last I telephoned her. The funny thing was, the person I talked to on the phone wasn't at all like the author of those many letters. The real Nicole was sensitive and well aware of her weaknesses and behavior patterns. I asked a lot of blunt questions, which she answered without hesitation. She spoke about her parents' old-world European values. Her mother was very submissive to her father, and Nicole has repeated that subservient pattern in her relationships with men. For instance, in Nice, France, she had fallen in love with a forty-four-year-old doctor, and they had founded the bed-and-breakfast together. Nicole did all the work—the doctor had patients to see—but Nicole let him take 70 percent of the money and leave her only 30 percent. She left France when she discovered he was having affairs with the B&B's guests. She walked away with nothing. When she started the toner company in Chicago, she also had been romantically involved with her cofounder. Again, she did all the work, but she let him keep 85 percent of the equity. He's received all the recognition for the company—he was named Entrepreneur of the Year, it's his name on all the plaques. They haven't been lovers for several years, but she's still never stood up for herself.

She admitted, "On the outside, my story looks like a success, but the truth is I've never been able to shake this low-grade-fever dissatisfaction with what I do. I'm exhausted. I've done all these things to make me happy, and none worked."

I flew to Chicago ten days later. I gave her a hug hello at the airport, which I knew was pushing it because she'd warned me that she used to be uncomfortable with hugs. She still is, but she tried. She's very attractive, sandy blond, about five feet nine, but a bit stiff in her carriage. She has a nice smile but only flashed it when I took pictures of her for my scrapbook. She spoke in full sentences with a Wisconsin accent, listened hard to every question, and frequently remarked, "Oh, that's an interesting question." She was unusual; on one hand, she spoke with perceptive introspection, but on the other hand she believed she didn't quite know herself, and I could feel that this was true.

We spent only a short time at her office, and the rest was spent around town in museums and restaurants, or just walking between places. She drives a metallic green VW Beetle that's a mobile billboard for her employer, audaciously and sadly smothered in huge logos. (No wonder she felt defined by her work.) She owns what's called a "3-Flat" in the Logan Square neighborhood, but she rents out the two best flats and lives on the third floor in what is basically an attic studio. "That's typical of me," she said. "I never think I'm deserving of the best space." This pattern was reproduced at her office. Even though she was the president of the company, she only kept a desk on the sales floor, while the CEO (her former lover) and others had private window offices.

"Nicole, how is it that the observant, selfless person you are is so out of whack with the Superwoman who wrote me all those stiff letters?"

"I've grown accustomed to hiding behind the guise of corporate bitch," she said. She felt it was unsafe to let her feminine side out in business. Admitting weakness can confirm what men used to think about women in the workplace, that they weren't tough enough.

"Yet you're not tough at all. You've said yourself—you let men walk all over you."

"I know." The truth was, she had trouble letting her feminine side out—ever. Not just in business. As if every situation was a business situation. Which it was, I guess, when she was involved with her business partners. "But it's time to ask, 'What do I really want to do with my life?' Not

'What does my corporation need?' or 'What do my business partners want?' "

I asked her when she first realized she needed to look inwards for solutions.

"I'm embarrassed to admit it. It sounds so petty. But a woman at work is from Czechoslovakia, and her relatives make crystal glasses. One day she was accepted by the Home Shopping Network to sell her crystal. And she was so elated. Absolutely joyous. And I was so jealous, because I couldn't even remember the last time I'd felt elated. I couldn't even remember what elation felt like. I hated my jealousy. And I knew I would always be miserable unless I stopped chasing this idea that I'll only be happy *if*—if this, if that."

Nicole started seeing a therapist shortly after. It was a safe place to tell her real story. To talk about her father, the carpenter, and about working for him as a young girl hanging drywall, digging a foundation, setting up a C-wall. And about her mother, who's always urged Nicole to avoid her fate by staying away from men (because they will control you). Nicole had gone to Japan to rebel against their need for safety. While her résumé showcased several successes, it hid some failures, too. She'd been fired three times, but only from stupid meaningless sales jobs. She didn't have much money—less than people might expect.

But these conversations were in private. In public, Nicole was still the "corporate bitch." One day, she went to a big self-help seminar, where a Very Successful Speaker wowed the audience. Nicole had an urge to be like that speaker. Maybe someday she could be a famous speaker. So she found the local chapter of a nationwide organization called Toastmasters. It helps people overcome their fear of speaking in public. They met every other Tuesday, and Nicole took turns getting up to speak in front of the small group. She loved it.

I asked, "Is it possible the real appeal of Toastmasters is just baring your soul in public—not being a famous speaker?"

She'd been wondering if that was her real motive. I'd already become convinced that she reached out to me so I would expose the real her.

Her first Toastmasters speech was of the genre she'd seen at that seminar. She presented herself as successful, and suggested that to become successful, one just needed to take "Baby Steps"—every day, do one thing toward your goal. She envisioned a workbook and an infomercial, the whole package.

The next time, she did something much quirkier. She interviewed a call girl and spoke about the life of hookers. The call girl was a client of one of her business customers; he set up the interview. It shocked the audience, a real downtown corporate crowd that was expecting another rehash of Baby Steps™. The time after that, she interviewed people in a plastic surgeon's office; the surgeon was also one of her customers. The audience was entertained, and even though Nicole wasn't talking about herself, she felt more herself than ever.

Her most recent speech was about what she called her "savior issues." It was her first time being really honest, publicly, about how her relationships with men were sabotaging her career choices.

We ended up sitting in her car outside my motel. She was driving up to Wisconsin to spend the night at her parents. This was winter; the cold was biting without the engine running. We had only minutes left together. I could sense her anxiety intensifying. Nicole had built up a hope that she would come away from this day with some resolve, some direction—some clarity. She knew she needed to leave the toner company. But the only thing that made her happy was public speaking. Did she really have any chance as a motivational speaker? She'd fantasized about it. She'd fantasized about a lot of things over the years. None had made her happy.

"Po, how am I to know the difference? How am I to know this isn't a mirage, like the other changes I've made?"

I said she didn't have to turn the public speaking into a career option to justify its value. It was worthwhile simply because it helped her be honest. "I've been all over the country," I said. "And what I've found is that, when you succeed and you're still unhappy, it's usually because in your heart you're conflicted about how you accomplished it or whether you really deserved it or, most likely, that you're conflicted about what you've presented about yourself to the world."

The way you tell a back story often determines where the story is headed. The past leads to the future, but the past is up for interpretation. By telling and retelling her story—to her therapist, to her Toastmasters group, and to me—Nicole was rewriting her past, opening the door to different futures.

I asked, "What is the one thing you *are* clear about, Nicole?"

She thought about that. "I'm realizing that whatever I do, it has to be one hundred percent *for me*. I get caught up in the current of men, doing their bidding, getting excited by whatever they're excited by."

"Well, what's the simplest way to bring that about? Do you really have to start a whole new career?"

This gave her some comfort. "Toner has been very good to me," she said. Toner was her bedrock. Maybe she didn't need to leave the toner business. Maybe she just needed to leave the company she'd founded with her former savior. Maybe she needed to do it alone.

"Is that *it?*" she asked.

"That's for you to say."

"How *do* you know?"

"Try that story out for a while," I suggested. "Live with it. See if it feels right."

"But what's *right* feel like?" she asked.

"Like it's the true story, not a made-up one."

"Am I supposed to be happy? Content? What should I be looking for?"

"I can tell you what people describe."

"What do they?"

"Like you're living your own genuine life, not someone else's. You stop comparing your life to some other imagined life in your head. Your like or dislike for what you do doesn't hinge on what happened that day, or even that month. The mind chatter stops, without being ordered to stop."

She paused for a long moment, holding on to the image framed by those words. We said good-bye.

In the next months, Nicole quit her job and parted ways with her co-founder. She hoped to negotiate a settlement, but she eventually decided it wasn't worth it to be tied contractually to him. She started her own supply company—it was still toner, but this one was for her, and her alone.

A year later, I returned to Chicago. Her company was doing very well, she said. Her proudest moment was when she discovered that her toner supplier had gone behind her back and started selling toner directly to her biggest customer. He'd thought she would let it slide, sort of "that's business." Instead, she immediately cut him off and found another supplier.

"You're standing up for yourself now," I said.

"Sometimes." She admitted that she'd been in a relationship until recently. It followed the same old pattern. He fell in love with her, thought she was his Perfect Woman, things got serious quickly, and then he real-

ized she wasn't nearly as strong as she first presented herself to be. He'd
berate her: "you're weak, you lied, you're not what I thought."

"So you dumped him?" I guessed.

"No, he dumped *me*. I put up with it. I felt like I'd brought it on myself,
that it was my fault. And it wasn't even like he was a great guy or anything.
He was short and fat and not very nice."

She was clearly dismayed. "The business is going well, and I know it's
good for me to run it alone, but that old urge is *so strong*."

"For some man to come along and take care of things?"

"I thought it would go away. I really have to fight temptation."

I nodded. It's a part of the story I still can't explain, only document.
People repeatedly reverting to old patterns, despite their own wishes. I assured Nicole she wasn't alone.

35 ||| The Once-Angry Minister

A NEW KIND OF SUCCESS STORY

What are we to do with this enhanced story of ourselves? Can what-we-do really be in alignment *that deeply* with who-we-are? I think it can, if we let "I'm going to be truer to myself" be the principle that drives our decisions every time we come to a crossroads. Through trial and error, we are pushed to greater recognition about what we really need. The Big Bold Step turns out to be only the first step.

No story demonstrates this more cleanly than John Butler's.

The first time we talked, John was in his law office in Santa Clara. He's about six feet one, with ruddy cheeks and short auburn hair and a diamond stud in his left ear. He still had the sweeping shoulders and tapered hips that he developed almost thirty years earlier, when he was ranked number two nationally in the 200-meter breaststroke. He's forty-seven now. John was preparing to shut down his divorce mediation practice so that he might become ordained as a minister by the Unity Church. This was a two-year program at Unity's world headquarters in Missouri. John expected to hear any day—and did, the next day, by letter. His application was turned down. The church told him he had "anger issues." John had spent his life struggling to overcome his anger—he thought he *had* overcome it—so this rejection was doubly devastating. It almost extinguished his hopes.

The next time we talked in depth, we met in the Portland, Oregon, airport and traveled down to the southwest corner of the state, to a two-stoplight town called Bandon-by-the-Sea. The Unity chapter in Bandon had given John a six-month contract as their interim minister, even though he was not ordained. Their regular minister was on sabbatical. John was two months into his contract (he'd come back to the Bay Area that week for training), and he absolutely loved it. It had convinced him

232 | Know Thyself

his instincts had been right. "Already I can't imagine not being a minister. I'm not even sure I can go into the ministry training program next year. Why wait two years to do something I've already gotten to do and am good at?"

While this jump from lawyer to minister sounds like one of those radical 90-degree turns, John's been narrowing in on this his whole adult life, and the theme that's brought him here has been consistent. When he was young, he was abrasive and quick to assign blame—and he found work that aligned with that personality. But his life has been a gradual step-by-step away from that hostility. This latest step has brought him to the other end of the spectrum; now he's calm, good-natured, and forgiving.

That journey began shortly after college. He had a personal motive for becoming a lawyer—he'd suffered a great injustice in court. John had started out as a carpet salesman for a building materials wholesaler. They stiffed him on $80,000 in commissions, so he sued. John hired a letterhead-litigator from one of San Jose's best firms to represent him, but the guy did a lousy job and was unprepared. John thought, "If this guy is supposedly the *best,* I'm in the wrong business." He took the LSAT a week later, paid the extra hundred bucks to be FedExed his score quickly, and persuaded Santa Clara's law school to take him at the last minute. He was sitting in property class a week later.

He flashed that same kind of bullheadedness after school, when he joined the San Jose district attorney's office. Within a year he was the lead misdemeanor attorney in the office. His specialty was drunk driving arrests. John went after everyone. He refused to settle. He was feverish with his righteousness. These people had done something *wrong;* they had to be *punished.* If that meant he had to work ninety-hour weeks, he would do it. If it meant he tied up the courtrooms, so be it. There was no excuse for letting offenders plead to a second or third offense as if it were their first offense. There was no excuse for not making them go to AA meetings and fulfill their community service. John became infamous in Santa Clara County courts, and soon no attorney wanted to take him on. They began to plead guilty without a trial.

A couple of things ended this vindictiveness. First, John realized how much of the anger he had for drunk drivers was actually misdirected rage at his father, who drank excessively when John was young. As soon as he made the connection, he no longer felt this hatred for the offenders. His zeal for prosecuting these cases was gone. The district attorney bumped him up to felonies, and his first two cases were ones that the DA wanted to drop because they were too hard to prosecute. But John couldn't do

that. When he saw blame, he would stop at nothing to get a conviction. One was a molestation case involving a patient at a mental institution, the other a child endangerment case. He took both cases to trial and won convictions, but they required an incredible amount of his energy. He could see that if he were to prosecute rapists and murderers, he would never escape from this cycle. His tendency to take these cases so personally, as if *he* were the victim, meant the cases would swallow him. He needed to learn not to take it so personally, something he would never do if assigned to criminal cases. So he quit and spent three months soul searching.

He thought about being a minister, but it was so far-fetched, "It was like a football player suggesting he wants to be a ballerina," John said. John decided to go into bankruptcy law. He got two job offers from firms that specialized in corporate bankruptcy. The first was from a hardball litigation firm that took everything to court. The second was less prestigious and less money, but from a boutique that preferred to negotiate, use workout sessions, and help the debtor's business turn around. John had a deep hatred of debtors (his wound from the $80,000 in unpaid commissions hadn't healed at all), but this second firm's approach tugged at him. John went with them. It felt right. He found in their methods a better solution for his own resentments, which he held against his parents and his ex-wife.

He spent four years there, then started his own practice. It was another notch down in pay and prestige, but he thought he'd be happier representing consumers rather than corporations. Consumer bankruptcies were usually uncontested; the injured parties were banks and credit companies who didn't take it personally. The whole process was designed to help a man turn his life around. Again, this felt right. John was very good

at it, and highly sought after. He was in therapy at this time, and he was realizing how much better he felt *talking things out* than bearing grudges and
fighting endlessly. One day after therapy, as he was sitting in the parking
lot, the thought occurred to him, "Why don't you become a mediator?"

He took a class on mediation with the goal of doing one divorce mediation by the end of the year. John became, rather quickly, the dominant
and most successful divorce mediator in Silicon Valley. He'd been married
for six years, had two children, and divorced during law school—he
brought his own experience to his mediation sessions, and he was often in
tears as he described his own experiences to the warring parties. He uti-
lized *Men Are from Mars, Women Are from Venus* techniques to help divorcees
communicate better in their sessions. John found the work very rewarding, and still does. But one of the keys to resolving marital separation
agreements is always to push the question, "What do you *really* want?" She
doesn't really want his car, she wants him to say he's sorry and to admit he
handled it badly. He doesn't really want the home, he wants her to forgive
him. And John Butler really wanted to be a minister. The thing was, he
didn't go to church and didn't really believe. But he still wanted to be a
minister! Somehow, it called to him, quietly. It didn't make sense, but the
idea of ministering to people's problems seemed the next step in his evo-
lution.

During this time, John took a theology class at San Jose State. It was
very academic and not very spiritual. He looked into seminaries, but he
didn't believe in any of those religions. Then he met a woman who was a
minister, and he fell in love with her, and started going to her church, and
they got engaged. John thought she was his soul mate. She was going to
make this transition easy. Their plan was, after the marriage, John would
become the co-minister of her church. He still hadn't found his belief yet,
but the God part wasn't the appeal of it to him. Shortly before the wedding, she called it off and broke up with him. No soul mate, no ministry,
no church.

"I see now that I was using her to make my dream happen," John said.
"And there was something false in that. I wasn't willing to do the work
myself. It was devastating, but it was a real test. Was I willing to make the
transition alone, without anybody's help? That's a lot scarier."

John went looking for a new church. He tried the Unity church in Palo
Alto, and more for ritual and solace than religion, he kept going back. The
Unity church did not convert him, not in the slightest. Slowly, gradually,
as he learned more about Unity's teachings, he realized here was a church
that he didn't disagree with or have misgivings about. Here was a church

that aligned with how he'd come to see the world. One of the distinguishing beliefs of Unity is that the world is not a battle between good and evil. There are not good people and bad people, the right and the wrong, the saved and the damned. Unity teaches that all people are inherently good, even if they might have made some mistakes. This is exactly what John had slowly gravitated to in his work! Then, Unity teaches "practical Christianity," meaning it models how to handle life's everyday difficult situations, which are their own reward when handled well. Unity ministers don't wear robes and aren't the congregation's conduit to God. John found in the Unity Church a way to add a spiritual dimension to his evolving skills in handling conflict resolution. With everything in alignment, his spiritual belief gradually came to him.

"But being religious was not enough," John said. "And bringing spiritual ideas into my mediation practice was not enough. I still had a calling to be the one delivering the sermon."

John joined the board of the church and became a well-regarded mediator for church conflicts, both at his church and at others. It was at one of these mediation sessions, for a Unity chapter in another county, that John learned their minister had to leave town on a family medical emergency. Who was going to deliver Sunday's sermon?

"I'd love to do the sermon," John found himself saying.

He had three days to prepare. He'd never felt more alive. His mentor attended, and so did his mother and father. When John talks about his father, his voice trembles and cracks with emotion. "After the sermon, he came up to me and blessed me. It was—" He choked up, then let go. "It was the first time in my life he blessed me. He said I had a gift."

Over the next couple years, John delivered an occasional sermon and took some weeklong classes at Unity's world headquarters in Missouri. (I discovered him through a friend who attends the Unity church in San Francisco, where John gave three sermons last year.)

When we talked last year, it amazed me that he was once an abrasive man, but he assured me that was the kindest word one might use to describe him. He understood himself enormously well and had nothing to hide. He was never afraid to reveal his weaknesses. I assumed he was going to be accepted to the ministry program—how could he not? He'd clearly done his work.

"Being told I had 'anger issues' was such a blow," John said, now nine months later. "I was infuriated at being rejected. I was angry at them. And yet every time I felt anger, it was like I was offering them evidence that I'm angry. *Of course* I'm angry, because I felt they were wrong, but I couldn't protest or appeal their decision, because they would see that state I was in and think they were right. Oh, it was a trap."

"How'd you get out of it?" I asked.

"Well, first, spending a lot of time forgiving them for what I perceived was their mistake. And then, kind of on the wings of that forgiveness, I realized they were probably right. I'd been a little on edge when I went for the week to Unity Village. I don't like being judged and evaluated. And they had these knickknack rituals that bothered me, sort of treated us like children. There was a dress code, just casual clothes, but I'm an adult. I dress appropriately. Then, I had to sign in for classes every morning, as if I might skip class. I'd paid over a thousand dollars for the plane tickets, hotel room, and rental car—was I really going to skip class? So these things put me on edge, and they could feel it when I was there. I had a bit of a grudge."

"So did you go back?"

"Yes, I went back for another week, to sit in more classes from the very teachers who had denied me permission to the program. That was a real test. It would have been so easy to see them as my enemy, my tormentors, and bear a grudge. When they saw I did not bear this grudge, and I was no longer bothered by the knickknacks required, they realized I was a better man than they had known."

"It sounds like you will get admitted to the program next year."

"Yes, they've indicated that, and I've applied. But I don't think I want to go," he said.

"Why not?"

"Because I love being a minister *so* much. I'd rather find another short-term position than sit in school. My contract is up in June. That will be a very tough decision."

He told me the story of how he received this position in Bandon, Oregon. When he was back in Missouri, he grabbed a newsletter for Unity ministers. In the back pages were classified ads from churches needing ministers. Bandon had advertised. John called and sent them a CD of his sermons, but he was told they already had two ordained candidates they were interviewing. A month later, they called back. Neither of the two candidates was quite right. Could he be there in four days and deliver the Sunday sermon? John agreed, but then was told they couldn't pay for his plane ticket, which was about four hundred dollars. He bristled. It was standard procedure to pay for a candidate's travel costs. He didn't want to be taken advantage of. Finally, on a friend's advice, he decided to drive, a twelve-hour trip, spend the night, give the sermon, and drive back the next day.

The congregation loved him. He was offered the six-month contract.

"I know it now seems like a dream come true, but it still was very hard for me to accept," John said. "Most of my friends and my mentor thought I shouldn't take it. I would have to pay other lawyers to take over my mediation cases, and wrap up a practice I'd taken years building, for what? For a six-month gig that led nowhere. That offered no next step, no future. My success is not measurable. I used to make $250 an *hour.* This pays $425 a *week.* It's not like I was unhappy with my mediation cases. I love that work. Plus, I really want to find a soul mate. Most of the people in Bandon are retired and older than I am." He went on with more excuses until I cut him short.

"But you needed to know if this was really for you," I argued.

"Yeah."

"Is it?"

"So much more than I ever anticipated."

Unity's chapel in Bandon is an aluminum-sided, aluminum-roofed barn across from an oil change shop off the coast highway. It's a humble place. There's no cross on the roof's peak. Inside, the walls are plastered and the ceilings are suspended and the light flickers from long fluorescent tubes. The floor is covered from wall to wall with cream carpet. There are no pews, just semicircular rows of ordinary metal chairs. I had no expectations, so I wasn't surprised. But now describing it, I'm at a loss—what makes it a church at all? It was entirely in the minds of the congregation. They hadn't inherited a place of worship. They'd started this chapter themselves, and the church required their participation or it would not exist. During the week there are children's classes, a writers' group, a science-of-mind class, a meditation class, a prayer support group, and at 9:30 on Sunday mornings, an adult class with about fifteen feisty people who wanted John to challenge them. This was incredibly refreshing. Most of them were retired. They'd come to tranquil Bandon from California's busy cities, but they weren't here to golf and play bridge. They'd gone north, not south. In their fifties and sixties, they were using this time for personal growth.

John had given them homework the week prior, and most had done the exercises. He'd asked them to write down their *limiting beliefs*—essentially, their opinions of themselves, reseen not as identity statements but as self-constraints. One woman's limiting belief her whole life was that she wasn't smart and couldn't learn—she'd realized she *did learn,* but slowly. Another woman's limiting belief was that she could never ask for help. She had to fix everything, and by herself. John urged her to learn the feeling of helplessness. "Wow!" she exclaimed, unable to imagine ever going there, but willing to think about it. Another woman said that her limiting belief was that there was never enough money. One of the principles of Unity is to be aware of our "abundance," that we already have plenty and we will not go hungry, that the world will take care of us. She had real trouble accepting this, and as a result she was preoccupied with the material world.

I began to get the hang of this exercise, and I wrote down the limiting beliefs that had stopped me over my lifetime—that my dream of writing wouldn't come true and I needed to find another career, that my divorce had wounded me, that being a parent was not compatible with my calling, that nobody would read what I wrote unless I was funny. . . . Many of the constructs John was teaching these retirees were ones I'd arrived at over the course of this book—that our fears should be attacked, not run from. From our deepest wounds come our greatest gifts. Everyone in this book has overcome his or her own limiting beliefs. They've discovered that their hard-earned skills mean more to them than the talents they were born with. John said, "Most of us can trace our problems back to two or three limiting beliefs." In his own case, he had believed he was a fighter, and so he went looking for fights—in the swimming pool, in the courts of justice, and in his family. That fighter turned out to be a shell, and inside was a man who hated to fight.

At eleven o'clock the chapel filled with about seventy people. John took the microphone and led the service. People felt free to interrupt with questions or joke lightly with him. During his sermon, he involved several as actors in a skit. He never bludgeoned them with scripture, and quoted poets and philosophers and politicians more than Christ's disciples. In a voice quaking with feeling, he told long stories from his own life, from times when he was challenged to love unconditionally or grant forgiveness.

He'd told me, "All week long, Sunday's sermon is on my mind. It really pushes me to think and observe. This is not about me lording over the congregation, me being better than them. I've got tons to learn. Delivering a weekly sermon accelerates that growth."

John's arc is, in my opinion, the clearest example of how I've come to think the question "What should I do with my life?" should be approached. What I so admired about John Butler's journey was *not* that he ended up a minister. Most people jump through life, asking what's next, and choosing based on where can they make the most money, what offers the most upside or opportunity. A conventional "success" story is one where, with each *next,* the protagonist has more money, more respect, and more possessions. I'd like to suggest an alternative "success" story—one where, with each *next,* the protagonist is closer to finding that spot where he's no longer held back by his heart, and he explodes with talent, and his character blossoms, and the gift he has to offer the world is apparent.

Changes
of Scenery

DEEMPHASIZING THE QUESTION
IN ORDER TO ANSWER IT

Answering this question makes me think of sweeping up a large spill. After one long, effective thrust of the broom, we have to reach back and come at it from the other side. That's where we are now. Backing away from the ideas recently discussed, this next sweep of stories explores the power of our environment over how we answer the question, then segues into travel and the adventure of working abroad.

I tracked a dozen people who'd recently realized that the too-competitive, rat-race pressure of their big cities was the source of their un-happiness. So they moved to small towns, which they chose either for their idyllic picturesque character, or because they'd grown up there and wanted to feel at home. A woman in Seattle moved to the hills of Ver-mont; a couple in Atlanta moved home to Lima, Ohio, et cetera. All of them struggled, and it was never the cure-all they hoped for. They grew bored, some because they couldn't find interesting work, others because they couldn't find interesting people. They missed the chaotic melting pot of the city. They still felt a need to be busy. The drop-off was too great. Many tried to split time, which was expensive and hard on relationships. Was there a way to get the best of both?

That was what people found in New Orleans. The Big Easy promised the perfect antidote: a big, culturally diverse city, free of rat-race tension. Unlike the Small Town Solution, nobody finds New Orleans uninterest-ing.

I first became interested in New Orleans four years ago, when my wife (then my girlfriend) took me there for Christmas. My wife was from Texas, but her mom grew up in the French Quarter and her dad in the Ninth Ward. All of her cousins and uncles still lived in and around NOLA. At Christmas dinner forty-five people sat down—just your ordinary-sized Catholic family. I had prepped for this dinner, peppering my girlfriend with questions throughout the plane ride. Most were tradespeople—nurses, electricians, forest rangers, salesmen, bookkeepers. But they didn't think of themselves that way. The most fascinating cultural indicator was that I was introduced to forty-five people, and *not a single one asked me "What do you do?"* Here I was, their cousin's new boyfriend, wanting to make a good impression, willing to pass whatever test they might have for me—and how I supported myself never came up. They figured if I could pay for a plane ticket to fly all the way from the West Coast, I must be doing all right.

I received a surprising number of stories from people who had either moved to New Orleans or left New Orleans. They were all college-educated, professional-class, in their twenties and thirties, and were tinkering with the effect of an environment on their ambition. They moved to New Orleans because they felt their ambition was running too high, like an engine, unsustainably, dangerously, burning too much oil. New Orleans succeeded in idling down their ambition, and helped them enjoy life. But frequently it succeeded too well, and their ambition shifted into neutral, and then just puttered out completely. Those who left did so because they needed a little social pressure, like a turbo boost, to remind them of what they could become with some hard work and a little opportunity. This was the constant tension of New Orleans—how to use its laid-backness effectively.

People weren't moving to New Orleans to party, or to slack. That wasn't the notion. In Chicago, or San Francisco, or New York, or Dallas, they adopted the bad habit of measuring themselves against others—by those external accomplishments. So they chased success, and often met it, but just as often at the expense of what they really wanted to do, or who they really wanted to be. New Orleans was a place to get in touch with what they really wanted to do. Offices are empty by 5:30—plenty of time at night to get in touch with their dreams. Then, more tinkering with that carburetor, because it is not a culture where people work hard at anything, or very passionately, or fight to make their dreams come true. So most dreams are in hobby mode. As one woman described it, "In Los Angeles, if you say you're a musician, you're asked where you've played, who your A-and-R rep is, what label are you with—in effect, *are you, or will you be, successful?* In New Orleans, if you say you're a musician, then people accept that you're a musician, even if you only jam one night a week at some dive with no audience. In New Orleans, a dream doesn't have to become a reality to be *real.*"

I went to New Orleans to observe this tinkering. On the first night, I was pulling into a parking space when the front wheel dropped down into a drainhole, which was missing a drain grate. The chassis crashed onto the concrete, damaging the underbody. I called for a tow truck and waited. A woman came out from the house. She said her husband's car had fallen into that hole a bunch of times. The city hadn't gotten around to replacing the grate in two years. I gave the tow truck four hours, then bummed a ride back to my hotel. So that was the tension of New Orleans—how to let the Big Easy work its magic on you, without getting stuck in a sinkhole. "New Orleans tends to quell motivation with the same success rate as an opium den," I was warned.

I interviewed nine people in depth. I'll share two stories, but the others equally contributed to my perceptions. The best place to start is with an obvious question: what makes a place, any place, *interesting*? It's not just the mausoleums, wrought-iron balconies, weathered Victorians, and vintage streetcars. I was told it's the friction—between old and new, blacks and whites, gay and straight, tourists and locals. Everyone agrees New Orleans is changing, but nobody agrees what it's changing into—and that's friction too. The density of a city makes collisions of cultures inevitable. Suburbs are designed for low density, to guard against that collision. Suburban land is zoned for a single use; it can only be developed in that way, and the geography of the land can only be interpreted one way. Cities foster multiple interpretations, multiple readings. In New Orleans, I heard diametrically opposed observations spoken with equal conviction.

For instance, jazz is a collision of musical styles. I was told that New Orleans is a great city for jazz musicians, which is to say for any kind of musician willing to collide with other musical influences. Charlie Dennert had moved here from Birmingham; his band, Quintology, was an example of where jazz was headed. But I was also told that the jazz scene here is a "museum culture," which shies away from the avant-garde in order to cater to tourists. So the brass band is still the cornerstone of jazz here. At best New Orleans is on the tailwind of traditional jazz. Evan Parker and Dave Holland, two of the foremost musicians of the last forty years, almost never come to town.

Another for instance: I was regularly told that very few people leave New Orleans; when they ask which school you went to, they mean which *high school*. They also ask which hospital you were born at. Someone whose family has only been here four generations can still think he's new to town, particularly if he hangs out with the Historic Preservation Society. But I was also regularly told that the intellectual capital that graduates each year from Xavier, Loyola, Tulane, Dillard, and the University of New Orleans flows out of town just like the natural resources flowed away over the last hundred years. *Nobody stays.* They go to Jackson to work for Nissan or WorldCom, or to Birmingham's medical industry and auto plants. Even the oil business has left town. The only jobs left are in the tourist industry, restaurants and hotels.

So which interpretation is accurate? Probably both. That's friction. That's what makes it interesting.

Marc Weidenbaum is thirty-four, tall and slender. He moved here a year and a half ago. He's an exotic here, because he's a Jewish kid from Long Island via San Francisco who talks too fast and wears a backpack.

"You don't see many backpacks here," he said. "The backpack is a staple of New York and San Francisco. It says you're coming from somewhere, and you're going somewhere else, and you have things you *need* that you can't be without. Here, backpacks are unnecessary. People look at me and think I'm way too old to have a backpack. But I don't carry as much in it as I used to. Look. I don't carry business cards anymore. People don't swap business cards here. In another year I'll probably kick the backpack habit entirely."

Marc's learned to talk slower. He's had to. People tuned him out. They just stopped listening. He still has what he calls his "internal ass kicker," but he can now go to the dentist and sit in the chair for half an hour and not get stressed out about all that time being wasted. The checkout lines are still too slow at the supermarket. He's gotten used to the fact that he cannot get *The New York Times* home-delivered here; now he enjoys the stroll down to Magazine Street to get a copy. Recently, he found himself saying aloud, "It really doesn't take much money to get by." He shocked himself.

"It's not like New Orleans is really cheap. The homes in this neighborhood [the Garden District] would all cost several hundred thousand dollars. Many a million plus. Just like in S.F. But in New York and S.F., it was unacceptable for someone with talent to just get by. It's not radically cheaper here, but it's completely acceptable—normal—to make just enough to pay rent and have beer money. And it's amazing how little you have to work to do that."

In this culture, free time is more valuable than money. People work just enough to maximize their free time. So Marc edits comics and listens to electronic music and publishes his own music criticism on the Web. For money, Marc is the national music editor for the website Citysearch.

When he arrived, he told people he did "content." They didn't know what that was. Back in San Francisco, he'd been Citysearch's editor in chief. He enjoyed the work but he hated the get-rich-quick mentality. Marc's dad still worked, happily, at age sixty-five—Marc had zero desire to score big and retire early. He decided to leave when he started seeing Bentleys while walking to work.

So he and his girlfriend had "that conversation," the one that our parents never had, about balancing two careers. She was a sociologist who wanted the stability of a tenured position. She wanted to be in a culturally active city. As an editor, returning to New York was his obvious choice. But he hated New York's superiority, the way New Yorkers talk like it's indisputably the best place on earth. Marc pushed for her to apply in the South, even though he'd never been—he wanted to be the outsider. She was offered a position at Tulane, they were both happy, and they stuck together.

"We made the right choice. I used to wonder, What if I lived here, what if I lived there, what would my life be like? I'm aware how my life is different because I'm here, but that's it. I don't wonder where I'd be happy. My mind's calmer. Here, when we go out, it's to *enjoy* the music and to dance. In New York, it was culture consumption. You listened to the music so you could be an expert on it. Everything had a purpose that related back to status." In New York, people engage in a sociology experiment on what life is. In New Orleans, people live their lives.

Marc's not afraid he will end up stuck in a drainhole. He used to want to be an English professor. He doesn't fantasize about that anymore, but he interprets this as a sign of his being at peace, rather than giving up a dream.

"I still bring a lot of big-city stress wherever I go," he said. "And the tenure track at Tulane is a prominent stress engine." He says this like stress is food, and without stress they'd starve. "The people we know who've made interesting life decisions still tend to define themselves in large part by their work. New Orleans hasn't rid them of that. But it's helped them make decisions about their work that are not what their friends or family expected, or what their background steered them to." It's helped them find their own course.

Six months later, I met up with Marc in Austin; we were both in town for the South by Southwest music festival. He'd recently gotten a contract to write a book about electronic music for Temple University Press; the previous week had been his last with Citysearch. The contract wasn't for much money, but that wouldn't matter in New Orleans.

Julia Kamysz Lane was one of those Tulane grads who came, got educated, and fled. She went back to Chicago, where she'd grown up and where there were lots of driven workaholics like her. But after five years trying to climb the ladder at advertising firms, she came back to New Orleans. The place had a tug on her. Here, she didn't feel pressure to be on a career track. She was twenty-eight and it was clear that she was complex beyond her years. For money, she read the mail for a fifty-two-year-old blind jazz musician, took him for walks, and ran his errands. "There are demons in New Orleans," she said, cryptically, then changed the subject. NOLA celebrates the weird. There are voodoo trinkets sold in all the shops, and I just figured she meant something mystical of that sort, as if she were using black magic to cure her workaholism. Then, later, she used the word "demons" again, and made clear that these were not generic demons, but *her* demons. She changed the subject again, but it was clearly a tease. *Chase this, I want to tell the truth.*

The moment was nine months pregnant. I felt Julia's hesitation, her urge to swallow her candor as she'd no doubt swallowed it time and again. So I began rambling about the harder periods of my own life. When I was done, she reciprocated.

She'd arrived at Tulane, eighteen years old, in the fall of 1990. She enrolled in premed classes. Her father was an electrical engineer, her mother a graphic artist. They didn't pressure her, but she had so much energy, and felt so bottled up in such a dark blind space, confused by what she desired to be versus what she could succeed at, and the only slim light of a path out was premed/med school/intern/resident/doctor/success. She put her blinders on, feigned confidence, and earned good grades. In the fall of her sophomore year, she went for her mandatory sessions with an academic counselor, who probed her thoughts about career choices. She does not remember what was said in those sessions, but she associates them with the incredible funk she fell into afterward, culminating with an F on a paper for organic chemistry. She got back to her dorm room and the walls started to spin, and she felt the floor sinking into a deep dark hole. She called her mother. Her mother called a counselor on campus, who suggested Julia get to the hospital. Julia's father was manic-depressive, so Julia's mother was scared but prepared that Julia might be as well. A friend—who'd feared that Julia was suicidal—drove her to the hospital. On the way, her friend said Julia should get back to her writing. Could all this come from swallowing her desire to be a writer?

Julia stayed on the campus psychiatric ward for a week. She did not take medication. She went to group therapy every day, and even there, she felt a competitive urge to outperform the others and prove she was functional. That Christmas holiday, she had a long talk with her father. His parents had emigrated from Poland. His parents had chosen his career as an engineer. He'd never had a choice, and he wanted her to feel free to choose. He was concerned about this blind drive in her. He told her, "When you talk about your biology class, you are so serious, and you sound so unhappy. But when you talk about working for the student newspaper, you love that, you light up."

Where was this blind drive coming from? Julia fantasized about controlling the world around her. She let steam out by writing letters that she would never mail. These were letters to her bosses, her family, ordering them what to do to fix their nagging, entrenched problems. It seemed like some twisted permutation of frustrated ambition. Being competitive was a default substitute for following her dream. Being better than others was a default substitute for being true to herself. And after graduation, this pattern recurred. She worked in advertising (a common compromise for people who want to write) and became fiercely competitive, felt like her life wasn't moving, switched firms, kept getting bored, learned every skill she could but wasn't happy, and one day—four years into it—someone asked her "What's wrong?" and she burst into tears.

She needed a break from the salary life. She worked at a Starbucks and felt like a complete loser. She moved over to a Barnes & Noble, which was a little better, and she met her future husband, but she still couldn't summon the courage to have a go at writing. What would it mean to fail at the thing you really want to do? What would be left to dream about? That's when she felt the call to return to New Orleans, and to join the freelance/part-time culture, where everyone gets by somehow, fixing cars on the side, working one day a week at the museum writing grants, or at Kinko's for the health insurance, or designing Web sites. It is a culture in which you *cannot* fail, because even to try is to be legitimate. In New Orleans her demons were guarding the path she had not taken, at eighteen, when she took her first wrong turn.

So Julia and her now-husband Brian, a photographer, came to New Orleans and have found a way to get by. She started writing and editing for free, and it always evolved into paying work. She still fought her workaholism, even here—for a while she was the managing editor of the local weekly *Gambit* and wrote some great stories uncovering petty graft being perpetrated on local merchants. But that urge to control came back, to tell every writer how to do the job, and she realized she had to quit and go freelance or the urge would ruin her again. Now she wrote book reviews and was writing an essay about race, informed by the blind jazz musician she worked for. He's black, she's white; they got a lot of stares on their walks. She feels the friction. It's interesting.

37 ||| Nobody Taught Me

THE BENEFIT OF BEING
AROUND LIKE-MINDED PEOPLE

Julia asked me, "Can writing schools really teach you to write?"
I never thought that was the litmus test. Writing school helped me by surrounding me with people who aspired to the same ideals I did. I'd been a
bond salesman—I didn't know any other writers, and I'd never even met
a writer. I didn't even know any *readers*. If the other traders and salespeople
read books, they never mentioned it. At school, for at least one night a
week, I sat down beside people who thought nothing was more important
than making a sentence sing . . . Who believed that having a story accepted
by a small journal with a readership of a thousand librarians was just about
the most prestigious accomplishment imaginable . . . Who had chosen,
like me, to compromise their love lives and work lives to carve out time
for being alone with their thoughts and a pencil . . . Who had received rejection letter after rejection letter, and who had been called "impractical"
by their parents. I can't emphasize enough the sway of being in a community of like-minded people. As New Orleans had its effect on Marc and
Julia, my writing school helped support the choice I'd made. Because the
hardest thing was not learning to write; the hardest thing was to *never
give up*.

The publication of my first novel was my great chance to quit working
and attempt to support myself by writing full-time. I imagined I might
maintain an income writing for magazines. But I was going to finish my
graduate degree around the same time. I would take the leap without my
community, my three-hour-a-week lifeline that had nourished me for
seven years. What would I do all day? Who would I talk to? I was accustomed to waking up every morning and going to the office.

So with two other writer friends—Ethan Canin (whom I'd met playing
pickup basketball) and Ethan Watters (who knew editors at magazines)—

I rented a second-floor flat in a dusty Victorian on Market Street in a no-man's-land between the Castro and City Hall. This would be a place where we wrote every day. It had six rooms, two bathrooms, a kitchen. The rent was intimidating, and we were on the hook for the whole nugget if we couldn't find some creative types to occupy the other three rooms. So we threw a party. We made up a postcard invitation, but the address, 2148 Market Street, looked too lonely floating in the middle of the card. Who wanted to come to "2148 Market Street"? What was it? A restaurant? A bar?

"We need an enticing name," one of the Ethans said.

"What about 'The Grotto'?" said the other.

"You can't steal Jim's name!" I protested.

Jim was another writer who rented the basement room in my house as his writing space. He called it the Grotto.

"Jim's on vacation. He'll never know."

"But *I'll* know!" I fought back.

"What about 'The *Writers'* Grotto'?"

"That's the same thing!"

"Not quite the same."

So we stole Jim's name, and everyone we knew came to the party, curious about what the Writers' Grotto was. They came, they got drunk, they danced, they lit off fireworks, set a tree on fire, climbed up to the roof, broke the toilet, ruined the carpet, and left, still unsure what the Writers' Grotto was.

"Do you *live* here?"

"No. Just work."

"Are you all writing a book *together*?"

"No. Just our own projects."

"How much does rent cost?"

"Two to three hundred."

"A month!?"

"Yeah."

"You can fly to Cabo every month for that!"

"I like to write."

"But you can write at home, for *free*."

We were going to get stuck with the whole rent. It was hard for people to understand what we were doing. There was nothing like it in the whole city. There were writing colonies, where people go and live and write for a month or two. There were writing conferences, where people take classes for a week. The rest of the time, writers cling to their outsider status, which they resent and defend at the same time, feeling it is somehow crucial to their sense of being special. At the conferences and colonies, writers notoriously got drunk and had affairs, so everyone suspected that was what the Grotto was really about—we had our clubhouse, the boys with the treehouse fort, a place to get drunk at two in the afternoon and screw women and never grow up. It took years before people stopped assuming the worst about the Grotto whenever they heard about it. Luckily, the three rooms were finally taken, by a filmmaker (David), a monologist (Josh), and a struggling freelancer (Tessa) who had written a couple pieces for a British daily. She was the only woman at the original Grotto. She became our den mother. She made tea for us in the afternoons and listened to stories about our love lives, which were small-time dramas compared to the ones she'd lived through. The beauty of the Grotto is, when I have a bad day, at least I went to the office. A bad day working at home is a sad and lonely thing, and if a few bad days land in a row then an editing job starts to sound pretty appealing.

Our daily life was structured by the routine of work. I didn't want to become a writer so I could escape from work, to *not* work, or to get rich on royalties so I'd never have to work. I wanted to work. I craved work, as much as a sled dog or a packhorse, work that fulfilled me. We got up, had coffee at home, read the paper, drove to the Grotto, and then just let the benefit of being around each other rub off. I learned how to write features from Ethan Watters, I learned screenwriting from David, and I learned to speak extemporaneously in public from Josh. Nobody *taught* me these things; they were doing it, and made it seem possible. We created an environment where taking creative risks was *okay*. Nothing was formalized—the sharing and reading of each other's work was entirely spontaneous.

"What are you doing?"

"Making tea. Want some?"

"What kind?"

"Earl Grey."

"Naw."

"What are you moping about?"

"I can't get started on this article."

"When's it due?"

"In, like, five hours."

"What's it about?"

"Rock the Vote."

"Why can't you get started?"

"Because the truth is, I hung out with them for two days, and I just realized now, *I didn't like them.*"

"Why not?"

"They were phonies. They just went around saying, 'Chicken is the bird of the People. Duck is the poultry of The Man.' 'UPS is the parcel service of the People. Fed Ex is the tool of The Man.' They made me sick."

"Geez, that's hilarious. You should lead with that."

And he did. (*Spin Magazine,* October 1996.)

Tessa made the most amazing transformation. She'd started life over in San Francisco after getting divorced in London. Not long before she found us, she'd been cleaning houses as a maid in order to get by. She'd only written a couple of articles before we met, but she was soon writing for all the British and Australian magazines. That gave her great confidence, and, buoyed—this is the amazing part—she remembered that she'd always wanted to be a jazz singer. If she could become a journalist, maybe she could become a jazz singer. She was in her early forties and hadn't sung since she was a young girl. "I was always told I had a great voice," she said. So she moved to Manhattan and two years later had a famous singer as her mentor and was represented by a top manager. And she was not just singing—she was composing too. Her community there has helped her just as our community had helped all of us. I'm not saying the community is everything, but it makes success possible. Did we believe in each other? Here and there, but not across the board. You would assume that's necessary, but it's not. The talent doesn't have to shine from the outset. Most people will perform if given a chance and a few role models.

After two years, rents started to creep up, and the landlord booted us to bring in some lawyers. We found a bigger place, this time with room for nine writers, more evenly balanced between guys and girls. It lasted another three years until the rents tripled (the mad rush of the dot-com boom). So we were out on the street, nine writers without a tree fort, and there wasn't anything left in the city to rent. Artists' cooperatives were all moving to the naval yards in Hunters Point and Alameda, but we didn't want to abandon the heart of the city. The only place left to rent in the city was an old dog and cat hospital above a parking garage near City Hall. It was scheduled to be demolished in two years to make way for a twenty-two-story condominium tower. It was huge; to make it pay, we were going to have to put twenty-two writers and filmmakers in there, and build the office walls and doors ourselves, put in skylights, rewire the electrical system—knowing with every hammer fall and screw turn that it would all be coming down in just two years.

But we clung together, and took a gamble on the pet hospital. We built the walls and taped the seams and mudded and painted and hung doors and threw another party to find thirteen others, and we became unwieldy for a while, until we got the hang of there being so many of us. We each have a chore—take out the recycling, clean the roof deck—and somehow, recently, we have the feeling that the Grotto would now survive the departure of any person or persons. For six years it was powered by the initiation energy we continuously supplied it; now it rolls onward with its own momentum.

I've learned that without structure, I become unstable and self-destructive fairly quickly. I have an ability to reimagine the world. I used to glorify this ability to pretend—it's the essential gift behind writing fiction, and it's a great coping mechanism for dealing with rejection. But I'm not proud of it anymore. Sometimes, when things get tough, I run away—run away into my imagination, run toward a new life, like so many empty pages, ready to be filled. Enough of that, turn the page and write a new chapter. I've run from my parents, run from my first marriage, run from job after job where I felt misused. My struggle now is to stay grounded and to *not* indulge my imagination. To stick with *this* life. I've turned from fiction to nonfiction not just because I can, or because the magazines offer work—I do it because I need to pay attention to the ways of real life. The Grotto verges on being a self-created utopia, a huge loophole in the work/play continuum, and sometimes I wonder if I'm allowing myself to live in a dangerous fantasy. But the structure and routine it provides keep me sane. I'm absent-minded, forget to pay my bills, can't return phone calls, forget birthdays—I used to embrace these traits because they were evidence of having a "writer's" personality. But now I think there is no excuse for not taking care of myself or treating others with decency.

Which gets us to the hard part I've been avoiding. Inevitably, getting into an environment of like-minded people, whether it's building your own Grotto or moving to New Orleans or making friends with other social workers or switching to a college in Washington, D.C., where there are other young people interested in politics—*inevitably,* it means you have to ditch your old support system, family or friends or coworkers or dorm-mates. You have to inflict pain on people who love you. Oh, they can still be your friends, still love you—but the seat you've saved for them at your Inner Circle has to be given to someone new. And this is never done without the sting of rejection and the collar of guilt. Why do so many people hush the longing to be someone different? It's not because they have to pay their student loans. It's not because the economy is in a lull. It's not because they don't have notions of what they'd like to be. *It's because they don't want to be the kind of person who abandons friends and takes up with a new crowd.* When is it running away, and when is it the best thing for you? It always looks like running away to those you're leaving behind. And if you've ever run away before, you're open to that criticism. But just like Carl Kurlander wondered if being in Pittsburgh would ever really be different from Beverly Hills . . . just as Ana Miyares got the courage to be rejected by her family by making friends with social workers . . . just as Rinpoche could find himself better by living around ordinary people in Phoenix than around monks in a monastery in India . . . just as Tim Bratcher took the heat off by moving to Atlanta . . . just as Bart Handford found his people on the second floor of the campaign headquarters in Arkansas . . . just as Bryce was under the sway of Big & Oily until he made friends with the other inspectors . . .

Put this power to work.

38 ||| The Romantic Depressive

"I know exactly what you mean," said Claude Sidi, stabbing his foie gras and chasing it down with a gulp of wine. We were enjoying lunch at a restaurant belonging to a friend of his. "Environment's everything."

His dad had worked for the World Bank's food and agriculture division in Africa and Asia, and Claude had always admired his dad's zeal for his work. Claude wanted to be a marine biologist, and maybe an aquaculture specialist, so he could travel to developing nations and help them grow fish. He advanced to the PhD stage, and was finally a marine biologist, with his own well-funded research project at a remote lab on the craggy Oregon coast. He woke to the smell of the ocean. Talked back to the fog and the elephant seals. Hiked through the rain forest.

"It was such a romantic place. Classically romantic. Absolutely stunning. But I got *really depressed,* right away."

"Why?"

He threw his arms out wide. "Not enough people! I was lonely! I realized, Fuck biology, I like *people*. I'd never been without people around. It was *terrible*."

So he quit and became a dentist in a big city full of interesting people. He *loves* it. Every day he sees his patients, they come in, chat, laugh, share stories, and Claude helps them in his own small way. He snaps pictures of his patients and can tell you the names of their dogs.

"So you're totally happy?"

"Yeah. I *love* it. Been happy ever since." He seemed it. "Let's have some dessert, huh?"

39 ||| On Planet Hug

I flew down to Los Angeles to attend Sunday Mass at Saint Agatha's as the guest of Ashley Merryman. Saint Agatha's services are stirring and vibrant affairs on any weekend, but this was also the day of their annual picnic in a park nearby. Saint Agatha's is located near the USC campus, in what used to be considered a bad neighborhood to be in at night. It's a one-of-a-kind church: Multicultural Catholic Gospel, with a fantastic rock band backing up the choir. The culture of this church is infectious; it was like we were on a different planet: Planet Hug. When I looked into their eyes, everybody seemed to have a world of hurt in their past, yet they were the warmest group I've ever met. I'm not a religious person, but I was stirred, and I sang and clapped and stomped, and when I pictured people in my life I wanted to pray for, my brother, or my stepmom, or an old friend, their image brought tears.

Ashley was the scrawny Irish redhead in a sundress with a big smile and an alto voice. She's thirty-three. Two years ago, she rebuilt her life with Saint Agatha's as the emotional center. Father Ken and the congregation had rescued her and taken her in when she was unemployed, had no car, no phone number, and was losing weight fast—the former conditions had triggered the reemergence of her eating disorder. She joined the choir and started attending a couple times a week. At St. Agatha's, strangers are *always* greeted with a warm hug and the line, "How can I help you?" Ashley had never been treated that way before. Back at the White House, where she used to work—and back in Hollywood, where she worked before the White House—the premise of every first meeting was, "How can *you* help *me?*"

Ashley let *how-can-I-help-you* reorient her mind. Her heart went out to all the little kids who attended. She began tutoring a few. She knew these kids needed an after-school education center, to keep them off the streets until their parents came home from work, so she approached Father Ken and asked if there was a room that could be used. This is another part of the culture that Father Ken has created—you don't complain, you don't tell other people what they should do. If you see a need, that's your chance to help. Ashley now runs this classroom/tutor center. She decorates the church and sweeps the parking lot as a police helicopter circles overhead. What's important to her now is getting Keisha to pass third grade or getting Gabriella on family health care.

The catch is—and this is why I've placed this story at this spot in the book—Ashley has to make a living. On top of rent for her spartan Culver City apartment, there's a car payment and then the $1,500 per month owed to Georgetown Law School. Those student loan payments really have her pinned down. So she's been working as a contract attorney for a Beverly Hills law firm. "Contract" attorney doesn't mean she works with contracts, it means she's paid by the hour and works from ten to six. A sort of attorney temp. It's a paycheck, not a career. She hates the work and the value system, but that's not unusual. If she promises a kid she'll be at the church at 6:30, she can live up to her promise. That's worth something, isn't it? I thought her life had balance. Her days were necessary sacrifices for her nights and weekends. Who hasn't been there? I admired her and I loved her friends. The kids adored her. Her refrigerator is covered with drawings they've crayoned for her. Wasn't this a good life? Wasn't she serving God? Wasn't that the message of Father Joe's sermon today—when helping people, you are serving God? That was Jesus' dying wish: out of love, do this for Him. People who need you *is* your destiny, and this destiny is a free gift from God.

I told Ashley I thought she should be content and proud of herself.

But she wouldn't have it. "I've found my community, but not my calling," she warned. "I'm not even sure God knows what I should do with my life."

"Come on, *this* is exactly what you should be doing with your life. Isn't it?"

"One of my classmates clerked for the Supreme Court. I'm not allowed to make a copy in the main copy room of my firm because I'm a temp."

"But look at what you've got here. Isn't it okay to be working only for the paycheck, if you come home to this?"

"I still feel like there's so much more I'm supposed to be doing. Supposed to have done already. I just don't know what it is. I was blessed. I went to a preeminent law school, the best film school, my parents didn't

beat me. I have an incredible sense I should have accomplished something. When people say I'm talented, it makes me feel worse. The blessing
has become a curse."

Over the course of her life, Ashley had done right by every piece of advice I might give her. She'd pursued her childhood inspiration. She'd
taken risks. She'd sacrificed, and worked for no pay in order to later get
hired. She'd been moved by the events of her day to get involved. She
made her contribution to the national dialogue, then returned to her chosen career (or tried to). And after all that, what was she?

An attorney temp who isn't even authorized to make copies.

How could this happen?

Or, maybe I should ask, am I giving bad advice?

Or, if St. Agatha's *was* the cause to devote her life to, how could she revise her own story so that she didn't feel like she'd failed?

Ashley said, "I've given myself permission to have a job that sucks for a
while."

"No, you haven't. You're still punishing yourself for it."

"I'm trying."

"Look at all the love you have in your life!" Planet Hug was in full gear
at the church picnic.

"Isn't it wonderful?" she said, cheering up, then tossing off a look that
mocked "How did I get here?"

When Ashley was eight years old, she read an article in *American Film
Magazine* about her hero, George Lucas. It said he'd gone to USC Film
School, so Ashley put the magazine down and told her parents that was
where she was going to college. Ten years later she moved into a USC
dorm and started film school. She graduated, and spent a few years work-

ing her way up in Hollywood as a reader, production assistant, and assistant to a creative executive.

The L.A. riots on the night of April 28, 1992, were a wake-up call. They were not far from her apartment. She was overtaken with this feeling that "something has to change." Not in her life, but in society. She had this Jeffersonian notion that everyone should serve their country for a few years. At that same time, Bill Clinton announced that were he elected, he would create a National Service Corps, later known as AmeriCorps. Ashley thought that was *so cool*. She decided to hit the pause button on her movie-biz career, and she drove her Honda all the way to Little Rock, completely unannounced. She got a room at the Best Western, and asked the desk clerk, "Where's the campaign headquarters?" By chance, there was a Clinton advance team right there in the lobby.

"Are you Clinton people?" she asked. "I want to be one of you."

"Come upstairs then," they said, and that was the beginning.

When Clinton won, she wasn't rewarded with a job, like Bart Handford. She probably should have come back to Hollywood. Instead, she was swept up in the excitement, and moved to D.C. She became a full-time but unpaid speechwriter for Al Gore. Most of the party hacks had law degrees and never practiced law. Ashley went to Georgetown at night for the respect it might bring her. She paid her dues, and eventually she was given a political appointment as speechwriter for the commissioner of Social Security. She was a Clinton official. Whenever she wanted, she'd call a friend in the White House and go over there for lunch. After sixty or seventy speeches, though, she lost her reverence for it, and according to Jefferson, that was the time to come home.

Was Hollywood ready to take her back? They said so. She took several informational interviews, and it was all, "Oh, we love you, you'll have no trouble getting work." During the 1990s, Hollywood had a great love affair with the White House. As a Clinton official, it was easy for her to get meetings with creative executives. But as soon as she quit—as soon as she moved back to L.A., and was no longer from the White House—as soon as her callback number began 310, not 202—Hollywood stopped biting. When she actually *needed* something from them (another production assistant job), they scratched their heads. It was the very week that the Monica Lewinsky scandal broke, and everyone wanted to ask her if Bill Clinton had hit on her. There seemed to be no reverence for the commitment she'd made. *Hey, I served the country!* Nobody cared. Ashley was told she was too old for the entry-level positions, and for the positions more appropriate to her age (twenty-nine), she was "unqualified."

—Unqualified!
—I gave five years to the country, dammit!
—Unqualified!
—I used to eat lunch in the White House!
—Too old!
—I'm twenty-nine!
—Did he hit on you?
—Hasn't anybody read Jefferson!?

Now, I know plenty of people who didn't start working in Hollywood until they were thirty, so I'm not sure what can be extrapolated from Ashley's rejection. But I *have* been encouraged to lie about my age in Hollywood. I figure when you start lying about your age, there's no telling what else you might fabricate.

Maybe, if she'd hung in there and kept applying, she'd finally land another P.A. position. But Ashley was a perfectionist. Her psychology was not resilient enough to handle a long period of rejection. She stopped eating almost completely. She made me promise not to mention how much weight she lost in how short a time, because anorexics might read it and find self-destructive "inspiration" in the information. "I got to the point where I couldn't finish a long sentence, because by the end of it I couldn't remember what I was saying," she said, to give me some indication how bad off she was. She didn't have the down payment for an apartment.

A lot of it was, her whole life she had defined herself by what she did. Suddenly that equation created self-hatred. It was killing her. She had to find a new way to define herself.

"Why didn't you go for help?" I asked. "A therapist or a doctor?"

"Because I didn't think I deserved it. Film school, law school, good family. I should be fine. I wasn't supposed to need help. I thought someone like me asking for help was selfish."

How she'd found Saint Agatha's was, she liked a television drama called *Nothing Sacred*. She read an article that the show's creator had gotten his inspiration from attending Saint Agatha's. She followed her curiosity, came to a service, and met Father Ken. "You're ours now," he told her, and sent her to a doctor.

How she found me was, some scenes for a movie were being shot near Saint Agatha's, and Ashley saw the arrow signs on the lampposts. She drove by the set, looked up the movie, and found that it was based on my second novel. Then she looked me up, and discovered the topic of my current book was the question she asked herself every morning as she drove into work. Again, curiosity. Her instincts were good.

Since meeting that Sunday in July, I've remained in contact with Ashley for over a year. Her attitude has changed. For so long she had been looking for her calling as a *profession* that she didn't realize her *people*, her community, could be her calling. But this is what she's come to accept. It just took a while. Every day there are young kids around St. Agatha's who need her help—and she has the variety of skills to get them help.

Her misgivings about her day job were softened the following summer, when she asked for a three-month leave to go to Belfast. After a week of being wishy-washy about her request, the firm eventually granted it. The job would be there when she got back. Maybe it wasn't so bad to have "just" a day job.

She went to Belfast because she heard about a female priest who had been excommunicated. The story pissed her off, and she wanted to investigate. She'd written a few essays for the *National Catholic Reporter,* and she shaped her research into a play, which had a well-attended reading at a local theater.

Her life no longer felt temporary; St. Agatha's wasn't just a place to rebound and move on from—it was worth hanging on to.

I corresponded with numerous people who were traveling in different parts of the world, hoping that while away they might figure out what to do with their life. Some returned with a new courage, and an insight into themselves that guided their decision. Many didn't, though. They had a good time, saw the world, and often wished they could keep traveling for the rest of their years. But insight into what they would do with themselves if they had to stand still? They weren't able to milk that rock.

So when it helped, how did it? What was the causal link?

I'll start with the subtlest effects, and in the following chapters describe a few more substantive ones.

For those who simply feel trapped under their responsibilities and can't summon the initiative to quit, exposing yourself to how other people live loosens the mind. "Look at how happy they are with so little money!" for instance. You comprehend how many ways there are to get by. Choosing a new way seems possible.

At home, at work, at school, there are always a ton of external inputs coaxing you in the direction you're already going. Deadlines, parents chirping in your ear, friends wanting you to go out. Your life has a momentum. Traveling can take you away from all those influences, quiet their din, and allow you a kind of silence to consider who you are as an independent entity. It can be uncomfortable if you're not used to it. You might come face to face with the fact that there's not much brainwave activity upstairs without all those influences to react to. "And when you start to think that you haven't been the pilot of your life for a long, long time, you have no other choice but to hear what your soul is saying," wrote one young man who found the courage to quit business school while traveling across Asia. "Am I the person I think I am if nobody is there to tell me who I am?"

Being uncomfortable is good. If you remain comfortable, you remain more or less yourself. The quickest way to make yourself uncomfortable is to travel *alone*. I found a high correlation between traveling alone and milking the rock. It takes courage to change your life. Sometimes, doing so, you feel all alone in the world. You can get used to this scary feeling by traveling alone, being by yourself for long periods of time, having to talk to strangers, having to get yourself from one city to another. You become accustomed to it. The fear of being alone will no longer stop you.

It also helped to travel without a plan. This was particularly true for young people who've segued from high school to college to a prize job they were recruited for without ever taking any great leaps of faith. They've never been off a path. With each step, they've known where it was likely to lead, even as they pretended they might opt out. They're uncomfortable with the prospect of not being associated with a respected school or company, since they've always had that. Traveling without a plan is a way to rehearse the improvisational approach, and opens your mind to the sense of adventure. You learn to trust the laws of chance. Perhaps, when you get home, you'll be willing to do the same.

When you subdue these fears, they no longer guard the gates, and you invite the truth into your life.

41 ||| Success Formula

Perhaps, in your travels, you will discover something that is worth devoting your life to.

Will you be ready for it?

Mike Jenzeh was an unlicensed commercial real estate broker in Silicon Valley in the early nineties, when the economy hiccupped and the market paused. He'd been hustling for five years. He was the stereotype of a pushy salesman. All his deals—thirty a year—came from cold calls. He drove a 240Z and wore a tie. Jewish, but not practicing, he came to America from Iran when the shah fell. He was afraid of commitment. He'd almost been married once, but had backed out. "My life was all about *me*," he said. "About me finding the light, following the heat." When the real estate market tanked—largely because of the cutbacks in defense spending—he couldn't close a deal to save his life. He worked eight to five and made no jack. He had no control over his life. Frustrated, he simply stopped. He stayed in bed all day reading books. He was almost thirty.

Mike read a lot of poetry and religion. "I realized that the only way out of this rut was to give up *myself*, to make it not about *me*. To give what I could in my own way."

He was particularly struck by a passage in Isaiah 58. It was written to the religious who were pointing fingers at others. Mike was so struck by this passage that he rewrote it in his own words—he recrafted it into the message he needed to hear. He called it his Success Formula.

> When you stop pointing fingers,
> Lying to yourself and others,
> When you give yourself to the hungry,
> And satisfy the desire of the afflicted,

Then your light will ride through darkness,
And your gloom will rise as the noonday sun,
And you'll continually find the desires of your heart in
scorched and dry places and strength in your bones,
And finally become like a watered garden,
Like a spring whose waters never fail.

He put this in his wallet. Hokey? Maybe. But he was ready.

With the vague idea that travel might be good for him, he cashed in some air miles for a trip to Costa Rica with his girlfriend. She wanted to snorkle and ecotrek. He didn't want to *consume* Costa Rican nature. He wanted to help these people from this friendly country. Providing jobs seemed the substantive way to help them. He was riding in a city bus outside San José, wondering if there was something they manufactured here that he could sell back in the United States. At a bus stop, Mike looked out the window and saw a leather shop. He got off the bus and went in. It was a little hole in the wall. Workers were bent over workbenches making leather goods—luggage and duffel bags. He met the master craftsman, who spoke some English. Could they make bags for him to sell in the United States? They could. Could they use vegetable-only dyes? They could. Were forests being cut down for grazing land for the cows? They weren't. Mike took some samples and came back to the Bay Area. His girl-friend thought he was crazy. "Why don't you get a job!" she screamed at him. She left him because she thought his life was going nowhere.

Mike went around to banks in the Bay Area, showing these well-crafted bags and his business plan, hoping to receive a loan for a small importing business. He always showed them his Success Formula. He made them read it. He wanted them to understand he wasn't just going to be a bag salesman. He was that bricklayer who was helping to build a cathedral. He was helping the families of those guys at the workbenches in Costa Rica. He got a loan, bought some bags, and began cold-calling on Silicon Valley software companies, trying to get them to buy his bags as giveaways. It wasn't an easy sell, but he was in business. He called his operation the Joseph Company. It was difficult to keep faith. Often nobody cared who he was helping.

A year into it, he met a banker in Oakland who made it her business to help disadvantaged communities. Her mission was much like his, except she had a lot of experience in what she was doing. She suggested Mike buy a small warehouse building in West Oakland, where unemployment was 50 percent, and use that as his domestic warehouse. This would qualify him for special community-development loans she could offer. "I can't buy a building! I'm selling bags out of my car!" But she loaned him the money to buy a small two-story building, and then she went down to Costa Rica with him. Impressed, she urged him to buy the factory in Costa Rica and move it to a tax-free zone near the San José airport. That seemed way out of his league, but she coached him through the process and loaned him the money. He bought a factory with fifty workers, and he has four employees in Oakland. That's his life now. The bags and leather goods are not a big operation. He rents half of his Oakland building to a tenant, and the factory in Costa Rica still has all *its* customers, only Mike is now the owner. He's married with a baby girl. When he quotes poetry, it's hard to imagine he was once a pushy salesman:

"No eloquent words of a man can replace the pathless forest or the quietness of a rock."

None of this would have flowered if he hadn't challenged himself to write down the standards by which he wanted to live, then let that guide him.

42 ||| Trafficking in Extremes

Did you ever dream of working abroad?

I went to Hong Kong to look for stories because the city seemed an accessible frontier. It was the most modern and cosmopolitan of all cities in the world, with every convenience one might be accustomed to, from Pilates classes to chicken-ginger wraps. Those who spoke English there did so better than I. Yet it bordered China, then was handed over to China, and remained the gateway between capitalism and communism. If I was looking for a little adventure, but I still wanted to have a career in traditional business, that's where I would move. So I went to find people who had done just that.

No sooner did I get there than I was told this wasn't *the* place to be. "Oh, you gotta go to Shenzen, in the New Territories!" "No, no, you gotta go to Shanghai! That's where it's really at." The frontier is a state of mind. People who'd come to Hong Kong had grown accustomed to it, and now some other city took on the symbol of the frontier. But I wasn't looking for the ultimate frontier. I wanted a place that anybody could move to, and be gainfully employed, yet was *interesting*—which I'd learned in New Orleans was created by collisions of diametrically opposed extreme contrasts. By that measure, Hong Kong was the most interesting city on earth.

Everywhere, freewheeling *über*capitalism collided with China's state-run central plan. For one tiny example of how freewheeling it is, consider the typical twenty-dollar Hong Kong paper bill. Except you can't, because there is no typical twenty-dollar bill. Many different banks are authorized to print currency, and their bills don't look alike. They're about the same size, but the Standard Chartered Bank's twenty is in different colors and a very different pattern and typeface from the twenty from the Bank of China or the Hong Kong and Shanghai Banking Corporation. This didn't bother anybody, and they all were honored as legal tender. I felt like printing some twenties myself. Multiply this concept by every layer of the economy, and you begin to imagine how entrepreneurial you might become if you lived there a few years. Businesspeople I met carried at least a half-dozen different business cards, ready to pounce whether I happened to be in real estate or semiconductors. The only reason this dynamism hasn't taken over the planet is that China stands in its way. In China, where entrepreneurism has met its match, the rules and customs for doing business are so convoluted and arbitrary that it will sap the spirit of all but Hong Kong's most relentless capitalists. There is no way to know how much money has to be spread around, no quoted price on bribing certain levels of bureaucrats. A deal is not a deal. Maybe your factory will get built, maybe not. The system must be worked continuously to have any chance.

So, despite the fact that so many businesses want to invest in China, many grow frustrated and focus instead on Hong Kong, which has become far and away the most expensive city in the world. Your basic Mid-Levels flat without a view would set an expat back $6,000 U.S. in rent every month. Out of frustration, I might move across the harbor to Kowloon and try to buy; a 1,700-square-foot flat sells for $1,100,000 U.S. How can all these taxi drivers and shopkeepers possibly pay their rent? Sure, I might be able to pay it, living on a hyperinflated expat salary, but how can a merchant hawking Baby Gap denim jackets for $2.50 in an open-air market possibly compete? The answer is, they *don't*. They're locals. The government builds housing for them and sells it at a subsidized rate. Eighty percent of the housing is nonmarket. The government erects endless skinny twenty-five-story apartment towers on every possible scrap of land; each floor has two 500-square-foot apartments, which are sold to locals for about $140,000 U.S. They're cheaply constructed. Those who can afford it hire private contractors to tear it up and redo it to their liking. Only Carl Sagan could convey how many of these skinny towers there are. *As many as there are blades of grass on a football field . . .* All the way in from the airport, a forty-minute drive, the harbors are lined with these towers, one behind the other, up into the hills. Imagine every brownstone in Manhattan as a skinny twenty-five-story tower, with no bigger footprint. Every row house in Baltimore. Every Victorian in San Francisco. There are more people per square kilometer here than anywhere on earth. I was told the populated side of Hong Kong Island was ten times as dense as Manhattan. Ten times!

This is a city in love with skyscrapers. There are almost a hundred more than fifty stories tall. In my neighborhood stood the fifth and sixth tallest buildings in the world. Yet, unlike Manhattan, above this skyline is a mountain, Victoria Peak, twice as tall as the tallest building. The mountain is covered in a lush green tropical forest. Sixty percent of Hong Kong Island is national park. Nature competes hard with capitalism. A fifteen-minute cab ride through the tunnel in the mountain dropped me into a series of gorgeous small towns comprising Mediterranean-style houses gathered around perfect sandy beaches on soft aqua bays surrounded by tropical forest. The ideal South Pacific kick-it-back repose is *right there,* three kilometers away, butting up against the city bustle, and holding its own.

The expat's life traffics through these extremes. Spending $4 a person on lunch in the markets, then dropping $150 a person on dinner in the ultrahip restaurants of the Lan Kwai Fong clubbing district. The workweek is spent anonymously in the concrete anthill, then the weekend is spent in a communal beach house on one of many nearby tropical islands, a quick ferry ride away. Sometimes it seems incredibly diverse, with English spoken in so many nuanced accents, from Singapore, Nepal, the Philippines, Canada, England, and regions of India. Other times the expat is painfully aware of being an outsider, floating in a fat cream on top, while 96 percent of the population are Cantonese-speaking ethnic Chinese who have been burned too many times by falling in love with or becoming friends with an expat who inevitably leaves after three or four years. Colonials have been coming here for four hundred years, and you're just another in a long line who wants to break some local's heart.

There's always a rapid turnover on the frontier, which means that even though you're young, you can be thrust into responsibility very quickly. This was the case with Allan Matheson. A year ago he was hanging out in Vancouver without a job, living with his parents and drinking away his meager savings. On a friend's tip, he learned of a job opening—the membership manager of the Canadian Chamber of Commerce in Hong Kong. Industrious but unqualified, full of potential but lacking any experience, he talked his way into the job and came to Hong Kong. Today, at the age of twenty-four, he's running the Chamber.

This is a big deal. A huge pipeline of money and people moves between Vancouver and Hong Kong. Both the United States and Canada allow investor visas, which means if you have a million dollars to invest here, you

can become a citizen. But the United States forces investors to choose—
they can be an American citizen, or a Hong Kong citizen, but not both.
Canada allows dual citizenship. So partly through investor visas, and
partly through ordinary immigration channels, almost everyone in Hong
Kong has either been to Canada to visit or has a relative who has done so.
Before the 1997 handover of Hong Kong to China, 40,000 people a year
moved from Hong Kong to Canada. They brought with them an insane
amount of money. These flows have stabilized now since the handover,
but the pipeline was built. In Hong Kong, there are 150,000 people who
carry Canadian passports, and over 30,000 were born in Canada. The reason they're coming back is that the top tax bracket in Hong Kong is 15
percent. I don't know what it is in Canada, but I'd guess three or four
times that rate.

So the Canadian Chamber is not one of those rinky-dink trade groups
that throws cocktail parties nobody attends. Business in Asia is done with
relationships, and so every Canadian company needs introductions to
Hong Kong and Chinese business partners. When they have a new product for the Asian market, they often look to Allan to make these introductions. If they want to take advantage of cheap Chinese labor, they ask Allan
for manufacturers. And it is through the Chamber that Canadian companies lobby the Hong Kong government to have environmental standards
enforced and racial discrimination forbidden. When the Chamber throws
a cocktail party, *everybody* comes, and businesspeople mix freely with
diplomats and government officials.

Is Allan up to it? Or will the result be the same as when twenty-four-
year-old guys took their Internet start-ups public? It's a scary thought.

Hong Kong has that anything-can-happen vibe. Nobody's promising the upside, but the possibility is there, even for a slacker like Allan.

"I was basically a lazy guy," he tells me, when we go out for burritos on Elgin Street. "My only work experience was as a data processor in a hospital foundation."

That was during college at the University of British Columbia. With graduation nearing and no clue what to do, he bought a Eurail pass an hour before his last exam. After a few months in Europe, he went on the Internet and found a language school in Beijing. He had taken one semester of Mandarin in college, which is not unusual. He arrived in Beijing and was quickly frustrated. These language schools are set up to attract U.S. dollars. They're filled with American businessmen and students, speaking English to each other. Allan wanted to immerse himself. So he walked over to Qinghua University, which was full of mainland Chinese students. He asked to attend their School of Business and Management. Their classes were only in Mandarin, and they told Allan his was not good enough. He persuaded them, "Well, listen, I won't pay you regular tuition. I'll pay you what I was paying that language school." He wanted to live in a dorm but they insisted on a hotel. In all other ways, he participated as a regular student, which is very unusual. At the end of the year, his laptop was stolen, which turned out to be insured, and the insurance paid him $4,500, far more than it was worth. So he came home to Vancouver to live with his parents and party on his $4,500.

Again, he had no clue what to do. Nothing seemed to pique his interest. One day he received a call from an old college friend, Stephanie (I later bumped into Stephanie on the street). She was flying through Vancouver on her way back to Hong Kong, and she was at the airport on a four-hour layover. Did he have time for a drink? He had all the time in the world.

At the airport bar, she mentioned this position was open at the Chamber. When she told him, the lightbulb went on. He wanted that job. He called and begged for four months. Finally they hired him. Which doesn't explain how he became the executive director seven months later. Nothing quite explains that. He was very good at being the membership manager, and the director happened to quit around the same time as one of her likely replacements also quit—the revolving door of expats left a hole to fill. The Chamber's board was recruiting from Canada, but Allan kept pushing them to hire him instead, and ultimately he convinced them. So far, everyone in town thinks he's doing a good job.

"I know I had never demonstrated that I had it in me," he said. "But I did. And I just had to get in the right environment, where I could really put all this energy to good use. Hong Kong turned me on. It turned me from a guy headed nowhere to a guy really doing something."

In Hong Kong, they appreciate that business is a form of diplomacy. It can serve a higher purpose in the struggle against communism and warlord feudalism. Capitalism begins with the basic concept of private property, which gives everyone with property a stake, and through that stake a desire to fight for individual liberty. Eventually, capitalism can create a middle class and bring prosperity. This isn't without significant trade-offs, of course, but many businesspeople in Hong Kong saw their work on these terms. They paid close attention to the political changes in Southeast Asia, and they felt that their work contributed, sometimes directly, to the weaving of an economic fabric that could hold these countries together despite political turmoil. One of those who thinks in this way is Brooks Entwhistle, who is thirty-four and is a banker for Goldman Sachs.

During the nineties, Brooks worked for the United Nations with the Carter Center, helping to administer first democratic elections—in Cambodia in 1993, in Liberia in 1995, and in Mozambique in 1997. He flew to these countries and was assigned a precinct. He ran get-out-the-vote efforts, then helped to validate the results. It was enormously satisfying work, to see democracy in action, to watch people get to vote for the first time in their lives.

"But Cambodia and Liberia did not stay democracies for very long," he said. "They quickly fell back into the hands of warlords and the military. To the Khmer Rouge in Cambodia and to Charles Taylor in Liberia. We learned that democracy cannot sustain itself without an economy, without people having a financial stake in it remaining free. Business is a huge democratizing force in India and northern Asia."

Brooks had put in two years as an analyst with Goldman right out of college. "But, you know, I didn't learn anything as just an analyst, didn't know any better. I learned to use the copy machine." So he went back to Goldman, both to learn how business was done, and to help them seed capitalism throughout undeveloped Asia. Their Hong Kong office has been open eleven years; it's grown from a couple dozen to a couple hundred.

"Doing business here is not one-dimensional like back in the States," he said. "You have to learn languages, or learn to work with translators and communicate despite the language barrier. You have to understand economic policies. You have to be willing to work with local governments. And mostly, you have to be willing to have genuine respect for other people's point of view. You can't be bullheaded here. You wear many hats and draw on many disciplines."

The shelves in Brooks's home are not filled with marketing primers, they're filled with political biographies.

"One of my greatest joys is getting together with our friends on Friday night. During the week, people have been off doing interesting work. One guy has come back from Vietnam, and he has a story to tell. Someone else has been in Indonesia, and a friend of my wife's has been in Taiwan on a deal. When we get together to talk, it's *interesting*."

He said this with a little regret, a sadness. I probed, and he admitted he was considering moving back to the States. His daughter was the same age as my son, and his wife preferred to raise her back home. Brooks was visibly torn. He would only hint at it, but I could tell what he was hinting at, since I'd had this conversation with many other people who had as much talent as he did. In his heart he knew that his years at Goldman were not intended to be the pinnacle of his career. He meant them as training for his future contribution to the big picture, a stepping-stone to a bold venture that might more directly push democracy into Asia. He didn't know what that might be, but he was trying hard not to forget those vague ambitions.

Relationships and Family

STRUGGLING TO SATISFY DUAL CAREERS

Perhaps, in your travels, you'll stop traveling, because you've found the place where you most belong. For a long while this won't seem like an environment/culture story, but I assure you that it is.

I knew Mark Kraschel fourteen years ago. We were friendly during the two years I was at First Boston, where he also worked. Six years ago he and a girlfriend showed up in the crowd when I read at a bookstore, but that was our entire interaction in all these years. We knew each other once, and I'd moved on with my life, and he'd faded back into the rabble of strangers. Shortly after I put word of this project on my website, my phone rang. It was Mark. He had changed his life. Radically. He termed it "career suicide."

"And it's all your fault." He laughed.

A few things about Mark, from when I knew him fourteen years ago: He was a tall, uncoordinated, pasty-faced redhead with a bitter sense of humor, but none of his jokes were his own—he repeated quick one-liners he'd heard over the wire. He earned about $160,000 a year as a money markets salesman. In the hierarchy of salespeople, money markets is bottom rung. Mark's special trait was that he could be brutally honest, particularly about himself. Mark never quite felt like he belonged—he loved it but didn't feel like he deserved to be there. He was no brainiac. He frequently quipped that you could teach a rhesus monkey to do his job (a borrowed line). Whenever someone wondered why the markets were moving, he'd answer, "Don't ask me, I'm a hick from Oregon." While everyone else on the floor had been recruited from the best business schools—Stanford, Wharton, Kellogg, et cetera—Mark had started with a two-week temp gig in the mail room, and brown-nosed his way into a sales assistant position on the floor. He attended business school in a night program at the University of San Francisco and was promoted from within, an extremely rare event at a firm so concerned with its employees' pedigrees. His mail-room-to-money-markets arc wasn't a point of pride with him. He credited luck and ass kissing. "I shouldn't be here," he'd confide, waving at the high-priced talent. "I should be selling these guys car insurance. I should be at H&R Block, filing their taxes." He frequently reminded me that he had a twin brother, an identical twin, who was living in Portland, married, making $30,000 a year as a real estate appraiser. "I'm a boring person," Mark would say. "I'm white trash. My brother is living the life I should rightfully be living."

Mark hung in there, and he survived the industry contraction after the '87 market crash. They kept him because he was honest, had a submissive ego, and by Wall Street standards was cheap labor. Most employees from the top firms like First Boston were able to cash in on the firm's reputation, trading down to less stressful jobs at less prestigious firms, often switching to the buy side to manage money. A few years later, Mark duplicated this trade into a position at Wells Fargo, where he patiently worked up the ranks, and, by the time I saw him six years ago, he was a vice president at Wells Fargo, managing four people and ten billion dollars. He'd paid his dues and outlasted the hotshots and grew to understand that Wall Street really isn't that different from any other industry. Life is a series of trades. Don't be a fool, and you can trade yourself right into the good life. Mark made $250,000 a year, bankable (salary). He lived in a two-thousand-square-foot apartment on the top floor of the tallest high-rise in Pacific Heights. He was thirty-three years old. Life was as good as it gets. Was he comfortable in his skin? More so, but not quite. Was he an interesting person yet? Not really. He knew his life was a bit of a yuppie stereotype. He couldn't make his relationships with women work. He started dating a beautiful twenty-seven-year-old German girl, and it felt like First Boston, redux: "What's a hick like me doing with a beauty like her?" He loved her. She was the one piece of his life that transcended yuppie stereotype. She made him interesting.

During this project, Mark and I spoke a lot over the phone. It did not carry the same immediacy as meeting in person. But our years as salespeople had taught us both to love the phone. We learned to recognize clients by the tone of their voice within the first syllable spoken. Introductions became unnecessary as our hearing developed an acuity. For a salesperson, the telephone can be as intimate as a candlelit dinner. And when Mark called out of the blue that day, it brought everything back. Faces change, but voices don't.

Mark called from Portland. He was sitting at a desk in the Portland Unified School District trying to sort out a bug in his Excel spreadsheet. He'd been pretending to work on it for hours. He was surrounded by "fat ugly women" who had made the school district their life, and there was a woman down the hall who was very upset that Mark wasn't "getting it." She was making his life hell.

"How long have you been there?" I asked.

"A few months. I was hired to handle their finance. I thought it would mean managing their investment portfolio. Turns out they needed a clerk to handle accounting on a prehistoric non-double-entry bookkeeping system. It sucks. I'm making twenty percent of what I was earning just two years ago. I can't believe how badly I screwed up."

"You're living your brother's life," I said.

"Except for the wife and kids and house part."

"Are you still with that woman I met?"

He laughed, like *No way.* "Nicole? You remember her?"

"No, I'm being polite and pretending like I remember her. I only remember you were with someone."

"Well, she's a big part of how I ended up here."

"Oh, this is a love story."

"I wish. We should talk. What are you doing tonight?"

I gave him my home number to call.

"Gotta hop," he said, which is how one says good-bye in the markets.

The rest of the day I was insatiably curious. What did he mean by "It's all *your fault*?" How had Mark fallen from such heights? I began writing down everything I could remember of him. We'd biked once in Marin and his legs, arms, and neck were badly sunburned. Another night I took him to an aerobics class, and he sprained his ankle within minutes.

I learned more that night and in the following weeks. It was quite a cautionary tale. It started two years ago.

"I was thirty-seven years old. I wanted to be married and raise kids. Nicole had had a hard time finding work in San Francisco, so she had gone back to Germany. I dated other women but I missed her. I had a great life but without someone to share it with, it wasn't so great. I flew to Frankfurt to see her every month, just for the weekend, for two or three days. That seemed crazy. And I started thinking. Why am I not happy? What's the point of life?"

He told himself the truth—his life had always been a little bit of a borrowed line. There had to be something more for him out there. He'd always admired how I had left sales and trading, despite having a talent for it, and gone on to find my true self. He also admired another coworker of ours who had moved to New Zealand. He respected the leaps we'd taken more than he respected any Big Swinging Dick on Wall Street. Wall Street pretends to take risks, but it's only with money—the big risk is with one's life.

"I wanted to be a citizen of the world," Mark said. "I'm a small-town kid from Oregon. Most people I grew up with never left. They're still here. I didn't want to lead a safe mundane life out of fear. My parents were dead. This ain't no dress rehearsal."

Mark contemplated giving it all up and moving to Frankfurt. He'd climbed up the ladder here, and he could do it again there. Once he considered this, the idea had a sway over him. He'd always felt like he got his start at First Boston out of serendipity and luck. He felt like an imposter. Was his whole life a fluke? This was his chance to prove it wasn't a fluke. If he could rebuild his life in Frankfurt, he'd finally feel like he belonged, right?

"When you meet with success, it's natural to wonder, 'Can I do this again?' So I tried to repeat it."

He marched into his boss's office and resigned, leaving a $250,000 job for nothing. Anyone on Wall Street would tell you he got the short end of the trade, but the sheer craziness of it had its own appeal.

"It's so easy to derail a career," he remarked. "It's scary."

He moved to Frankfurt. He talked to a headhunter and a guy from Deutsche Bank and one from J. P. Morgan. The language barrier was a much bigger impediment than he anticipated. And the labor laws made it difficult for them to hire a foreigner. Without a job, Mark didn't feel like a man. He got depressed and gave up after a month. He called Wells Fargo and begged for his old job back. They turned him down.

He moved into his sister's apartment in Seattle. He traded several steps down the prestige curve and ran money for a regional dealer. This was called "proprietary trading," and it was not like what he'd been doing at Wells Fargo, where he kept their money safely invested at reasonable returns. Prop trading is day trading, and it requires a daredevil philosophy. Much as Mark wanted to think of himself as a daredevil (based on his recent life decisions), he really didn't fit in. It was not the kind of investing he'd learned. Very quickly, his boss threatened to fire him, so he quit.

He called Nicole in Frankfurt and begged her to move to New York City with him. She agreed after he proposed marriage and bought an engagement ring. In New York, he figured he'd have no trouble getting a job resembling the one he had at Wells Fargo. Wall Street was booming with Internet money. But in every interview, Mark had to explain why he'd ditched Wells Fargo, and this story didn't fly in New York. It was a big black mark. He had dozens of friends in the business. Nobody helped him out.

"When you check out, you realize how few friends you have. Most of those networks of friends are worthless."

He became a financial writer for Standard & Poor's. He hated it immediately but lasted a year. Nicole was a stock broker, which required her to schmooze clients most nights. Mark complained they weren't spending any time together. He pushed her to get a job that she could leave at the office. She didn't want to hear it. At the end of the year, Nicole moved back to Germany. Mark wasn't invited. Once again, Mark called Wells Fargo and begged for his old job back, or any job. They told him to forget it. So Mark gave up and dropped out.

"I was burned out on life."

Mark knew one other guy who had checked out from Wall Street. Talbott now owned a little marina on Candlewood Lake, near a tony enclave called Sherman, Connecticut. Mark went upstate and became a gas boy. Talbott couldn't pay him to pump gas, but Mark was welcome to the tips. Mark slept on the couch in the marina office. They drank beer all day, watched pornos, scarfed hot dogs, and waterskied. At times this life seemed like a salvation, but it was degrading to pump gas. Most of the customers were Wall Street brokers with summer homes on the lake, a constant reminder of exactly how Mark had fucked up. To get tips, he had to tell them he was working gratis.

"A lot of people think they might be happier just working the dock at a marina," I suggested.

"That's what I thought. Say fuck it, give up, enjoy life. Some people can do that. I wanted that to be me but that's not me and I knew it."

Eventually Talbott's wife asked Mark to leave. She was a nurse. She was jealous that she had to change bed pans all day while her husband bummed with his buddy. Mark bought a bicycle and decided to ride across the country. It would be a pilgrimage. He filled his water bottle, packed his toothbrush, and pedaled into the sunset. He made it as far as Chicago. Twenty days on a hard seat alone with your thoughts is more than enough time to contemplate your navel. He wanted to work, had to get a job, felt disgusting. In Chicago he jumped on a plane and flew to Portland. He rented a room in the dank basement of a police officer's house for a month until he was hired by the school district, when he was able to rent a down-town loft. Recently he'd started dating a lesbian. The way he said that, it was as if he was still using women to make himself interesting.

"That's it," he said. "That's my whole fucking story. The moral of which is, I'm back where I began. Who am I? I'm a hick from Oregon. I have a shitty job, I'm alone, and I'm envious as hell of my brother, who has a beautiful little kid."

But that wasn't the end of the story. This is an environment story, re-member? We haven't got to that part yet.

A month after calling me, Mark flew down to San Francisco for the day to beg for his old job again. He hoped that offering his apology in person might loosen the resentment that had cemented against him at Wells Fargo. It didn't. We had a drink that night at the Elite Café on Fillmore Street in Pacific Heights, and afterward we walked over to his old apart-ment building at 2000 Sacramento Street. The doorman had changed.

"When I was young in the city, I always wanted to live here. It repre-sented success to me. The tallest building in the neighborhood. It was full of very old rich people. And I threw it away."

Mark blamed himself entirely. His fault was being ungrateful for how life had blessed him. That didn't sound quite right to me. He didn't take the big leap out of greed—he did it for love, right? But I was grateful he didn't resent me, since my leap had been one of his inspirations. We talked about my book. I told him I was constantly worried I would give readers false inspiration.

"Are you worried someone's going to blame you?" he asked.

"Not really. But I want to offer fair advice. I want to be responsible. Re-sponsible to the consequences of failing, yet also responsible to that un-born person inside who's struggling to get out."

"Why? Who cares? What's wrong with holding some things in?"

I said, "Because if you don't let that person out, it can haunt you, it can ruin you, and you will resent life, and resent others who have more courage than you, and most of all, it very likely will find its own way out, ripping a big hole in your life."

"Or you could rip a big hole in your life trying to let it out."

"Maybe."

I took him to the airport.

That night I couldn't sleep. Mark's story made me question my entire project. No matter how realistic the stories were that I'd found, there was no doubt that I had a slant. Why was I bent on encouraging people to change their lives? Because I've watched my generation stop reading books, stop reading the newspaper, stop voting in local elections? Because I've watched money/salary become a proxy for respect, and then a synonym for respect, and then the only kind of respect that counts? Because I have seen us judge books we have not read, politicians we have not heard, musicians we have not listened to, referendums we have not debated, and fellow citizens we have not met? Because I have seen us torn apart by jealousy for what others our age have accomplished, rather than celebrating those accomplishments? Because I have seen us glorify those who make decisions over those who enact decisions, prefer being a consultant to being fully engaged, being an investor to being invested in, being an adviser over being politically involved, being an expert over being partisan, being a news analyst over being a news gatherer—all in fear of the inflexible boredom of commitment?

Well, so what? Who am I to know better? Mark was right. Who cares?

I planned on going to see Mark in Portland the next month, but it never came together. That was because Mark got a call from a headhunter. Headhunters can be a little cagey, but this one explained he was looking for a portfolio manager to work in the UAE.

"The what?"

"The UAE. The United Arab Emirates."

Would Mark come to Manhattan to meet with him? Mark had never heard of the UAE, but he was excited that *anyone* would consider hiring him again as a portfolio manager. What the hell? A few days later he was sitting in the open-air café of the Helmsley Palace lobby, talking to the headhunter. Then Mark met with two men. The job was with the Abu Dhabi Investment Authority, which managed the country's excess wealth from the sale of oil. It was sort of like the Alaska Permanent Fund and was supposed to help the nation and its people remain prosperous after the oil is gone. One of the things about Arab business culture is, they never tell you directly if they appreciate you. You hear secondhand. So Mark had no idea what they thought of him or who his competition was. He did learn how he'd been recommended for the job—two of his old bosses at First Boston had put in a good word for him. That meant a lot to Mark.

When Mark got home to Portland, the headhunter had already called to say he wanted to offer Mark the job.

"What do you know about the UAE?" he asked, calling me and everyone else he knew.

"Nothing," I said.

"I'm scared," he said. "I've heard terrible things about the Middle East."

He was scared because he wanted to go. "Anything's gotta be better than this."

The headhunter offered to fly him to Abu Dhabi and see the country. Mark said no. He was afraid he might lose his courage, and he was afraid—deep down—that they would figure out he was an imposter and didn't deserve the job. The last two years had crippled his confidence. The more time his employers spent with him, the more chance they had to rescind the offer. So Mark took the job, sight unseen, and moved to the Middle East.

"I go tomorrow," he said, another call. "What the fuck? I wanted the adventure, right? You're either able to say yes to the unknown or not."

"Wear sunscreen," I said.

"Will you come visit me?" he asked. "You gotta, for the book."

"Ah, man. I just got back from Hong Kong."

"Nothing like seeing it with your own eyes."

"I'll try. It's a long way."

"Work the trade, man. Make it happen."

"I'll try."

At last we get to the culture/environment part.

Mark Kraschel, hick from Oregon, found his place at long last in Abu Dhabi. This was completely unexpected. He went there blindly, seeking only adventure. But within months he was saying, "Now I wonder what all the fuss was about! I'm living on cloud nine, drive a brand-new Beemer, and am trying to figure out how to get my twenty-one-year-old Romanian girlfriend back into the country without marrying her." After a night out smoking *chicha* and drinking tea with his expat buddies, he'd come back to his empty office around 11 P.M., where the call to me was on the house. "I play squash at lunch and golf three times a week. I live in a spacious apartment overlooking the Gulf. My commute is less than five minutes. I work with a great group of very wealthy people. Life is good. Wells Fargo can kiss my ass."

Most of this was bragging, and Mark was using common symbols of success as evidence of his happiness. But even on a psychological level, the UAE was a great fit for him. The job he had, and the lifestyle he led, were almost identical to the ones he had in San Francisco. He was managing ten billion dollars, same as at Wells. Nice apartment? Check. Foreign girlfriend? Check. Sports car? Check. Outdoor recreation? Check. The piece that was different was the culture. He finally felt like things were right in his life because the culture made sense to him.

First, a few basic facts about the UAE. It was granted independence from Britain after World War II. When oil prices shot up in the early 1970s, the country was transformed overnight from a poor nomadic culture to one with one of the highest per capita incomes worldwide. Only about 20 percent of the population are native citizens. The rest, like Mark, have moved there in the last twenty-five years from other Arab nations, Sri Lanka, the Philippines, and recently Eastern Europe. It is a land of opportunity, full of shocking contrasts. There's no crime, no beggars, no tax limits, and no speed limits. More Mercedeses per capita, but also the highest vehicular death rate anywhere. A strict prohibition on premarital sex, as in any Muslim country, but one of the highest rates of STDs in the world. The government is run by Muslims, but the cities are grotesquely westernized, overrun by McDonald's and Pizza Hut.

Mark fell in quickly with the British expat contingent. He was one of only two Americans around, so Mark Kraschel, Mr. Boring, was suddenly exotic. He had a funny accent and an unusual vocabulary and one hell of a story to tell. Everyone wanted to meet him. It didn't take a girl on his arm to make him interesting. Remember, Mark was an identical twin; his whole life he'd sought the feeling of being unique. At last he was the outsider, not shadowed by a parallel self. Is it possible that being an outsider is what someone might need to feel at home? Plus, Mark had risen again to his old level, proving that he deserved this. It wasn't a fluke.

Mark was relieved to be off the career roller coaster and enjoy some stability. He thought he'd had stability at First Boston and at Wells Fargo, but now he realizes that a two-year contract *wasn't* security. He was always one bad trade away from being shown the door. The work culture in the UAE is old-fashioned, like something out of our early 1960s.

Mark explained, "In the U.S., the trend in the labor market is to make you disposable. I was a replaceable commodity. That's no way to live a life. I lived in fear. Job security is an important thing. People in the States are so used to it now they don't know any better. Companies here don't lay people off. I have a job I love and I have no chance of being fired. It's much more civil. They appreciate seniority and respect people who've put in the time. None of this worshiping the young hotshot. I work a thirty-eight-hour work week and get a two-month vacation. Two months! I'm appreciated by my coworkers. You can't imagine how good that feels. It's a sweet thing to have a good job and be proud of it."

Relationships between men and women were also old-fashioned. The Muslim influence rubbed off on the expats. They were big on formal introductions. Most women stopped working once married. The men are expected to support their wife, or wives, in a style they are accustomed to. Women demand their men put up or shut up after a year. It's not like in the States, where either side might string the other along for years before they're ready. In the States, the expectation for what marriage should be is so high. The Muslim way is much more pragmatic.

"They just want somebody to be with," Mark said. "It's not this American ideal of finding a soul mate. It's simple. Do you have fun together?"

"You don't want to find a soul mate?"

"My expectations are not huge. I want a woman comfortable with being a wife."

"Meaning not needing her own career?"

"My mom was a single career woman," he said. "I dated women like her for a long time. I tried to make it work with Nicole. Two careers, two countries—a ship can't have two captains. I respect how they do it here. It's more workable. I want someone who's around."

"You don't want your kids to go through what you went through."

"Yeah. I know that sounds unenlightened, but I would disagree. They have *sharia* marriage here, as defined by Muslim law. It's a no-fault marriage, and it's an explicit arrangement, where things are worked out in advance, like the level of financial support, and whether you live in the same or separate bedrooms—"

"—Separate bedrooms?"

"Men and women lead separate lives here. The women go out with the women, the guys hang with the guys, and nobody feels guilty about it. The Muslim men can have multiple wives—"

"—Now I see the appeal."

"It's not for the sex. Guys who need sex on the side keep mistresses.

The multiple wives is a pragmatic thing. Nobody wants to be alone. So a Muslim's second wife might be his first cousin, so she won't be a spinster. It's a way of assigning responsibility for who is going to take care of people. Everyone is taken care of. Same as at work. There's a stability in not having unrealistic expectations."

"You're going to sound like a misogynist."

"Guys in the States treat their women with no dignity. It's so casual it's demeaning."

Maybe I didn't agree with it, but I found some empathy for what Mark was saying. I'd been on both sides. My ex-wife was from Tacoma, Washington. She had a West Coast feminist mentality. When I introduced her, it was important not to label her as "my wife," because that made her feel like a piece of property. She was her own person. I bought into that philosophy of equals and learned my way around these minefields, but after we got divorced, I was in another universe with Michele, who's from Texas and has very different expectations of how a woman should be treated. It's disrespectful to her if I don't make it clear she is the most important person in my life when I introduce her. I *always* say, "This is my *wife*, Michele."

Mark talked a good game but it was not so easy to shake his American expectations. He had fallen in love with a young Romanian woman named Elena. She had been working as a cocktail waitress earning $200 a month. Elena had no desire to keep getting her ass pinched every night. She was only twenty-one, and considering she was from a formerly repressed country she might want a few years of freedom, right? No thank you. She wanted security. She took Mark back to Romania on vacation to meet her family. He did manage to get her back into the UAE without marrying her, but it took a few weeks, and once she showed up she put it to him: "Are you going to marry me?"

"I balked," he said. "In that moment, I didn't *know*."

"Do you have fun together?"

"Absolutely. Ahh, man . . . We'd never talked about marriage before. She caught me by surprise."

"So how did she react to you being Mr. United States 'I Can't Commit'?"

"She ran out."

"When?"

"Yesterday."

"Why didn't you say yes, you dope? All that jive you gave me about not expecting too much?"

"Eastern European women are different. It was a little presumptuous. I mean, a marriage is a thing that should be talked about a little, shouldn't it? What do we expect, what do we want, how many kids . . ."

"Hah! You still need a *little* bit of soul mate, don't you?"

"Maybe a little."

"Will she come back?"

"I don't know."

Elena came back two hours later, and they went to work on finding an in-between.

I was happy for Mark. I respected that he needed a culture where "a ship doesn't have two captains," and I recognized that he arrived at this solution only after five hard years trying to balance his career with Nicole's. He moved to Germany for her, and then to New York for her—he tried. But not many couples are going to find solace in his story. *Honey, I'm leaving you for another country.* Dual ambitions will tear many relationships apart, inevitably, but no couple wants to accept that possibility. They want to find a solution. They recognize there are going to be some sacrifices, but the bottom line is, *breaking up is not acceptable.*

There are no right answers for how couples handle their dual ambitions, so I want to tread there only lightly. Yet it's important to talk about, because fears of hurting your relationship can hold you back from finding your dream. I'd like to offer two portraits of happy couples. They're at spots that a lot of couples fear and fantasize about. The first is a couple whose dreams, once so aligned, are beginning to part. The second is a couple who've quit their careers in order to work together.

WHEN PATHS BEGIN TO PART

Tom and Jennifer Scott first contacted me from an Internet café in Chiang Mai, Thailand, where they'd heard about my book. I imagined word of my project being passed along like an old 95-cent edition of *Tropic of Cancer*. Tom and Jennifer were four months into their five-month sojourn and Tom was dreading the trip's end, because he was no closer to figuring out what he wanted to do with the rest of his life than he had been on the day he left the States. They were refugees from Washington, D.C., where they'd spent the last eight years working in politics. They did not intend to return to D.C. They'd cleaned out their apartment, sold their car, and put their possessions in storage. They were not quite thirty.

Tom was waiting for an epiphany. He anticipated that without the intense daily obligations of national politics, his head would be clear to do the big thinking he never had time for.

"I really thought that one night I'd wake up in my sleep and realize, 'This is what I want to do,' " he said later.

The first month, he suffered withdrawal from politics. He was watching CNN every night from their hotels in New Zealand, trying to get the latest on the disputed presidential election. The second month in Australia and the third month in Malaysia, he reveled in the trip, procrastinating on that big thinking he'd planned. This last month he was no longer sleeping well as reality was setting in and the Decision was haunting him. You have thirty-six days to decide. You have twenty-two days to decide. Fourteen days . . .

For the record, I'll say here what I told Tom when he landed back on our shores: Do not wait for the kind of clarity that comes with epiphanies. In the nine hundred plus stories I heard in my research, almost nobody

was struck with an epiphany. It was one of my biggest surprises. Most people had a slim notion or a slight urge that they slowly nurtured until it grew into a faint hope which barely stayed alive for years until it could mature into a vision. Most people feel guilty about wanting what they want, and they feel foolish for wanting something impossible, and those censoring voices will bark like a pack of junkyard dogs, night after night. Don't doubt your desire because it comes to you as a whisper; don't think, "If it were really important to me, I'd feel clearer about this, less conflicted." My research didn't show that to be true. The things we really want to do are usually the ones that scare us the most. The things you'll not feel conflicted about are the choices that leave no one hurt.

Jennifer never had as hard a time. She'd been a speechwriter and then the deputy chief of staff for a Washington State Republican congressman who represented two wineries in the Columbia and Yakima valleys. From her first meeting with the winemakers she was intrigued. A lot of foodies develop an appreciation for wine, but Jennifer kept abreast of the industry's needs, and she even took a class on the history of the wine industry. The culture of D.C. turns everyone into expert spinmeisters, so she figured she had the skills to handle public relations for a winery. The day before she left her job, she called the two wineries and asked for some contacts in Napa Valley. As they traveled through New Zealand and Australia, she kept dragging Tom to vineyards for tastings.

The day she and Tom landed back in the States, she felt like a string of lucky stars steered her right into a job in the industry. They flew into Reno, and in the airport won $1,800 in a slot machine. They bought a car with it, and, thinking she had to *be* in Napa to get a job in Napa, drove down to find an apartment. Within hours they found a lady who had a cottage available for five weeks—enough time to see if they liked it. Tom was already lobbying for his backup plan, which was to return to D.C.—but Jennifer wouldn't hear it. She wanted 100 percent commitment. Tom had never seen her so passionate and determined. She called the names she'd been given, was referred to a PR firm, went in for an informational, and three days later was offered a job. She felt the guiding hand of destiny making it easy. Her first day on the job she filled out forms, and her second day I drove up to Napa to keep Tom from going stir crazy.

The sun was high overhead, the temperature a pleasant 78; Tom was in shorts and sandals, drinking chilled bottled water and otherwise completely miserable. On the other side of the country that morning, Jim Jeffords left the Republican Party, giving control of the Senate to the Democrats and throwing a monkey wrench in President Bush's agenda. This was the sort of inside baseball D.C. goes nuts over. Tom was three thousand miles away, sitting in his cottage, reading about it on the Internet, calling old friends, suffering painful withdrawal.

Tom was incredibly interested in my book. He said he'd been asking himself this question every day for the last two years.

"But I don't have any idea how to answer it," he said.

That said, he didn't want help. He preferred talking about the last eight years. He squirmed whenever I asked for more detail about his notions of what's next. He dreaded having to make a decision, but at the same time he liked being at this crossroads. He enjoyed the sense of infinite potential. He had a rare chance to reinvent himself into whoever he wanted to be. I realized he didn't want me or reality to take that away.

This was the first time his and Jennifer's paths had diverged. They met in 1992 at a bipartisan event for the delegations from Washington State. Tom was working for Democrat Al Swift, Jennifer for Republican Slade Gorton. They discovered they'd both grown up in Bellevue, lived only three blocks apart when at the University of Washington, and had birthdays only five weeks apart. Meeting at last was the closest thing to destiny they've ever felt. Lucky stars. They moved in together; they could see the Capitol from the balcony of their apartment.

Tom loved it. Many people get into politics because they care about the issues, but end up hating the game. The people who are happiest in Washington actually love the game. That was Tom. "Every day, we won or we lost. We won if we got our message picked up by the media and into the minds of the voters. And tomorrow, we woke up and played the game again." The issues mattered to him a great deal, but not as much as winning did. He became shrewd at second-guessing every so-called fact or statistic thrown his way. He slowly accepted and understood the necessity of compromise as a way to build a consensus. He learned that in D.C., having a lot of money doesn't make you important. Nobody in D.C. makes that much money. Your importance is measured by how many people work for you, and how many people you can influence.

They didn't know how long they would stay. The average job tenure for congressional staff is 2.3 years, so they both had to scramble a few times for new positions. Al Swift told them early on that they'd know it was time to leave when they drove past the Capitol and no longer had a sense of awe. Elections provide natural opportunities to leave, and every election a few of their friends would peel off for new lives. In the way Tom envisioned his life, someday he and Jennifer would peel off too. He never expected it to last forever.

On their vacations they scoped out other places to live. They were drawn to quaint, picturesque towns, the Charlestons, Blowing Rocks, Galways, Santa Fes and Napas. They'd stay in bed-and-breakfasts and fall in love with the setting, trying to imagine starting life over. But they'd always get stuck at the same thought: *What would we do here?*

"You're about to find out," I said.

"I'll figure it out," he said, bucking up. He'd decided that Place was more important to his Happiness than Job. Or, $H = P > J$.

From the moment they first came here on vacation, Tom and Jennifer thought Napa was the right kind of place to raise children. Not anonymous like suburbs, not crime-ridden like cities. Plenty of open land.

"For the longest time, I felt the people out in the hinterlands, the people back in the state, didn't understand what we were doing in D.C. They didn't get the game. Didn't know how to play it, didn't respect it. I guess I looked down on them and thought they were naïve."

"What changed that?"

"I started traveling with the senator back to the state and meeting people. And I slowly realized they're the ones who know what's important in their lives and what really counted. They were the ones who were grounded. It changed my entire perspective of our life in D.C. How unbalanced it was."

Napa is even more of a one-industry town than D.C. The valley was preparing for that coming weekend's Vintners' Association Charity Auction, which is the biggest black-tie event of the year, lasting three days. It was the perfect opportunity for newcomers like Tom and Jennifer to meet everyone in the industry, but tickets cost $2,500 each. They tried to volunteer and discovered there is a three-year waiting list. To be a volunteer!

The guy who coordinates the valet parking has been doing it for twelve years and holds the position like a tenured professor.

Tom didn't want to work in wine, which felt frivolous compared with politics. He spoke eloquently about free trade versus logging, salmon versus dams, and veterans' benefits versus budget constraints. The more we talked the clearer it seemed to me that Tom had never lost his love for politics. But he had a hard time honoring that.

He explained that on Capitol Hill, every press secretary is drilled to think in terms of an average Family of Four. What will this *tax cut* mean to a Family of Four? How will *school lunch money* affect a Family of Four? Tom was better at thinking about what a Family of Four needed than he was at thinking about what *he* needed.

I think he was suffering from having spent his entire adult life in politics. He'd flown to D.C. the day after college graduation. He didn't know anything else, and his intellectual curiosity was making him second-guess whether he was happy. He'd watched other friends go off to Wall Street, Hollywood, and Silicon Valley and make so much money. He reminded me of George Bailey in *It's a Wonderful Life.* When I told him so, he admitted that's exactly how he felt.

"Maybe it *is* curiosity," he said. "But how do I tell the difference between common curiosity and a future passion? I have these thoughts. These notions. Things I'm curious about. Things I've never had a chance to explore."

Tom was repeatedly asking, *Could I be happy doing ____?* H = ? Happiness isn't a difficult standard to meet. He could be happy doing any number of things, fill in the blank. Beware of happiness chasing. The higher standard (and it's not for everybody) is to ask, *Is doing ____ why I am here? Will ____ be meaningful to me? Is ____ what I want to contribute to the world?*

"There's a lot of Clinton alumni in Sacramento now working for Governor Davis," I said. "Why don't you call them up?" Sacramento was only an hour east.

"Do you know anything about local politics?" he asked.

"Actually, I do. My first gig as a writer was covering San Francisco politics. I did it for two years."

"I don't mean to insult anyone, but the game's not as interesting at this level."

I'd already interviewed people who'd left Capitol Hill to work in Los Angeles, San Jose, and Sacramento. Tom was accurate that it was minor league by comparison, but people adjust.

I said, "It might give you the balance you need."

He didn't really want to talk about it anymore. Focusing on it was making him uncomfortable. "I'll figure it out," he said again.

I realized I should shut up. He didn't want to solve it. He wanted some time to play and be curious. Eventually, like George Bailey, he'd remember what gave his life meaning.

A few months later, Tom started working on a local campaign.

WORKING WITH YOUR SPOUSE

Nancy Latham is thirty-two, but looks younger, with a quiet baby-girl voice. She looks down and away a lot when she speaks, toes the gravel with her work boot. Two years ago, Nancy was an installation manager at a small telecommunications company in Seattle, daydreaming of escaping from the corporate grind. She'd attended good schools but didn't have much initiative or ambition. By her nature, she was a ski bum. Nothing she liked more than kicking it on the slopes, slumming it in the bars, crashing on fold-out couches.

Coming out of college, she wasn't too resourceful in hunting for her first job. She scanned the classifieds in the newspaper, eventually found one as an office manager. It took her three years to get bored with that. She didn't look hard for what to do next. Her dad owned a small company that sold and installed business phone systems. He'd founded it in 1985, after thirty-five years as a gray flannel suit. He seemed happy, so Nancy thought why not?

She liked it. Didn't get itchy, didn't think much about what her life was adding up to. Nancy didn't care about phone systems, but she cared about seeing the business succeed. Phone systems were the macguffin, the company's plot device, the thing they happened to sell. It could have been software or tortilla chips or insurance, it didn't matter. Building the company was fun, in and of itself. It had that family-business feel. What she didn't know was that all along her dad was trying to get out of the business and retire. In her fourth year, the company was sold to some big telco, and everything she liked about the job was gone. It was suddenly just *phone systems.* Nancy had a couple of new bosses, and was no longer a manager. The demotion was embarrassing. They moved her to an office in Kent, and she

suddenly had an hour-long commute every day, each way. She was road rage waiting to happen. She gave two weeks' notice.

But phone systems was still a growing industry, so she had another job offer in no time. Not being a particularly brave person, she resolved to take the job and swallow her pride. There was just one thing. She drove over to their office to tell them, "One week vacation's not going to work for me. I need more." This seemed idiotic—who can live on only a *week* vacation? But they said no. One week, that's it, same for everyone.

—I'm a ski bum! I can't live on only a week!

On the Richter scale for life-changing moments, Nancy's hardly rates. But for the first time, driving home from that visit, she woke up to the seriousness of these choices she was making, the endless compromises of how she'd really prefer to live.

Suddenly these ski-bum fantasies burst into her consciousness. She wanted to spend more time with her husband, Ross. She wanted to be a bartender. Or a helicopter pilot. Do traffic reports. Maybe they could own a bar. Maybe own a bar, and park the helicopter on the roof, and call the joint the Traffic Jam. And do traffic reports. Sure, she'd be a white-collar dropout, but if she did this with Ross, maybe she wouldn't feel the shame of that.

What I'm about to tell you is going to sound like she's purposeful and direct and the master of her own destiny, but really, she's not—she's simple.

She went home that night, a Thursday, and when her husband Ross came home, she said—*Honey, I've made a decision.*

—Okay. Is it something I should I sit down for?

—Yeah.

He sat down. —Go ahead.

—I'm buying a business.

He laughed. She was only half serious. Wouldn't that be nice, though? Ross was a telecom consultant, and not enjoying it much more than Nancy was.

So, the business-to-business classifieds only come out twice a week. On Sunday, Nancy grabbed that section out of the *Seattle Times*. Why not? It's where she had found her first job.

Businesses for Sale:
ESPRESSO STAND . . . naw . . .
JANITORIAL SERVICE . . . nope . . .
RESTAURANT . . . mmm . . .
NURSERY FOR SALE. No nursery skills necessary, just people and
   business skills. Will train.

Hey, now that looks interesting.
—Ross, you gotta call this guy.
—No, you call him, you can do it.
—No, I don't know what to ask. Please?
On Monday, Ross called. The owner was fifty-two years old, an ex-drummer from Texas, and his wife wanted to go back to the South. His company wasn't a regular nursery. Its name was Big Trees, and that's what they specialized in. When the owner started the business, he didn't know a thing about trees, so he was confident he could train Ross and Nancy. He promised that if they bought it, he would stick around for two months and make sure they knew the ropes.

Ross and Nancy drove up to Big Trees. It was a warm July day. The Snohomish River Valley lies thirty miles north of Seattle. Emerald green dairy pastures run for miles. At its edges, evergreen hills climb into snow-capped mountains. It's a postcard from any angle. Big Trees sat plumb in the middle on twenty-eight acres. A large aluminum-sided barn had been fashioned into plain offices for the staff of twelve (now nineteen). Some serious heavy equipment stood out back, including a hydraulic spade truck, which operated a four-bladed spade that is big enough to bite the root ball of an eighty-foot, sixty-ton tree right out of the ground. The acreage was surrounded by a nursery of diverse trees—bigger than you can buy at a local nursery, but still young—most are ten to twenty feet. Umbrella pines, jacquemontii birches, weeping willows, katsuras, paperbark maples, pyramidalis. They sell three thousand trees a year to places throughout Greater Seattle.

Nancy and Ross fell in love with the place instantly. The owner was really nice and reassuring. Trees weren't brain surgery, he said.

They drove straight to the library and checked out four books on trees and four books on how to buy a business. Where would they get that kind of money? The books said sometimes banks will finance the purchase, paying down the debt over ten years with income from the business. The books also said they should get an attorney. Ross knew an attorney, and the attorney knew a banker, and . . .

—Can we tell him the price?

—I don't think we should say the price.

—I don't want to come across like we have something to hide.

—It was about on par with the cost of buying a really big house.

—Yeah. A really big house.

. . . so for collateral, the bank wanted their house, as well as their unfinished cabin in ski country. Until then, that house was their rock, and that cabin was their dream. What if they lost their house? They had a real bout with fear. The scope of this loan was way out of Nancy's comfort range, and the gears of the transaction had begun to turn, and Nancy panicked. Started to lose sleep. Cry. I asked her how she got over that fear.

—I don't know how I got over that, said Nancy.

—It was when the bank okayed the ski cabin, said Ross.

—Oh right. The bank wanted us to finish building the cabin.

—Because it was better collateral finished than half-finished.

—Sure, but the message to me was, "You can still go ahead with your life." That was symbolic.

I suspected that Nancy's dad had helped her. But other than by being a role model, apparently not. He certainly could have, because he's wealthy, and maybe he would have, if Nancy had asked—but she didn't want to.

As the day neared, they started to realize: *I may never have to work in an office ever again. I am my own boss. And it's trees!* Trees!

On September 10, less than two years ago, they signed the papers and were handed the keys to the barn and the keys to the trucks. They went out to breakfast with the old owner to celebrate, and then they came back to the barn to start their new life.

"When we were going through the purchase," Ross said, "we'd try to imagine ourselves here, in this life, and ask, 'Is that *me?* Can I do that? Will I like that life?' I had doubts, because it was so different. My life was putting on a suit, getting on a plane, going to a meeting, flying home. But I'm amazed how much that life *wasn't* me. This *is* me."

The business has grown a little, but it hasn't really changed. They're doing more environmental work—they won contracts to reforest the banks of salmon streams throughout King and Snohomish counties.

I asked them if they ever feel like they dropped out from the professional ranks, and if that ever bothered them. But it didn't. They had no trouble embracing this life as the good life. But they both, separately, mentioned they expected a class divide between them (the managers) and their nineteen employees (the labor). But that hasn't been the case. They socialize together by night, and everyone grabs a shovel by day.

Nancy and Ross live spartanly, because the profits go to the bank. They bring their dogs to the barn. They wear what they want to wear. They carry walkie-talkies and drive big equipment. People *love* trees. Trees are like books—they have an intangible psychic significance far beyond their utility.

The couple is so ecstatic about this new incarnation that they can't describe it or talk about it without pausing to wonder, "Do I deserve this? Do I deserve such a wonderful life?" It came so easily to them, it doesn't feel like they *earned* it. It's like they're afraid if they can't explain it, justify it, the dream might end. They keep trying to figure out *why us,* why were we worthy among the millions of unhappy people out there?

They don't have many answers. But once they were at their ski cabin, and they found an old list in a coffee table drawer. They'd made this list back in 1997. They'd been driving out to their half-finished ski cabin, and they were playing a Tony Robbins audiotape that Ross's sister had sent them. They didn't know who he was, and they weren't turned on by his message or anything, but it was a long drive and they had time to kill, so, inspired by his tape, they made a list. Goals. Things they would like to someday do. Nothing unusual. Work together, work outside, work for themselves, that sort of thing.

The list stayed on the coffee table in their cabin for the weekend, then was soon relegated to the drawer, then the back of the drawer, and long forgotten. But when they found the list, they thought, "Maybe this is how it started."

—I think, we put it out there, in our heads.

—We didn't do anything about it, but *subconsciously* . . .

—If it's there, you tend to get to those goals.

—Just write it down.

So here's what I wanted to know: How much of their bliss is attributable to running their own business, how much to working outside with trees and trucks, and how much to getting to work together as husband and wife? The answer, sort of, is yes, yes, and yes. The threads are knotted tight. They never would have fallen in love with the company if it sold, say, toner. And Nancy never would have taken on the debt or the responsibility without Ross to shoulder it with her. Nancy's friends can't believe she enjoys going home with the same guy she works with, sees him all day every day and doesn't get sick of him. But that probably says something about her friends, and their husbands. Nancy can't explain why it works so well and doesn't try. That's who she is.

46 ||| Where Fears Hide

Trust me for a moment on where this is headed.

I remember wanting what Nancy and Ross have. I remember wanting that *so badly*. When I was young and drifting, I fantasized about working alongside my girlfriend, and occasionally did. It was always my first fix. Sharing made everything more interesting. And in the later years, when she became a reporter and editor, sharing writing was when we were closest. She got me started, long ago. When I was twenty years old, she presented me with a notebook to write down my thoughts. For twelve years, she was the first reader of every word I ever wrote.

When I left her (I didn't have "reasons," I was confused, our relationship's patterns were forged when we were very young, and I felt trapped by my past, and despite therapy and writing and painting metaphorical visualizations of the Man I wanted to be . . . instead I gave in to temptation, had an affair, then felt terrible shame that became an even bigger wedge, drove away my friends, slept at the office . . . and started over, started over with nothing but my mom's couch and my soccer cleats and my ability to write, except—)

. . . anyway, when I left her, I *couldn't* write. How could I write? I need regularity and calm, and had neither.

For eleven months, I sat down every weekday morning and tried to complete the magazine assignments that I had due. I would string sentences together, but could not "hear" their effect. Everything sounded flat, and it was. A piece of writing has to seduce the reader, it has to suspend disbelief and earn the reader's trust. I lacked these facilities. I was in a state of permanent disbelief, not worthy of anyone's trust, and quickly ruined any seductions I started. Out of obligation, I turned a few articles in, but they were rejected outright with a kill fee, or were sent back with the instructions "throw this away and start over." I grew discouraged and was unsure if I'd ever be able to write well again. My second novel arrived in bookstores during this time (I had written it before I threw my life away), and it was receiving strong praise, which only made me feel *worse*—"look what you used to be able to do!" *Look at what you'll never be able to do again.*

How did I get past this? My work wasn't yet the topic of therapy, but my love life was. During therapy, I found I was evaluating other women with my old expectation that, ideally, we should be very alike. I'd never learned to appreciate differences. I concentrated on learning this, which was embarrassingly hard, and when I got a little strength I was able to look back and see that I had used my ex-wife's support for my writing as a crutch. I was that guy whose leg had probably healed long ago, but was afraid to let go of his crutch. On my journey toward being a writer, this was a major test, and I'd been ignoring it. So what if I had two best-sellers if I couldn't write alone? Do you remember the story of John Butler, who wanted to be a minister? He faced this same test. He wanted to be a minister, so he fell in love with one, and hoped to marry her and be her co-minister. They broke up and he had to find his way to being a minister by himself. It's a very common test. Often the crutch is not your lover—it might be your company, if your success has only occurred at this one company, or it might be a mentor, or an agent, or a business partner. Whatever we have relied on too heavily along the way. Whatever we secretly fear we could never succeed without.

So I deliberately attacked my weaknesses as a writer—my lack of various reporting skills. I procrastinated calling strangers, and I had a strong tendency to rely on my imagination rather than research. I never wrote straight nonfiction. My ex-wife had these skills, so I never had to learn them myself.

I'd been assigned articles about Silicon Valley—a big topic in those years—so I used these assignments as means to retrain myself. I got on the phone, I went to see people, and I stopped fictionalizing events to serve my ends. I wrote only what I saw, and I dug to find where reality was weirder than fiction. I fought hard for access to events that had always been shrouded in secrecy. Not even the people who knew me best were aware that this was what was driving me. I only talked about it with my therapist. I was not trying to wrestle Silicon Valley, I was trying to heal. I was trying to learn the skills I had relied on my ex-wife for. The book that came of those three years, *The Nudist on the Late Shift and Other True Tales of Silicon Valley,* put me on the cover of magazines. I was interviewed hundreds of times, and I was held up as one of the foremost experts on the

Valley. Maybe I was, but that didn't matter to me. I was enormously proud that my weaknesses had become strengths. I never tried to explain my real motives—I might have, but nobody ever asked, "Why did you write this book the way you did?" True writers have a lot more invested in *the way* they've written their books than in what those books happen to be about. The way I wrote that book was a meaningful accomplishment for me. Far more meaningful than being a Silicon Valley know-it-all.

This period of chaos that had threatened to snuff out my writing ended up being a gift that made me a far better writer.

I'm married again now. Is Michele supportive and helpful? God, yes. And I hope I'm helpful to her. We have an incredibly rich marriage, with many bases of connection. When it comes to my work, I relish her support but don't cling to it. It's healthier. I do not overindulge. I'm careful not to let my work be an obsession that gets between us. I know that if writing is my dream, then it's my responsibility alone. I never again want to use another person that way.

This was the biggest surprise: in the years after the divorce, out of that pain and sadness came an ability to empathize with people I interviewed on a level I had never reached before. To empathize is to be able to see the world through other people's eyes. I too knew the feeling of wanting life to end, the feeling of not wanting to cause any more pain, of having hurt the one person who loved me the most, of believing I was broken, of having a hole in one's self, of not being able to get out of bed, of wanting to throw it all away and start over again, and again, and again . . . and when I would sit down with subjects to talk about life, I had a new respect for their emotions, a respect they could feel, and they talked to me differently, they revealed themselves differently . . . and I realized I had never been good at interviewing before because I did so only on an intellectual level. My therapist listened to me for three years, and from her I learned what it meant to listen. Before my divorce, I was only interested in my own life, for that was the only life I could truly relate to. I could only learn from firsthand experience, from my own mistakes. I was uninterested in history. Afterward, other people's lives became rich and cathartic for me. I was able to live a little through them, and accept some of their wisdom. Sometimes I don't even have to hear their story—just being in their presence is instructional.

With a book like this—a book of stories—I recognize that some readers will be hungry to extract the intellectual components, but they won't genuinely feel for the people I've written about. They need to make their own mistakes. This book might help them argue away some misconceptions, but it won't release their fears. The suggestion that they even have fears will seem ridiculous. Who doesn't feel fearless at twenty-five? I wasn't afraid! I was ready to try anything! But that brazenness is usually hiding something. For the first six years out of college, my biggest fear was that the working world would push my wife and me apart. My choices were ruled by that fear, but I never would have called it a fear. I would have advertised it as one of the few things that I knew mattered to me. I would have called it self-knowledge. You want to know where your fears are hiding? Tell me what you know about yourself. Tell me what you can't live without.

47 ||| The Lottery Winner

Most of the people in this book are Generation X'ers or baby boomers. A few of the most important stories are of those older and wiser, but the bulk aren't. Why have I chosen that? Why not more from my parents' generation, or my grandparents'? They've asked this question too; they still do. They might answer it a little differently, with their own perspective, but shouldn't that be included? I did collect their stories, maybe a hundred or so, and I found many tragic or dramatic, but very few did I seek out and research in depth with the intent to include here. Why? I went with my gut. The stories that spoke to me—that made me want to pay for plane tickets and hotel rooms and rental cars and sometimes leave my family—were from my own generation.

Prior generations went through something that's had time to percolate into a story. This story is filled with common placemarks, and to even mention those placemarks conjures a known meaning, a legacy. For my grandparents: the Depression, World War II, the social conservatism of the fifties, the Cold War. For my parents: civil rights, Watergate, Vietnam, feminism, the huge spike in divorce, the return of former housewives to the workplace. On the shelf at my mom's house, and on the shelf at my dad's house, are the excellent books that tell this story. They've been on those shelves since I was a child.

There's a common reaction when we hear tales from other generations. The reaction is, "I can't compete with that. Nothing momentous like that will happen to me." And it sends us back into thinking we have no story, into a sort of creative futilism, rather than stubbornly working to build a story with the few leads life does present. My generation's story hasn't had time to percolate. Or we've missed our chances to do so. As a result, many people of my generation have *a harder time telling their own story and finding its meaning.* They don't have the placemarks and legacies to draw on. They use irony to poke fun at the hole in the center.

It's that hole I'm aiming at. The stories in this book are of people who've taken what life has offered, good and bad, and said to themselves, "I'm going to learn from that. I'm going to change."

The tension between generations is a common theme in these pages. So many have had to challenge their parents' philosophy of life, fighting to get across that *just because we're doing it differently is not a sign of disrespect.* The young people in this book do understand their parents' choices. Every single one has told me, "If I were in their shoes, I would have done the same thing."

Chi Tschang was one of these young people.

Chi is a twenty-five-year-old schoolteacher at one of the most successful public charter schools in the country, the Academy of the Pacific Rim, which is in Hyde Park, Massachusetts, about a half-hour southwest of Boston. APR is an educational "start-up," and is still very much in start-up mode, meaning the core group of young teachers works start-up hours, eight in the morning until nine at night, and is often in on Saturday. They have a sense of ownership in the school, though there are no stock options to say so. It was founded five years ago by a Harvard Business School grad who was interested in education reform, took a trip to Japan, and was inspired by Asian education techniques. Its first class will graduate high school in spring 2003; all will go to college, and many to the best colleges in the country.

APR has no entrance requirements; its students come from low and middle-income neighborhoods. Sixty-five percent are African American, 25 percent Caucasian, 5 percent Hispanic, and 5 percent Asian. When they come to the school, in the sixth grade, many can't read or write. A third flunk their first year and take sixth grade again. By ninth grade, only a tenth flunk, and by the end of high school they will be top students applying to the Ivy League. In education, this is the true measure of success—getting kids who would have floundered in public schools and sending them to really good colleges. Chi says the benefit is mutual—it's made him a better person. He's in his third year here, and he's enormously proud of what he's helped build. He fights on the front line of one of the most important issues facing our country, and he's not merely "making a difference"—he's winning the battle.

Yet his father refuses to acknowledge that Chi is doing something good. He never asks about Chi's work. He wants Chi to be a doctor or a lawyer, or at least make money. Last summer, when Chi flew home to Fresno, he timed his father to see how long before he brought this up. Chi walked off the plane, greeted his family, and headed toward baggage claim. Fifty-three seconds after his arrival, his dad let fly, "So, how's business school sound?" Fifty-three seconds!

"He loves me to death," Chi said. "But he pretty much disowned me for my choices."

I told him that's a pretty strong word.

"He hates it. He says, 'So, I guess you'll be a teacher the rest of your life?' "

"Why such a strong objection?"

"It's a common hypocrisy in Asian immigrant culture. We prize being educated, but we don't respect educators. My dad believes in Confucian circles of responsibility. You take care of yourself first, then your family, then strangers. In his mind, I'm helping poor black kids before helping myself. He doesn't believe that I like this, that I feel it's good for me, that I'm doing this *for me* as much as for my students."

"Has he ever visited the school?" I asked.

"No. Never even come to Boston."

"This kills you, doesn't it?"

"In Chinese families, we are raised to respect our elders."

"Respect, or behave?"

"Respect their wisdom about how to live."

"So you feel a ton of guilt, huh?"

"Yeah."

"Do you think about going off to make money?"

"Never. I love what I do. I remember, the summer after college, I told my dad I was joining City Year, an AmeriCorps program, to tutor kids in a housing project in Providence. My dad e-mailed me back. . . ." Chi tightened up.

"What'd he say?"

"He said, 'I regret ever sending you to Yale. I refuse to support you as long as you are doing this.' And he meant it. It broke my heart, but it didn't change my mind one bit. He couldn't believe his son would choose to do something *any* high school grad could do. He'd invested a lot in me, a lot of time and a lot of money. He was mad he wasn't going to get a return on that investment."

"Wow, Chi, the way you say that, it's like you're not mad at him. Like you agree with him."

"I can see his point of view."

At Yale, Chi was the head of "Ex Com." During the days of dot-coms, they had Ex Com at Yale, with very different motives. Ex Com was the nickname for the Executive Committee, the ten students who ran Dwight Hall, which was the community service center at Yale. Yale had been transformed by an article that ran in GQ, "The Death of Yale," which accused Yale of completely neglecting the slums of New Haven that surrounded the school. In response to the article, Yale students got involved in huge numbers. During Chi's years, 80 percent of students performed community service in seventy various programs run through Dwight Hall. Not all were do-gooders at heart; putting in time was prestigious. Chi was shocked when, upon graduation, five of the ten members of Ex Com abandoned community service and went off to McKinsey Consulting, Goldman Sachs, law schools and medical schools. Were they prestige whores? Or did two years of volunteering entitle them to get theirs? Chi didn't harbor any resentment, but he was a little confused by it, and even more confused by his own plans. He had none.

Chi's degree was in history, but his favorite subject was urban studies. The summer after graduation, he stayed on to help two of his professors. That summer popped his belief in what he calls the Academic Bubble World Myth—the notion that a student can "know" a subject merely by reading books about it and writing papers, without ever having experienced it firsthand. Everything Chi had learned about urban studies had come from lecture halls and library stacks, rather than the streets. "What do I really know?" Chi kept asking himself. He joined City Year to fill in this void.

City Year groups students into teams of six. Chi's team—most of whom were only high-school graduates—were placed in a housing project in a Hispanic neighborhood of South Providence. They wore red jackets and were paid a stipend of $138.52 a week. During the week, he volunteered at an elementary school. Without any parental support, Chi lived on food stamps. He ate a lot of thirty-nine cent hamburgers at McDonald's. He would hear stories of his Yale friends at Goldman Sachs dropping a thousand bucks on brunch.

Chi keeps a memento from that year in his wallet. It's an Amtrak stub, for a thirty-dollar ticket from Providence to New Haven. After Chi purchased it, he had only thirty dollars left to his name. He showed me the stub, and I took a picture of it.

I asked him to tell me why it was so important to him.

"It reminds me I can be happy without money. It was, financially speaking, my lowest point. But even at my low, I was still happy."

I thought there was a little more to it. "It sounds to me like it mirrors the story of your dad that you've told me so often. The stub says to you that you are following in your father's footsteps, even if he doesn't recognize it."

"Yeah. I guess it does."

The story Chi told me many times goes like this: his dad had grown up in Taiwan, moved to Singapore when he was eleven, and was in Hong Kong for high school. When he came to Chicago for college, he had only seventy dollars in his pocket. During the summers, he would take the train to New York, where he would work as a dishwasher in Chinatown restaurants, living in a cot in the back room with the other employees. He went on to Duke Medical School, and now runs a pathology lab at Saint Agnes Medical Center in Fresno. Rags to riches.

Chi, like many Asian Americans, is very aware of being what they call "lottery winners." A parent's choice to come to America radically improved their chances of thriving. Chi traveled through China last summer, and he was shocked by the Chinese preteens working long hours with no hope for an education. If not for the choices of his parents and grandparents, that could be Chi—nine years old, malnourished, pulling a cart piled high with rice bales. He's extremely grateful for this opportunity. But how should he use his winning lottery ticket? This question tears at his mind and soul. Is he obliged to secure the riches, prestige, and job security that his ancestors never dreamt of? Does he owe that to his family and his heritage and the 1.3 billion Chinese who never won the lottery? Or is this opportunity a chance for more than material gain—is it a chance to do something great, to *be* Great?

312 | Relationships and Family

Chi wrote me, "Call me romantic, but deep down I want to be great. I want to believe in a cause or an idea bigger than my individual financial or career progress. Deep down, that's why I can't get myself to look seriously at law or business school applications. Tell me, is there really anything—anything at all—'great' about working for a firm or corporation? And so here I am, chasing greatness."

Chi never considered being a teacher while growing up, but at the elementary school he discovered how rewarding it was to work with kids. At a City Year roundtable discussion, he met one of the founders of the Academy of the Pacific Rim, which was then two years old. Chi interviewed for an opening, and the next fall started teaching sixth graders. (He now teaches eighth and tenth graders.)

That first year stripped him of every notion he'd learned at Yale. "At Yale, we were taught that people in the cities are poor because of factors outside their control. I used to think that inner-city kids only needed to connect. They needed love and understanding. And so if they were disorderly in class, I would let it go as a way of making them my friend, currying their favor. And they kicked my ass. They abused me. If I gave an inch, they would take a mile. I couldn't connect with them. They did not respond to kindness, they took advantage of it. My class would be continuously disrupted. I learned the hard way. What they need is someone to teach them habits that lead to success later in life. They need someone to tell them when they've done something wrong. Kids face a thousand choices, and they need someone to teach them to make the right choices. How to handle social situations, how to take responsibility and not make excuses. I've become much more conservative by working here. It's the last thing I expected. It's much more like how my father raised me, with tough love. I wrote a little essay about my changing perspective, and I sent it to my father, who's a real conservative."

"What'd he say?"

"He said 'Good job.' It was only the second time he'd ever said that. The other time was when I got into Yale."

I spent a day in the classrooms at Academy of the Pacific Rim, and I witnessed this tough love in action. I was also there at night, for a poetry slam. APR occupies two floors of an old glass factory. They have no auditorium or gymnasium, but the heat is on, and the lights work, and there's not a scribble of graffiti anywhere. The kids wear khaki pants with either a red polo shirt or a white button-down; at the high school level, they're allowed a blue button-down in the rotation. School days begin with a schoolwide gathering for announcements (there were 295 students at the time). Every morning, one student is chosen for having shown excellent character, and their teacher gives them the Gambatte Award. *Gambatte* is Japanese for "Fight to the end!" Then the students join hands—like at a church. Classes begin and end with similar rituals—with the students standing silently at attention, prepared to learn, the teacher pronounces "Good morning!" and students take seats. This is followed by a five-minute quiet period, where students read a passage and write answers to a question or two. It's very quiet. The students meet with their adviser every Friday to review grading; Chi has had the same ten student advisees for his three years—he knows their parents well, and he has their home phone numbers memorized. When a student drifts off in class, or makes a time-wasting remark, or whispers to a friend, the teachers dock them a break or send them to the office with a quick, curt remark, midsentence. Students are not allowed to ruin the learning environment for others. They're also not allowed to disrespect their environment—they can't go to lunch until they vacuum their homeroom's carpet and Windex the windows. The night custodian only cleans the bathrooms. The rest of the school is cleaned by the students. Rather than athletics, they take tai chi every day. They're young, boisterous, fidgety—junior high schools are very hard places to learn, but at APR they manage to keep these outbursts out of the classroom. At the end of the day, it's an odd sight. As the students file out, they shake their teacher's hand and look them in the eye. Then, as they leave the school, they shake the principal's hand and look her in the eye. Coming down the staircase, they gaze at a big mural, *The Road to College*. Their school day lasts two hours longer than at other schools, though most of the additional time is spent in study hall, completing their homework. The school year is six weeks longer. The teachers are paid a bonus of up to $5,000 a year if their students perform well.

None of this quite explains the school's success. It'd be a police state if it was only rules and slogans. "We teach character," Chi said. "I didn't know what character was when I came here. I was chronically late, and my body language was distant. I had to learn character in order to teach it, and I'm a much better person now. I handle situations better." *Handling situations* is how character is routinely coached. When a student is sent to the office, they're not merely punished. They fill out an incident report on themselves, which they review one-on-one with the disciplinary officer. The situation that got them in trouble is replayed in conversation, moment by moment, and the students are repeatedly asked how they could have handled the moment differently. It's drilled into them that they make choices. They become aware, and they stop acting without thinking.

This same concept of moral choices is applied in the classroom. In their English classes, they write essays on whether high school students should be required to do community service. In their history classes, they debate Supreme Court cases, and are pushed to justify how they would vote. Every Friday, during the advising period, the students are presented with a moral dilemma and asked to write in their journals about how they would handle it. They are never asked to memorize—they're only asked to demonstrate exemplary character: perseverance, integrity, respect, responsibility, courage. The highest honor in the school is not a 4.0 GPA—it's to receive the Gambatte Award for exhibiting character. This can be for an act of generosity, or for resisting peer pressure, or for avoiding a fight.

Chi has stayed true to his path by continually emphasizing these virtues and applying them to his own life. He treated me with enormous respect—he insisted on picking me up at the airport, found teachers I could stay with, made sure every teacher (and most of the students) knew who I was before I'd arrived. When I had a question, he wrote me long earnest essays ruminating on his answer. During winter break, when I couldn't make it down to Fresno, he drove up to the Bay Area. His correspondence over the year's time showed him maturing and his beliefs clarifying. The issues he focused on seemed more to the point. "The truth is, I don't really think about what I should do with my life," he said, late in the year. "I love my school, and I stopped thinking about it."

I challenged him, though. He was leading an unbalanced life. He'd had only one date thus far that school year, and it was a very good date that he hoped would go farther—and yet, even then, during dinner, he was half-thinking about his next day's lesson plans. When I'd call him on his cell phone late at night, he'd commonly still be at school. He eats most nights at a small family restaurant on his route home to Jamaica Plain; they close at 9:30, and Chi slips in right before the door closes to get take-out. On Friday nights he works at Rosie's Soup Kitchen from five until eight, then drives the van the rest of the night, delivering meals. With the performance bonus, Chi earns about $43,000 a year. That figure stepladders up a decent amount each year, but he did the math and it's about $5.00 an hour, considering his hours. APR is a start-up—the teachers are learning what works and what doesn't, refining their lesson plans and their methods. It's very intense. But I smell danger anytime a work culture romanticizes the hours they log. Of the forty school staff, only three have children, and of the teaching staff, only one.

I argued that it wasn't responsible to trust these students' futures to the goodwill of super-dedicated teachers. That's not a stable organization.

"You can't call this a true success until you transition toward a sustainable lifestyle," I warned him. "Or burnout will undermine the success you've had."

"It's on our minds all the time," Chi admitted. "Some of the teachers are about to get married; we're facing a challenge." Yet he went on to argue that in most companies, 20 percent of the people do 80 percent of the work. APR was no different. Contributions are always unequal. He was only giving lip service to the notion of scaling back his commitment. I warned him not to confuse commitment with hours. And I warned him not to use work to fill the void of not having a girlfriend or much of a social life. But I understood this feeling. When I was his age, I slept four hours a night in order to carve out three hours of writing time each day. I had no social life.

"Maybe it's okay for now," I said, pulling back on my critique. "But you can't stay a start-up forever."

Chi gave so hard because the students needed it. Clearly. And yet, his journal reflections, which he shared with me, indicated he viewed himself in the context of his peers at Goldman Sachs and McKinsey Consulting. At the dinner table of his inner circle, he'd be surrounded by Yale friends who'd gone off to make money, and at the head of the table would sit his father. A teacher or two might be allowed an appetizer—and maybe *I* would be there too, now that we are friends—but for the main course, he'd face the people who represented the lives not taken. Chi spent a lot of time at this table in his mind. And so the hard work was a way to compete. If his friends at Goldman Sachs were working until midnight, he would work until midnight. If his friends were at high-tech start-ups, he was at an educational start-up. If they bragged of intensity, Chi would admonish them that they don't know a thing about intensity. If his dad told the story that showed off his dedication and perseverance—"When I arrived in Chicago, I had only seventy dollars in my pocket"—Chi could prove he was his father's equal. And when the topic turned to why keep doing what you're doing if you're already a success, Chi could top them all:

"A few weeks ago, I have a conversation with a parent," he wrote in one of his journals. "A forty-year-old woman who works as a crossing guard and moonlights as a clerk at an Osco drugstore—who pulled me aside and, in the most heart-felt way imaginable, asked me—practically begged me—not to leave the school until her two middle-school daughters graduated from high school. Eat your heart out, Mastercard—those five minutes of gratitude were as priceless as it gets. A teacher, you say? Nah, call me the luckiest guy on earth."

Kurt Timken grew up in northern Ohio living a life of privilege. His father was the CEO of the Timken Company, a Fortune 150 multinational corporation known for steel and ball bearings. The company had been founded by Kurt's great-great-grandfather a hundred years ago. Kurt followed in his father's footsteps to the Phillips Academy Andover, and later to Harvard Business School. He was being groomed to fill his dad's shoes at the company, just as his father filled his grandfather's shoes, and so on. He trained four years at the family company, and then another three years in management at Rockwell. But the long hours destroyed his marriage to his college sweetheart, and when he got divorced he started asking the big questions about why he's here and where he could make a real impact.

At thirty years old, he spit the silver spoon out of his mouth, listened to an inner voice, and after a major test of his conviction, he's now a police officer working the graveyard shift in El Monte, California, which is a few highway exits east of East Los Angeles, one of the highest-crime cities in the state. He works the graveyard shift because that's when the hot 911 calls come in, and the drugs are moved, and the transvestite prostitutes work the streets. It's when the beer hits the bloodstream and, under the influence of alcohol or coke or meth or greed, people do terrible things to each other. The graveyard shift is when he can make an impact.

His shift begins at 6 P.M. with a briefing from the sergeant, and runs twelve hours and fifteen minutes. Most of that time he is alone in his patrol car, hunting for "bad guys." He had me sign a waiver, and he issued me a flashlight and Level 3 body armor, similar to the one he wore underneath his uniform. Handgun rounds will not pierce the armor but will still cause blow trauma. He explained where the different gang turfs were divided, and rattled off the addresses of seedy apartment complexes where crimes were commonplace. He taught me how to approach a car of gang-bangers and use my spotlight to blind them. Then he rechambered his shotgun, which is kept locked to the grille above our headrests. He pointed to a button. "This is the switch that unlocks it, in case something happens to me out there, and you need a weapon." It was around then that I stopped thinking that what Kurt has done is really cool and started wondering whether the risk was worth it. Did I really need to witness an El Monte night? Yes, if I was going to shed my TV-inspired, schoolboy-fantasy preconceptions. Yes, if I was going to understand Kurt and tell his story.

While getting dressed in the locker room, Kurt had said, "Everybody needs fuel for their engine. Making seven figures on Wall Street is cheap wood, it burns up too fast. I need something that burns well. That's sub-stantive. That's real." By the end of the night, I understood what he meant.

Kurt is five-ten, thick, tanned, freckled, with a solid jaw and brown hair swept over the side. When remembering his past, he speaks slowly with his eyes nearly closed, like he's going back to that old place in his mind. He still has many friends from the world he left behind, and in a way, he returns to his past every day to get away from what he sees in El Monte. He lives in a spotless luxury condo on the oceanfront at Venice Beach. There's a hot tub on his deck and a restored antique Brunswick pool table in his living room, and upstairs, in the center of the master bedroom, a two-person steam shower. After a shift he'll sit in there and forget, and wash the night away. He calls the condo his "countervailing force." Kurt likes the dichotomy. There's no shame about his background. He drives to El Monte in a Mercedes ML 320, license plate NYSE TKR.

Kurt's great-great-grandfather built carriages. He had some ideas about how wheels and shafts turn, and the kind of stress that is put on ball bear-ings when there is a heavy top load and side load. This was going to be even more important in automobiles. He penciled out designs for the first tapered roller bearings, which could handle those two loads better than standard bearings. It took awhile, and the auto industry was reluctant, but Timken bearings became the new standard, and are used to this day in every vehicle where wheels meet shafts.

After Kurt graduated from Pomona College, he did his four years of training at the Timken Company. They sent him to France and India, and he found it fun and interesting, but with his whole life ahead of him he

didn't hold it to an especially high standard. That changed after Harvard Business School. You come out of HBS thinking that you can change the world in an instant, and you're hungry to find the place where you can make that happen. The years start to add up, and pretty soon it's natural to wonder, "Is this really the choice I want to make?" The family expected him to train at Rockwell and come home when he was thirty. But Kurt was working eighty-hour weeks there, as was his wife, at Disney corporate. They rarely got to see each other, and when the marriage fell apart, Kurt was bitter about what work had wrought. It seemed like you had to choose: do you want a marriage or a career? He would have preferred a relationship, but it was too late.

"I spent almost ten years in business. I was at great, innovative companies, with super management, not trapped in layers of bureaucracy. I received great evaluations, and frequent promotions, and was always challenged and given responsibility. And I was still not hopping out of bed in the morning, excited to get to work."

Kurt had always been interested in law enforcement. He didn't know anything about it. He'd never known a police officer. He'd never seen a trailer park, never hung out in a bad neighborhood. He felt it in his gut, not his brain. Business was about growing the bottom line; if it helps people, it does so indirectly. Kurt needed to serve people directly.

At Harvard, Kurt took marketing with a fairly famous professor named John Quelch. Quelch taught the Monkey Law. The monkey swinging through the jungle must never let go of an old vine until he has a firm grip on the new one. That's how businesses operate, and that's how people trained in business operate.

"I decided to violate the Monkey Law," Kurt said. "And plunge into the jungle, without a plan. I went into Rockwell and gave them my pink slip and said thanks."

His father tried to be neutral, but it was very hard for him to understand. He'd invested a lot in Kurt. They were of two generations; Kurt's dad never had a choice about whether to fill his own father's shoes. Kurt tried to explain that in our generation, it's important to look around a little. Kurt, though, couldn't get hired in law enforcement. He went a whole year being rejected. It was the first time anyone had ever said no to him. It was a real shock. You come out of Harvard pretty much thinking the world works for you. In business, you can move laterally between industries, and most of your skills are transferable. But in law enforcement, as in medicine, you start over from *scratch*. The FBI turned him down, the LAPD turned him down, the L.A. County Sheriffs turned him down. They took one look at him and saw a bookworm. He didn't *need* the job; would he be there as backup in a gunfight? Law enforcement is a nepotistic career; most officers got into it through a cousin, uncle, father. Kurt kept taking the different cities' physical and mental tests, and polygraph tests, passing them all, and that's when Kurt's dad came in with unexpected support. He was offended that nobody would hire his son. "Keep taking the tests," he urged. "It'll happen."

Finally, Kurt paid his own way through the Rio Honda Police Academy. He graduated fourth in his class, and still—nobody would hire him.

"It was a test of my resolve," Kurt said. "It was not going to be handed to me."

Some guys Kurt went to the Academy with were hired by El Monte. They bugged their chief to hire Kurt. The chief sent Kurt over to the Community Relations Anti-Gang Unit. This was the prevention arm of their task force, and it tried to get ex–gang members jobs and teach them life skills. They told Kurt if he would volunteer for a whole year, he'd have a job on the force at the end.

A whole year?

"Yup."

So you went two years without a job?

"Yup."

Without even any real idea what was involved?

"I was learning. In all my interviews, I was learning. And at the Academy I learned. And at Community Relations I learned."

Did he feel like he belonged in the community of cops?

"Not really. I live a different life than most of them."

So why?

"I was hungry to do it. I thought the glove would fit. I'm a bulldog, real tenacious, and a quick thinker—I would be good at it and it would have real purpose."

Still, though. Two years. It's amazing he didn't give up.

Kurt reached for his wallet and pulled out a photocopy of a note. It was written by his great-grandfather to his great-great-grandfather, the inventor. The sons were having trouble getting the auto industry to adopt their father's tapered bearings. The note read, "Dear Father, I hate to think we are putting troubles on your shoulders. We'll hang in there like grim death. We've got grit if we don't have sense."

Kurt explained, "I carried this in my wallet, and whenever I despaired, I read it again. I knew it didn't make sense that I wanted to be in law enforcement, but I had grit."

In his year volunteering, Kurt revamped a defunct tattoo removal program, and turned it into one of the most successful in the country. He put in twenty to forty hours every week. He became a gang specialist, building an intelligence base about the five gangs in El Monte. At the year's end, the El Monte Police Department kept their word. A job was waiting.

On his Sam Browne (his belt) he carries a Colt .45 pistol with seven rounds in the magazine and one in the pipe. He carries pepper spray, a flashlight, a tape recorder for statements, a key ring for his baton, two sets of handcuffs, a department-issued cell phone, and a small holder for five rounds for his backup pistol, a .38 Special jammed into his back pants pocket. In his pockets he carries gloves for a fight, a leather sap, and a second cell phone. All of this adds weight. The weight is not measured in pounds. The weight is measured in the somberness and seriousness of his profession.

Around the department and before the briefing, the office chatter was of the five new bonus positions that the chief would be hiring, and of the acting sergeant's promotion that night to sergeant, and of who would take the fourth K-9 if his partner became a detective. Kurt slipped into this chatter easily. He didn't quote Hegel at these guys, didn't throw out business school maxims. They all put Timken Bearings in their boats, but they don't connect Timken Bearings with Kurt Timken.

No sooner did we leave the lot than Kurt had me running license plates through the onboard computer, hoping to find a GTA, grand theft auto. Every Honda and Toyota I saw, I ran their plate hoping for a hit. It was the lottery. The more plates I ran, the more likely I'd get a hit. We did this with zeal. If we spotted either make, Kurt would gun his cruiser and ride up the car's ass until I could make out the plate. This would scare the shit out of the driver, which was the whole point.

"Sometimes they freak out and take off, and then you've got probable cause."

There were a lot of Hondas and Toyotas. We were looking for bald heads, or ski caps pulled low to hide bald heads. It was night, so we flashed our spotlights on every face that passed. Every pedestrian on the sidewalk, every juvie hanging out on their front stairs, every bicyclist crossing the street—we blinded them with the spot. We watched their hands, to see if they threw anything away. More probable cause.

"You couldn't do this in Beverly Hills," Kurt said. "They'd be on the phone complaining to the city council a second later."

We were on our way to investigate a report of a potential child abuse case. Reading the statement, which was taken from the nine-year-old boy's teacher, it seemed very likely his big sister had simply kicked him in the groin before school. But we had to make sure, which would mean ruining some nice immigrant family's night. This was a Level 3 Priority call, and not the most effective use of our time. Before the shift, I sat with the 911 dispatchers for an hour, watching the calls pile up. Level 1 calls were for imminent bodily harm, Level 2 for imminent harm to property, and Level 3 for sleepers. Kurt decided we needed to pick up the dispatcher's dinner from Denny's, so that they'd cut us some slack the rest of the night and leave us to hunt bad guys.

On the way, Kurt barked "known prostitute" and spun a U-turn on Garvey and pulled tight to the curb, where a transvestite was standing under the bus stop sign. We talked to him/her for a while. I recognized her from the intelligence database Kurt had assembled in three-inch binders he kept in his trunk. There were about seventy transvestites who worked El Monte. Most came in from Hollywood; only a dozen lived in the neighborhood.

"You working tonight?"

"I'm waiting for the bus."

"Have I arrested you before?"

"No . . . Wait. Maybe. At the donut shop that time."

"Are you on any drugs?"

"No."

We stepped out for a chitchat. Kurt held a pen light to her dull eyes to check her pupils, which were constricted, indicating heroin. But her pulse was racing, indicating meth. I found a tie-off strap in her purse, but no needles. Kurt talked to her long enough to conclude her small pupils were a chronic condition, from overuse, and the pulse was from codeine, the poor man's methadone. He checked her for tattoos and showed me the back of her hand, where the heroin crusted up under the skin like extra knuckles when a vein was missed. Many times he assured her he wasn't taking her in, and tried to use this to pry a little information out of her for her profile in his database. She was friendly but didn't trust him.

"Do me a favor," he said. "Don't work here tonight."

"Okay," she said.

Kurt works the prostitutes because nobody else on the force was doing it. It was how he was trained in business—find where you can add value and improve the situation. Make an impact. A few have become priceless informants for Kurt. Prostitutes are both perpetrators of crimes and common victims of crimes. Not only hooking; they'll move drugs, steal wallets, and set up johns to be rolled by gangs. The johns drive in from all over Greater Los Angeles. Seventy percent of the prostitutes are transvestites, because that's what's popular, and because the transvestites seem to enjoy their work more than the women do. El Monte is one of the last places in Southern California where hookers still strut the streets. When he started on the force, Kurt wanted to crack down right away, but that's not how it's done, and he's had to slow down, build the database, and wait until the chief tells him it's time.

"Law enforcement is twenty years behind the corporate world, in terms of its culture. Here they promote by seniority, not by contribution. We don't have a customer, other than the city council. They don't demand better performance. So the culture is, don't stick out, don't rub elbows, stick to what is. Work your beat and don't come up with new ideas. A lot of officers in El Monte are good enough to wow our bosses, but they don't."

Kurt hasn't let this mindset infect him. He never just works his beat, never plays it safe, never hesitates to be the backup when another car is assigned a call. We never code-seven to eat. "My idea of law enforcement is not pulling cats out of trees," he said. "That's why I'm in El Monte."

There's a deadly cycle of violence here. Kids grow up watching their mothers and fathers drink and fight, and then they do the same. The El Monte Flores gang runs El Monte, except for when it kowtows to the MA, the Mexican Mafia. The Mexican Mafia is a prison gang. When inmates get paroled, they're often sent to El Monte, and given housing vouchers which are good at a number of seedy motels on Garvey Street.

It's here we go hunting.

With lights off, we gun into the parking lots of these motels, hoping to surprise someone. The attitude is always suspicion; we presume guilt and look for probable cause. Kurt pushes me to learn this.

"Why could I pull that car over?"

"Fog light out."

"And that Infiniti?"

"No license plate."

He flashes his spot into the car. Four young men. Another U-turn. We pull them over, blind them, approach. I shine the light on their hands. We do their wallets one by one. We run them for warrants. Kurt chitchats. He asks them flat out if they're gangbangers.

"No, *paisanos,* man," the driver says. Just four guys getting off work at the plant. One admits he's on parole.

We could ticket them for the license plate, but then they wouldn't have a car to get to work. The tough call is when they don't have a driver's license, or their license is suspended. Kurt doesn't want to take them in, but people who don't have driver's licenses tend to flee the scene of an accident, and nothing pisses citizenry off more than being the victim of a hit-and-run.

We scare the life out of a drunk driver, but don't take him in. We tell a pregnant woman at the bus stop not to work this corner tonight. We tell two juvies to get home, it's after curfew. One of his transvestite informants tells him that the driver of a certain taxi is moving dope; the soda can he's carrying has a false bottom with a lot of meth inside. We scope out every taxi we see.

This work trains the mind. To be a good cop in El Monte, you need to be suspicious. You need to believe that every bicyclist is moving dope, every woman at the bus stop is a man selling blow jobs, every ski cap is hiding a bald head. Every tattoo is gang-related. Every hand you can't see is holding a bag of dope or a weapon. Every Monte Carlo belongs to a gangbanger, every El Camino to a Title 8, every Lincoln Continental to an MA. Every windowless Toyota minivan is a possible getaway vehicle for an armed robbery. In every car parked behind a warehouse is someone sleeping, or someone getting their dick sucked. Every restaurant, unless otherwise known as friendly, will have someone working in the kitchen who will piss or spit in your food because you locked up her brother. The number 13 is for the thirteenth letter in the alphabet, *M,* or Mexico, i.e. the Mexican Mafia, the real bad guys. Apartment complexes breed criminals. A mouth whistle is a sign that we've been spotted. It probably sounds terrible, to live night after night in this frame of mind, but the alternative is worse. Catch them before they commit more crimes. Make it hard. Crack down on the little things. When all you're doing is harassing guys coming home from their busboy jobs, it feels like a power trip gone bad. "But when I catch a bad guy, and take him off the street, it feels so incredibly rewarding. It's what I live for."

If the law of business is the Monkey Law, the law of the street is, Nobody Tells You the Truth.

"I couldn't believe this at first," Kurt explained. "Where I grew up, you always told the truth. In business, you always told the truth. I'd never been lied to before. Here, nobody ever tells the truth. Even to a police officer. Especially to a police officer."

He tests me on this. When we question people, he continually tosses the situation my way: "Do you believe her?"

I shake my head. "A second ago she said she got off baby-sitting. Now she says she's waiting for her sister who's in the laundromat."

"Right. Because . . ."

"Because who would wait outside on a cold night like this?"

Again, another. "Do you believe her?"

"She pointed that way but now she's walking the other way."

Again, "Do you believe him?"

"That he was beat up by his roommate with a pipe?"

"That he was robbed."

"No."

"Why not? There was no money in his wallet."

"He had a Big Gulp and two bags of chips he'd just bought."

People are drunk. They lie terribly when drunk. Just by not being drunk, we're sharper than they are, faster, quicker.

"He won't tell us where he lives."

"Let's follow his dog home."

We use our *brains*. This was my big surprise. How much we had to use our minds to get the jump, to process the situation, to assess the risk, as it was happening, before bad things happened, to read the signs, to call for backup—and the stakes were shockingly high. You had to play it right. You had to be a move ahead. Before anyone gets suspicious of an informant, make a big show of taking her away in handcuffs. Before cruising into an apartment complex known for gang activity, send another out back to catch any runners as they jump the fence. Before going into a warehouse with the alarm blaring, call for the helicopter to patrol the roof, and call for the K-9s to sniff the burglars out.

This underworld exists. But why choose it? Not for the eight-weeks-plus vacation, though that sure makes it nice. Not for the three-day workweek, though that's sweet too. When I was up in the police helicopter, an off-duty officer was filling his tank at a gas station and witnessed an armed robbery of the station attendant. He pulled his gun, was shot in the leg, and still managed to take down both perpetrators and get them into custody. We were above the scene in a minute and a half. Patrol cars had already reached the gas station and had it under control. It was a big deal. It's very likely that if the officer hadn't been so ready to intervene, he wouldn't have been shot.

Is this a way to live, being suspicious, always hungry to intervene? One of the things I've learned from this book is, don't pretend what you do doesn't shape you. Can a steam shower and the Venice Beach sun wash off what gets rubbed in at night? Kurt's been in a lot of fistfights and scrums, and he's pulled his gun many times, but he's never had to fire it. This is his third year on the force. I told him about Cynthia Ringo, a sex crimes investigator in Atlanta who had to quit after two years because it was making her jaded about the human character.

"Was she young?" Kurt asked.

"Yeah. Early twenties at the time, I think."

"If I was in my early twenties, doing this, it would get to me, too. But you learn how to protect yourself, keep your distance, and you just know yourself better. And when you've had to fight to know yourself, you don't give that ground back, not to anything."

Kurt is a good man; he doesn't seem poisoned by his calling. If anything, the work seems to intensify his goodness, refine it, give him a spine, strengthen the spine, straighten it. He's working his turf, a turf defined by city limits on the east and north and Peck Road and Interstate 10 on the west and south. It's a bigger challenge to tackle than any he could face in business, but it's not so big that he can't make a significant impact, and not so big that he doesn't feel, every night, like he made this world just *that* much better, taking that bad guy off the street, protecting that woman from her drunk husband, steering gang members into the workforce, giving the new Americans in this city a chance. Crime is bad in El Monte, but crime is down in El Monte; there are many reasons for this, but when Kurt steps out of his steam shower at dawn, and crawls into bed, he knows *he's* one of those reasons. And after five or six hours' sleep, he'll wake, and hop out of bed, and be excited to get back there.

FEARS ARE INHERITED, TOO

I learned that you're much more likely to answer the question with integrity if you've worked things out with your parents. Some of the things we think we need from our work, like the respect of peers, might be things we really never got from our parents. Or we inherited their fears. Sometimes it goes deeper than we think. This story is one brief example.

A year ago, Marc Sirkin was a thirty-year-old managing engineer who spoke the language of Business 2.0, worked nonstop at his third start-up, had a house in Carlsbad and a half million dollars of stock in IXL. He thought his problem was that the NASDAQ was crashing, and he had to readjust his financial expectations. He offered to talk with me about this.

I blew him off.

Three months later, Marc Sirkin's IXL stock was worth nothing, but he'd adjusted to that. He still thought that building websites for companies was the good life, as lucrative as an advertising firm or management consulting. His problem was that it was kind of boring now, and he had to adjust to how fun, or unfun, one's work should be. He offered to talk with me about this.

I blew him off.

Then another three months later . . .

Marc Sirkin's father's multiple sclerosis finally killed him, and Marc went back to the Bronx to spread his dad's ashes in Monument Park, behind the left-field wall in Yankee Stadium. Yankee Stadium was their temple. Harold took Marc to opening day every year when growing up. Harold developed MS when Marc was ten; by the time he was twelve, Harold could no longer throw a baseball. On this trip, Marc wondered why he lived in California, not back in White Plains, and he realized, in a kind of epiphany, that his entire life had been defined by his avoidance of his dad's crippling illness. When he was seventeen, he lied to his mother and told her he'd received a baseball scholarship to Florida State. He needed to get away, and he'd never gone back. He'd been running from the illness his whole adult life.

In the eight weeks after the funeral, Marc lost twenty-five pounds, but more surprising were the traits he'd shed from his psyche. That inexplicable anger he'd been carrying for years, that led him, occasionally, to put his fist through a wall? It was gone. Those get-rich-quick schemes he was always coming up with? That constant hunger to have more money? Gone. The whole reason he'd learned computer engineering was how much money you could make doing it. That was the Marc his friends knew. Scheming. Intense. But much of his personality consisted only of symptoms of a deep unwillingness to confront what had happened to his family when his dad developed MS.

Mark offered to talk with me about this, and this time I didn't blow him off.

He was on a crusade to get to the bottom of these things. He said there was a huge hole in his self.

I asked him what his dad did for a living.

"He was a CPA, and miserable doing it. A few years ago he sent me a poem he had written, way back in 1977. It was about how his pinstripes were his jail bars, holding in all this sexual energy, urging himself to come out. 'Come on out, motherfucker, I know you're in there.' It was called 'Who's in There?' "

"Did he stick at it for the money?"

"Yeah. You know, to provide."

"Do you think your urge to get rich quick is a way to avoid being trapped like him?"

"Sure. It would mean freedom."

"Sounds like you inherited from him this notion that it's one or the other, money or jail time."

"I used to think I'd be happy if I had money. But when I had money—when I had that half million in my account—I wasn't any happier. I was less happy."

He asked me if business was as empty as he'd started to think it is. I told him no—if you're in it for the right reasons, it can be incredibly gratifying. I asked him what he thought he was going to do.

"I thought I'd quit and get an MBA. I convinced myself I wanted one. I had all the applications lined up—Wharton, Stanford, UCLA. But then I was laying in bed, wondering what the hell I'd do *after* I got an MBA. I realized I only wanted an MBA to help with how people *perceived* me. It wasn't going to help me figure out what *I* needed."

"What will?"

"I think I want to move home. Back to the Bronx, or to White Plains. My wife's from Jersey. She wouldn't mind either. I don't know if I'd be able to find work. But something's telling me that if I'm going to reorient my life, and try to find what's meaningful to me, I need to start *there*."

I told him he should probably listen to that.

Marc did listen to that.

Three months after we spoke, Marc Sirkin sold his house in Carlsbad and drove across the country with his wife and two girls. They moved in with his mother, temporarily, in the house he grew up in. He turned down several jobs and went to work for the March of Dimes instead, rebuilding and administering their website. This was a cultural shock, but it was good for him. He couldn't get used to being home for dinner *every single night*. He no longer carried a cell phone. He started to read books—not software manuals, but *real* books. When he woke up, he wrote down his dreams.

A month ago, I went to see him. I told him I wanted to meet his whole family, so he drove them down to meet me at the Christmas tree in Rockefeller Center. His mom even brought her boyfriend.

"Moving home has been even *more* of a factor than I expected," Marc said. He couldn't exactly explain why. He was no longer on a crusade. He'd calmed down. He was trusting what this new lifestyle was bringing him, without trying to know what that might be in advance. He said that working from only nine to five felt like stealing. He'd be the last to leave, and he still walked out feeling guilty.

"In a year, I went from wanting to change the world to wanting to get rich to wanting to make a decent living to just wanting to fit in. And you know? I *like* fitting in. It's good for me."

WILL I HAVE TO PUT MY ASPIRATIONS ASIDE?

Some quotes, to warm up the next topic:

"I've thought about this question every day for the last five years. But soon it won't matter anymore. I'm going back to New York to marry my girlfriend, and I figure, when we have kids, they'll bring us *so* much joy, it simply won't matter anymore what I do with my life."

> —from a thirty-five-year-old attorney in the Justice De-partment. He's a former candidate for Congress in the Eighth District who dreams of being a sports agent, but is afraid there's no way in.

"I'm afraid to have kids yet. I need to accomplish more with my work first. I know it's selfish. But it's also responsible. I don't want to end up being one of those moms who, fifteen years from now, develops terrible regrets, throws a midlife tantrum, sleeps with my husband's best friend, and secretly resents my kids because I gave it all up *for them.*"

> —from a thirty-three-year-old senior editor for a maga-zine, who's accomplished *plenty,* but whose mother ex-hibited all of the above.

"I always assumed I would get swept away into Mommyland if I had a baby. This wasn't a comforting thought. And by Monday I'd started to panic, and I realized, I'm not ready for this! But it was too late. By then I was already pregnant. Two years later now, it's changed my entire outlook on life, and yet, I've never been swept away into Mommyland, even though I stay at home and take care of the baby and arrange play dates and go to the zoo with other mommies. The truth is, the question of what to do with my life is back on my mind, it's there all the time, and my craving to figure it out is as intense as ever. Obviously, I can't mention this when I go to the zoo."

—from a thirty-four-year-old mother/MBA who always wanted to find something that really engages her.

"Because I'd recently lost my job, while my wife still had hers, our revised plans called for me to stay home after our daughter was born. I had every intention of finding a new job after six months. That milepost passed a year ago. I've had interviews, but not the desire. I'm perfectly content. How long this will last, I have no idea, but it suits me fine. I realize my daughter's probably not the only factor. I used to work sixty-hour weeks. That's what 'work' conjures to me, a one-dimensional life. No wonder I'm scared to go back."

—from a thirty-one-year-old former computer engineer.

"I'd kinda always wanted to be a science teacher, but I never had the guts to give up the big commissions and, I guess, my superiority complex. That was my image of a man. When my son was born, it freed me, in a way. I was no longer trapped in that image of Man the Provider. I found myself loving my son in a way I had been afraid to relate to anyone else. Nurturing, I guess. It wasn't sudden, but my son helped me see what was important."

—from a thirty-eight-year-old former real estate broker, studying toward his teaching credential.

I accumulated a hundred stories from recent parents, and I could make only one broad observation: many of our fears and misconceptions about our careers stem from our fears and misconceptions about being a parent. We treat one or the other like a highly explosive liquid compound which we've heard has to be handled gingerly. When it comes time to mix them, we'll do this studiously, in the laboratory, under controlled conditions. We do so deliberately, with a plan.

Many of us grew up watching our parents go through a midlife crisis. Our parents jumped into their adulthood quickly, saddling themselves with responsibilities like mortgages and children, and often compromising their dreams to support the family without quite realizing that's what they were doing. Later, they wanted to recapture the youth they'd abandoned too soon.

Now it's our turn, and is it any wonder we're wary of taking on responsibilities before we're ready? We're extending our youth, getting married later and waiting to have children. If we have a midlife crisis, it's the other side of our parents' coin—we realize that endless youth isn't endlessly fulfilling. It gets old. One by one, we add those meaningful responsibilities into the mix. We do this with great ceremony. They've been built up in our minds as threats to our freedom, so to undertake them is now "courageous." Even if we get married young, or have children young, we usually don't do it blindly—we have pretty strong expectations about the tradeoffs we're making, and we have a script for how we're going to manage. We pray we get it right.

Despite this careful planning, so many people reported that it did not go according to plan. It was more meaningful than they expected, or less, or more stressful, or less. It was easier to mix these explosive compounds, or harder. What people expected and what they discovered often had no correlation. Which suggests that our expectations often do us no good. They get in the way. Our expectations are frequently only veiled versions of our wishes and fears.

Becoming a parent can trigger a return of meaning, a sort of *meaning audit*. The relationship with your child is so meaningful it can reveal just how meaningless other things in your life are. And people deal with this information in opposite ways. Many people suddenly are relieved of the burden of finding meaningful work. They're perfectly content to punch the clock; family provides meaning now. If they can afford to, they'd rather stay home with the kids. But just as commonly, this meaning audit compels people to hold a higher standard to their life; they can no longer waste half their waking hours on some job that doesn't do it for them. They don't want their child to watch them lead a dispassionate life. Almost half the people in this book are parents.

Katt Clark was one. Katt and I began corresponding as she was facing a very tough decision—whether to give up her dream for her daughter.

What was compelling about her story was that this was not the first time.

The first time was in the mideighties. In high school, Katt stood out. She was different. She was not accepted into any clique. She had an outspoken personality, and she was embarrassingly big and strong. Six feet two, and bulked up with muscle. The only place in high school that she did not feel weird and out of place—the only place where her size was not socially awkward—was on the track team. She threw the discus 175 feet and the shot put 50 feet, which placed her second in the state of California. Her goal was to compete in the Seoul Olympics in 1988. She was a natural, and she was driven. She took all the rejection and poured her revenge into the weight stacks. During her senior year, she had scholarship offers to attend the best track colleges in the country. But she leveled with herself. She really didn't like school. She didn't feel comfortable at school.

So she joined the marines as an enlisted person. The marines had a track team that sent its athletes to the Olympic Trials. She told her recruiter this was her goal. He promised her that she could join the Camp Pendleton team, and she would do nothing but prepare for the All-Marine Team and the Olympic Trials.

A year later, the All-Marine Team was two months away from being chosen for the Olympic Trials. Katt's distances were certain to qualify her for the team. But then, disturbingly, she lost some of her strength. She couldn't leg-press her normal workouts. Her throws fell short. She tried to fight through it, train harder, run six miles a day. She started to fear she'd not be selected. She wasn't feeling well and wanted to vomit. At the last minute, she went in for a physical.

She was at work on base, waiting for a phone call from her coach to be notified whether she made the team. When the phone rang, instead it was the team doctor. Katt was eight weeks pregnant. She thought this was impossible, because she was on the pill. Being a mom was the last thing on her mind. But the news put the biggest smile on her face. The doctor told her that if she wanted to keep the baby, she would have to give up her training fairly soon.

The baby or the Olympic Trials.

The choice was easy for her. The father was not in the picture. She wanted the baby. A few days later, that other call came—she'd made the All-Marine Team. She turned them down. There was no question.

Her daughter, Marlaena, grew into the most beautiful girl. Katt raised her alone, devoting her life to parenting. She never regretted it, and never thought about track again. Katt developed endometriosis, and after two miscarriages and four laproscopies, she gave up ever having another child. For work, Katt became an executive assistant to various CEOs of Silicon Valley companies. Marlaena was the world to her. They're like sisters. Telepathic. They could always guess what the other got for Christmas. When one was asked a question, the other one answered. Sometimes they answered together, using the same words. They adopted three dogs and three cats. Every day, Katt would take a break from work at 2:30 to pick her daughter up after school and take her home, before returning to work. Marlaena's softball and volleyball trophies lined the mantel. Her pictures are all over Katt's desk. Despite scoliosis, Marlaena batted .306 in softball. She was the third-chair flautist in the Bay Area's Honor Chorus.

Fast-forward to last year. Katt decided to do something about that col-

lege degree she never went for. She enrolled part-time at De Anza Community College. And one day, on a lark, she went down to the track coach's office. She was afraid to knock, so she wrote down his phone number and called him when she got back to her car. She explained her situation, and wanted to know if she was still eligible to throw the shot and discus. He looked her up, found her state records, and told her he would absolutely love to have her on the team. She would have to carry a full academic load, though—part-time students aren't allowed to participate in NCAA athletics. He introduced her to a trainer, who flogged Katt back into shape. After thirteen years, Katt had added weight, but at thirty-two was able to regain all her strength in a few short months. The following semester, she enrolled in fifteen units and joined the track team. She was working at her job every day, attending classes three nights a week, and working out five nights a week. Her form was perfect. Already, she was throwing farther than she had at nineteen. This strength gave her a renewed confidence in herself.

"I wanted to go to state, I wanted to work towards going to the Olympic Trials again in 2004, I wanted to recapture my youth that was taken away when my wonderful daughter was born," Katt wrote me, shortly after. It sounded, at the time, like an inspiring story—a woman who waited until her daughter was old enough to regain her dream.

When Katt left for work in the morning, Marlaena was still asleep. When Katt came home at night, Marlaena was going to bed. "From her attitude, I knew that she wasn't happy, and yet all I could think about was what made *me* happy," Katt said. When the semester ended, Katt chose to work nights at a metaphysical bookstore during the Christmas rush. Marlaena was an excellent student, but had developed terrible testing anxiety. Her finals would be in early January. She needed her mom to tutor her, but Katt didn't have time. Two days before Christmas, Marlaena confronted her mom.

"Mom, I am lonely. You are never home anymore."

Katt was facing the choice again. Marlaena's critique jolted her out of Selfish Mode, and she now hated herself for having lost touch with the one person who meant more to her than anything. But what to do with this natural talent she clearly had? It was now or never. When the semester resumed, should she go back to the team? Should she continue her classes? She'd always wanted to be a high school teacher. Could she pursue that—find another outlet for her desire to transform?

She invited me down to talk with her about it, but I was reluctant to be involved in such a crucial decision. I backed off. It echoed times in my life that were shameful to confront, like how selfishly I had handled leaving my wife. I thought of Carl Kurlander, whose mom had left him to be an actress when he was fifteen. When I was fifteen, my mother gave us up to my father in order to try to become a stockbroker. I *never* thought of that as selfish. Hell, I made it harder for her—I balked, refused to move into my dad's home, once ran away (to my mom's). I was the selfish one. Was the stress I caused a factor in why she had to go back to being a secretary?

I waited two months before going to see Katt again.

She had dropped the track team, and shortly after dropped her classes altogether. She spent her nights going over homework with Marlaena. She could feel her strength eroding. Her muscles itched to be used. Occasionally she resented her sacrifices. They snipped at each other. But then Marlaena received her grades, which were excellent.

"That's when I knew I had made the right decision," Katt said. "My time invested made a difference. Any resentment I had vanished."

I commented that it sounded a little too Hallmark—*Being a Mother Makes It All Worthwhile. . . .*

She clarified. "The most frustrating thing about parenting is not the sacrifices—it's when you try everything and they still won't eat, or they shut you out and won't accept your comfort. You feel helpless. And the opposite is the most fulfilling—when being there for them actually helps." So the fulfillment wasn't in merely being a mother—it was in being a *great* mother, in spending a lot of time with her daughter and really being aware of what she was thinking and feeling—having that telepathic-like connection.

They went to an NSync concert together. One weekend they went down to Pebble Beach for the Pro-Am to ogle the celebrities. Katt became girlish around Marlaena. It was pretty clear that she was reliving a bit of her lost youth with her daughter, but nothing was wrong with that. Katt never talked about her decision as a sacrifice. She loved spending time with her daughter. It made her happy.

Katt also felt a clarity in having a singular purpose. When she could fudge her various responsibilities, the many directions of her ambition tore her apart. When Marlaena made the stakes clear, Katt could embrace that one thing, and enjoy doing it well.

"I'm trying to accept myself for who I am," she said. "One of the reasons track was so important to me is my size. How big I am. When I was working out, even though I'd get bigger, I felt immune to how people looked at me. I want that confidence." She started dating again.

So is her story a cautionary tale? Is it what every parent with a career plan fears? On one hand, she had to give up her dream. Twice! On the other hand, she found being a mother incredibly rewarding, despite the sacrifices (not to mention having to raise Marlaena without a husband). I tell Katt's story here because it reflects the ambiguity I found in the whole of my research.

Katt was philosophical now. "I think of Marlaena as the greatest gift. It's not for me to criticize or change the nature of this gift. It's like when you witness a miracle. My job is to accept it, as it is, whatever it brings."

I thought that was wise, and I remember it when I get stressed about having less time for my own needs. That's pretty much how I got over the mental hurdle—by learning to give up control, and accept whatever kind of gift I would receive. My wife, Michele, had always wanted children, and was vocal about it. I was never sure. One day, she put it in different terms.

"I've been on the pill since before I ever had sex. I'm tired of preventing my body from doing what it does naturally. I want to stop *not having* a baby. If it takes years, that's okay."

Those words changed me. I saw my life on different terms. It wasn't my freedom I'd been protecting—it was my monopoly over life. I was a control freak masquerading as a bon vivant. And that's not who I wanted to be. So I decided to let nature take its course. That's still how I think of it— we have very little plan. We'll find out.

Huge numbers of young people are choosing to never have kids. Now that I am on the other side of that choice, it makes me sad. But I have no doubt why they've opted out. Becoming a parent is routinely characterized by new parents as a "life-changing" event. It's played up to be a significant break from what was. If I ever mentioned I was considering becoming a parent to someone who already was a parent, they eyed me sternly and played God for a moment, and delivered a clear warning: "Your life's going to *change*." For good and bad, they would imply, but *say goodbye to who you used to be* was their point. It came across as a threat. Anyone who enjoys their life would wonder, "Geez, I'm already happy. Do I want to screw it up?" I can't tell you how much it helped when one of my Hollywood producers, a father of three, leveled with me: "In the fall, on Sundays, you can't watch all four quarters of the football game. You catch a few plays and watch SportsCenter after they've gone to bed. Otherwise, life goes on." On the television show, most of the other writers had babies or toddlers; we still had a blast. This was eye-opening.

Does your life change? Sure. Do you make sacrifices? Absolutely. But nature takes care of us. We get nine months to prepare. For the first half year of babies' lives, they only need love and milk. They sleep more than they're awake. *You have time to get accustomed to these rhythms.* Life changes, significantly, but at a pace we're built to handle. In the same way women have the hormones that loosen the hip ligaments in order to let a baby move through that canal, we have the psychiatric makeup to adjust to being a parent. Not everyone, but most. People have managed to raise kids since the beginning of time. Most of the great men and women from history had kids—the notion that your career success hinges on being child-free is overplayed. If you need to wait, that's legit. If you don't ever want to be a parent, fine. But telling yourself it's for your career is not a fact, it's a fear.

When I was in New Orleans, one young man who was not yet a parent, but considering it, said, "I've noticed that people who don't have kids never quite see themselves as a success, and people who do have kids never see themselves as failures." It seemed dead true to me, but why? Are kids an "achievement" that makes you feel like a success? Not quite. I stared at his quote for six months before I could see the cause and effect: *having kids will teach you to be accepting.* Not to be submissive, but to be patient. Tolerant of minor delays. You don't measure yourself on the conventional success/failure spectrum. Many parents talk about how it's made them better people, and this is one of those ways—it forces the mind to be a little more flexible.

Another benefit is that it teaches the joy of being generous. By giving so much to our kids, we become accustomed to how satisfying this is. We open ourselves up to a whole range of emotional rewards that we didn't give much credence to before. We find these rewards not only in our kids, but everywhere.

When you put these gifts together, and recognize them, you don't end up in the usual me-or-my-child trade-off, sacrifice or be selfish. You discover that your child has given you a new outlook, maybe one that solves your permanent unease.

This next story, of Rick Olson and his son, Patrick, illustrates this beautifully.

51 ||| The Mechanic Gives 100 Percent

CHILDREN HELP YOU REMEMBER WHAT'S IMPORTANT

Since Rick Olson was now a long-haul trucker, and regularly crossed the country in three days, he was willing to meet me with his eighteen-wheeler anywhere on my travels and take me to the next place I needed to be. Later, I took him up on that, but for our first meeting I wanted to meet him near his home in Pittsburgh, and specifically, to re-visit a place in Pittsburgh called the Incline. The thing to do at the Incline is ride an old mining tram to the top of Mount Washington, which offers a spectacular view of the Golden Triangle downtown and the river fork where the Monongahela joins with the Allegheny to form the Ohio.

On a Saturday afternoon three years ago, Rick came up here with his son, Patrick, then seven. That day began a chain of events that led Rick, now forty-two, to change his life.

So we came here first.

Rick liked Nascar, hunting and fishing. He played ice hockey and was learning the guitar. He smoked. He almost never drank; on the Fourth of July he'll buy a case of long-necks. That lasts him a couple months during the hot weather, but the rest of the year he has no taste for it. His cowboy boots were splattered with mud. He's six-one, medium build, skinny legged. His voice hits many high notes; there's a drawl in it, even though he's originally from Minnesota. His most distinctive feature is the bone structure of his eyebrows; they're slanted in an upside-down V, so the look on his face is permanently receptive and compassionate. He stood with his fingers jammed in his front pockets, his shoulders in a shrug.

Patrick was not his biological son, but from the moment Rick first picked him up and held him, at ten months old, the bond between them was permanent. Rick had met Patrick's mother, and married her, and divorced her, and none of that really mattered. Rick said, "She and I were brought together to bring him and me together." Patrick needed a dad, and Rick was it. After the divorce, Patrick really looked forward to his Saturdays with Dad. And this one particular Saturday, he woke up and told his dad he wanted to go to the Incline.

They rode up to Mount Washington and then stood at the railing at the overlook. Rick had been here a hundred times in his life. Patrick started to look around and ask questions.

"Hey, Dad, look at that sign flashing on Three Rivers Stadium."

"Hmmm." Rick had never noticed the sign before.

"Hey, Dad, look at that boat on the river. What kind of boat is that?"

Rick had seen boats like that his whole life, but didn't know what they were called or what they carried. So he pointed out a sand barge.

"Hey, Dad, how do they get the sand out of the railcars and onto the barges?"

Again, he didn't know. So they looked around, scanned the visual field for clues, and figured it involved a big crane and a funnel.

"Hey, Dad, which building do you work in?"

Rick pointed out his downtown tower, where, at the time, he was a corporate lawyer.

"What's that building next to it?"

It was a perfectly logical question for a kid to ask, and Rick had walked right past that building every day for five years, but he didn't know. How could he not know?

"Hey, Dad, look at that bridge."

"Hmmm."

"It's painted blue and gold. Pitt colors."

Rick had driven across that bridge a thousand times, and while he knew it was colored, he'd never associated it with Pitt.

"Hey, Dad, can we wait here until the Geyser goes off at the Point?"

"Sure."

"Hey, Dad, which river goes south to north? Is it that one, or that one?"

Every schoolkid in Pittsburgh learns about the oddity of how the rivers meet and one seems to flow upstream. Rick had moved here when he was seventeen; he'd lived here twenty-two years, and he'd never learned such an obvious thing. He'd never thought to ask. He'd never really paid attention to things like that. But today, Patrick was *making him* pay attention. They didn't snap a picture and go after five minutes like most people. Patrick stood there for *two hours,* asking question after question, noticing

thing after thing that Rick had never in his life noticed. This had a profound effect on Rick. It was like his son was sent to him to teach him to
pay attention and treasure the moment.

Three years later, Rick turned to me from this very same spot. "My eyes
were more open that day than they ever had been with him. I loved my
son dearly. But until that day, my mind was always six hundred places. I'd
never focused on him one hundred percent."

After two hours, they walked down the street for an ice cream cone, and
then they went back to Rick's apartment, and Rick made his son dinner,
played with him, put him to bed, read him a story, kissed him good night,
and came downstairs to his couch. Rick sat there and tried to figure out
what had just happened. But something *had* happened.

One thought kept recurring, haunting him: "I'd been here twenty-two
years, and never noticed all those things. What else in life have I been
missing?"

Rick was a corporate lawyer specializing in radio station mergers. He
nicknamed himself "The Mechanic," meaning he was good at closing deals
but terrible at bringing in business. He'd been passed over for partner and
didn't make much money, forty or fifty thousand a year. The hours were
long, and he'd been doing it too long to enjoy it anymore. Doing it for
what? Doing it only because he'd always been doing it, ever since Henry
the Eighth? Certain memories came back to him, like the time his wife
had gallbladder surgery. On the way over to the hospital, a partner handed
Rick a cell phone and suggested he make calls while in the waiting room.
Or like the time his son had to sit in his office all night while Rick met
with clients. Or all those vacations he'd supposedly gone on, but every
morning at 7 A.M. was checking the hotel fax machine and returning calls

before his family woke. It was suddenly so clear to Rick: your job runs your entire life. Even if you work only eight hours a day, it stills controls your life. What you wear and when you wake up and when you eat and when you come home and when you go to sleep are all *scheduled around work*.

"I had a permanent edginess back then," Rick explained, though it was hard to imagine because he was now so peaceful. I commented on that, and he said, "It really has so much to do with multitasking. Even as I'm talking to you now, I'm trying to remember everything I want to tell you, and it hurts my brain to think two lines at once. I've become that sensitive to it. But I used to think six lines all the time. And stupidly I was proud of it. I thought it was who I was, but I see now it was a symptom of my work. And I see now that multitasking creates a sense of guilt that you're selling everyone short, including yourself. God forbid anyone accuses you of being less than one hundred percent there, because then you're just defensive. That defensiveness, and that guilt, become a skin you wear every day, a skin you wake up in. You talk too fast, you drive too fast. I felt twenty pounds lighter when I shed that skin and learned to pay attention."

Rick's wisdom always came out perfectly like that. He had become a great philosopher, but not by reading books (he read Tom Clancy and Robert Ludlum) or talking to other philosophers. He hadn't met many other people who'd changed their lives, and he hadn't told his story to many strangers. I don't think he realized how eloquent he sounded. He'd spent all that time alone in his truck, driving, being in the moment, noticing the road, the view, the beauty of the country, and somehow, because of that, when it came time to talk, these articulate words spun from his lips.

That day with Patrick pushed Rick 80 percent of the way toward quitting. So he went looking for the other 20 percent. He called his father in Minnesota, a retired engineer, and told him he needed to quit. His father said, "You're thirty-eight years old. You gotta stop squeezing into a round hole if you're a square peg. You're going to have a heart attack in five years. You've won it all and lost it all several times, playing a game you just don't want to play."

The rest of the 20 percent came when Rick started playing ice hockey again in the adult leagues. Shortly into the season, Rick crashed into the boards at a flukey angle. He woke up later in Presbyterian Hospital, and was told by the doctor that his ankle was shattered into eleven pieces, both of his legs were broken, and his heel had been sheared off. Rick heard this and started laughing.

"Why are you laughing?" the doctor asked.

"They just unlocked the gate. This is my chance to walk away."

"You won't be walking anywhere for a while."

"That's fine by me."

His rehabilitation took ten months. He couldn't leave his bed. He had a house he'd recently bought that was halfway torn up in a remodel. He had bills he couldn't pay. He had a Siberian husky that couldn't get out, and peed on the living room carpet. He had to declare bankruptcy. He endured two lengthy surgeries, the insertion into his body of fourteen inches of steel plate and seventeen screws. But the whole time, he was laughing because he was finally free. He didn't have to quit. He'd already stopped. It was liberation without exposing himself to the usual critiques.

"The injury was the Great Precipitator," Rick told me. "The link in the causal chain. The accident could have made me need the money more. But I was looking for my catalyst."

He was going to have to start over no matter what he did. The only question was . . . where?

For twenty years, whenever work got frustrating, Rick's retort was, "I'd rather drive a truck." He'd done so one summer in college, for a student moving company. So he fell back on this old skill.

"I needed to do something different," he explained. "I didn't anticipate that I'd fall in love with the job."

We went out to the bulk terminal where Rick's beast was kept. It's a 1998 Century Class Freightliner with 450,000 miles on its 330 Cummings engine. He's due for a new engine soon. On the passenger seat is a cooler, in which he stores sandwiches and milk. Behind that seat is a small closet in which he hangs several outfits. Behind this is a guitar, and behind that a mattress and bedding. Rick sleeps here rather than in motels, and he eats what he buys in grocery stores, avoiding fast food. He spends 60 percent of his life in this rig. His only indulgence is his stereo system; he listens to Steve Earle and John Prine. Rick makes 32 cents a mile, which at three thousand miles a week works out to $52,000 a year.

Long-haul trucking has cleaned up its act. CB radios have been replaced by satellite computers and cell phones. It used to be about making a statement; today it's about making a living. In the old days, you could bank a lot more, but you took your life in your hands, and everyone else's on the roads. A full tanker weighs 65,000 pounds, and that's now considered a very serious responsibility. There's a professional ethic taking over the industry. Recruiting is aimed at drivers who handle the clients well and the hazardous materials procedures with care. The company takes care of maintenance; drivers don't need to be mechanics. Drivers can't work more than twelve days straight; eight or ten days is the usual, then a few days off. They can't drive more than ten hours straight, or sixteen hours out of every twenty-four. Your permit logs can't show you made it from Chicago to Tennessee in four hours; it has to be six hours, an average of 64 miles per hour. Always 64 miles per hour, or else the driver and his company get fined.

Rick's employer is Schneider, whose trucks you will recognize on the highways by their orange cabs and their shiny steel tankers. Inside those tankers are liquid chemicals, like latex resin, oils, water treatment, or haz mats. Because of their dangerous payloads, tanker guys are the elite among truckers. Rick's not in the strip clubs at night, and he doesn't hang out in the truck stops telling war stories.

I met his buddies, an incredibly diverse group—a former accountant, a southern bigot, a Ukrainian immigrant, a former Wendy's franchise owner, a former army officer. They have in common only one trait: they don't like being told how to do something. It took me a while to understand this. Because I would have thought if Rick's sleeping in his cab, and he's on the road ten days out of every fourteen, his life is even more controlled by his job than when he was a lawyer. But Rick said no, and his buddies backed him up. The difference is, Schneider gives him an appointment: have this tanker in Jackson, Mississippi, by 8 A.M. on Tuesday. The rest is up to him. Rick decides when to leave, what roads to take, when he wants to stop, sleep, eat.

"Most jobs, you're consumed by answering questions about why you're doing what you're doing and how you're doing it. And in the hallways, everyone's complaining about how they're second-guessed by their bosses. In this job, we're *never* told how to do it. Just make your appointment, drop the load, and relay home. I have autonomy. I have a window seat, with a view that changes every mile. Nobody ever comes into my office without asking. I enjoy this job, but I'll be the first to admit it's not like what you do. It's not my passion. I'm doing this for the wages, and I'm doing this because it doesn't eat me alive. So when I come home, I pick up Patrick and take him out to our house, and I'm one hundred percent there for him. I have several days straight with no distractions. Can you see what kind of a turnaround that is, from where I was three years ago? He knows the difference. Patrick tells me all the time how much more he enjoys me now. Everyone does. I went to Rome for a wedding last month. The bride called me yesterday and said, 'It's amazing how relaxed you look in the pictures.' I'm always being told that. My dad tells me that. 'You look so relaxed.' "

We hit the road for a while.

I kept thinking how hard it was for Rick to quit—how it took having his leg shattered to get him out of there. It suggested how deep the need for prestige is rooted. So I asked him, once he'd broken the vise-grip, did that need for prestige evaporate? Or does it still haunt him? Does he struggle with being a "prestige dropout"?

"When I drive by the Golden Triangle, I never feel a magnetic tug toward those downtown buildings," he said. "I didn't leave any unfinished business there. I *had* my chance. I was turned down for partner but I can't say I never had the opportunity. Several times I was given the resources to become a rainmaker, and I didn't have it in me. I had some good years. It was a good ride in life's amusement park. I wouldn't appreciate what I do now if I hadn't spent so much time in an office. I wouldn't appreciate Patrick so much if I hadn't not been there for him earlier on."

I thought about the other truckers I'd met at the bulk terminal. "No disrespect to your friends, but do you ever miss the intellectual stimulation? Being surrounded by smart people?"

"Hah! People think that's an issue, but really ask yourself, how many stimulating conversations have you ever really had in an office? You talk about work. My legal work was a glorified version of filling out forms. There was not a big intellectual challenge in it. I'm not trying to put down the law. My best friend is a lawyer, a good one, who hangs his own shingle and loves it. One man's hell is another man's salvation. So what I get in trucking is the benefit of perspective from very diverse people. They're not brilliant, but they've seen things I'll never see. I learn from how they see the world. I'll take that any day over a bunch of other white, college-educated smart alecks like myself. And anyway, I get a lot of intellectual stimulation trying to teach Patrick about the world. Because he asks good questions. He asks more interesting questions than anybody I've ever worked with."

It always came back to Patrick. Almost every question I asked him, he'd work through his thoughts and evaluate what he'd said so far and gravitate, back again, to the thing that brought him most meaning. I could tell you more about Rick's life on the road, or about how, months later, we were crossing Wyoming and saw a herd of a thousand antelope. Everything Rick saw, he wanted to show to Patrick. It comes back to Patrick.

They read *Harry Potter* every night they're together. This helps, because Patrick is at a remedial reading level in school. He loves chess. He's starting to sing in glee club. He's a weenie on the baseball field, but he's tough at hockey, taking after his dad. He's in the Scouts. Rick and Patrick bought a house together, picked it out together, a few months after that Saturday at the Incline. Patrick liked the peach tree in the backyard. Rick managed to hang on to it through his bankruptcy. It cost only $36,000, which boggled my mind. Patrick picked out the bathroom tile, and they laid it together. "We're growing into it together," Patrick said. He has his father's facial expressions, especially the upturned eyebrows, quizzical, as if I were about to say something, and he was waiting patiently for me to say it.

THE HARDEST THINGS ARE THE MOST LIBERATING

I learned that the hardest things are the most liberating. Such as for Kurt Slauson.

It's very important in this story, when the point comes, not to get bogged down wondering why Todd Slauson, Kurt's older brother by two years, committed suicide at twenty-nine. Nobody really knows. Kurt and his family were thrown into a state of impenetrable unknowing, of retroactive guessing, without any conclusions, even to this day. They couldn't make sense of it. Todd wasn't around to ask. So when I tell this story out loud, I've seen that listeners want to ask questions about Todd, not about Kurt. They want to figure out that which cannot be known. So you'll know a tiny, tiny bit of how confused and frustrated Kurt felt, but the answer is not there, and I won't try to chase it or speculate about it here. I promised the family that. This is a story about Kurt, not about Todd.

I first heard a little of Kurt's story from a guy in New Orleans. I'll share exactly what I learned:

My friend K. is thirty-one and married with a new daughter. He's a chef in Seattle but is about to move to some remote resort town in eastern British Columbia, near where his wife's from. When I first met K. (studying English at the University of Montana), he was solidly en route to becoming a scholar of contemporary avant-garde poetry, the far-out stuff stemming from Pound, and had completed his coursework at the University of Victoria for his Ph.D. when his brother, a roommate of mine in Montana, trekked into the woods and shot himself with a deer rifle. The brother, T., was older by a few years, a solid ESPN-watching outdoorsman type who worked at a sporting goods store and fly-fished, hunted elk, et cetera. He was a great guy and lived the life people in cities with desk jobs dream about. Still, he committed suicide (bashing my own belief that dedication to fishing was some sort of mental salvation) because, among other unknown reasons, he didn't seem to be "headed anywhere." And a few months after the suicide, K., seeing his brother in himself, dropped out of his Ph.D. program and went to culinary school in Seattle, a career swing that seemed and still seems out of the blue—he wasn't a natural cook and had never pursued it even as a hobby. But he graduated at the head of his class and is happily employed, loves his work, and works hard to support his wife and new daughter, all thoughts of Ezra Pound forgot.

He gave me Kurt's e-mail address, and I sent off a missive. I didn't try to insert myself or push. I simply offered to listen if he needed to talk. If he had unresolved issues, maybe it would help him to hear that other people have gone through a similar swing.

I didn't hear back.

That was fine, but after a month I started to wonder—if Kurt was moving to Canada, maybe his e-mail address had changed. Had he ever received mine?

So I called information for Kelowna, British Columbia, which is a six-hour drive east of Vancouver, in the middle of the Okanagan Wilderness. They had his phone number. I called and left a message.

A week later, his wife Laura telephoned. Kurt had received my e-mail and phone message, and they'd been talking about whether it was a good idea to contact me. She thought it was because he still had a lot of unresolved issues, was holding a lot in. She thought he should talk to *someone*. She'd worked at a bookstore in Victoria and had sold my books. I described my research as plainly as I could, and she said they'd talk some more.

Another month into the summer, Kurt left me a message. I could hear the reticence. We traded messages for a while. I think we were both nervous. We got used to the timbre of each other's voice, replaying the messages.

Finally, in August, I reached him. His voice was deep and scratched; he peppered his words with a raw slang. A meat-and-potatoes guy's guy. He may have been a poet, but he wasn't used to showing his weakness. He asked how I was doing my research, how I was choosing people, and how did I see his story fitting in? I said I didn't know. From the little I'd heard, his story spoke to me. It was that simple and straightforward. How was the book organized? I didn't know that either. Did I have a message? He was snooping for a hidden agenda. He realized I didn't have one. That seemed to pacify his edge. He paused . . . considered it . . . and said, "Okay."

Five minutes into his story, he stopped and said he'd feel a lot better about this if we were talking over a couple of beers in person. "It's a little too intense to talk about over the phone."

"What's your schedule like?"

He was sitting around, waiting for his landed immigrant application to come clean. Until then he couldn't work. I was welcome any time.

"I'll be there in two weeks."

A few hours into our time together, after a few beers, Kurt felt he needed to tell me *why* he'd let me into his life. "I thought your process would lead to something good," he said. "I wanted to be part of it. Maybe my story will help someone else out there, who's going through what I went through."

I hoped it would.

He had been thinking about what he wanted to tell me. My imminent visit had pushed him to reflect. It had led him to track down his high school English teacher, who, in his sophomore year, had turned him on to poetry and lit a fire in him. She was now in South Carolina. He also called old friends to tell them how much they meant to him. "You hadn't even got here yet, and yet you started some good things," Kurt said.

And what were his unresolved issues? I felt them right away. He had an emotional distance from the things he should have most dearly embraced. They'd bought a new house in a pretty subdivision at the base of a mountain. Kelowna is renowned as the Napa Valley of the North; it has an exquisite charm, not quite rural, not suburban, the best of both, with a picturesque old town center on the lakefront. Kurt showed me his house with a stiff real estate agent tour, and he copped to this stiffness. "Isn't it great?" he said, and then a moment later, hearing the hollowness in his voice, he covered with, "Maybe I'm just not used to being in a subdivision yet."

This was also true of his feelings for his daughter, Maya. She'd turn one in a week. She brought Kurt joy, but when talking about her he fought awkwardly for words. It's hard for a new parent to describe what it's like, but I was a new parent too, and there's a comfortable self-deprecating conversational ritual that centers on poopy diapers and feeding times and hours of lost sleep. Kurt was uncomfortable with such talk—it was like he was trying to *sell me* on how great his new life was. Again he caught his

own false note. "Maybe I'm not yet acclimated from my old bachelor bohemian poet life," he suggested, even though it had been two years since
he'd read a word of poetry. Four times he made some version of this comment. He was clearly holding his emotions back. He had a great new life
here in Kelowna, and yet he couldn't seem to enjoy it, or wasn't letting
himself embrace it.

He suggested a pint and a smoke might loosen him up, so we went
down to the harbor and took a seat under the warm sun. Soon the amber
ale blurred our sense of the moment, and we rode its daze back in time.
Kurt is tall and slender, freckled—his most distinctive feature is a birth de-
fect called Poland's Anomaly; his left forearm is shorter and some of his
fingers are only a couple knuckles long.

Since he was sixteen, Kurt had always wanted to be a professor of poetry. He knew this going to college at the University of Oregon, where he
wowed the TAs and hung out with grad students. He knew this at the
University of Montana, where he received his master's. He wrote his own
poetry but it was academia that called to him. This was esoteric analysis.
His shtick was the history of shared influences, placing contemporary
poets in a continuum from the nineteenth-century Romantic tradition.
He was highly focused on language, not artifice, nor craft or metric standard. Most of this terrain had been trammeled a thousand times by every
graduate student in the country; it was hard to offer novel commentary. It
was as if the deeper he got into it, the less air there was to breathe—a thousand scholars in the same room, suffocating on each other's carbon diox-
ide. At the University of Victoria, this asphyxia started to wear him down.
He passed his grueling second-year exams, for which he had to practically
memorize every word from fifty novels, forty poets, twenty playwrights,
and one hundred years of American Lit. He was a leading presence in the
department, but at night he watched hockey games rather than read for
pleasure. What could he do but grind it out and hope his spirit came back
when he started teaching? For as long as he could remember, he'd told
everyone he wanted to do this. His career choice had a momentum of its
own. How could he tell his wife and family who'd supported him all these
years that he no longer wanted to do it? On the cusp of success, there was
no love of poetry left. He was unable to pen his thesis. He could find not
a drop of inspiration. He could no longer sleep. He was filled with dread.

One Monday in November of that year he got a phone call from his
brother's boss at the sporting goods store in Missoula. "Todd didn't show
up for work. Has he called you?"

The next day, with still no word, Kurt flew to Montana. They found Todd's car parked up near Schwartz Creek, on elk hunting grounds. Search parties began combing the mountain in grids. This was a heavily wooded area. For six days, Kurt and his father sat around the house, wondering if they'd ever find him. They were going to call off the search party that day. It started to snow, covering any tracks they might find. Two miles into these woods, they found Todd's body with his brains blown out. Beside him was the deer rifle he'd used. In the stock of the rifle he'd carved a note. He'd carved it with a penknife. The note read, "Sorry, can't hurt anyone anymore."

Sorry, can't hurt anyone anymore.

Telling me this, Kurt cried frequently. Not with the sadness of Todd's death, but with the sadness of his brother, sitting there on the north slope of their beloved hunting grounds, taking the time to slowly carve this note. How long might that note take to carve? What kind of grief was he in during that time? "I can hardly bear to think what he was going through. It breaks my heart even to imagine that time passing. A penknife. A fucking penknife. That took a long time. A rifle butt is hardwood. Plenty of time to get a grip on himself. Plenty of time to change his mind and hike back to the car."

Sorry.
Can't.
Hurt.
Anyone.
Anymore.
S.
O.
R.
R.
Y.

"You want to know one of the weirdest things?"

"What's that?"

"His best friend from high school had come out that week to go hunting together. So he wasn't lonely at the time. Russ was sleeping on the couch. His favorite companion, his chocolate lab, Angie, was sleeping on his bed. At 4 A.M. Russ heard the screen door slam; it woke him for a moment." Kurt sobbed some more, lit another cigarette, rubbed at his eyes.

"It's terribly sad. He was the last person you'd ever suspect would do something like this."

After the funeral, Kurt went back to Victoria to write his thesis. He got nowhere. He was overwhelmed with grief. He'd wake up in a cold sweat. He was so depressed, he started to wonder why more people didn't kill themselves. Why the hell not? Life is hard. Kurt drove around, screaming at the brother in the passenger seat who was no longer there. "I was so mad at him. I was so incredibly pissed off at him. In Catholicism, we're taught that suicide is a selfish act, and that's how I felt. I thought what he'd done was so selfish. I wanted to scream at him. And I did. In my mind, that's all I could think: 'You could have called us!' 'If you were unhappy, you should have said something!' 'You had options! You had other choices!' 'You could have changed!' 'It might have been hard, but you could have started over!' 'If you felt guilty for something, we could have forgiven you!' I couldn't get past this anger. And then one day, I turned it on myself."

"What do you mean?"

"I realized, yeah, I was yelling at him. But I might as well have been yelling at myself. Maybe I *was* yelling at myself: *I* can change. *I* can start over. *I* have other choices. I don't have to stick it out with poetry. I can find something else to do. I can finally tell people how unhappy I am. I *have to*, or I'm going to end up like my brother."

"And how'd you end up a chef?"

"That was all I could do in my grief. I could hardly read. I watched the Food Network and started reading cookbooks. Every day, Laura would come home, and it was all I'd done that day. So, once, she says, 'Why don't you just become a chef?' And I was defensive. 'What? You don't think I can finish my thesis?' But it was planted in my head. She'd given me permission to consider it. And so at a Christmas party, after I'd had a few drinks, I just said it out loud. 'I'm going to cooking school. What about that?' "

She told him it was a good idea.

"Fucking A, let's do it then."

A month later he called her at work to tell her they were moving to Seattle.

A culinary academy is where a cook is turned into a chef. I'd talked to other people who, like Kurt, had turned to cooking after a midlife crisis. There's something about nourishment, and nourishing others, that helps people to heal. Half the student body of most culinary schools are people in emotional transition. This was true of Kurt's class, too. Half were

twenty-year-olds who didn't want to go to college; the other half were former nurses, alcoholics, accountants, caterers, who needed a second lease on life.

Kurt said emphatically, "Changing my career saved my life. You tell people that. You put that in your book. *Changing my career saved my life.*"

There's a romantic notion of being a chef as creative person, an artist working in the food medium. Cooking school jolts that naïveté. "Being a chef is fucking *brutal*," Kurt warned, even as he said, "I knew *at once* it was for me." The hours are terrible. You get no holidays or vacations. At school, if the master chef doesn't like your soup, he might throw it on the floor and tell you to clean it up.

Kurt didn't say this outright, but it was clear from his comments that he loved the physical intensity of cooking in a restaurant, 120 steaks going on the grill, firing and plating, no time to be pensive or lost in space. Later, watching him whip up some Vietnamese *pho,* I could see he grooved on the action of chopping vegetables, flashing his knife skills, talking about a good fish stock. It was the polar opposite mental state of being an academic, where the joy is in letting the mind wander, with few deadlines, and the product of one's labor is intellectual—an obscure idea, or a few good lines of verse. Kurt no longer wanted to live in his mind. He needed the pressure, needed to be pushed, needed rules and standards that were enforced, needed to be part of a team, with a customer who would send it back if it wasn't cooked right. He'd found that he was much happier with his mind squeezed down to a peanut, and he could take a break from the kind of terribly sad thoughts that preoccupied it.

It was those thoughts that returned, time and again, as Kurt talked about his life. I could see these thoughts rock him, see them cloud his face, and his heavy voice would stop, could go no longer, and he'd be overtaken. I put my hand on his shoulder.

"Were you close?"

"Growing up, we played hockey and lacrosse together. We were always close. When I lived in Montana, we were chums. I lived in that house with him. He had a hard time when I left for Victoria. I'd been paying the house bills and ran the ship. When I left, it went to hell in a handbasket."

"Why?"

"Todd always had champagne taste, but he lived on a beer budget. Dad bailed him out a lot. He was never a great student, and he didn't aspire to a career. He'd been a bartender for a while, and he really liked being the assistant manager at the sporting goods store. But he liked *things,* the things that making a little more money might afford. He had to have the newest sneakers, or the latest skis, or the coolest car. The gym membership, golfing at the country club. He liked that image of himself. They gave him a sense of power. He always wanted what other people had, but he never had any desire to put his nose down to work for those things."

"When was the last time you saw him?"

"About a month before. He'd met a girl at our wedding that summer. . . ." Kurt paused a second. Something flashed in his mind. A memory. He finished the sentence, but it was clear that thought was his preoccupation. It made him sob again.

"Did something happen at your wedding?"

"He, uh, gave a speech." Kurt almost can't say it.

"What did he say?"

"It was not very articulate. It was rambling, and not just for the delivery did it come off a little odd. He talked about how he felt, seeing his little bro get married. It was clear he felt awkward. 'Here's my little bro, getting married before me!' And about how he'd watched me get my master's before him. When I got that degree, he really thought of it as an achievement, a sign of true success. It was just an English degree, which you and I know at best can bring you not much coin, maybe thirty grand a year. But to Todd it was the thing he could *never* get. He was so proud of me when I graduated. But in that speech, it was those words he kept using, 'before me,' like it was a competition. All these milestones I'd reached before him. I haven't been able to watch our wedding video."

I said, "In your mind, do you think that your getting married, and your imminent PhD, were making Todd feel inadequate, like he was a failure? Do you feel like that was one of the causes?"

Kurt couldn't speak. He held his lips tight. He nodded. I don't think he'd admitted this to anyone. He gathered himself, and added, "Sometimes he thought of me as the privileged one. Sometimes I think if he were still alive, and if he were to come here, to Kelowna? With the life I have now? If he saw my daughter? He'd be a great uncle for Maya. I know that. But I also think that my daughter would be a fragile blow to him."

That was one of the saddest things I'd ever heard. Kurt was blocked from letting his love out for his daughter, because he felt that his successes had made his brother be unhappy.

"Kurt, can I say something?"

"Please."

"You have to give yourself permission to enjoy your daughter and your wife and your home."

"I know!" he sobbed, having no idea how to do such a thing.

"You've earned this life you have. It wasn't a privilege. It wasn't handed to you on a silver platter. My god, you've had to fight for every bit of it. You weren't lucky. You paid for it with sweat and tears."

"You think so?"

"God, Kurt, listen to your own story. It's a heroic story."

"Thank you."

"Listen, my friend. You *have* to give yourself permission. You cannot do this to Maya. You cannot let her grow up in a house where you associate the birth of your daughter with the death of your brother. You have to uncouple those events. You have to free yourself to love her completely. You can't let this go unresolved for years. You have a responsibility to her!" By now I felt an incredible urgency in my voice. I wasn't yelling, but I was saying this with a ferocity.

Kurt said, "Have you ever done anything like that?"

I had.

"Will you tell me about it?"

"My baby was going to be born last March. I'd bought a new house with Michele, and we'd gotten married in October. My life was filling with these joyous things, but I couldn't let myself enjoy them, because I felt guilty. Terribly guilty for how I'd left my ex-wife, and how badly I'd hurt her. I'd needed to move on, but I'd never quite let myself move on, carrying this guilt for four years. Some of this guilt descended from my parents' divorce, and from how they'd fought for decades afterward. I projected some of my mom's pain onto my ex-wife. She and I had become civil, and we talked on the phone every six months or so. But I could never tell her about Michele, or about our house, because that always hurt her more. It was twisting the knife. She'd hang up the phone, or tell me never to mention Michele's name. So last February, I was taking stock, and trying to prepare for being a dad. And I realized I had this unfinished business. I had to tell my ex-wife, even if it meant hurting her. I had to do it, because I didn't want to run into her at the grocery store a year later, with my son in my arms. Or pull up at a stoplight and see her in the next lane, with my son in his car seat behind me." Now I found myself crying into my beer, tears running down my cheeks as I imagined those moments.

"Why not?"

"Because that wouldn't be fair to my son. My love for my son shouldn't be complicated. It shouldn't be dragging a parachute of guilt behind it. I owed that to him. He wasn't born yet, but I owed it to him. So I called my ex-wife up, and I asked her to have tea one morning."

"And you told her?"

"Yeah."

"Did it hurt her?"

"The thing was, *no*. She was happy for me, proud for me. She'd come *so* far, healed herself, that she had no resentment. That was the greatest gift, I think, that anyone has ever given me—the permission to love my son without any regrets. I was so much more ready for him to be born."

I'd never told this story to anyone. I'd never put it into words. But here I was, telling it to Kurt, and I think it was helping him, but it was also really helping *me*. I had no guilt left, but I had memories of guilt, and sometimes I didn't know what to do with those memories.

After some time, Kurt said, "Todd's not around to give me that gift."

"Well, maybe you can have that conversation in your head. You need to tell him, 'I earned this life. I have a right to love my daughter.' "

"Like how I used to yell at him, even though he was gone."

Nobody could say why Todd Slauson killed himself. But in the absence of knowledge, we try to craft theories. Kurt's mind had stitched together a theory, which he had harbored in secret, which was saddling him with guilt.

Two men, drinking, sitting in the sun, letting time pass, letting their pasts drift away, giving themselves permission to come back to the present, and seize it like the way, when you've swum underwater the entire pool length, you break the surface and inhale.

The
Appropriate
Time Frame

WHEN IS IT TOO LATE TO START OVER?

A few blocks from the Chancery Lane tube stop in London, I darted through an alleyway and stepped up into 11 Stone Buildings, which was both an address and the name of a chamber of barristers, as a firm of lawyers is termed in the British legal system. I asked for Sidney Ross. I was escorted back outside, four doors down, and into the basement, where Sidney welcomed me into his office. Sidney is seventy years old. After twenty-seven years as a professor of chemistry with tenure, he gave up his security to start a new career in law. His legal specialty is matters of inheritance, such as trusts and estates, but he's also had some fun representing defendants in professional misconduct cases, i.e., white-collar crime. He is not a famous lawyer, nor a rich one—just a happy one. I sat down on his piano bench beside his electronic-organ keyboard.

"When I feel like a bar of rehearsal, I rehearse," Sidney asserted. "Many chambers look askance at this, but in mine, nobody gives a damn as long as I don't frighten the horses. I do what I want with my life and when I want to do it. If I want to go to Venice for five days in October, I put it in my diary, and nobody says I can't do it."

He has sung in choirs most of his adult life. On Tuesdays he sings the Eucharist at Church of Saint Andrew by the Wardrobe. That coming weekend, he'd arranged for a cat-sitter so he and his wife could go to North Oxfordshire, where Sidney would sing and his wife would ring church bells. Sidney often walks to work from their home in Islington, 2.5 miles north. He is an avid reader of "police procedurals," a genre of detective novels. His wife is a scientist, as are their twin daughters—one at MIT, the other at IBM. For most of his life, Sidney was a scientist, too. He has a master's degree in solid-state physics, and a doctorate in inorganic chemistry. When he became a professor, "tenure" meant what it's sup-

posed to imply—lifetime employment. But he was pushed into early retirement and rather than beg some other university to give him a class or
two, Sidney admitted to himself that sheer stupidity had taken him into
chemistry in the first place.

When the war broke out in 1940, Sidney's elementary school in London's East End was evacuated. Sidney was awarded one of only three
scholarships from the London County Council to attend Christ's Hospital, an elite school founded in 1552. "And they'd been wearing the same kit
ever since," Sidney teased. "Long blue gown, knee britches, shirt and collar with bands. I felt quite conspicuous parading in that gear." He was nine
years old. The British school system forces students to narrow their area
of study early and often. Sidney was only thirteen when he specialized in
science. It was his worst academic subject. He didn't like the teachers who
taught the language arts in which he excelled. "I simply made a daft choice
out of personal pique," he said, chastising himself. "I never asked anybody's advice. It wasn't a sensible or rational decision." The system didn't
intervene to straighten him out. "I didn't figure in their calculations. The
school was unashamedly elitist. They were not interested in changing
their system for the benefit of students. We were lucky to be getting such
a quality education. If one made a mistake, one had to take the consequences." The consequences were sticking with it through his high school
certificate, which in turn determined his university entrance requirements.

In those days, chemistry had artisan connotations: grubby overalls in a
laboratory. If Sidney had studied Greek, he would have gone on to Oxford
or Cambridge. Because he studied physics, he went to a small technical
college affiliated with the University of London. "The higher echelons

were barred from me because I was not from the higher echelons." His parents were Hungarian immigrants. Sidney put in two years with the Signal Corps, and this class structure dissolved in the military. Soldiers rose through the ranks based on merit. It was very liberating. England didn't create anything like the G.I. Bill we had in the States, but the romantic notion of a classless society was similar. In the 1950s, this widely shared sentiment led to the first real Socialist government. "We all wanted to be part of something that was going somewhere," Sidney explained. "I wanted to build the new Jerusalem. I thought I could make my contribution to this enterprise by teaching other students how to *think*." He got an assistant lectureship at a college in London that he'd prefer not to name. Many of the students were older and attending university classes again because they felt they'd missed something the first time through. They were highly motivated and a pleasure to teach.

This growing social consciousness peaked in the mid-1960s when the prime minister, Harold Wilson, touted "the white-hot technological revolution." Suddenly scientists like Sidney were highly regarded. Research money was made more widely available on the promise that if English scientists built a better mouse trap, the world would beat a path to their door. Sidney published papers on the electrical properties of various materials and consulted for private companies on diabetes drugs. While his work was reputable, he described some of it as "sheer graffiti," meaning the system rewarded teachers for pumping out papers and never gave them credit for being great teachers. So even in the heyday of a technological revolution, chemistry was hitting a false note for Sidney. By the late 1970s, "the white-hot technological revolution had burnt down to dull ashes," and it was apparent to Sidney that chemistry was no longer attracting talented students. His students took chemistry because it was one of the only things on the menu. They hadn't passed the minimum requirements. Their minds were on subjects where there was more money to be made.

Sidney was bored. "I started to cast about for something to occupy my mind."

He cashed in a life insurance policy he had taken out twenty years prior and took his wife on holiday in Norway. There, he resolved that upon his return he would take steps toward a part-time prelaw degree. He had no intention of changing careers. It was purely an intellectual endeavor. He had always enjoyed reading what he called "legal reminiscences." Why not take a correspondence course?

"Upon my return, I went down to an old office in the city, which looked like every solicitor's office I had ever read about in Dickens—dark, heaps of dust on yellowing papers attended by an elderly gentleman—and exchanged a check for the forms. At night, I sat at my desk and applied myself to their version of what I needed to know in order to satisfy the whim of the external examination board." For four years, he mailed his assignments off to a tutor, who marked them up and sent them back. This was not associated with any law school. "I was studying law simply because I wanted to study law. I took a course because I thought I'd do it better within a framework where there was something to get out of it at the end." It was merely a hobby with structure.

That changed when his university decided it needed only half of its chemistry professors. They couldn't sack Sidney, because of his tenure contract, but they could make him feel unnecessary, and they induced him to retire early by offering a payoff of twenty thousand pounds. It surprised me that's all it took. They might have considered him old, but he hadn't saved enough to stop working. How long would twenty thousand pounds last? He was still going to have to find another income. "What I was doing was pointless," he said. His wife encouraged him to make a clean break. She had recently left science and trained in the gem business.

"I finally listened to where my talents are," Sidney said.

Now, if anyone ever had the justification to say, "It's too late to start over," it would be Sidney. I assumed he came from a generation where people postwar were happy to have any job at all. Instead, Sidney described decades of idealism and techno-boom much like the ones I have lived. He talked about the promise of social mobility that began when his parents emigrated from Hungary and continued with his daughters becoming chief scientists in America at institutions that two decades ago would never have allowed women at the top. I pressed Sidney quite a bit about this moment at the precipice, when he was about to enroll in law school at the University of London alongside students thirty years younger. Law school is grueling. Wasn't he scared of starting all over as a minion? Wasn't he afraid the young kids would outwork him? Wasn't he afraid his life would become unbalanced? Wasn't he afraid that when he went looking for a job as a barrister, nobody would hire him?

"If I had those fears," he said, "I simply put them out of my mind."

Even as I was inspired by his twilight bravery, I was dissatisfied by this answer. What if you can't put it out of your mind? What if you can't conjure this necessary illusion? Sidney's actions were new-era, but his attitude was very old-school: *I simply put it out of my mind*. I'd been trying to gain some perspective on this question, "When is it too late to start over?" and too often I heard the obligatory "It's never too late," which always struck me as one dimensional. Surely there are times when it's too late, no? But I never could define these conditions. Everyone I asked had embraced a sink-or-swim philosophy, i.e., *you'll get over your fears if you're in a situation where you simply have to.* I still don't know what to make of it. Sidney didn't seem scared of the huge loss of status associated with falling from professor of chemistry to legal peon. He implied that status games and competition for competition's sake were largely the make-work of young people looking to prove something to themselves. If you know your own worth, it's easier to handle. "I was simply not interested in competing with anyone else," he said.

It's safe to say that if Sidney had known what was coming, he might never have done it. He wouldn't use the words "discrimination"—maybe because he's a lawyer—but he was certainly discriminated against repeatedly. Despite graduating in the top 3 percent of his law school and rightly expecting to be highly sought-after, no firm would take him on. He applied to twenty-four different chambers, and each one rejected him. Time and again, he was told "It would be difficult to fit you into the structure of our chambers." Or "Your age would create stresses in our structure that we're not interested in undergoing." In the United States, when you pass the bar exam you're entitled to practice law and hang out your own shingle. Not so in England. The first year of employment is a compulsory internship; an established barrister agrees to take responsibility for you, train you, ensure that you learn the ropes. You cannot practice law without having completed the year under this sponsorship system. Despite being a top graduate during the beginning of an economic boom, Sidney was shut out from earning a living. He became depressed, even though in his heart he felt certain it would work out all right.

Nine months after passing the bar exam, Sidney heard about a vacancy at 11 Stone Buildings. He applied and was interviewed by a prospective "pupil master," who asked Sidney if he would have a problem being taught by someone fifteen years younger. "Not at all," Sidney replied. On that basis, a job was offered in good faith. The next day it was rescinded, then put in limbo. The head of chambers, the firm's top banana, wanted to interview Sidney. He seemed to bear a grudge, as if he suspected the other attorneys of doing an end-run on his authority. He fought with those who wanted to hire Sidney, and they compromised. Sidney was offered a job, but only for six months. At the end of that time, he would not be allowed to stay under any conditions. (It was common to split one's year and learn two specialties, but usually at one firm.) In the meantime, Sidney was advised to lie low and avoid the head of chambers.

What could he do but accept, and hope it worked out? Sidney began quietly drafting documents for his pupil master and a colleague. As in law school, he was doing work commonly done by those thirty years younger. But Sidney didn't mind. "I made the percentage decision," he said. "I had moments of depression as others got 'the shot' on interesting work. I didn't think I was entitled. I believed I would succeed on my merits eventually." That August, when one of his bosses was on summer vacation, Sidney went looking for a document in his office. On the desk was a synopsis of a textbook this barrister had contracted to update, with many arcane thirteenth-century references to Markets and Affairs. Little of the book was written, and it was due to the publisher. When his boss returned, Sidney pleaded his case to help with the book.

"I'm a published author."

"You are?"

"Over sixty articles and two books. I'd be happy to help out."

Sidney finally started to curry favor. Come October 9, his six-month internship deadline came and went. Sidney was officially a "squatter," but by avoiding the head of chambers, he heard no complaints. "I didn't want another period of probation. I preferred to sit it out." For one senior member he wrote an opinion of whether a farmer's milk quota could be sold separately from the land apportioned to that quota. It was about £2,000 worth of work, for which he was paid £250. He had no grounds to demand more. He was skating on thin ice.

At the end of the year, the head of chambers came into the office of the clerk. He was quite cross. He needed help on a case, and his junior barrister was away on holiday. The clerk told him that Sidney Ross was available. Old animosities resurfaced. *Is he still here!?* But there was nobody else to perform the research, unless the head of chambers wanted to spend his holiday in the library himself.

"As it was, I did a first-class job on it," Sidney remembered. "From then on, I did a 'volte-face' from pariah to jewel in the crown. The head of chambers got me involved in his large-scale fraud cases, which took us as far as Singapore and Hong Kong. With the caveat that I needed to look a little more respectable—I hadn't bought a new suit in many years—he persuaded me to accept a position as permanent member of the chambers."

Sidney went to the tailors on Fleet Street to have a suit made. When he showed up at work in it, the entire staff pretended not to recognize him.

He loves the law. He has a mind that loves puzzles, and cases are puzzles—timelines, cross-references, stories with motives. That said, the law is not just brain candy to him—all he's had to go through to get here is what makes it so special. He doesn't mind representing the occasional white-collar criminal. "I gave thirty years to this country. I've earned the chance to enjoy myself." We spent the entire afternoon at the restaurant he frequents, emptying a bottle of wine. Why not? As Sidney pointed out in many ways, "The moral is to not set yourself goals which don't leave you any freedom to maneuver."

He's often called by people who want to know the secret of his success. He has none. He sat it out and endured until his chance came. In one of his favorite "police procedurals," a mergers-and-acquisitions banker realizes that the life he's leading is not fit for a human being. "That's very much how I felt," Sidney reflected. "I hit the point where I knew I ought to do something while my faculties were still reasonably intact, and not waste the rest of my life."

KEEP IN MIND EVEN WHAT YOU CAN'T DEFINE

These last few stories are reminders to keep an eye on your Big Picture. By that I mean not everyone's got it figured out just yet, but in the meantime you can build skills that you might be able to draw on when the time comes to make *your* contribution, X. Maybe you can't even define X, but that's no reason not to prepare for the day you do figure it out.

People who can define it usually keep their Big Picture to themselves. Big Pictures sound too audacious and far-fetched. My wife has one. She didn't tell me about it for three years. I keep her secret a secret, but I thought it was incredibly cool that she had one. I remember that feeling, back when I was a bond salesman, and I dreamed that someday I would write books. Mentioning this invited smirks. *Yeah, right. YOU?* I learned to keep my mouth shut.

Phil Caplan had been telling me his story for a while. One afternoon, we were sitting in his corner office, twelve stories up, high enough that we could look over the Potomac at Washington's many monuments. Phil is the kind of guy other people go to for advice, so he had told his story many times, and it usually impressed them. But something about it suddenly wasn't adding up. On paper, he was on top of the world. Why was he so incredibly interested in my book? The people *most* drawn to my book didn't have it figured out. Phil was managing a venture hedge fund for Northern Virginia's hottest investment bank, FBR. Before that, he was President Clinton's staff secretary, which is one of the coolest jobs to have in the White House. Many Clinton alumni thought Phil had masterminded the perfect exit transition, segueing from one corridor of power to another. He was set. His story should have been all in the past tense. Except there were clues.

1. He was absolutely feverish about my book, an indication of something unresolved.
2. His office had no mementos from his years in the White House or working at AmeriCorps—the past was not cluttering his future.
3. He asked me quite a few questions about Seattle and Washington State, as if that might be in his future.

Then it came to me—he was still looking for his X! He hadn't forgotten about his Big Picture.

I called him on it. "This isn't the end of the story, is it?" By *this* I meant the investment bank and its hedge fund. "Everyone thinks this is it, but you know better, don't you?"

He paused, leaned back, and smiled.

I took a guess. "You going to run for office in Washington State? Governor? Senator?"

"I'm not sure," Phil said. "I've thought about it. My wife's from the Pacific Northwest. I ran the state's operation for the ninety-two election. A politician has to *be* from somewhere. If I put my time in there . . . Or maybe it's running a company. I'd like to lead people. CEOs are heralded as our leaders today. I think I can do a good job."

"It's okay if you don't have it figured out. As long as you don't stop figuring."

"I appreciate you saying that. I've had these windows into these two worlds, politics and the New Economy. And I don't want to burn through my experiences like some trash novel that's gone from my mind as soon as it's finished. I want my experiences to add up. I want them to be useful, and to come together. I don't really know how they fit together, but I think about it all the time. They have to add up to more."

I admired Phil, because he took his responsibility to his Big Picture seriously, even though it might have come in and out of focus a few times. Phil had unique integrity. Most people who work in politics have no intention of ever becoming a politician. Phil saw his years in the trenches as training that he would draw on when it was his time to run. When he decided to leave the White House, in 1999, it surprised everyone around him.

"Everyone thought I had the greatest job in America," he said.

"Did you?"

"I did."

The White House is about a five-hundred-person organization. There's the president, his chief of staff, and his cabinet, and then everyone else is divided into nine departments. The whole world wants to sway the president, and their opinions come in through these nine offices. Mayors who want to talk to the president come in through Intergovernment Affairs. Congresswomen come in through Legislative Affairs. Health and Human Services issues come in through the Office for Policy Development. Religious issues come through Public Liaison. Can you imagine, for a moment, the huge number of people who want to sway the president? The center of this funnel, which pipes all these concerns up to the president, is the Office of the Staff Secretary. It is the center at the eye of the storm. It is the gatekeeper of access. The staff secretary decides what the president needs to see and not to see. After a few months of getting to know each other, President Clinton and Phil took care of business mostly by paper. Phil would write one-page memos, summarizing the opposing positions of constituents. Then Phil would make a recommendation, and at the bottom put two boxes for the president to check:

____ Agree   ____ Disagree

Sometimes Phil would present two options for the president to choose. Option 1. Option 2. Phil controlled the autopen, and was authorized to sign on behalf of the president for anything except a bill from Congress.

"Wow!" I exclaimed, when Phil explained this to me. "You were practically running the day-to-day business of the country!"

"I don't like to think of it that way," he said. "I was sorta the president's personal assistant."

"It sounds incredibly cool."

"It was."

"So why did you leave two years early?"

"Well, I never pretended that *I* was somebody important. It wasn't *me*. It was the *chair.* My power and influence came from sitting in the staff secretary's chair and having that business card. The Secret Service didn't open doors for Phil Caplan, they opened the door for the staff secretary. CEOs didn't return Phil Caplan's phone call, they returned the staff secretary's call."

"You didn't think you deserved it?"

"That's not what I'm suggesting. I just didn't let it go to my head. I knew our term there was finite. And I knew that when it was over, and I stepped outside, I would be a normal guy. I wanted to know that I could succeed in life without flashing that business card, without having to say I come from the White House. In Washington, you can build a career as a lobbyist leveraging the two years you worked on Capitol Hill. But I didn't want to be riding out my years, with my best years in my past, begging old friends for favors. That possibility made me very uncomfortable."

"Because it would have been a waste of your potential?"

"Exactly."

"Why'd you leave politics for business? And why two years early?"

"I wanted the education. I wanted to learn business. Throughout the nineties, I could see that business leaders in America were more trusted than politicians. A lot of successful businessmen ran for office, and their business experience was seen as a real asset. They were fiscally responsible. They had proven their ability to motivate their employees. They took care of their employees. I realized that working in business would be good training, and I might learn traits and habits and ways of leading that would serve my future. People don't normally talk this way about business, but they should. They talk about the military this way, that a few years in its culture is good for you. Well, I realized I'd worked in politics my whole life, and I didn't have any business experience, and a few years would be good for me. And as soon as I realized that—I was thirty-five, my clock was ticking—I knew I had to do it, even if it meant leaving the best job in America."

Phil took this need for an education so seriously that he was willing to completely humiliate himself. He went across the river to meet with one of FBR's founders, Russ Ramsey. Russ was only three years older than Phil—the kind of guy someone like Phil might normally be competitive with. Russ had a crazy life and didn't have time for all the work he had to do, let alone errands like picking up his dry cleaning. Russ needed a bionic personal assistant, someone smart but egoless. Capable of both attending meetings on Russ's behalf *and* getting his lunch. Russ called this a "Personal COO."

Phil suggested, "Well, at the White House, we call that the staff secretary, and if I can do for you what I did for the president, I think I could help you."

They agreed to a deal: Phil would receive a hundred times better education than any business school could give him. In return, he agreed to do *anything* that Russ needed for two years, no matter how humiliating. The job would pay about the same as Phil was making at the White House, which wasn't much. After the two years, assuming they were still friends, Phil would be given real responsibility and autonomy.

Phil sat at a little desk in the corner of Russ's office. He showed me the office—the desk is gone now—and it's an office 100 percent surrounded by glass. One side looks out over the Potomac toward Georgetown. The other side is a fishbowl looking onto the sales and trading floor, where about seventy macho guys and girls could watch Phil sitting at his little table. One year he's practically running the country, the next year he's a peon—because he believed in learning this point of view. Phil hired Russ's secretary, he helped out Russ's mom, and he dropped off Russ's car at the repair shop. But he also became the voice of Russ wherever Russ was stretched too thin to be there himself. Deal negotiations, pitches from start-ups, board meetings. By being willing to be subservient, Phil learned business at its highest level, without having to work his way up to that point.

Before the two years were up, Russ and Phil went out and raised $200 million for a hedge fund. Phil is managing it—to be clear, not choosing the investments (he doesn't have *that* kind of experience).

Now the question is: How long will this suck him in? Will he become trapped by the fat salary, the house big enough for his kids to have their own bedrooms? I don't get the feeling that will be a problem with Phil. I don't think he's going to forget.

"Do you know the story of Bob Graham?" he asked.

"From Florida?"

"The senator, then the governor. When I was twenty-two, I read about this thing he pioneered. He called it 'work days.' He would regularly go out and work an entire day doing different jobs. Cutting sugar cane in the Everglades, picking in the citrus groves, the assembly line in a car factory. He walked in the shoes of the people he represented. It wasn't a photo-op. He wanted to understand them. I was profoundly influenced by this. I still think about it."

"Well, remember, you're going in my book. You've got too much to offer the world not to shoot high. If people like you don't become leaders, then *who*?"

"I appreciate that," he said.

With most people I got to know, we would agree to check in again in a few months, or maybe next year. With Phil, that wasn't the appropriate measuring increment.

"I'm going to look in on you in ten years," I vowed.

"Ten! Not five?"

"The bigger the picture, the longer it takes," I said. "That's okay. I can wait."

BUSINESS IS A TOOL TO SUPPORT WHAT YOU BELIEVE

Joe Belanoff's Big Picture came into focus in the last couple of years. He's forty-four. If you don't know where you're headed when you begin, it can take that long, easily. But it's worth it.

Joe is an easygoing, amiable guy. We met the first time at his office, which was inside a law firm in Menlo Park, but I'll reveal later what his office is for and what he's doing there. He's not a lawyer.

Ironically, Joe worked at this very law firm the summer after college, 1979. He was an English major at Amherst and figured he might go to law school, but one summer in the xerography department cured him of that idea. He drove back East to look for a job. Early in his trip, he stopped at Lake Tahoe and gambled for four days. He knew how to count cards, and he raked in $1,200.

"So when I got back East, and I went in for interviews, I had a *story* to tell people," Joe explained.

And who would be impressed with a card-counting gambler? Wall Street. The attraction was mutual. Wall Street was the antithesis of his summer bent over the Xerox in a suffocatingly quiet law firm, where it would take seven years to make partner. Wall Street was going to work with a track suit on. As long as you made the firm money, it didn't matter if you were unshowered or stubbed your cigarette out on your own shirt. In October 1979, Joe went to work for Mabon Nugent. They specialized in technical arbitrage, the simultaneous buying and selling of the same security—for instance, buying gold at 500 while selling gold futures at 520. Joe was one of the first guys on Wall Street to trade bonds versus bond futures. He was good at it, and by the time he was twenty-five, he'd left, and with a few friends started their own arbitrage shop, Miller Tabak & Hirsch (now Miller Tabak & Co.). The goal on Wall Street was early retirement, and starting their own firm was the fast way to that end. Get their money and get out. None of them expected to still be working at age thirty-five.

But Joe's Big Picture gyroscope kicked in, mucking up that plan. He realized he didn't want to retire at thirty-five. He wanted to find his life's work, and he hoped that once he found it, he would be of use to people his whole life. At the end of a trading day, what did he have besides money? Numbers on a page. He wasn't a "stuff" kind of person, so he didn't need the money *for* something. He'd taken advantage of market inefficiencies. Was that going to be the full sum of his contribution to the world—eradicating market inefficiencies by taking advantage of them? His was a very narrow life. He hadn't learned anything new in several years.

Joe started thinking about what he really wanted to do with his life. His girlfriend was in med school, and he found what she was learning very interesting. He enrolled in premed night classes at Hunter College and NYU, showing up in pinstripes. He took four semesters of science and the MCATs while holding down his day job—hoping this wasn't a mistake, a mirage. The doctors he talked to were down on their profession, frustrated by reductions in their compensation inflicted by HMOs. But those concerns never seemed to matter when they were in a room with a patient. Joe longed for that human contact, making a difference in people's lives. He began medical school at Columbia when he was thirty-one. When he told people on Wall Street that he was leaving, it was very hard for them to fathom.

"Currency is the only currency on Wall Street," he explained. "I still have lots of friends from those days. I ask how's it going, and they tell me where the long bond is at."

During medical school, Joe gravitated toward psychiatry. One reason was his desire to be active his whole life—psychiatrists were leading good lives, well into their sixties, without burning out. Scientifically, he was interested in the brain as an organ, which we know so little about. And he loved the window into people's lives that psychiatry affords. Psychiatrists spend more time with their patients than any other doctor. Joe was fascinated with the cases he saw. The Ivy Leaguer who claimed George Bush senior was having an affair with his wife, Princess Diana. The college student who was in the ER after a suicide attempt. The lightheaded ballet dancer who everyone thought was simply starving herself, and turned out to have hyperthyroid. By treating them with the right medication, he was able to help them resume their lives. Indirectly he helped their friends and family, made their lives easier too. This work had a ripple effect.

Joe came to Stanford for his residency, to work with the department chairman, Dr. Alan Schatzberg, whose particular interest was psychotic depressives. Psychotic depressives are not manic depressives. It's a very common form of depression but one that few people talk about because there is no approved treatment for it. They often have no previous signs of depression or illness. They can be CEOs or doctors. Half of them suffer only a single episodic bout, which never returns. It starts with lots of stress, which leads to their feeling depressed. Then they become incredibly suspicious. Their brains begin to piece together clues wrongly, weaving closed doors, glances, and whispers into the pattern of their suspicions. They suspect their coworkers of manipulating to get them fired, suspect spouses of having affairs, and often think they're about to die or be killed. This advances to the point of hallucinations. They become "crazy," in the old-fashioned way, and 20 percent commit suicide. One hundred thousand cases of psychotic depression are logged in the United States every year, which means almost two thousand people a month commit suicide under its spell.

Unfortunately, the only available treatment is electroshock therapy. I didn't know this still went on—I thought that since Ken Kesey exposed its horrors in the sixties, it had gone the way of bloodletting. I was wrong. So I went down to Stanford Hospital to watch. They still have a case a day. Patients are knocked out with general anesthesia. A current is run through the patient's brain until it forces a seizure, which medically is a tremendous release of neurotransmitters that basically triggers a cold reboot of the brain. The patient will have to undergo electroshock six to ten times in thirty days.

Joe arrived at Stanford and was disturbed that electroshock therapy was the prevailing treatment. "I kept asking, 'This is the best we can do?' These were very sick people, receiving very crappy treatment. In the age of Prozac, we were still using these medieval methods."

Dr. Schatzberg had been hunting for a cure for some time, and Joe enlisted to do his research. This kind of biomedical research is very hit and miss, and miss, and miss. You press forward, testing assumptions derived from the little that's known so far, and most of these assumptions don't test out. Eventually, your triangulation might come up with a target, a very particular brain receptor that needs to be juiced or neutered. To borrow the lock-and-key metaphor, this receptor is the lock, and then you start all over again looking for the key that fits that lock. Most keys fit about twelve locks, which creates all number of side effects. So you hope for a key that, ideally, would fit only your target lock.

Psychotic depressives have elevated levels of cortisol, a long-acting adrenaline that's usually triggered by stress. Their research narrowed in on a type of brain receptor with a superaffinity to cortisol. This was the lock. Where was the key? Joe read up on metastatic cancer tumors that were pumping out cortisol. Back in 1980, a cancer researcher in Europe had tried a compound called C-1073 on these cancer cells, and in the course of twenty minutes he discovered that it blocked both cortisol *and* progesterone. This researcher was not looking for a progesterone controller, but he knew that was a big deal—a complete accident, but a big deal—and the compound has been used throughout Europe to control progesterone ever since. It was such a big deal that its implications for cortisol were overlooked, and never explored. Joe read this, and wondered if C-1073 might work on psychotic depressives.

They wrote to the FDA and received approval to try it on five patients. This was around Christmas, 1996. All five patients got better right away, and none experienced side effects. "These were unbelievably sick dudes," Joe said. "To get them back to their life was so rewarding."

At this point, the two doctors faced a choice. Should they license their discovery to a big pharmaceutical company? Or should they pursue it themselves? They were doctors, not biotech executives, and unfamiliar with the regulatory procedures required to bring a drug to market. Despite this, the fastest way to get it to market was to do it themselves. "Two thousand patients every month were committing suicide," Joe explained. "We decided we had a responsibility to take the fastest approach. I'd made a promise to myself that I would never do business again. I liked my doctor life, my patients, my classes, my students. I didn't want to run a company. But it was the right thing to do."

Joe went back to his closet and dusted off his suits. He took leave from Stanford. A local venture capitalist funded a larger trial of thirty patients at six academic hospitals. The drug showed similar miracle results. Joe raised another $26 million to conduct a final, pivotal trial, which is currently in process. His law firm lent him some office space, and he's in there with about twelve employees. Their company is Corcept Therapeutics.

This may be the fastest way to get C-1073 to market, but nonetheless they're required to do all the FDA trials. It requires a great deal of patience. Every month, another two thousand suicides. Joe has gone back to seeing patients one day a week at Stanford, and he teaches one course every fall. He has two kids, six and ten, and doesn't work in the evenings.

Imagine making that significant a contribution—saving twenty thousand lives a year. Joe didn't invent a cure. He discovered what was already there, and in that sense, he was lucky, but he never would have discovered it if he wasn't looking for it. I think that's a fairly good illustration of how to live up to your own notions of a Big Picture—it doesn't require genius or heroics. You'll discover something if you keep looking.

"I used to use business to make money," Joe said. "But I've learned that business is a tool. You can use it to support what you believe in. I'm using business to extend research and treat my patients."

NO BIG PICTURE IS TOO BIG

If business is a tool to support what you believe in, Deni Leonard takes it to another level. For him, it's not just a tool, it's more like . . . a magic power. Business is one of many magical powers he can conjure to fight for his Big Picture, which is to economically empower indigenous groups around the globe. His other powers include law, education, governance, and international relations. He is a Native American from the Warm Springs reservation in Oregon, and he lives in Mill Valley, north of San Francisco. He is fifty-six years old, but the fruitful phase of his career has only recently begun. This is according to plan, and it's because he *planned* for it to take this long that I was so impressed. What patience! What vision!

Here's how I heard about Deni. After one of our weekly pickup soccer games, I was raving to another guy about how I loved the multicultural aspect of soccer. It's one of the few places where people can embrace their national or ethnic identity and still play together by the same rules. Soccer assimilates without breaking down heritage and style. Where else can we see such a great thing? Our schools are bogged down in identity politics, every kid wanting to belong to a disadvantaged-hyphenated-minority, while our business markets tip in the other direction, every company pushing itself to be professional, i.e. colorless. This country's becoming so diverse. We need more examples of integration sans cultural annihilation. My friend said I ought to meet Deni Leonard. He'd met Deni only briefly, but had kept his business card.

Deni was exactly what I was looking for. I followed him around several days throughout the year, and I also took several people in his circle to lunch. I attended one of his conferences, in which he educated tribal leaders on how to finance and build power plants on their reservations. Once a month, on Saturday afternoons, Deni gathered with the other members of the Water Mushroom Club at Café Trieste to drink red wine and listen to the waiters sing opera. The Water Mushroom Club is a multiethnic, multigenerational network comprising business leaders who've decided to stop chasing minority set-asides and find other ways to compete outside the white man's mainstream. It's one of a dozen networks Deni has a hand in founding.

You're familiar with the term "parallel universe"? A parallel universe is in our midst but we can't see it. Well, that's sort of like what Deni's up to. He's spawning an entire parallel economy, using sources of capital you didn't know existed, building factories and power plants you'll never see, on land and in neighborhoods you'll never go to, and selling the output to customers you didn't know were buying. If it continues to grow according to plan, it will slow or reverse the migration away from reservations . . . it will diversify Native Americans away from their reliance on gambling casinos . . . it will restore lost traditions . . . it will bring jobs to inner cities . . . it will teach young people self-reliance . . . it will give tribes an identity they can be proud of.

Deni is medium height, solid. His skin tone is quite brown and etched with scars from his youth. His hair is graying only slightly; he wears it swept back and neat, with a pinky finger's worth of ponytail hiding in back, often tucked into the collar of his dress shirt. He wears top-dollar banker suits and ties. He has a sly sense of humor, chuckles a lot. He's often hard to pin down—never evasive, but will switch the subject to a different venture mid-sentence. He seemed to enjoy my confusion when I tried to chronicle everything he does. So with the caveat that I might have missed half of it—that I probably saw only a little of his parallel universe—here is a bit of his story.

He didn't leave his tribal land until he was nineteen. He attended San Bernardino Valley College and worked as a grocery store clerk at night. He was profoundly affected by the assassination of Bobby Kennedy and the Vietnam War, and by the time he was twenty-five, he was an antiwar leader. This was 1969. He had tons of energy and no sense of how to direct it other than through protest. The army decided to make an example of him. At his draft hearing, he said that as a person of color, he couldn't go kill other indigenous people. They sent him to boot camp anyway. On the walls were framed pictures celebrating the army's history, including many photographs and drawings depicting the slaughter of Indians. He protested again, and was told his pacifist ways were undermining troop morale. They came one night at three in the morning and dragged him off

to his court-martial. He explained that he was bound by a treaty never to pick up arms—this was a treaty his forefathers had signed with the U.S. government. Now the government was telling him to pick up arms? He refused. They imprisoned him in the Presidio stockade (a half mile from where he lives now). For seven months he was treated terribly, and the day he walked out, his stories triggered an investigation into brutality. The stockade was shut down; he was its last prisoner.

Deni went up to the mountains east of Eureka, into the lands of the Hupa tribe. He went there to think. To intensify his thinking, he fasted for ten days, drinking only water. After several days, in a slight delirium, he began to have a vision for his life. It was a raw vision, somewhat impractical, hallucinatory but genuine. Was fighting back the best use of his energy? Why were Indian ways disappearing? Tribes had their own land and their own sovereignty over it. Why were they losing people, why was their wealth draining away?

He realized that everyone in the sixties who wanted to help Indians was, in fact, making them dependent. When a check shows up every month in your mailbox, you're the one who loses, because you lose your own survival skills. The handout system had turned Indians into eunuchs. Assimilation had gone too far. Education was nothing less than a cognitive drug. When you lose your identity, you lose your source of power. How could they regain this power? First, there were 107 tribes in California alone—if they could *connect,* and work together, they would have a collective power. Second, young Native Americans needed to have their identities restored. Tribes had fought for political sovereignty, but they had never paid attention to their economic sovereignty. They had neglected learning business.

Deni walked out of those mountains determined to write a new curriculum that embraced ethnic identity and emphasized self-reliance.

He wrote a business plan that set out his objectives for the next twenty years of his life. He would train himself for five years in four different areas: education, business and banking, indigenous government, and international relations. "I had to learn the white man's ways to save the non–white man's ways," he explained.

I won't go into the details, but he stuck to his plan marvelously. Five years in each skill set. Degrees from Harvard's Kennedy School and the University of Oregon. He taught at Berkeley and the University of Washington. He consulted with the Department of the Interior and the Department of Education. He learned investment banking and insurance underwriting. He traveled the world helping indigenous groups defend their rights in Samoa, Saipan, Mexico, Ecuador, and New Zealand.

In 1990, at the age of forty-six, he began to take that raw vision he had in the mountains and refine it into something practical and solid. This took another five years. He formed an investment bank and several other financial service firms under a subsidiary, DLA Financial. The basic premise was that reservations are special economic redevelopment zones. Corporations on these lands do not have to pay taxes. At the same time, commercial banks are pressured to lend a small portion of their portfolio to economic redevelopment zones; they do this in order to stem federal regulation. A small amount of initial seed capital—from tribe bank deposits, for instance—could be vastly multiplied using a variety of loans and tax advantages. In addition, the federal government has a purchasing program called Section 8(a), instructing the government to purchase from businesses that are owned by Indians, native Alaskans, and Hawaiians. Whatever they brought onto the reservation—courtesy of government tax breaks—they could turn around and sell back to the government—courtesy of more government breaks. The tax laws and the purchasing programs were already in place, waiting to be played. Indians didn't need cash aid, and they didn't need any more help.

Deni started with a single piece in the midnineties. The key was to stop the flow of money off reservations. Many Indians kept their scant deposits in non-Indian banks. Deni taught tribes to set up their own co-op banks, and then he managed their assets for them, like a mutual fund. This was the seed capital to get started. He kept working up the food chain. Native American companies were buying worker's compensation insurance from national firms—again, pennies on the dollar flowing off the reservation, never to return. Deni underwrote their insurance. Payroll services were next—more pennies on the dollar to keep around.

Then he became aware of a gross injustice, which he quickly foresaw as a huge opportunity. Indians were paying twelve cents per kilowatt-hour of electricity, almost twice the national average price of seven cents. Deni began financing the construction of cogeneration power plants. Co-gen plants are small; they're powered by natural gas, are built around jet engines, and each turbine costs about $1.3 million. They produce electricity, which can be sold in the newly deregulated power markets, and they produce lots of steam, which can be used to heat buildings on the reservation or to create even more electricity. Rather than buying electricity at twelve cents, why not make your own, at two cents, and sell the leftovers at seven cents to pay for the whole thing?

Well, why not?

Nobody could see a reason why not, other than it wasn't the sort of ambitious thing tribal councils normally did. How would they pay for it? Deni would float the bonds. Who would buy the bonds? Deni's customers. Who were these customers? Banks. It sounded like white man's hocus-pocus to them. Which was exactly the point. White men did this stuff all the time.

What if there were no buildings nearby on the reservation to heat? Build a large greenhouse and create an herb farm, growing organic herbs for the farmers' markets! For every objection, Deni had yet another way to add jobs and make money. He kept working up the food chain. He trusted that if it worked with small cogeneration plants, it would work with a big geothermal plant. So he raised $180 million to build a 250-megawatt plant for the Elem Pomo Indian tribe. After enough cogeneration plants had been built, he started to wonder, "Why pay someone else to do this?" And so he purchased a power-plant construction company. He folded his banking company into a larger holding company, United Native Depository Corp., and created the first and only publicly traded company majority-owned by Native Americans.

Then he discovered another gross injustice. There was a ton of oil wells on reservations in the Southwest. Indians were routinely paid a 10 percent royalty on their oil when the going rate was 20 percent. Many of these wells had nearly dried up anyway. Deni found an inventor in Odessa, Texas, who could clean oil wells by flushing them with water and a small concentration of a surfactant he'd invented. Wells usually dried up because salt would make the ground swell, clogging off the veins that the oil moved through. This surfactant caused salt to drop out of water; I saw it demonstrated in a glass of dissolved salt water. The salt undissolved and fell to the bottom. When this same process occurred underground, the wells returned to 60 percent of their peak levels. Deni offered to flush everyone's wells. He would pay for it; each well would cost about $6,500. It would cost them nothing; they would split the additional earnings. Again, it sounded too good to be true. Those wells had been dry for years! You're going to make us money off them? At no cost to us?

Deni was turning dust into oil, turning land into power, and turning nickels into dollars. Here's how he'd turn a nickel into a dollar: he worked with an immigration attorney named Eugene Wong. Eugene would be contacted by businesspeople in Indonesia who wanted to come to America. Eugene would secure them an investor visa, an EB-5. This normally requires an agreement to invest a million dollars, but three thousand EB-5s are set aside each year for investing in special economic zones. These can be had for a half million dollars. Eugene sends the money to Deni, who uses it as seed capital, and pairs it up with another $9.5 million in bank loans, which he's free to invest in something safe and predictable, like a power plant. Thus, nickels into dollars. Is it a trick? It seems so. Too good to be true. More white man's magic.

So where do all these dollars go? Back into education. Deni is a board member of no less than fourteen councils, task forces, and associations. They've created an American Indian Charter School in Oakland, and nearby, a Native American Cultural Center. He's helping strengthen the only Native American–run university in the country, DQU, which is two hours north. DQU is an impoverished school, terribly underfunded by the state (another gross injustice!) and struggling to survive. But Deni sees these students as the future leaders of the businesses that'll spawn on the reservations. He'll give them a reason to go back to the land they came from.

His list of projects is endless. Every time I called him, it was something else.

"What are you working on today, Deni?"

"Oh, we're building an ecotourism resort in Costa Rica run by Indians."

"What are you working on today, Deni?"

"Oh, a billionaire in China owns the world's biggest sapphire, and he wants to put it on display at the Pequot casinos in Connecticut. I'm trying to insure it."

"What are you working on today, Deni?"

"Oh, I'm learning a little about hydroponics."

"What are you working on today, Deni?"

"Oh, we're trying to repatriate this dead guy's bones back to Hawaii."

"What are you working on today, Deni?"

"Oh, a water theme park to be run by the Morongo tribe in SoCal."

I could write a story on any one of these ventures. Deni resembled a venture capitalist, continually shopping for opportunities, hooking people up, throwing his weight around when deals stalled. But he waded into the morasses that venture capitalists feared: government regulation, politicking and lobbying, the cacophony of school districts, the idiosyncrasies of military requisition procedure. Bureaucracies didn't behave like bureaucracies when he came calling. The waters parted. He said it's because he speaks their language. "They hang funny things on the wall and speak a language you can't understand," he said. "They have ways of doing things. If you respect their ways, they'll work for you. If you respect their *sovereignty*, they'll continue to help you."

Deni reinforced so many of the lessons I'd learned during my research. Patience, long-term planning, resilience. That when you embrace your true identity, you will discover a productive power you never imagined having. That no Big Picture is too big. That you must be willing to speak the language of others (that you must walk in their shoes). But it is the one I first mentioned—that business is a tool to support what you believe in— that I keep coming back to.

For the past nine years, I was the chairman of Consortium Book Sales & Distribution. It is based in St. Paul, Minnesota, and is the exclusive distributor of some of the finest independent publishers in the country. My relationship to the company was always odd; I had no equity and only occasionally received a nominal stipend for being one of its three directors. It's not really much work—it's more of a responsibility. The company grew 500 percent during this period, and ran fine with minimal guidance. I was appointed to the position back when I worked in small press publishing. It's the one stray orphan from those years still tagging along in my life. I did it because it was fun; I did it because I'm very good at it. I did it because I believe in books. Books have been my classroom and my confidant. Books have widened my horizons. Books have comforted me in my hardest times. Books have changed my life.

The thing is, book publishing is an absolutely crazy business. Most books lose a lot of money. Large publishers smooth out this roller coaster by being big and spreading their risk. Small publishers ride up and down this roller coaster with total abandon, going in and out of bankruptcy, narrowly averting meltdown by taking out a third mortgage on their homes, et cetera. Small publishers routinely take levels of risk that any classically trained businessperson would find completely unacceptable. They're either that stupid or that smart.

I like to do my part to make sure that the books I treasure so deeply don't become endangered species. It's one way I give back. I could donate money as well, and do, but I've found the best way to help is to do what I can to ensure that these small publishers have a distributor that is on a sound financial footing. The distributor is the backbone of their network. It is the custodian of their trust. It lends them money, encouragement, and manpower to help them survive the occasional freefall. At the same time, a distributor should never profit at its publishers' expense. It wouldn't be right, morally. Greed has no place.

This past year, we lost both our CEO and our owner. Both decided they wanted out after nine years. The responsibility of holding down the fort and replacing them fell to the directors, and we weren't looking forward to the work involved. I considered resigning but knew that would only leave the company weaker.

We began to market the company. From my years writing about Silicon Valley, I knew dozens of rich young men with time on their hands who might like to own the company. But I didn't call them. Largely due to what I've learned from this book, I thought about the question differently from how I might have before. Rather than asking, "Who has the money to buy this company?" or "Who has the experience to buy this company?" I asked myself, "Who has the *character* to own and run this company?" Who would be a worthy custodian of our publishers' trust? Who has demonstrated the moral sobriety this company needs? Who will do what is best for publishing, rather than what is best for himself?

And I came up with a name: Don Linn, the former investment banker turned catfish farmer whom I visited in Mississippi. He truly loved books, and if he could motivate farmworkers then he would do great with our twenty Spanish-speaking warehouse workers. He was a whiz at finance. If he'd learned agribusiness, he could learn book distribution. He'd made moral choices in his life. He was not in it for the quick profit.

I e-mailed him to ask if the farm was sold yet.

The ink was almost dry.

Did he have a job at a biotech start-up yet?

Not yet . . . biotech was tough to break into.

Did he still want to move to a big city?

He did.

Did the Twin Cities count as a big city?

Big enough. What did I have in mind?

I told him only the basics, and then we sent him our offering memorandum. I didn't push him at all. I knew how easy it would be to sell him on it. But I'd learned that it's either a fit or it's not—our publishers wouldn't be served by someone I'd hornswoggled into a deal. Don flew to Minnesota two weeks later to meet the staff. He became excited. He came back, weeks later, with accountants and lawyers to kick our tires. By this time, I'd beaten the outgoing owner into submission, and he'd agreed to a reasonable price, and to take a note rather than all cash. It was not that much money. We had plenty of other willing buyers, but the staff and the directors and the publishers all loved Don. They were nervous because he had zero book experience, but once they met him they were quickly won over by the same traits I was. His business mind was very keen. He showed them respect.

Don moved to Minnesota two months later. He found a furnished condo—his family wouldn't join him until the summer—and he began taking Spanish classes. He took to the business much like everyone else in this book—he loved being a book guy, and because he loved it, he seemed innately great at it. He kept us on as directors, and I have faded back into the wallpaper, there only when called upon. I made not one penny on the deal, but it was richly rewarding to have done a good thing.

"I have only one demand," I said, before signing his letter of intent. "This is just between us."

"Shoot."

"I'm not dropping you from the book. Everything between us as directors of the company might be private, but everything you've told me up until now is fair game."

"Deal."

I'd committed the cardinal sin of journalism—I stepped into the frame and changed the outcome. I felt funny about it. It's okay if our writing changes people's minds, but not if our actions do. It's like tampering with a crime scene before the police photographers show up. Who knows what Don Linn would be doing today if I hadn't sent that e-mail? Maybe he would be floundering and miserable, suffering his inevitable punishment for leaving Wall Street behind.

But I'd rather help than watch. I'd rather have a heart than a mind. I'd rather expose too much than too little. I'd rather say hello to strangers than be afraid of them. I would rather know all this about myself than have more money than I need. I'd rather have something to love than a way to impress you.

57 ||| Closing Remarks

ALL STORIES ARE UNIQUE

There will always be those who say it's impractical. I respect that we have to be practical in our approach, and we have to live up to our responsibilities. But to call it impractical is a cliché, and ignorant of the economy we live in today.

While writing this book, I was invited by Michael Dell, of Dell Computer, to be on a panel at a gathering of the Business Council, a group of over one hundred CEOs from some of the biggest companies in the country. Together, they pretty much *are* the economy. Or a huge chunk of it. It was an honor to be invited to address them. My panel would last an hour, and I was one of five participants, so I would probably only get one shot to deliver a coherent message. I might never again speak to such an influential crowd. This was my chance. If you had a few minutes to address the leaders of the economy, what would you say?

We had a great lead-in. Before our panel, the podium was turned over to Dr. Lawrence Summers, the president of Harvard and a noted economist. He reviewed some frightening demographics for any CEOs in the audience who were bullish on the economy. He asked the question, "Where will the economic growth come from, if at all?" In the preceding twenty years, we've had the wind at our backs. The number of prime-age workers (ages twenty-five to fifty-four) increased by 54 percent. The percentage with a college degree increased by 50 percent. In other words, the economy has grown since 1980 largely because the number of people participating in the economy has grown.

Looking ahead to the next twenty years, during which many baby boomers are expected to retire, we can expect no growth in the number of workers. The percentage that are minorities and immigrants will increase by 50 percent, and there will be no change in the fraction with a college degree. In other words, unless these trends are changed—or unless there are unforeseen boosts in productivity per worker—the economy won't grow much, if at all.

In other words, audience, if you sell John Deere tractors, there will not be people with lawns to mow. If you sell Boeing airplanes, there won't be people to fly in their seats. If you sell Tide soap, there won't be people who need their clothes washed.

It was a pretty intense moment as this sank in.

Could the most powerful CEOs in America change something about that? That's what this conference was for. The entire next day's schedule was devoted to education reform. The notion was, it would be up to the educational system to transform the unproductive and uneducated into productive consumers.

The question our panel was asked to address is, "What do employees want?" What would it take to get more commitment out of them, more ideas out of them, more value out of them? The panelists chipped in with their ideas about benefits, flextime, day care, free M&Ms on Wednesdays, stock options, small companies versus large ones, cubicles versus private offices, and various methods of showing standout individuals a little extra appreciation. At this point, the conversation was passed to me.

I leaned forward in my seat. "What do people *really* want?"

They want to find work they're passionate about. Offering benefits and incentives are mere compromises. Educating people is important but not enough. We need to encourage people to find their sweet spot. Productivity explodes when people love what they do. We're sitting on a huge potential boom in productivity, which we could tap into if we got all the square pegs in the square holes and the round pegs in the round holes. It's not something we can measure with statistics, but it's a huge economic issue. It's a great natural resource that we're ignoring.

The tone in the room shifted. One by one, CEOs stood up and shared anecdotes that concurred with my thesis. The value in their companies came from the employees who were passionate about being there. The extra effort came from them. The new ideas came from them. They took it upon themselves to teach and lead others. Was it just that they were driven? Was it just that they were well educated? No, and often those traits were distractions. Often these dedicated people weren't executives. They could be at any level of the company. They were the company's sustaining force. Every CEO wanted more of this kind of employee—if only there were a magical way to recruit them. Vague? Yes. Impractical? Not at all.

So it's time to define the new era. Economic growth will not come from one particular sector, or from companies that adopt whatever management method is in vogue—this will not be an era of blanket solutions; instead, growth will come one company at a time, from companies that focus on doing what they do, and doing it better.

And in the same way, individual success will not be attained by migrating to a particular "hot" industry, or by adopting a particular career-guiding mantra (your metaphor pollution is no good here); instead, the individuals that thrive will do so because they focused on the question of who they really are, and from that found work they truly love, and in so doing unleashed a productive and creative power they never imagined. The organizations that fuel this growth are as likely to be in shipping, defense, or education as they are to be in technology. The individuals that power this growth are as likely to be truckers, lab technicians, or teachers as they are to be MBAs.

Those who are lit by this passion will be the object of envy among their peers, and the subject of intense curiosity. They are the ones who, day by day, will rescue this drifting ship. And they will be rewarded. By money, sure, and responsibility, undoubtedly, but there is no reward more gratifying than enjoying a job well done.

I live in a different world now. Or one I perceive differently, thanks to the openness of the people I've met. I feel like I've rediscovered my *awe*. Let me explain what that means. I used to look at the world through the eye of a magazine writer, filtering out the ordinary while waiting for the sensational and buzz-worthy to trigger my muse. There were so many people I didn't listen to, so many stories I passed on, because I couldn't imagine them grabbing the attention of my news-hungry editors.

By writing this book—as a *book,* not as a series for magazines—I have opened up my filter and learned to see the extraordinary in the once cast-away ordinary. Good stories used to be rare; now they're everywhere, and better than anything I used to find.

Largely, the stories herein are of people who've learned to do what's right. At the hardest turning points of their lives—suffering from layoffs, divorces, and illnesses—they discovered the courage to build something better. Whether their initial instincts were logical or mystical, their story soon became anchored in deeply felt experience. They've left the world of money and status behind to find a more genuine connection to other people. They didn't let conventional notions of class restrict their options.

Their responsibilities didn't keep them from their purpose—they were part of their purpose, often the most important part. Combined, they make the world a better place, one encounter at a time.

I don't think of the people in this book as having the best stories out there. Rather, they're the ones that came into my life. Once I heard a story, I was willing to get on a plane, and I was willing to be honest. In order to know people personally, I might have gone to great lengths, but I didn't go to great lengths to discover them.

If some of the stories are amazing, it suggests to me that amazing stories must be everywhere. If the stories are inspiring, then inspiring stories are everywhere. If the stories are ordinary—which is how I think of them—then many ordinary people, everywhere, are daring to be true to themselves.

I began this book with nothing more than a glimmer. I was sitting in my office, staring into space, unable to write, when I asked myself: What was on people's minds? A lot were wondering what to do with their lives. That big, obvious, threatening, looming question. Without thinking, I got up and knocked on my friend Ethan Watters's door, threw myself down on his minisofa, and asked him what he thought of the idea. "How would you do it?" he asked, naturally. I didn't know. I had one instinct: Writing about my own friends would be cheating. I needed to sample real people from around the country. "How would you find them?" he asked. I didn't know. I secured votes of confidence from my agent and my ex-editor (who had left publishing, but I trusted his opinion, and it turned out he came back to books two months later). I set to work trying to figure it out. I didn't know where I was headed, but this seemed like what I needed, to plunge into the unknown, guided only by my muse.

I didn't know that I would meet so many wonderful people. I never expected how honest they would be with me. I didn't know that I would learn so much from them. I didn't know that this book would become a vehicle for me to express a new voice. I didn't know that my desire for this book would survive my son's birth, or the catastrophe of September 11, or our parents' falling ill. All that unfolded for me later, like a reward for trusting my instincts.

Here's my point: Usually, all we get is a glimmer. A story we read or someone we briefly met. A curiosity. A meek voice inside, whispering. It's up to us to hammer out the rest. The rewards of pursuing it are only for those who are willing to listen attentively, only for those people who really care. It's not for everyone. If we are the victim of an injustice, it is up to us to find a meaningful way to channel our anger. If we suffer a terrible crisis, only we can transform this suffering into a launching pad for a new life. These are the turning points from which we get to construct our own story, if we choose to do so. It won't be easy, and it won't be quick. Finding what we believe in and what we can do about it is one of life's great dramas. It can be an endless process of discovery, one to be appreciated and respected for its difficulty. Don't cheat. Treat this as the one true life you get.

Now, an admission: Conducting my research in a haphazard, grass-roots, word-of-mouth style has its faults. We all start somewhere, and my starting point was heavily steeped in the perspective of techies and MBAs, whom I used to write about. This book has taught me so many other ways of looking at the world—I've outgrown that old mindset, thankfully. I worked hard to expose myself to as many viewpoints as possible—but! . . . But when I began, I didn't know how universal this question was. And so my pool of nine hundred interviews was only ankle-deep in some areas, and I now wish I had more diversity, more working-class stories, more stay-at-home parents, more couples. Please don't condemn me. We all start somewhere. I'm just one person, with a family to take care of, and I can't be away from home too much. So I recognize my wish for more, and I hear the Call in that wish, and I'm propelled by that Call. And I know what to do. Be assured that while you're reading this, I'm out hearing more stories, doing my work, hammering out the rest.

Never enough money, never enough time! This threat hangs out there like a veto. And I recognize the book's not much practical help on this front. I know some readers would prefer a careful audit of each subject's finances to discern exactly how they made a dollar stretch. As hard as it was for the people in this book to make it work, I recognize that it always looks so much easier in retrospect. There's a natural inclination to put some distance between yourself and those here—*they're not like me, they don't have my problems.* Part of that inclination is to forget just how tough it really was, or maybe not forget, exactly—maybe *ignore.* Don't ignore Rick Olson's bankruptcy. Don't ignore that Chi Tschang lived in a housing project. Don't ignore that Mary Ann Clark had five children to raise. Don't ignore that those who have college and postgraduate degrees had to earn them grade by grade. Don't look for a story just like yours—there is no story just like yours. Open up your filter and you will recognize that all stories are unique and all stories are worthy. Your story is unique. Find your story. I hope this book helps people find their story. It helped me find mine. Until I met these people, I never thought I had a story.

Never enough time? On the contrary—the saving grace is time. The people in this book didn't fix their situation overnight. For most, it took many attempts over many years. When I began my research, I thought this was a weakness in their stories; I wished they had exhibited more commanding control over their changes. Now I admire their patience, and I find it more interesting that they've made their changes despite lacking control.

Now I wonder—why was it supposedly more admirable for someone to have made their change cleanly and overnight? Why did I ever want stories that weren't clouded by luck, pain, and ghosts? Why was that the kind of story I thought I wanted to hear? Answer: Because that's the storytelling convention. The Self-Made Person. We've been boxed in by that myth. We've edited our lives to sound more like that myth. We've judged ourselves negatively because we haven't measured up to that myth. We've stopped trying because we know we don't have mythic strength.

I'm glad I never found the stories I was originally looking for. Instead, I found true stories, full of messy complications, with wonderful outcomes nevertheless.

I hope the stories in this book have broken that myth's grip on what stories are supposed to sound like.

When you tell your story, embrace your luck, pain, and ghosts.

I hope this book has challenged how you categorize yourself (and others). Perhaps you identify yourself by your age, your gender, your race, the number of kids you've raised, or where you live. Perhaps you identify yourself by your profession. At one point, I considered organizing this book by all those supposed categories. I hope what I've done has portrayed another way to think about it. We're not identified by what we *do*—our identity is anchored in *what we've had to overcome to get there*. And we share those challenges with far more people than just those who talk like us or share our occupation. We all share this human experience. We are all looking for "rightness." We are all struggling to transcend the way our class has defined us. We are all trying to know ourselves. We are all looking for an environment that nurtures our soul. We are all trying to balance the needs and desires of our families. We are all trying to keep the Big Picture in mind. This unites us, not divides us.

So finding your calling is not "the answer." Callings are vehicles that help us let our real selves out; callings speed up the process. You can find your calling, or you can find your people, or you can find an environment that nurtures you—they all lead to the same place. Many people get there without ever finding their calling. Head in that direction. Seek, adjust.

Seek, learn. We grow into our true selves, our whole selves, overcoming our fears and the limits that once trapped us.

So many good things happened to me on the way to pursuing my dream.

Writing a little every day taught me to pay attention and not sleepwalk through life—it made this a richer experience. My dream helped me to resist temptation when I was young, and I have been better at resisting temptation ever since. My dream gave me direction during my divorce, and forced me to overcome my shyness. My dream led me, eventually, to this book, and to finally figuring out how to connect to others.

Not all dreams come true. But this very real transformation is available to everyone.

Now I'm walking with Carl Kurlander in Squirrel Hill. Now I'm walking with Chi Tschang through Jamaica Plain. Now I'm walking in the snow with Nicole Heinrich through Logan Square. Now I'm walking with Ashley Merryman through Culver City. Now I'm walking in the rain with Ana Miyares through Little Havana.

I keep my memories of these people close by. I want to hang on to their influence on me. We write and call each other. Sometimes I reread my notes taken during our conversations. Inevitably time will erode memory and I will be left with only fading highlights, and then only fond feelings. There's no way I can remember it all. So, for my sake, in order to have it in one place, I'll repeat some of the most important things I learned:

A calling is not something you know, it's something you grow into, through trials and mistakes. Work shouldn't just be fun. Work should be like life—sometimes fun, sometimes moving, and defined by meaningful events. Attack your fears, rather than shy away from them. Bring what you do in alignment with who you are. Freedom is the confidence that you can live within the means of something you're passionate about. Failure's hard, but success at the wrong thing can lock you in forever. Don't be seduced by artificial love. Be open to defining experiences. Don't mistake intensity for passion. You don't find your purpose above the neck, you find it below the neck, when you're transformed by what you have witnessed. You can get good at what you need to to serve what you believe in. Get your mind 80 percent of the way there, then go looking for the catalyst. Look backward as much as forward, inward as much as outward. Nothing helps like knowing you're not alone. There's a powerful transformative effect when you surround yourself with like-minded people. Create an environment where the truth is invited into your life. If you develop the character, the odds are pretty good you can succeed. Success is defined as when you're no longer held back by your heart, and your character blossoms, and the gifts you have to offer the world are apparent. Don't cling to a single scenario, allow yourself many paths to the same destination. Give it a lifetime to pay off. Things you work hardest for are the things you will most treasure.

I used to think life presented a five-page menu of choices. Now I think the choice is in whether to be honest, to ourselves and others, and the rest is more of an uncovering, a peeling away of layers, discovering talents we assumed we didn't have. I used to treasure the innocence of first love. Now I treasure the hard-fought. I used to want to change the world. Now I'm open to letting it change me.

||| Acknowledgments

I received a tremendous amount of support during the researching and writing of this book. My agent, Peter Ginsberg, encouraged me to share my own story alongside everyone else's. My editor, Jon Karp, recognized where he was happy and returned to publishing in time to shepherd me through the entire process. My U.K. editor, Geoff Mulligan, had faith this question was valid on both sides of the Atlantic. As the manuscript evolved, my production editor, Janet Wygal, let me bend every rule about how material is supposed to be submitted. My wife, Michele Bronson, taught me that family and work are not in competition. She never stressed out about the task I'd undertaken. Her calm kept me calm. She rescued me from the inevitable stormy doubts that plague any book middevelopment. She and Jon read the manuscript at two partial stages before its completion.

My assistant, Anne Ferguson, kept so many conversations going with so many people when I was on the road or locked in my writing closet. There isn't room here to thank everyone who shared their life with me, but there are a few dozen who left an indelible impression. The following invested significant time with me, even though I did not portray them in the book: Anabel Pelham, Anthony Wilson, Evan Aaronson, Janie Noble, Jocelyn Blumenthal, Katherine James, Laura McClure, Lynn Millner, Ron Spinhoven, and Steve Etzine.

In addition, the following people contributed something that had particular meaning to me—maybe an exchange that refined an idea, or a turn of phrase I adopted, or a bolt of honesty while undergoing a difficult turn in their life. They set the tone; their letters and calls fueled me: Adrienna Corrales, Alan Becker, Allison Deegan, Anne Marie Gallagher (who contributed her analysis of why mother stories are so hard to tell), Ben

Sternberg, Bill McNeely, Candice Ebbesen, Carl Berger, Carol Johnson, Charles Barnes, Chris Worth, Christine Cassady, Cindy Danielson, David Ash, Deborah Bryant, Diana Kapp, Elizabeth Auffenberg, Elizabeth Soutter, Erica Smith, Gloria Siler, Gregory Giagnocavo, Harry Dickran, Heidi Anderson, Jen Silver, Jenny Partridge, Jeremy Gelbwaks, Jon Locke, Joie Bernabe, Jude Barry, Julie Heynssens, Justin Hensley, Kate Lynch, Kristin Zhivago, Lane Pietro, Lashandra Oglesby, Maggie Lambert, Margaret Shum, Mark Johnson, Mary Leonard, Mathew Adams, Michael Wong, Michelle Quarles, Nancy Bauschinger, Patty Spiglanin, Paul King, Paul McKay, Philip Dampier, Rizwan Din, Rowan Beach, Sarah Booth, Shelbi Scott, Steve Rehmus, Tom Hale, and a woman named Katie who never gave her last name.

In some locations I relied heavily on locals to get my bearings and learn local customs. In New Orleans, thanks to Erik Vidal, Jessica Goldfinch, Rob Walker, Stewart Yerton, and particularly Brian Oberkirch, who explained his theory of what makes a place interesting. In Washington, I'm grateful to Brian Steele, Jill Zuckman, Kathy McShea, John Edgell, Tom Kalil, Shabbir Safdar, and Daniel Pink. In Miami, thanks to Monique Cattogio. In Hong Kong, I'm indebted to Porter Erisman, Rich Robison, Kenn Cukier, and my son's babysitter there, Teresa.

||| A Reading Group Guide

Now that you've read *What Should I Do with My Life*, we highly recommend discussing it with your friends, family, or book group. We suggest the following questions as fodder for those discussions.

For information on how your book group can contact Po Bronson directly, go to www.pobronson.com.

ARTISTIC CHOICES

1. When Po's memories were triggered by the stories of others, he chose to weave fragments of his own life into the narrative. How did this enhance or detract from your experience of reading the book? Did his doing so encourage you to think about your own memories, or did it get in the way?

2. Journalists are supposed to be impartial. They're not supposed to care overtly for the people they write about. In rejecting that method, Po seems to be suggesting that caring for others is necessary for a meaningful life. Do you agree? What would Po have gained or missed had he adopted a journalist's customary detachment?

3. Most of the stories have positive outcomes, but the subjects have to endure a painful period to get there, and they still experience some regret and uncertainty afterward. Did you find the overall picture rosy or sad? Did you expect to find it otherwise?

4. Po chose to include several stories of people who are still struggling, or who have found only part of their solution. He also chose ordinary

people rather than famous ones. Why do you think he made these choices? How do those choices influence the overall tone of the book?

5. Was part of your enjoyment of the book derived from the fantasy of being welcomed into the intimate lives of strangers? Did some of your enjoyment come from the knowledge that there's someone out there who might be willing to listen to your life story? How important to your enjoyment was receiving concrete wisdom from the stories?

6. Po recorded the stories of more than nine hundred people. This suggests that he wanted to represent people from all walks of life, but he freely admits that his research was heavily biased toward the kind of person he used to be (and the kind of people he used to write about). Does this bias compromise the legitimacy of his conclusions? In what ways has *your* perspective been limited by your past experiences?

7. Po categorized the stories in a way that highlights the psychological issues we all have in common. He rejected methods of categorization that would have sorted people by profession, age, or class. Thus, the story of a diver is followed by a that of a political appointee, and a mother's story is followed by a trucker's, etc. What is the author trying to say about the way people usually identify themselves?

8. Po clearly chose *not* to write a how-to guidebook. But he seems torn between two ambitions—his desire to be a serious chronicler, which required that he record the stories straight, and his desire to help readers, which led him to distill helpful insights. In your opinion, when did he go too far in either direction? Do you work in a field in which having a desire to help others means you are taken less seriously?

STRATEGIES & MACROINFLUENCES

9. Did you think any of these people should have stayed put rather than leave their old lives behind? Whose choices did you question or criticize? For instance, did you question Carl Kurlander's decision to write Louie Anderson's autobiography rather than his own? Did you wince when Evan Hambrick went back to Corporate America? Did

you accept or reject Mark Kraschel's appreciation for Muslim culture? Did you respect Katt Clark's decision to set aside her Olympic dreams for her daughter a second time?

10. Many of these people left professions in which they either already made a lot of money or would have been wealthy had they stayed. What message did you extract from this—that it's necessary to resist the temptation of money, the sooner the better, to avoid being locked in by golden handcuffs? Or do their stories suggest that it's okay to aim for money now and postpone your calling until later?

11. Kat James, Warren Brown, and Jennifer Scott are among the many who believed they were being steered toward the right decision. Do you believe in destiny, or a guiding hand? If so, what should you do when the universe seems to be making it extremely difficult to succeed? Is that a sign you're heading in the wrong direction?

12. Po concludes that a calling isn't something you *know* in the absence of experience; it's something you *grow into*. Many of the people in this book weren't able to figure out where they really belonged until the second half of their lives. How should this influence the way we counsel students who want to find their answer now, not later?

13. Every industry has a culture. And every culture is driven by a value system. Po urges us to recognize how these value systems have shaped us, for better or worse. What is the culture of the industry in which you work? What does it value in a person, and what doesn't it value?

14. How have you and your spouse (or partner) helped each other in your pursuits? How have you hindered each other? Have you chosen partners because they helped you succeed? Po confesses that he used the support of his first wife as a crutch—that he didn't take sole responsibility for his own situation. Do you agree that generous support from others can lead us to neglect our responsibilities?

15. Roughly half the people in the book are parents. The other half aren't—at least not yet (either because they've delayed parenthood, or they haven't found their partners). Did you respond to the stories of

people who have children differently from the way you did the stories of childless subjects? Did you relate more to one type than the other?

16. When you've had to counsel friends or family who are facing an agonizing decision, how have you balanced the need to be supportive with the need to be realistic? To what extent is your counseling strategy reflective of your own successes and failures?

17. Po says that we're all struggling to transcend the way our social class defines us. He seems to be saying that the inequity between classes is a wound in our collective psyche. Do you think class is that relevant? Does it actually affect an individual's enjoyment of life?

18. At LSU, Mike Blandino's Buddhism taught him to find his answers in his state of being, not in doing. In Indiana, Barry Brown was influenced by the sermons of an old-time Calvinist. Mike Jenzeh was guided by Isaiah 58 of the Old Testament. At the Unity Church in Bandon, John Butler taught that what we consider our strengths are *limiting beliefs* compensating for our biases and weaknesses. At St. Agatha's in Los Angeles, Father Joe preached that helping others is the way to serve God. How does religion affect your pursuit of the answer to the question of what to do with your life? Do you agree with your church's teachings?

FINDING YOUR STORY

19. What pursuits have you been called to over the course of your life? Have you listened to those calls? Which have you acted upon, and which have you chosen to pass on, or set aside for later?

20. Write a one-page memory of a time during your childhood or teen years in which you managed to succeed at something that you had been afraid to try or were convinced you would fail at.

21. In the first section, Po portrays various ways of arriving at "that sense of 'rightness,'" such as analyzing your skills, watching for synchronicity, and helping others who have suffered similar tragedies and losses. Po also says that we're as likely to stumble into a place that feels right as to arrive there by reasoned planning. When telling your story

to others, which of these methods would you say you have used to make your decision seem "Right"? Could you tell a version of your story in which you use a different method?

22. Po concludes that it's in hard times that we're forced to overcome the fears and doubts that normally give us pause. To what extent have the changes in your life been self-selected, during good times, or forced upon you, during hard ones? When you've suffered hardship, has it altered what you consider important? Have you allowed hardship to change your life, or have you fought to get back to normal?

23. Po warns against editing out important pieces of our stories in order to make them more presentable to others. "Embrace your luck, pain, and ghosts," he suggests in one chapter; in another he writes, "look backward as much as forward," and that we should chase away preconceptions of what our stories are supposed to sound like. He contrasts the Résumé Version with the Work-In-Progress Version of ourselves. How do you describe yourself to relative strangers in a public situation? How do you portray yourself differently in a private situation? What failures do you rarely bring up? Do you agree that in public situations we should be more revealing of our "real story"?

24. In the chapter "The Brain Candy Generation," Po says the true search is for what you believe in—what kind of world you want to live in. In what ways are you making the world a better place—even if it's just one quality interaction at a time?

25. Po tells Tom Scott that happiness is too easy a test; rather, we should ask what will be fulfilling to us. Leela de Souza found fulfillment when she stopped asking what would make her happy and instead asked to what she could devote her life. Mike Jenzeh's life improved when he gave up the notion that it was all about himself. Yet these stories are balanced by those of Warren Brown, who stopped suppressing what made him happy, and Kurt Slauson, who had been denying himself permission to enjoy his life. Have the most fulfilling periods of your life also been happy ones? Is happiness essential?

26. Bart Handford tells Po the parable of the three bricklayers building a cathedral, suggesting that even menial work can be meaningful if it's

contributing to something you believe in. Have your most meaningful accomplishments required a lot of menial work?

27. Po suggests that temptations can come in many forms: in the form of money, respect, love, or convenience. Write a one-page memory about a time in your adult life when you resisted one of these temptations.

28. In the chapter "The Ungrateful Soldier," Po recounts C. S. Lewis's assertion that belonging to an Inner Ring is a powerful, wayward desire. Po asks Tim Bratcher who is sitting at that table—who's in his Inner Ring. Are there ways that you've used status as a surrogate for individual expression? To what elusive ring do you long to belong? Are there people in your life (or in your past) whom you don't respect and yet are still trying to prove wrong?

29. Both Stephen Lyons and Chi Tschang tell Po that if you can develop into a person of good character, your chances of succeeding in life improve dramatically. What do they mean by "character"? What's an example from your own life of good or bad character?

30. In the chapter "On Planet Hug," Ashley Merryman learns to stop asking of others, "How can you help me?" and begins asking, "How can I help you?" Try living this way for a week, asking others how you can help them. Keep a list of your encounters. At the end of the week, who do you feel compelled to help, and who not?